9, 10, 11,

20, 21,

23, 31

# Global Issues 88/89

**Editor**

**Robert Jackson**
California State University, Chico

Robert Jackson is a professor of political science and
Director of the Center for International Studies at the
California State University, Chico. In addition to teaching, he
has published articles on the international political economy,
international relations simulations, and political behavior. His
special research interest is how northern California is
becoming increasingly linked to the Pacific Basin. His
overseas travels include China, Hong Kong, Portugal, Spain,
and Morocco.

**Annual Editions**
*A Library of Information from the Public Press*

Cover illustration by Mike Eagle

**The Dushkin Publishing Group, Inc.**
Sluice Dock, Guilford, Connecticut 06437

# The Annual Editions Series

Annual Editions is a series of over forty volumes designed to provide the reader with convenient, low-cost access to a wide range of current, carefully selected articles from some of the most important magazines, newspapers, and journals published today. Annual Editions are updated on an annual basis through a continuous monitoring of over 200 periodical sources. All Annual Editions have a number of features designed to make them particularly useful, including topic guides, annotated tables of contents, unit overviews, and indexes. For the teacher using Annual Editions in the classroom, an Instructor's Resource Guide with test questions is available for each volume.

## VOLUMES AVAILABLE

Africa
Aging
American Government
American History, Pre-Civil War
American History, Post-Civil War
Anthropology
Biology
Business and Management
China
Comparative Politics
Computers in Education
Computers in Business
Computers in Society
Criminal Justice
Drugs, Society, and Behavior
Early Childhood Education
Economics
Educating Exceptional Children
Education
Educational Psychology
Environment
Geography
Global Issues
Health

Human Development
Human Sexuality
Latin America
Macroeconomics
Marketing
Marriage and Family
Middle East and the Islamic World
Nutrition
Personal Growth and Behavior
Psychology
Social Problems
Sociology
Soviet Union and Eastern Europe
State and Local Government
Third World
Urban Society
Western Civilization, Pre-Reformation
Western Civilization, Post-Reformation
Western Europe
World History, Pre-Modern
World History, Modern
World Politics

Library of Congress Cataloging in Publication Data
Main entry under title: Annual editions: Global issues.
  1. Civilization, Modern—20th century—Addresses, essays, lectures—Periodicals. 2. Social prediction—Addresses, essays, lectures—Periodicals. 3. Social problems—20th century—Addresses, essays, lectures—Periodicals. I. Title: Global issues.
909.82'05        ISBN 0-87967-733-3

Fourth Edition

Manufactured by The Banta Company, Harrisonburg, Virginia 22801

# Editors/ Advisory Board

# To The Reader

In publishing ANNUAL EDITIONS we recognize the enormous role played by the magazines, newspapers, and journals of the *public press* in providing current, first-rate educational information in a broad spectrum of interest areas. Within the articles, the best scientists, practitioners, researchers, and commentators draw issues into new perspective as accepted theories and viewpoints are called into account by new events, recent discoveries change old facts, and fresh debate breaks out over important controversies.

Many of the articles resulting from this enormous editorial effort are appropriate for students, researchers, and professionals seeking accurate, current material to help bridge the gap between principles and theories and the real world. These articles, however, become more useful for study when those of lasting value are carefully *collected, organized, indexed,* and *reproduced* in a *low-cost format,* which provides easy and permanent access when the material is needed. That is the role played by *Annual Editions*.

Under the direction of each volume's *Editor,* who is an expert in the subject area, and with the guidance of an *Advisory Board,* we seek each year to provide in each *ANNUAL EDITION* a current, well-balanced, carefully selected collection of the best of the public press for your study and enjoyment. We think you'll find this volume useful, and we hope you'll take a moment to let us know what you think.

As the twentieth century begins to draw to a close, the issues confronting humanity are increasingly complex and diverse. While the mass media may focus on the latest crisis for a few days or weeks, the broad, historical forces that are at work shaping the world of the twenty-first century are seldom given the in-depth treatment that they warrant. Research and analysis of these issues, furthermore, are published across a wide variety of sources. As a result, the student just beginning to study global issues is often discouraged before he or she is able to sort out the information. In selecting and organizing the materials in this book, the needs of the beginning student have been kept in the forefront.

Each unit begins with an article providing a broad overview of the area to be explored. The remaining articles examine in more detail some of the issues presented in the introductory article. The unit then concludes with an article or two that not only identifies an issue but suggests positive steps that are being taken to improve the situation. The world faces many serious problems, the magnitude of which would discourage even the most stouthearted individual. Though identifying problems is easier than solving them, it is encouraging to know that many of the issues are being successfully addressed.

Perhaps the most striking feature about the study of contemporary global issues is the absence of any single, widely-held theory which explains what is taking place. Therefore, a conscious effort has been made to consider a wide variety of ideologies and theories. The most important consideration has been to present global issues from an international perspective, rather than from a purely American or Western point of view. By selecting materials originally published in many different countries and written by authors of various nationalities, the anthology represents the great diversity of opinions that people hold on important global issues. Two writers examining the same phenomenon may reach very different conclusions. It is not a question of who is right and who is wrong. What is important to understand is that people from different vantage points have differing perceptions of reality.

Another major consideration when organizing these materials was to explore the complex interrelationship of factors that produce issue areas, such as Third World development. Too often discussions of these problems are reduced to arguments of good versus evil or communism versus capitalism. As a result, the interplay of the complex web of causes is overlooked. Every effort has been made to select materials that illustrate the interaction of these forces.

Finally, the materials in this book were selected for both their intellectual insights and their readability. Timely and well-written materials should stimulate good classroom lectures and discussions. It is hoped that students and teachers will enjoy using this book.

I would like to thank Ian Nielsen for his encouragement and helpful suggestions in the selection of materials for *Annual Editions: Global Issues 88/89.* I would also like to thank James Hutchinson for providing some invaluable research assistance. It is our continuing goal to encourage the readers of this book to have a greater appreciation of the world in which they live. We hope they will be motivated to further explore the complex issues that the world faces as we approach the last decade of the twentieth century.

Robert M. Jackson

*Editor*

# Contents

## Unit 1

### Global Issues: A Clash of Views

The two articles in this section present distinct views on the present and future state of life on earth.

## Unit 2

### Population

The six articles in this section discuss the contributing factors of culture, politics, migration, and AIDS on the world's population growth.

The concepts in bold italics are developed in the article. For further expansion please refer to the Topic Guide and the Index.

# Unit 3

# Natural Resources

Fifteen selections divided into four subsections—the international dimension, raw materials, food and hunger, and energy—discuss natural resources and their effects on the world community.

The concepts in bold italics are developed in the article. For further expansion please refer to the Topic Guide and the Index.

The concepts in bold italics are developed in the article. For further expansion please refer to the Topic Guide and the Index.

# Unit 4

## Development

Twelve articles divided into two subsections present various views on world development in the nonindustrial and industrial nations.

The concepts in bold italics are developed in the article. For further expansion please refer to the Topic Guide and the Index.

## Unit 5

## Conflict

Six articles in this section discuss the basis for world conflict and the current state of peace in the international community.

The concepts in bold italics are developed in the article. For further expansion please refer to the Topic Guide and the Index.

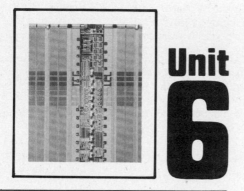

# Unit
# 6

## Communications

Five selections in this section examine the impact of communications on the world's cultural, economic, and political balance.

The concepts in bold italics are developed in the article. For further expansion please refer to the Topic Guide and the Index.

# Unit 7

## Human Values

Five articles discuss human rights and values in today's world. The effects of disease, education, and religion on the world's cultures are examined.

The concepts in bold italics are developed in the article. For further expansion please refer to the Topic Guide and the Index.

# Topic Guide

This topic guide suggests how the selections in this book relate to topics of traditional concern to students and professionals involved with the study of global issues. It is very useful in locating articles which relate to each other for reading and research. The guide is arranged alphabetically according to topic. Articles may, of course, treat topics that do not appear in the topic guide. In turn, entries in the topic guide do not necessarily constitute a comprehensive listing of all the contents of each selection.

| TOPIC AREA | TREATED AS AN ISSUE IN: | TOPIC AREA | TREATED AS AN ISSUE IN: |
|---|---|---|---|
| **Agriculture, Food, and Hunger** | 1. Life on Earth Is Getting Better, Not Worse<br>9. The Heat Is On<br>13. State of the Earth<br>16. A Crisis of Many Dimensions<br>17. The Hidden Malice of Malnutrition<br>18. Grains of Hope<br>19. Tomatomation<br>28. Women on the Sidelines | **Economics** | 7. The Global Phenomena of Immigration<br>15. Converting Garbage to Gold<br>16. A Crisis of Many Dimensions<br>19. Tomatomation<br>20. New Directions for Oil Policy<br>22. Power Without Nuclear<br>23. Shapes of a Renewable Society<br>26. Dance of Debt Isn't Over Yet<br>27. The Next Earthquake<br>29. Children in Darkness<br>30. Rural Industry<br>31. The Strategic Challenge of the Evolving Global Economy<br>32. Japan 1987<br>33. Dismantling the 49th Parallel<br>34. Strains in the Welfare State<br>43. Detectives in Space |
| **Communications** | 42. A World of Communications Wonders<br>43. Detectives in Space<br>44. The Regional Solution to a Global Problem<br>45. Uprising in the Philippines<br>46. Gambling on Glasnost | | |
| **Cultural Customs and Values** | 5. Baby Makes Three<br>7. The Global Phenomena of Immigration<br>15. Converting Garbage to Gold<br>23. Shapes of a Renewable Society<br>24. A Village Called Nanpur<br>28. Women on the Sidelines<br>44. The Regional Solution to a Global Problem<br>47. Smallpox: Never Again<br>48. Children in South Africa's Jails<br>49. How the Japanese Beat Us in Schools<br>50. Gandhi<br>51. Agenda for the Twenty-First Century | **Energy: Exploration, Production, Research, and Politics** | 1. Life on Earth Is Getting Better, Not Worse<br>12. The Lessons of Chernobyl<br>13. State of the Earth<br>15. Converting Garbage to Gold<br>20. New Directions for Oil Policy<br>21. The World's Shrinking Forests<br>22. Power Without Nuclear<br>23. Shapes of a Renewable Society<br>27. The Next Earthquake<br>43. Detectives in Space |
| **Development: Economic and Social** | 4. The Politics of Population<br>5. Baby Makes Three<br>6. Cities Without Limits<br>16. A Crisis of Many Dimensions<br>18. Grains of Hope<br>21. The World's Shrinking Forests<br>24. A Village Called Nanpur<br>25. International Stratification and Third World Solidarity<br>26. Dance of Debt Isn't Over Yet<br>27. The Next Earthquake<br>28. Women on the Sidelines<br>30. Rural Industry<br>31. The Strategic Challenge of the Evolving Global Economy<br>43. Detectives in Space<br>44. The Regional Solution to a Global Problem<br>47. Smallpox: Never Again<br>50. Gandhi | **Environment, Ecology, and Conservation** | 2. The Cornucopian Fallacies<br>3. 5 Billion and Counting . . .<br>9. The Heat Is On<br>10. 46 Nations Agree on Pact to Protect Ozone Layer<br>11. Transboundary Pollution<br>12. The Lessons of Chernobyl<br>13. State of the Earth<br>14. Treasure Among the Trees<br>15. Converting Garbage to Gold<br>16. A Crisis of Many Dimensions<br>21. The World's Shrinking Forests<br>22. Power Without Nuclear<br>23. Shapes of a Renewable Society<br>43. Detectives in Space<br>51. Agenda for the Twenty-First Century |
| | | **The Future** | 1. Life on Earth Is Getting Better, Not Worse<br>2. The Cornucopian Fallacies<br>3. 5 Billion and Counting . . .<br>6. Cities Without Limits<br>8. The Future of AIDS<br>9. The Heat Is On<br>14. Treasure Among the Trees<br>21. The World's Shrinking Forests<br>23. Shapes of a Renewable Society<br>35. The Great Siberia in the Sky<br>42. A World of Communications Wonders<br>43. Detectives in Space<br>51. Agenda for the Twenty-First Century |

| TOPIC AREA | TREATED AS AN ISSUE IN: | TOPIC AREA | TREATED AS AN ISSUE IN: |
|---|---|---|---|
| **Health and Medicine** | 4. The Politics of Population<br>8. The Future of AIDS<br>12. The Lessons of Chernobyl<br>14. Treasure Among the Trees<br>17. The Hidden Malice of Malnutrition<br>29. Children in Darkness<br>34. Strains in the Welfare State<br>47. Smallpox: Never Again | **Political and Legal Global Issues (cont.)** | 26. Dance of Debt Isn't Over Yet<br>27. The Next Earthquake<br>33. Dismantling the 49th Parallel<br>37. Ambiguous War<br>39. The Nuclear Arsenal in the Middle East<br>40. Foundation Stone, Stepping Stone<br>43. Detectives in Space<br>46. Gambling on Glasnost<br>47. Smallpox: Never Again<br>48. Children in South Africa's Jails |
| **Industrial Economics** | 12. The Lessons of Chernobyl<br>15. Converting Garbage to Gold<br>20. New Directions for Oil Policy<br>22. Power Without Nuclear<br>23. Shapes of a Renewable Society<br>31. The Strategic Challenge of the Evolving Global Economy<br>32. Japan 1987<br>33. Dismantling the 49th Parallel<br>34. Strains in the Welfare State<br>43. Detectives in Space | **Population and Demographics (Quality of Life Indicators)** | 1. Life on Earth Is Getting Better, Not Worse<br>3. 5 Billion and Counting . . .<br>4. The Politics of Population<br>5. Baby Makes Three<br>6. Cities Without Limits<br>7. The Global Phenomena of Immigration<br>29. Children in Darkness<br>47. Smallpox: Never Again<br>51. Agenda for the Twenty-First Century |
| **International Economics: Trade, Aid, and Dependencies** | 16. A Crisis of Many Dimensions<br>20. New Directions for Oil Policy<br>25. International Stratification and Third World Solidarity<br>26. Dance of Debt Isn't Over Yet<br>27. The Next Earthquake<br>31. The Strategic Challenge of the Evolving Global Economy<br>32. Japan 1987<br>33. Dismantling the 49th Parallel | **Science, Technology, and Research and Development** | 9. The Heat Is On<br>10. 46 Nations Agree on Pact to Protect Ozone Layer<br>12. The Lessons of Chernobyl<br>13. State of the Earth<br>15. Converting Garbage to Gold<br>17. The Hidden Malice of Malnutrition<br>18. Grains of Hope<br>19. Tomatomation<br>22. Power Without Nuclear<br>35. The Great Siberia in the Sky<br>39. The Nuclear Arsenal in the Middle East<br>42. A World of Communications Wonders<br>43. Detectives in Space<br>47. Smallpox: Never Again |
| **Military: Warfare and Terrorism** | 35. The Great Siberia in the Sky<br>36. On the International Uses of Military Force<br>37. Ambiguous War<br>38. The Future Course of International Terrorism<br>39. The Nuclear Arsenal in the Middle East<br>40. Foundation Stone, Stepping Stone<br>41. Arms Control<br>43. Detectives in Space<br>45. Uprising in the Philippines<br>48. Children in South Africa's Jails<br>51. Agenda for the Twenty-First Century | **Third World** | 3. 5 Billion and Counting . . .<br>5. Baby Makes Three<br>6. Cities Without Limits<br>16. A Crisis of Many Dimensions<br>17. The Hidden Malice of Malnutrition<br>18. Grains of Hope<br>21. The World's Shrinking Forests<br>24. A Village Called Nanpur<br>25. International Stratification and Third World Solidarity<br>26. Dance of Debt Isn't Over Yet<br>27. The Next Earthquake<br>28. Women on the Sidelines<br>29. Children in Darkness<br>30. Rural Industry<br>31. The Strategic Challenge of the Evolving Global Economy<br>36. On the International Uses of Military Force<br>43. Detectives in Space<br>44. The Regional Solution to a Global Problem<br>47. Smallpox: Never Again<br>50. Gandhi |
| **Natural Resources** | 2. The Cornucopian Fallacies<br>9. The Heat Is On<br>11. Transboundary Pollution<br>13. State of the Earth<br>14. Treasure Among the Trees<br>15. Converting Garbage to Gold<br>16. A Crisis of Many Dimensions<br>20. New Directions for Oil Policy<br>21. The World's Shrinking Forests<br>23. Shapes of a Renewable Society<br>43. Detectives in Space | | |
| **Political and Legal Global Issues** | 4. The Politics of Population<br>7. The Global Phenomena of Immigration<br>10. 46 Nations Agree on Pact to Protect Ozone Layer<br>11. Transboundary Pollution<br>12. The Lessons of Chernobyl<br>13. State of the Earth<br>16. A Crisis of Many Dimensions<br>25. International Stratification and Third World Solidarity | **Women** | 28. Women on the Sidelines |

# Global Issues:
# A Clash of Views

Imagine a clear, round, inflated balloon. Now imagine that a person begins to brush yellow paint onto this miniature globe. Symbolically the color yellow represents *people*, for in many ways the study of global issues is ultimately the study of people. Today, there are more people occupying the earth than ever before. In addition, the world is in the midst of a period of unprecedented population growth. Not only are there many countries where the majority of people are under age sixteen, but because of improved health care, there are also more older people alive than ever before. The effect of a growing global population, however, goes beyond sheer numbers, for a growing population impacts on natural resources and social services in unprecedented ways. Population issues, then, are an appropriate place to begin the study of global issues.

Imagine that our fictional artist dips the brush into a con-

tainer of blue paint to represent the world of *nature*. The natural world plays an important role in setting the international agenda. Shortages of raw materials, drought and crop failures, and pollution of waterways are just a few examples of how natural resources can have global implications.

Adding blue paint to the balloon also reveals one of the most important concepts found in this book of readings. Although the balloon originally was covered by yellow and blue paint (people and nature as separate conceptual entities), the two combined produce an entirely different color: green. Talking about nature as a separate entity or about people as though they were somehow removed from the forces of the natural world is a serious intellectual error. The people-nature relationship (symbolically represented by the mixing of blue and yellow paint) is one of the keys to understanding many of today's most important global issues.

The third color added to the balloon is red. It represents the "*meta*" component—i.e., those qualities that make human beings more than (or beyond) mere animals. These qualities include: new ideas and inventions, culture and values, religious and spiritual qualities, and art and literature. The addition of the red paint immediately changes the color green to brown, again emphasizing the relationship between all three factors.

The fourth and final color added is white. This color represents *social structures*. Factors such as whether a society is urban or rural, industrial or agrarian, planned or decentralized, and consumer oriented or dedicated to the needs of the state fall into this category. The relationship between this component and the others is extremely important. The impact of political decisions on the environment, for example, is one of the most unique features of the contemporary world. Historically, the forces of nature determined which species survived or perished. Today survival depends on political decisions—or indecisions. Will the whales or bald eagles survive? The answer to this question will be the result of governmental activities, not evolutionary forces. Understanding this relationship between social structure and nature (known as "ecopolitics") is important to the study of global issues.

If the painter continues to ply the paintbrush over the miniature globe, a marbling effect will become evident. In some areas, the shading will vary because one element is greater than another. The miniature system appears dynamic. Nothing is static; relationships are continually changing. This leads to a number of theoretical insights: (1) there is no such thing as separate elements, only connections or relationships; (2) changes in one area (such as the weather) will result in changes in all other areas; and (3) complex relationships make it difficult to predict events accurately, so observers are often surprised by unexpected processes and outcomes.

This book is organized along the basic lines of the balloon allegory. This brief, two-article unit demonstrates the lack of agreement among the so-called experts. Unit two focuses on population. Unit three examines the environment and related issues (e.g., agriculture and energy). The next three units look at different aspects of the world's social structures. They explore issues of development (for both industrial and nonindustrial societies), conflict, and communications. In the final unit, a number of "meta" factors are discussed. However, you should be aware that just as it was impossible to keep the individual colors from disappearing and blending into new colors in the balloon allegory, it is also impossible to separate these factors into discrete chapters in a book. Any discussion of agriculture, for example, must take into account the impact of a growing population on soil and water resources, as well as new scientific approaches to food production. Therefore, the organization of this book focuses attention on issue areas; it does not mean to imply that these factors are somehow separate.

In this unit, it is evident that when people are part of the situation they are commenting on, they cannot see the complete, objective picture. Their views are affected by the social structure to which they belong and the particular vantage point they have. Furthermore, because the global situation is always changing, there are always opportunities for further controversy and debate.

In the lead article, Professor Julian L. Simon argues that the quality of life is improving. Describing a variety of historical trends, Simon argues that the declining costs of basic necessities, along with advances in health care, support his hypothesis that the quality of life will continue to improve. In contrast, Lindsey Grant criticizes the assumptions implicit in the Simon analysis. Grant argues that many of the problems people face today are historically unique. Though the two authors look at the same world, they come to different conclusions. Their clashing viewpoints establish a theme that runs throughout the remainder of this book.

## Looking Ahead: Challenge Questions

Does either Simon's or Grant's analysis follow the assumptions presented in the allegory of the balloon? If so, how? If not, how are the assumptions of the authors different?

Both authors point to connections between different factors. What are some of the relationships they cite, and how do the authors differ in terms of the relationships they emphasize?

How do the authors use history to support their arguments?

What are some of the positive factors that are available to help people solve the problems they face?

How will the world be different in the year 2030? What factors will contribute to these changes?

What major events during the twentieth century have had the greatest impact on shaping the world of today?

What do you consider to be the five most pressing global problems of today? How do your answers compare to those of your family, friends, and classmates?

# Life on Earth Is Getting Better, Not Worse

**Julian L. Simon**

Julian L. Simon is professor of economics and business administration at the University of Illinois at Urbana-Champaign. His address is College of Commerce and Business Administration, University of Illinois, Urbana, Illinois 61820.

This article draws on his book, *The Ultimate Resource* (Princeton University Press, 1981, 415 pages, $14.50).

If we lift our gaze from the frightening daily headlines and look instead at wide-ranging scientific data as well as the evidence of our senses, we shall see that economic life in the United States and the rest of the world has been getting better rather than worse during recent centuries and decades. There is, moreover, no persuasive reason to believe that these trends will not continue indefinitely.

But first: I am *not* saying that all is well everywhere, and I do not predict that all will be rosy in the future. Children are hungry and sick; people live out lives of physical or intellectual poverty, with little opportunity for improvement; war or some new pollution may finish us. What I *am* saying is that for most relevant economic matters I have checked, aggregate trends are improving rather than deteriorating. Also, I do not say that a better future will happen automatically or without effort. It will happen because men and women will use muscle and mind to struggle with problems that they will probably overcome, as they have in the past.

## Longer and Healthier Lives

Life cannot be good unless you are alive. Plentiful resources and a clean environment have little value unless we and others are alive to enjoy them. The fact that your chances of living through any given age now are much better than in earlier times must therefore mean that life has gotten better. In France, for example, female life expectancy at birth rose from under 30 years in the 1740s to 75 years in the 1960s. And this trend has not yet run its course. The increases have been rapid in recent years in the United States: a 2.1-year gain between 1970 and 1976 versus a 0.8-year gain in the entire decade of the 1960s. This pattern is now being repeated in the

F. BOTTS/U.N. FOOD AND AGRICULTURE ORGANIZATION

Mother and child selling fruit in a **West African market. Food production per person has risen worldwide over the past 30 years. Africa's food production per capita has declined recently, but for political, not economic, reasons, says author Simon.**

From *The Futurist*, August 1983, pp. 7-12, 14. THE FUTURIST, published by the World Future Society, 4916 St. Elmo Avenue, Bethesda, MD 20814.

> Rising income and life expectancy, declining pollution and disease, plus the unique human talent for creating new resources all point to a brighter future ahead.

poorer countries of the world as they improve their economic lot. Life expectancy at birth in low-income countries rose from an average of 35.2 years in 1950 to 49.9 years in 1978, a much bigger jump than the rise from 66.0 to 73.5 years in the industrialized countries.

The threat of our loved ones dying greatly affects our assessment of the quality of our lives. Infant mortality is a reasonable measure of child mortality generally. In Europe in the eighteenth and nineteenth centuries, 200 or more children of each thousand died during their first year. As late as 1900, infant mortality was 200 per 1000 or higher in Spain, Russia, Hungary, and even Germany. Now it is about 15 per 1000 or less in a great many countries.

Health has improved, too. The incidence of both chronic and acute conditions has declined. While a perceived "epidemic" of cancer indicates to some a drop in the quality of life, the data show no increase in cancer except for deaths due to smoking-caused lung cancer. As Philip Handler, president of the National Academy of Sciences, said:

The United States is not suffering an "epidemic of cancer," it is experiencing an "epidemic of life"—in that an ever greater fraction of the population survives to the advanced ages at which cancer has always been prevalent. The overall, age-corrected incidence of cancer has not been increasing; it has been declining slowly for some years.

### Abating Pollution

About pollution now: The main air pollutants—particulates and sulfur dioxide—have declined since 1960 and 1970 respectively, the periods for which there is data in the U.S. The Environmental Protection Agency's Pollutant Standard Index,

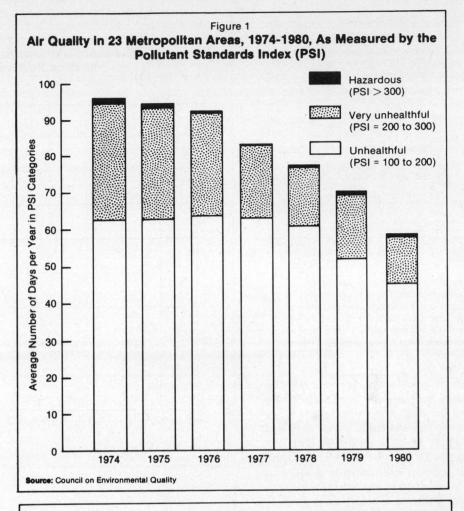

Figure 1

**Air Quality in 23 Metropolitan Areas, 1974-1980, As Measured by the Pollutant Standards Index (PSI)**

Hazardous (PSI > 300)
Very unhealthful (PSI = 200 to 300)
Unhealthful (PSI = 100 to 200)

Average Number of Days per Year in PSI Categories

**Source:** Council on Environmental Quality

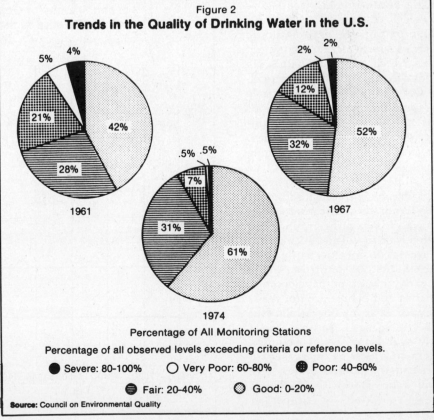

Figure 2

**Trends in the Quality of Drinking Water in the U.S.**

1961

1967

1974

Percentage of All Monitoring Stations

Percentage of all observed levels exceeding criteria or reference levels.

● Severe: 80-100%   ○ Very Poor: 60-80%   ◉ Poor: 40-60%

⊜ Fair: 20-40%   ◌ Good: 0-20%

**Source:** Council on Environmental Quality

# 1. A CLASH OF VIEWS

F. BOTTS/FAO

West African schoolboy eats lunch. Youngsters like this may reasonably expect to live amid greater abundance than their parents did if present trends continue, argues author Julian Simon.

which takes into account all the most important air pollutants, shows that the number of days rated "unhealthful" has declined steadily since the index's inauguration in 1974 (see Figure 1). And the proportion of monitoring sites in the U.S. having good drinking water has greatly increased since record-keeping began in 1961 (see Figure 2).

Pollution in the less-developed countries is a different, though not necessarily discouraging, story. No worldwide pollution data are available. Nevertheless, it is reasonable to assume that pollution of various kinds has increased as poor countries have gotten somewhat less poor. Industrial pollution rises along with new factories. The same is true of consumer pollution—junked cars, plastic wrappers, and such oddments as the hundreds of discarded antibiotics vials I saw on the ground in an isolated Iranian village. Such industrial wastes do not exist in the poorest pre-industrial countries. And in the early stages of development, countries and people are not ready to pay for clean-up operations. But further increases in income almost surely will bring about pollution abatement, just as increases in income in the United States have provided the wherewithal for better garbage collection and cleaner air and water.

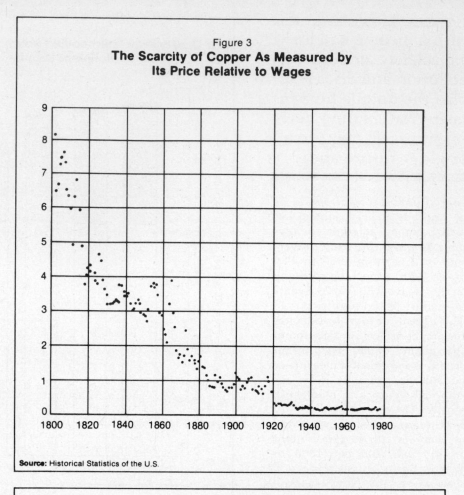

Figure 3
**The Scarcity of Copper As Measured by Its Price Relative to Wages**

**Source:** Historical Statistics of the U.S.

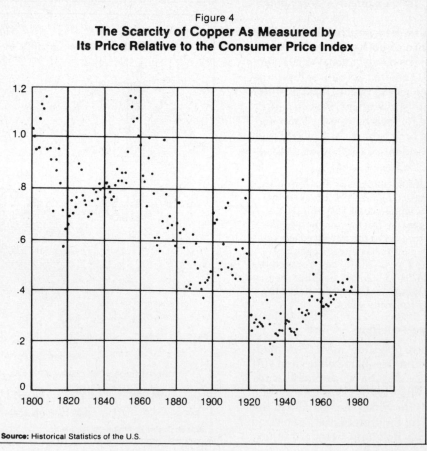

Figure 4
**The Scarcity of Copper As Measured by Its Price Relative to the Consumer Price Index**

**Source:** Historical Statistics of the U.S.

## The Myth of Finite Resources

Though natural resources are a smaller part of the economy with every succeeding year, they are still important, and their availability causes grave concern to many. Yet, measured by cost or price, the scarcity of all raw materials except lumber and oil has been *decreasing* rather than increasing over the long run. Figure 3 shows an enormous decline in the price of copper relative to wages in the U.S.; this relative price is the most important measure of scarcity because it shows the cost of the material in the most valuable of goods: human time. Figure 4 shows that the price of copper has even been declining relative to the consumer price index.

Perhaps surprisingly, oil also shows a downward cost trend in the long run (see Figures 5 and 6). The price rise in the 1970s was purely political; the cost of producing a barrel of oil in the Persian Gulf is still only perhaps 15 to 25 cents.

There is no reason to believe that the supply of energy is finite, or that the price will not continue its long-run decrease. This statement may sound less preposterous if you consider that for a quantity to be finite it must be measurable. The future supply of oil includes what we usually think of as oil, plus the oil that can be produced from shale, tar sands, and coal. It also includes the oil from plants that we grow, whose key input is sunlight. So the measure of the future oil supply must therefore be at least as large as the sun's 7 billion or so years of future life. And it may include other suns whose energy might be exploited in the future. Even if you believe that one can in principle measure the energy from suns that will be available in the future—a belief that requires a lot of confidence that the knowledge of the physical world we have developed in the past century will not be superseded in the next 7 billion years, plus the belief that the universe is not expanding—this measurement would hardly be relevant for any practical contemporary decision-making.

Energy provides a good example of the process by which resources become more abundant and hence cheaper. Seventeenth-century Eng-

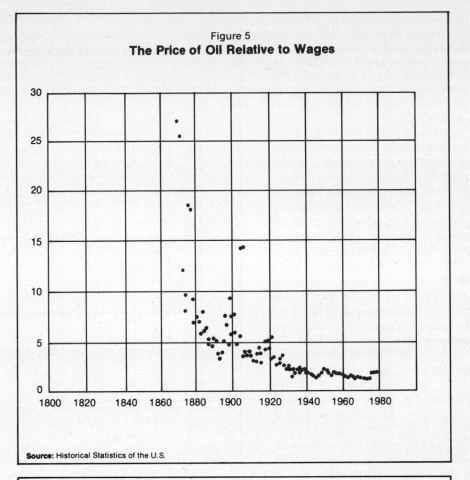

Figure 5
**The Price of Oil Relative to Wages**

**Source:** Historical Statistics of the U.S.

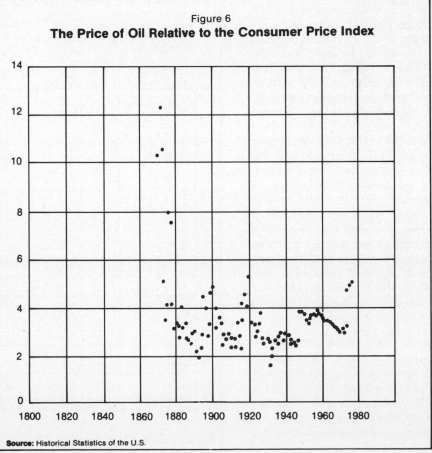

Figure 6
**The Price of Oil Relative to the Consumer Price Index**

**Source:** Historical Statistics of the U.S.

# 1. A CLASH OF VIEWS

land was full of alarm at an impending energy shortage due to the country's deforestation for firewood. People feared a scarcity of fuel for both heating and the vital iron industry. This impending scarcity led inventors and businessmen to develop coal.

Then, in the mid-1800s, the English came to worry about an impending coal crisis. The great English economist William Stanley Jevons calculated then that a shortage of coal would surely bring England's industry to a standstill by 1900; he carefully assessed that oil could never make a decisive difference. But spurred by the impending scarcity of coal (and of whale oil, whose story comes next), ingenious and profit-minded people developed oil into a more desirable fuel than coal ever was. And today England exports both coal and oil.

Another strand in the story: Because of increased demand due to population growth and increased income, the price of whale oil used in lamps jumped in the 1840s. Then the Civil War pushed it even higher, leading to a whale oil "crisis." The resulting high price provided an incentive for imaginative and enterprising people to discover and produce substitutes. First came oil from rapeseed, olives, linseed, and pine trees. Then inventors learned how to get coal oil from coal, which became a flourishing industry. Other ingenious persons produced kerosene from the rock oil that seeped to the surface. Kerosene was so desirable a product that its price rose from 75 cents to $2 a gallon, which stimulated enterprisers to increase its supply. Finally, Edwin L. Drake sunk his famous oil well in Titusville, Pennsylvania. Learning how to refine the oil took a while, but in a few years there were hundreds of small refiners in the U.S. Soon the bottom dropped out of the whale oil market: the price fell from $2.50 or more a gallon at its peak around 1866 to well below a dollar.

Lumber has been cited as an exception to the general resource story of falling costs. For decades in the U.S., farmers clearing land disposed of trees as a nuisance. As lumber came to be more a commer-

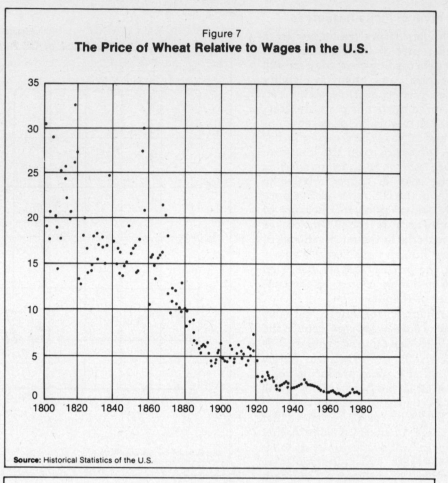

Figure 7
**The Price of Wheat Relative to Wages in the U.S.**

**Source:** Historical Statistics of the U.S.

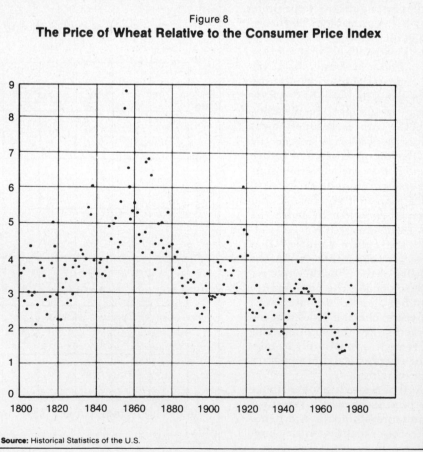

Figure 8
**The Price of Wheat Relative to the Consumer Price Index**

**Source:** Historical Statistics of the U.S.

10

cial crop and a good for builders and railroad men, its price rose. For some time, resource economists expected the price to hit a plateau and then follow the course of other raw materials as the transition to a commercial crop would be completed. There was evidence consistent with this view in the increase, rather than the popularly supposed decrease, in the tree stock in the U.S., yet for some time the price did not fall. But now that expectation seems finally to have been realized as prices of lumber have fallen to a fourth of their peak in the late 1970s.

## More Food for More People

Food is an especially important resource, and the evidence indicates that its supply is increasing despite rising population. The long-run prices of food relative to wages, and even relative to consumer goods, are down (see Figures 7 and 8). Famine deaths have decreased in the past century even in absolute terms, let alone relative to the much larger population, a special boon for poor countries. Per person food production in the world is up over the last 30 years and more (see Figure 9). And there are no data showing that the people at the bottom of the income distribution have fared worse, or have failed to share in the general improvement, as the average has improved. Africa's food production per capita is down, but that clearly stems from governmental blunders with price controls, subsidies, farm collectivization, and other institutional problems.

There is, of course, a food-production problem in the U.S. today: too much production. Prices are falling due to high productivity, falling consumer demand for meat in the U.S., and increased foreign competition in such crops as soybeans. In response to the farmers' complaints, the government will now foot an unprecedentedly heavy bill for keeping vast amounts of acreage out of production.

## The Disappearing-Species Scare

Many are alarmed that the earth is losing large numbers of its species. For example, the *Global 2000 Report to the President* says: "Extinctions of plant

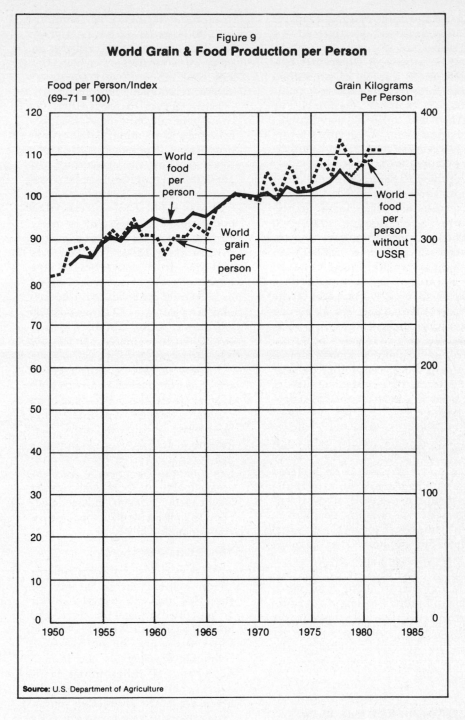

Figure 9
**World Grain & Food Production per Person**

**Source:** U.S. Department of Agriculture

and animal species will increase dramatically. Hundreds of thousands of species—perhaps as many as 20 percent of all species on earth—will be irretrievably lost as their habitats vanish, especially in tropical forests," by the year 2000.

The available facts, however, are not consistent with the level of concern expressed in *Global 2000*, nor do they warrant the various policies suggested to deal with the purported dangers.

The *Global 2000* projection is based upon a report by contributor Thomas Lovejoy, who estimates that between 437,000 and 1,875,000 extinctions will occur out of a present estimated total of 3 to 10 million species. Lovejoy's estimate is based on a linear relationship running from 0% species extinguished at 0% tropical forest cleared, to about 95% extinguished at 100% tropical forest cleared. (The main source of differences in the range of estimated

11

losses is the range of 3 to 10 million species in the overall estimate.)

The basis of any useful projection must be a body of experience collected under a range of conditions that encompass the expected conditions, or that can reasonably be extrapolated to the expected conditions. But none of Lovejoy's references seems to contain any scientifically impressive body of experience.

A projected drop in the amount of tropical forests underlies Lovejoy's projection of species losses in the future. Yet to connect these two events as Lovejoy has done requires systematic evidence relating an amount of tropical forest removed to a rate of species reduction. Neither *Global 2000* nor any of the other sources I checked give such empirical evidence. If there is no better evidence for Lovejoy's projected rates, one could extrapolate almost any rate one chooses for the year 2000. Until more of the facts are in, we need not undertake alarmist protection policies. Rather, we need other sorts of data to estimate extinction rates and decide on policy. None of this is to say that we need not worry about endangered species. The planet's flora and fauna constitute a valuable natural endowment; we must guard them as we do our other physical and social assets. But we should also strive for a clear, unbiased view of this set of assets in order to make the best possible judgments about how much time and money to spend guarding them, in a world where this valuable activity must compete with other valuable activities, including the preservation of other assets and human life.

## More Wealth from Less Work

One of the great trends of economic history is the shortening of the workweek coupled with increasing income. A shorter workweek represents an increase in one's freedom to dispose of that most treasured possession—time—as one wishes. In the U.S., the decline was from about 60 hours per week in 1870 to less than 40 hours at present. This benign trend is true for an array of countries in which the length of the workweek shows an inverse relationship with income.

With respect to progress in income generally, the most straightforward and meaningful index is the proportion of persons in the labor force working in agriculture. In 1800, the percentage in the U.S. was 73.6%, whereas in 1980 the proportion was 2.7%. That is, relative to population size, only 1/25 as many persons today are working in agriculture as in 1800. This suggests that the effort that produced one bushel of grain or one loaf of bread in 1800 will now produce the bushel of grain plus what 24 other bushels will buy in other goods, which is equivalent to an increase in income by a factor of 25.

Income in less-developed countries has not reached nearly so high a level as in the more-developed countries, by definition. But it would be utterly wrong to think that income in less-developed countries has stagnated rather than risen. In fact, income per person has increased at a proportional rate at least as fast, or faster, in less-developed than in more-developed countries since World War II.

### The Ultimate Resource

What explains the enhancement of our material life in the face of supposed limits to growth? I offer an extended answer in my recent book, *The Ultimate Resource* (1981). In short, the source of our increased economic blessings is the human mind, and, all other things being equal, when there are more people, there are more productive minds. Productivity increases come directly from the additional minds that develop productive new ideas, as well as indirectly from the impact upon industrial productivity of the additional demand for goods. That is, population growth in the form of babies or immigrants helps in the long run to raise the standard of living because it brings increased productivity. Immigrants are the best deal of all because they usually migrate when they are young and strong; in the U.S., they contribute more in taxes to the public coffers than they take out in welfare services.

In the short run, of course, additional people mean lower income for other people because children must be fed and housed by their parents, and educated and equipped partly by the community. Even immigrants are a burden for a brief time until they find jobs. But after the children grow up and enter the work force, and contribute to the support of others as well as increasing productivity, their net effect upon others becomes positive. Over their lifetimes they are a boon to others.

I hope you will now agree that the long-run outlook is for a more abundant material life rather than for increased scarcity, in the U.S. and in the world as a whole. Of course, such progress does not come about automatically. And my message certainly is not one of complacency. In this I agree with the doomsayers—that our world needs the best efforts of all humanity to improve our lot. I part company with them in that they expect us to come to a bad end despite the efforts we make, whereas I expect a continuation of successful efforts. Their message is self-fulfilling because if you expect inexorable natural limits to stymie your efforts you are likely to feel resigned and give up. But if you recognize the possibility—indeed, the probability—of success, you can tap large reserves of energy and enthusiasm. Energy and enthusiasm, together with the human mind and spirit, constitute our solid hope for the economic future, just as they have been our salvation in ages past. With these forces at work, we will leave a richer, safer, and more beautiful world to our descendants, just as our ancestors improved the world that they bestowed upon us.

# The Cornucopian Fallacies

## The Myth of Perpetual Growth

"Cornucopians" such as Julian Simon and Herman Kahn argue that the limits to growth have been greatly exaggerated. But their arguments simply ignore or dismiss the most critical issues that environmentalists warn about.

**Lindsey Grant**

Lindsey Grant is a former deputy assistant secretary of state for environment and population affairs and Department of State coordinator of *The Global 2000 Report*. He is a consultant to The Environmental Fund. This article is adapted from his Environmental Fund report *The Cornucopian Fallacies* (1982, 34 pages, $3.00 plus 65¢ postage and handling), available from The Environmental Fund, 1302 18th Street, N.W., Washington, D.C. 20036.

An intense if intermittent debate is under way between environmentalists and a pair of traveling "cornucopians," Julian Simon and Herman Kahn, who manage to appear in a remarkable number of forums to press their case. The environmentalists, drawing extensively upon the 1980 *Global 2000 Report to the President*, warn of threats to the ecosystem and to renewable resources such as cropland and forests generated by population growth and exploitative economic activities. The cornucopians say that population growth is good, not bad (Simon), or that it will solve itself (Kahn), that shortages are mythical or can be made good by technology and substitution, and generally that we may expect a glorious future.

The debate has strong political overtones. If things are going well, we don't need to do anything about them—a useful argument for *laissez-faire*. If something is going wrong, the environmentalists usually want the government to do something about it. The debate thus gets mixed up in the current reaction against "petty government interference" and a generalized yearning to return to earlier, more permissive economic and political practices.

One could hardly object to having a couple of cornucopians urging people to be of good cheer and stout heart, were it not for the danger that they may convince some citizens and policymakers not to worry about some pressing problems that urgently need attention.

The cornucopians' argumentation, however, is seriously flawed as a tool for identifying the real and important present trends.

There is an asymmetry in the nature of the arguments of the environmentalists and the cornucopians. The environmentalist—the proponent of corrective action—is (or should be) simply warning of consequences if trends or problems are ignored; he does not need to *predict*. The cornucopian, on the other hand, must predict to make his case. He must argue that problems will be solved and good things will happen if we let nature take its course. Since nobody has yet been able to predict the future, they are asking their listeners to take a lot on faith. They say, in effect, "Believe as I do, and you will feel better." Simon says explicitly that his conversion to his present viewpoint improved his state of mind.

The cornucopians have made assumptions and chosen methodologies that simply ignore or dismiss the most critical issues that have led the environmentalists to their concerns:

• The cornucopians pay little attention to causation, and they project past economic trends mechanically.

• They casually dismiss the evidence that doesn't "fit."

• They employ a static analysis that makes no provision for feedback from one sector to another.

• They understate the implications of geometric growth.

• They base their predictions on an extraordinary faith in uninterrupted technological progress.

Let us look into some of these cornucopian fallacies—the reasoning processes and omissions that characterize Simon's and Kahn's analyses.

### Extrapolating Past Growth: The Wrong Methodology

Simon argues that the past is the best guide to the future. Perhaps, but much depends on what part of the past you look at. He devotes most of his effort to demonstrating in various ways that mankind's eco-

---

**In Memoriam**

This issue of THE FUTURIST was just going to press when we learned of the untimely death of Herman Kahn. Rather than revising the article, the editors elected to run it in its original form, in recognition that Herman Kahn's ideas—and the debate—live on.

---

From *The Futurist*, August 1983, pp. 16-22. THE FUTURIST, published by the World Future Society, 4916 St. Elmo Avenue, Bethesda, MD 20814.

nomic lot has improved in the past century or so, which is not an issue.

Simon bases much of his argument on an econometric study of past correlations between the number of children and economic growth. This approach leaves unanswered the question: Which, if either, phenomenon caused the other one? Or is this simply a process of using complex mathematical relationships to obscure the commonsense proposition that the children shared in a period of prosperity?

Cited in increasingly simplistic terms, that study remains the basis for Simon's views, but his subsequent efforts have been directed almost exclusively to a search for errors in the statistics of *Global 2000* or indeed of any environmentalist, on the assumption that a shaky statistic undermines the credibility of the method.

Kahn is more nimble polemically, but there is less evidence of any systematic undergirding for his projections. He extrapolates mid-twentieth-century growth trends with a line of reasoning that comes very close to economic vitalism. His specialty is impressive graphic presentations of the future, but examination suggests there is more of the airbrush than of intellectual discipline in those graphs.

In one of his major works, *The Next 200 Years*, he projects per capita "gross world product" at $20,000 in 2176 A.D., but his evidence raises a doubt whether these are constant dollars, current dollars, or imaginary ones. As best one can gather from the text, this projection is based on a freehand plot of "S-curves" (slow/fast/slow) of GNP growth for different categories of countries, drawn roughly from the U.S. and European experience.

There are two problems with this method. First, analogy can be a dangerous process. To predict the future performance of the poor countries based upon the past performance of the rich countries may involve too loose an analogy to justify the faith put in it. The analogy assumes that the underlying factors are substantially similar. They are not. In contrast to Europe when it industrialized, poor countries today tend to have faster population growth rates, no colonies where capital can be mobilized, lower incomes (probably), extreme foreign exchange problems, no technological lead over the rest of the world, and no empty new worlds to absorb their emigrants.

Second and even more important, gross national product (GNP)—or "gross world product"—is neither tangible nor real except in people's minds. It has no life of its own. It is simply a way of giving a numerical abbreviation to a sum of economic activities. It is determined by underlying realities: the availability and quality of land, water, industrial raw materials, and energy; technological change; the impact of population change on production and consumption; the productivity of the supporting ecosystems; labor productivity; and so on. Kahn simply projects GNP without analyzing the forces that generate it.

Proof of past success is no assurance of future well-being, and the mechanical projection of economic curves is hardly a reliable guide to the future.

Most of us would agree that the general condition of mankind has been improving for a sustained period, at least until the past decade. Indeed, the scale of the growth is a new thing on earth; and the very magnitude of the growth of population and of economic activity is the source of the issue. For the first time, population and economic activities have grown so sharply as to bring them into a new relationship with the scale of the earth itself.

The hallmark of recent history has been this explosive growth, supported by and supporting an extraordinary burst of technological change and mankind's first intensive exploitation of fossil fuels. The central question for the future is not "Did it happen?" but rather: "Can such growth be sustained, or does it itself generate dynamics that will bring the era to an end? If the latter, what will the changes be, and what if anything should mankind be doing to forestall them or shape them in beneficial directions?"

## Ignoring Climate Change

As a single example, let us take the question of carbon dioxide in the atmosphere. It takes little imagination to recognize that $CO_2$-induced rainfall and temperature changes, rising sea levels, and perhaps the necessity to curtail fossil fuel use could influence future economic activities. To most of us, the fact that human activity is changing the very chemical composition of the air we live in would seem adequate justification to bring the issue into any consideration of current trends affecting the well-being of mankind.

*Global 2000* devoted 14 pages to man-induced effects on the climate, focusing primarily on $CO_2$ but dealing with other issues as well. It concluded that agreed climate projections are not currently possible to make, but it called attention to the problem: "The energy, food, water and forestry projections [in the report] all assume implicitly a continuation of the nearly ideal climate of the 1950s and 1960s. . . . The scenarios are reported here to indicate the range of climatic change that should be analyzed in a study of this sort."

Simon seems to have ignored the carbon dioxide issue.

Kahn discusses the problem along with other possible causes of a warming trend. He concedes that a warming trend might raise the level of the oceans, but argues that "this would hardly mean the end of human society. Major shifts might be forced in agricultural areas and in coastal cities." He concludes, "It seems unlikely now that the carbon dioxide content will ever double unless mankind wants it to happen." Thus, he cheerfully dismisses this problem and thereby illustrates the curious inversion of his logic.

Why does he dismiss substance for "prediction"? He dismisses the real issues for fear they would lead his readers to lose faith in the future he has promised them. Would he not better join the environmentalists and concentrate on telling his audience that, if they want that future, they may need to take the carbon dioxide problem seriously?

Which intellectual approach is the more valid way of attempting to understand current trends affecting human welfare?

If you seek a sense of what will shape the future, examine the issues generated by population and economic growth; do not simply extrapolate the growth. Economic changes cannot be studied in a vacuum.

### Doctoring the News

One cannot escape the feeling that some of the Simon/Kahn rebuttals of "bad news" are directed more by polemical ends than by an effort to get at the truth. Such casual hip-shots are more likely to generate doubts about the writer's credentials than to convince readers that bad news is false.

For example, Simon makes points by using gross totals rather than per capita figures and shifts sources to manufacture trends. On world population, for example, to show that "U.N. and other standard estimates" have been steadily lowering their projections of anticipated population in 2000, he starts with a 1969 U.N. worst-case scenario, higher than their "high" series, then moves down to a later U.N. "low" series projection, and winds up with a 1977 Worldwatch Institute figure, justifying his inclusion of the Worldwatch figure by saying that Worldwatch is U.N.-supported. Through these devices, he manages to show the projection declining from 7.5 billion to 5.4 billion. In fact the U.N. projection for 2000 has remained remarkably constant, the median projection having fluctuated between 6.1 and 6.5 billion since 1957. And Lester Brown points out that his Worldwatch figure was not a projection but a proposed timetable.

Also, to prove that *world* air quality is improving, Simon, in *The Ultimate Resource*, cites statistics on *U.S.* air quality in the early 1970s. His data are dated and limited, but they are nevertheless gratifying. He pays the environmentalists whom he excoriates the ultimate compliment of appropriating their work. If U.S. air quality has stabilized or improved in some ways in the past decade, it is at least in some measure the product of environmental efforts such as the Clean Air Act.

Kahn generally takes a subtler line. He, too, points to improvements in air quality, but he is quite willing to accept the need for some expenditures on air quality and

other environmental measures and he includes "possible damage to earth because of complicated, complex and subtle ecological and environmental effects" among eight "real issues of the future." In effect, his technique is to admit the possibility of environmental problems but to avoid focusing on them or attempting to measure their importance; he moves quickly on to extolling the brightness of the future and attacking those he deems pessimistic.

The cornucopians slight the resource and environmental issues that the environmentalists consider the most important questions to be examined.

### The Lack of Feedback

The cornucopians stand breathless on the edge of wonderful new expectations. Simon writes: "Energy . . . is the 'master resource'; energy is the key constraint on the availability of all other resources. Even so, our energy supply is non-finite. . . ."

Certainly there are remarkable possibilities implicit in our growing awareness of what can be done with energy. But energy does not solve all problems.

The Sorcerer's Apprentice learned that immense power is not always benign to those who set it in motion. All of us have learned many sobering things about nuclear power since 1945.

Any projection for continued expansion in the use of energy must ask the question: What are the implications of developing the energy for the environment and for resources, and what are the consequences of its use likely to be? The same question should be asked about projections calling for continuing expansion in the use of chemicals, or indeed of any physical resource.

*Global 2000* undertook to carry out as much as it could of this kind of interactive analysis and found that the state of current knowledge did not permit it to be carried very far. Nevertheless, it undertook to examine literally hundreds of such interactions.

The agricultural projections, for instance—themselves central to other major projections such as population and GNP—require certain assumptions about intensification of agriculture, a doubling or

trebling of chemical fertilizer inputs (to a point where man-made introduction of nitrogen compounds into the biosphere will exceed the natural production), parallel increases in herbicides and pesticides, and reliance upon monocultures. These assumptions in turn generate questions concerning desertification, the conversion of forest and loss of forest cover, the effect of intensive agriculture on soil productivity, the impact of increased fertilizer application on watercourses and fisheries and perhaps on climate, and the risks associated with pesticides and monocultures—all of which relate back to the initial assumptions about agricultural productivity and eventually to GNP and population assumptions. The degree of confidence concerning different interrelationships is made clear, and reference is made to the technologies that can help forestall or mitigate the harmful interactions foreseen.

There is nothing remotely approaching this sort of interactive analysis in the works of the cornucopians. Kahn simply projects economic growth and assumes that the necessary inputs will be available and that environmental problems will be surmounted. Simon does not address these questions in any integrated fashion. One may question whether they are even addressing themselves to the real issue.

The speed with which technology is changing, the demands for economic growth posed by population growth, and the effort to raise living standards in developing countries are combining to force change at an unprecedented rate, which makes the study of the future more important than ever. The principal purpose of future studies should be to look as far ahead as possible, to study the implications of current and projected activity, to see how different sectors and issues interrelate. This process is anything but static. It should be a continuing process of probing and testing the potential consequences of different activities and directions of growth, of identifying the issues that need attention and the potential directions for beneficial change.

It was the lack of and the need for this capability that *Global 2000* highlighted. A follow-up study made specific recommendations as to how the capability might be improved within the U.S. government. Simon and Kahn, standing aside and reassuring everybody that the future looks good, seem strangely irrelevant to this entire process.

## The Infinite-Earth Fallacy

Neither Kahn nor Simon successfully deals with the simple facts that the earth is finite and that no physical growth can be indefinitely sustained. Let us cite three mathematical examples of the power of geometric growth, and preface them with the warning that they are not predictions:

• Even if the entire mass of the earth were petroleum, it would have been exhausted in 342 years if pre-1973 rates of increase in consumption had been maintained.

• Assume that we have one million years' supply of something—anything with a fixed supply—at current rates of consumption. Then let us increase the rate by just 2% per year (very roughly the current world population growth rate). Now, how long would the supply last? Answer: 501 years.

• At current growth rates, how long would it take for the world's human population to reach the absurdity of one person on each square meter of ice-free land? Answer: about 600 years.

These things won't happen. Resource use won't rise in a geometric curve until a resource is exhausted, then plunge suddenly to zero. There will be changes in real prices, adjustments, and substitutions—the whole pattern of constantly shifting realities that makes prediction impossible. The population will never remotely approach such a level. Long before then, birthrates will fall sharply, death rates will rise, or both.

However, the examples dramatize that the outer limits to current growth patterns are not so very far away. Populations have exceeded the carrying capacity of local environments many times and have sometimes paid the price of a population collapse, but human geometry for the first time requires that we think in terms of the relationship of population and economic activities to the entire earth.

World population has risen from about 1 billion to about 4.5 billion in about six generations. The demand for resources and the environmental impacts have been more than proportional, because per capita consumption has risen. This is not a mathematical fantasy or a projection for the future. It is a description of current reality. What the mathematical examples above suggest is that there are real limits, and not so very far away, that lead inescapably to this conclusion: Indefinitely sustained growth is mathematically impossible on a finite earth.

Kahn and Simon offer several responses to this point, none of them satisfactory.

• They fudge the problem by shifting the calculations. They project the potential longevity of supply of raw materials based on *current* demand rather than on increasing demand. Kahn and Simon have both used this technique. Since they are also assuming rising populations and rising per capita consumption, this is not an argument. It is a moonbeam. The calculations above should have disposed of it permanently.

A more sophisticated variant is to say that GNP will rise, but not resource consumption, because we will be more efficient and we will be consuming more intangibles such as culture. Very likely, within limits. However, nobody has yet drawn a model of sustained growth relying upon the consumption of operas to feed the multitudes.

• They suggest that the problem is so far away as to be irrelevant to those living now. Simon, in a bit of sophistry that he has probably come to regret by now, says: "The length of a one-inch line is finite in the sense that it is bounded at both ends. But the line within the end points contains an infinite number of points. . . . Therefore the number of points in that one-inch segment is not finite." He then extends the analogy to copper and oil. He argues that we cannot know the size of the resource "or its economic equivalent," and concludes, "Hence, resources are not 'finite' in any meaningful sense."

This kind of argument is really pretty shocking. An inch of string is

finite, even if it can theoretically be cut into infinitesimal pieces. The earth is finite, even though we may differ endlessly about how much of a given resource may be available.

• Kahn says that population and consumption levels will stabilize in two centuries. If he paints with an airbrush, it is a broad one. He projects population stabilization at 15 billion, but allows himself a margin of error of two—i.e., the population may be somewhere between 7.5 and 30 billion, or a rise of something between 67% and 567%. Most of us suspect that population will stop growing *somewhere* within that range.

He does not attempt to explore whether the resource base would support the 15 billion population he posits, or what the ecological and environmental effects of such population and consumption levels would be; he simply announces that we can handle them. He thinks that prosperity will lead to lower fertility, but he does not ask whether the population growth itself will in some countries preclude the prosperity he expects. He offers no capital/output analysis to suggest how world consumption levels will progress from where they are to where he hopes they will be. In short, he states a dream without attempting to explore how it will be realized or what the effects of its achievement will be.

• Simon says different things at different times. Sometimes, he advocates population growth without limits of time or circumstance, and he speaks of resource availability and population growth "forever" without recognizing the crudest of barriers: lack of space. Elsewhere, he advocates "moderate" population growth. Still elsewhere, he urges that we not worry about the effects of geometric population growth, since it has never been sustained in the past, and he documents his remark by showing how population growth has been periodically reversed by pestilence, invasion, and famine. Is this the man who professes such warm feelings toward his fellow humans?

Most of us agree that population growth will eventually stop, if only through the operation of the Four Horsemen. Most of us hope that it will be stabilized by limiting fertility rather than through hunger and rising mortality. It is this goal that leads many environmentalists to advocate conscious efforts to limit fertility. Kahn thinks it will happen automatically (but does not know how). Simon, apparently, isn't dismayed at the alternative.

## Technology As a Faith

Technology is knowledge. It is very difficult to predict knowledge if you don't have it yet, and technological trends are among the least predictable of the forces that will shape our future. The cornucopians are justified in reminding us forcefully of technology. A lot of people from Malthus on have underestimated it, and some environmentalists still ignore it.

Let us agree on one point: The world has been experiencing a burst of remarkable technological growth.

Although Kahn and Simon seem to have missed this point, *Global 2000* assumes that this rate will continue for the next 20 years. This approach may be faulted as too sanguine, but it is perhaps the safest projection given the relatively short time frame.

From here, however, we move to an article of faith among the cornucopians that the more pragmatic among us do not share: that the recent high rate of technological growth will continue *indefinitely*.

Yet Simon's advice to use the past as a guide argues against too much faith. Human history has been characterized by spurts of technological growth alternating with periods of slow growth, dormancy, or retrogression.

Technology may continue its recent phenomenal growth. It may not. It is an act of faith to assume that it will.

In addition, technology is not necessarily benign. It shapes us, as we shape it. Right now, it may be making communications cheaper,

## "Technology may continue its recent phenomenal growth. It may not. It is an act of faith to assume that it will."

while it makes unemployment worse. It helped to generate the spurt in population growth that now concerns the environmentalists. New industrial and agricultural technologies have created many of our present environmental problems. Other technology will almost certainly help us to correct our mistakes. A sensible observer with a feeling for history would be justified in assuming that those solutions will in turn generate new problems to be addressed.

If one chooses *not* to stake human welfare on unsupported faith in technology, a certain caution seems in order. Mankind will not have suffered if population growth is less than the advance of technology makes possible, but it may suffer very seriously if hopes for technology prove too high and if populations outrun the ability of science to support them.

## No Limits to Debating

If this article reflects a jaundiced view of the cornucopians' methods, it is not meant to discourage the debate. We can learn from each other.

We are all—cornucopians and environmentalists alike—trying to understand and describe a world in vast change. The technological growth on which the cornucopians pin their hopes is itself part of that change, as are the population growth and the environmental byproducts of technological growth that concern the environmentalists.

We are all—except perhaps for a few nuts who enjoy human misery—interested in seeing the modern im-

provement in human welfare continue.

Cornucopians by their nature tend to emphasize *solutions* where environmentalists emphasize *problems*. An interchange can be useful. Do the environmentalists overstate difficulties and fail to recognize new directions that can be helpful? Have we explored the opportunities presented by the oceans, by recent breakthroughs in biology, and by electronics and data processing as thoroughly as we have explored the dangers from desertification, deforestation, and acid rain? Have we pressed for the elimination of legal and administrative impediments to beneficial change as eagerly as we have pressed for restrictive legislation?

If we urge the cornucopians to recognize the problems, we should share their interest in promoting technological change that will help to address the problems.

Those of both persuasions should remember that this is no single battle at Armageddon. Solutions will create their own problems, and problems their solutions. We should perhaps all recognize that only change is constant. And change is very fast right now.

We would ask of the cornucopians that they accept as much. Growth such as we have witnessed cannot be indefinitely extended. We must all seek a sustainable relationship between people and the earth. Most particularly, we must work out the implications of population growth. The issue cannot be: Should it stop? The questions are only: When should it stop? And how?

# Population

Beginning students often oversimplify when they discuss the world's population. For instance, they often associate the "world population problem" with women having too many children. In fact, because there is great diversity between regions in terms of population dynamics, the reality is that there is not a *single* population problem, but many population problems. For example, in Africa, where there is a large rural population, there is both a high birthrate and a high death rate. Life expectancy is in the mid-fifties, and there are many health problems. Latin America has a different set of circumstances. The largely urban population has a much lower death rate than that of Africa, and while the birthrate is dropping, it has not dropped fast enough to stabilize the population. As a result, many areas of Latin America have the fastest growing populations in the world.

The world's population situation is not restricted to rapid growth and too many people. In some areas, governments do not believe there are enough people. In the oil-rich Gulf States (e.g., Saudi Arabia), governments pursue a pronatal policy. Currently, large numbers of foreign workers have immigrated to these countries to work in the oil fields and at other, related projects. Consequently, the governments are pursuing policies that encourage large families so that eventually their own population will be able to replace the foreign workers.

Population demographics also vary a great deal from nonindustrial countries to the industrially developed nations. In North America and Western Europe, women, on the average, are having two children or less. Population in the United States is growing primarily because people are immigrating to the country, not because people are having large families.

In 1987 global population reached 5 billion, a gain of 2 billion people in just 27 years. The lead article in this section discusses the implications of this historic occasion. The issues of this unprecedented number of people in terms of urbanization and Third World development are introduced.

In the articles that follow, these and other population issues are examined in greater detail. Margaret Wolfson, for example, discusses the politics of population. During the past decade, there has been an increased awareness of the linkage between population growth and development policy. As a result, governments have been adopting policies to increase populations in a few cases, but more

often, they have been pursuing population growth rate. A case in versial policy of limiting parents to Julian Baum's article.

The movement of people is the articles. The transformation of the nantly rural to urban is examined, e enon of the supercities which i movement of people from the countr movement of people from one c analyzed. According to Charles K raises many questions. How does identity when it must absorb large r ple? Where will it obtain the reso integrate these new members into society?

The population section concludes Acquired Immune Deficiency Syndr problem. Whereas all of the other a are concerned with population growt the possibility of population decline The author speculates about the from the disease if a cure is not fou

Making predictions about the f population is a complicated matter, b forces at work and considerable va region. The danger of oversimplifi be overcome if people are going t ingful opinions and policies.

## Looking Ahead: Challenge Que
What are the basic characteristi tion situation? How many people the population growing?

How do population dynamics the next?

What regions of the world are of international immigrants?

How does rapid population gr ment, social structures, and the views itself?

How does a rapidly growing p World country's development pl

What potential impact does A growth, social values, and econ

# Unit 2

# 5 BILLION AND COUNTING...

**Each year, the earth's population grows by a number equal to the population of Mexico.**

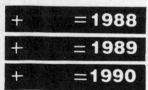

**Nigeria's population is expected to surge from 100 million to 532 million by the middle of the next century. That would give Nigeria a population equal to all of Africa today.**

## Timothy Aeppel

*Staff writer of* The Christian Science Monitor

**Washington**

For the first time in history, there are more than 5 billion members of the human family. And this number is expected to double again before the global population stabilizes late in the next century.

In the 15 minutes that it takes to read these two pages, more than 2,200 people will be added to the world's population. Each week, we add the equivalent of another Houston; each year, another Mexico.

But the problem of population goes far deeper than numbers. Analysts agree that many advances of the 20th century, such as falling death rates and rising incomes, could be reversed unless more is done to control population growth.

The current expansion of human settlements poses unprecedented environmental challenges. For example, the clearing of tropical forests for new cropland is thought to contribute to the gradual warming of the earth's atmosphere, known as the greenhouse effect.

"The fact that we've reached 5 billion means that we've managed to overcome high mortality," says Dr. Nafis Sadik, the new head of the United Nations Fund for Population Activities. But, she adds, it also underscores the need for effective family planning.

The UN will observe the "Day of the 5 Billion" on next Saturday. It is promoted as a day to "contemplate a future in which population will eventually reach 10.2 billion."

UN officials work with three population scenarios, each showing the level that world population will stabilize at under different circumstances. The middle-range projection is 10.2 billion, which assumes steady progress in bringing down global birthrates through education and family planning.

So far, actual population growth has fallen in this middle range—despite ups and downs along the way. The unanticipated success of China's controversial family planning program, for instance, is offset by failures in other regions.

A balance between births and deaths is the ultimate objective. In recent years, nations throughout the world made strides in health and sanitation which helped boost the number of babies that survive as well as the length of individual lives.

In most industrialized countries, this pattern led to a natural decline in births. As incomes rise and knowledge about family planning spreads, families tend to limit the number of children they have. Indeed, some Western European countries have even begun to see a natural decline in their populations.

Most developing countries have made significant progress in slowing their growth rates, stirring hope that they would follow in the footsteps of the industrialized nations.

But analysts now worry that a number of countries may be stuck in a "demographic trap"—where rapid growth outstrips the ability to advance

# Population growth, 1750-2100

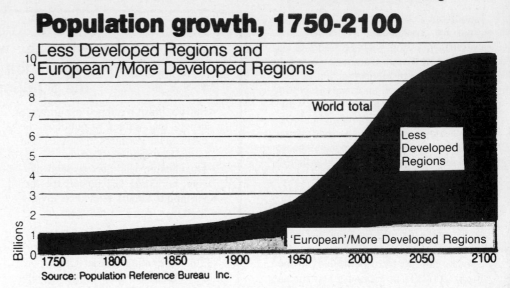

Source: Population Reference Bureau Inc.

socially and economically. Nigeria's population, for example, is expected to surge from 100 million to 532 million before it levels off in the middle of the next century. That would give that nation a population equal to all the people living in Africa today.

"We're putting enormous stress on the world's natural systems," says Lester Brown, president of the Worldwatch Institute, a Washington-based research group. "And in some parts of the world, those systems are deteriorating."

The result, says Mr. Brown, is economic decline. In parts of Latin America and Africa, for instance, real incomes have fallen in recent years. "Declining living standards in rapid population growth areas is not hypothetical anymore, it's happening," says Brown.

The link between population and economic prosperity remains controversial, however. Some economists argue that a growing population boosts a nation's economy—providing a larger pool of workers and expanded markets for manufactured goods. This was certainly the case for Europe and North America during the Industrial Revolution, when populations grew rapidly along with wealth.

But, compared with today, the population surge that fed the factories of the Industrial Revolution was a blip on the screen. The key elements behind today's growth include:

**Urbanization.** By the year 2010, more than half the world's population will live in urban centers. Cities in developing countries are mushrooming

especially fast—with expansion fueled by migration from the countryside and the natural growth of urban populations. In 1950, only three of the world's 10 largest cities were in the developing world; by the year 2000, all but two of them will be in developing regions.

**Age.** About half the people in the world are under age 24. This has ominous implications for the future, since these younger people will start having children in coming years. As a result, even if birthrates fall rapidly, growth is now inevitable well into the next century.

**Expansion in developing regions.** Nine out of 10 babies born today are in the developing world. This tends to make these countries even younger on average than the world total. It would be a mistake, however, to view these

nations as a single bloc. Some countries, such as South Korea, have dramatically cut population growth and appear on the verge of joining the ranks of industrialized nations.

The most disturbing trends, meanwhile, are in Africa, South Asia, and Central America. These regions have rapid population growth coupled with quickly deteriorating resource bases.

"One doesn't need to be an ecologist to know that if you're cutting down 27 trees for every one planted—as is the case in Africa—you'll eventually denude the continent," says Werner Fornos, president of the Population Institute, a Washington-based group that advocates population control.

The key challenge is to feed these ever-growing numbers of people. Countries such as Brazil have plenty of

# World's 10 largest cities
(population in millions)

| | 1950 | | | 1985* | | | 2000 | |
|---|---|---|---|---|---|---|---|---|
| 1 | Greater New York | 12.4 | 1 | Tokyo/Yokohama | 18.8 | 1 | Mexico City | 25.8 |
| 2 | London | 10.4 | 2 | Mexico City | 17.3 | 2 | São Paulo | 23.97 |
| 3 | Rhein/Ruhr, West Germany | 6.9 | 3 | São Paulo, Brazil | 15.9 | 3 | Tokyo/Yokohama | 20.2 |
| 4 | Tokyo/Yokohama | 6.7 | 4 | Greater New York | 15.6 | 4 | Calcutta | 16.5 |
| 5 | Shanghai | 5.8 | 5 | Shanghai | 11.96 | 5 | Greater New York | 15.8 |
| 6 | Paris | 5.5 | 6 | Calcutta | 10.95 | 6 | Shanghai | 14.3 |
| 7 | Greater Buenos Aires | 5.3 | 7 | Greater Buenos Aires | 10.9 | 7 | Seoul | 13.8 |
| 8 | Chicago/N.W. Indiana | 5.0 | 8 | Rio de Janeiro | 10.4 | 8 | Rio de Janeiro | 13.3 |
| 9 | Moscow | 4.8 | 9 | London | 10.36 | 9 | Greater Beunos Aires | 13.2 |
| 10 | Calcutta | 4.7 | 10 | Seoul | 10.3 | 10 | London | 10.5 |

*1985 is the latest year for which figures are available
Source: United Nations

## 2. POPULATION

land, but cultivating it will lead to massive deforestation.

Sharon Camp, vice-presidnet of the Population Crisis Committee, says the combination of environmental decay and regional food shortages is putting the world on a collision course with famine. But careful planning and vigorous population control could avert disaster, she says. "What happened in the last population doubling is that a lot of countries lost what little wiggle room they had left," Dr. Camp says.

A 1983 study by the UN's Food and Agriculture Organization found that, even using the most advanced farming techniques, 19 out of 117 nations will not be able to feed themselves in the year 2000. If farmers use less intense farming, the number of countries that are facing shortages jumps to 65.

Such dire projections have helped make family planning a top priority in many countries. "Contraceptive supplies that used to last for months in some developing countries are being cleared out overnight," says Camp. "It's spreading like a prairie fire."

Meanwhile, the Reagan administration has dramatically altered the United States policy on population control.

At an international population conference in 1984, the United States

---

## No one knows exactly when the world's population clicked past the 5 billion mark.

But that hasn't stopped a number of groups that wanted to publicize the event. The Washington-based Population-Environment Balance organization was first through the gate, heralding last July as the turning point. Others tended to favor March or April of this year.

The United Nations designated July 11 as the "Day of the 5 Billion," reflecting official UN projections that the 5 billionth baby will be born this month.

"This is what the statisticians call the fallacy of misplaced precision," says Sharon Camp, vice-president of the Population Crisis Committee. What's important, she says, is what these rapidly growing numbers

mean in terms of the human condition.

Observers say it would have been nice if all groups agreed on a single date, but that was impossible. The UN, for instance, uses official population figures, which some nations juggle for political purposes.

Carl Haub, a demographer with the Population Reference Bureau, says one of the things the UN didn't factor in was the recent jump in China's birthrate. That nation— which accounts for one-fifth of the world's population—has a highly effective birth control program.

Even a slight increase in such a large country can substantially alter global demographic trends, says Mr. Haub.

---

announced that population was a "neutral" factor in development. The US has also withdrawn support from the UN's Fund for Population Activities

and the International Planned Parenthood Federation, citing these groups' involvement with programs that offer abortion as a family planning option.

---

# How regions compare
(in millions)

| | Population estimate (mid-1987) | Crude birthrate | Population 'doubling time' in years (at current rate) | Population projected to 2000 | Population projected to 2020 | Percentage of population under age 15/older than 65 | Percentage of population living in cities |
|---|---|---|---|---|---|---|---|
| Africa | 601 | 44 | 24 | 880 | 1,479 | 45/3 | 30 |
| Asia | 2,930 | 28 | 37 | 3,598 | 4,584 | 34/5 | 32 |
| North America | 270 | 15 | 101 | 296 | 326 | 22/12 | 74 |
| Latin America | 421 | 30 | 31 | 537 | 712 | 38/4 | 67 |
| Europe | 495 | 13 | 272 | 507 | 502 | 21/13 | 73 |
| Soviet Union | 284 | 19 | 79 | 312 | 355 | 26/9 | 65 |
| Australia, New Zealand, and South Pacific Islands | 25 | 20 | 59 | 29 | 35 | 28/8 | 71 |

Source: Population Reference Bureau Inc., 1987

# The Politics of Population

## Margaret Wolfson

*Margaret Wolfson is a senior staff member at the Development Center of the Organization for Economic Co-operation and Development, where she is responsible for research in the inter-relationship between population and development. She is the author of several books on the management aspect of development assistance, on population policies, and on how to implement them through workable population programs. The views expressed in this article are solely those of the author and do not necessarily represent those of the OECD.*

A few years ago, an American specialist on family planning, Carl Djerassi, brought out a book with the intriguing title *The Politics of Contraception*. It proved to be not, as one might have expected, a study of the political considerations that shape the determination of population policies by national governments or the implementation of those policies through the actions of individuals, but rather a scientific appraisal of current contraceptive technologies. It would seem that the "politics" of the case, in the more narrowly accepted sense of the word, still awaits a similarly scientific analysis. We know that over the past three decades, countries in increasing numbers have decided that the achievement of their national objectives required a policy for population. But what prompted these decisions, whether they were appropriate for the situation, in their timing and context, and whether, as the twentieth century draws to a close, they will still remain valid, are questions about which we know very much less. This article does not presume to offer any clear answers; the intention, much more modestly, is simply to suggest for consideration what seem to be some of the principal factors behind the decisions themselves and the way that they are likely to work out.

### Fewer is Better: Anti-Natalist Policies

Perhaps our starting point should be the fact that so *many* countries today have formulated an explicit population policy of one kind or another—a phenomenon largely unknown on the political scene until after the Second World War. The industrialized countries of the world, disturbed at the rate at which their national populations are shrinking, have policies intended to try to reverse the trend. More surprising is the growing number of *developing* countries which have adopted population policies mostly, though by no means always, in the direction of curbing a rate of population growth deemed to be too high. We have become so accustomed to the prognostications of the Club of Rome, aid agencies, development specialists, ecologists and, of course, demographers warning of the dire consequences of failing to check the population growth that has proved to be such an astounding phenomenon of the post-war developing world, that we tend to forget that in most regions, the countries most severely affected by a population explosion, in fact, now do have policies to try to contain it. By 1983, 35 developing countries had an official policy to reduce their population growth rate, and in 34 others, the government supported family planning activities, although for other than demographic reasons—usually for reasons of health or as a human right. The exceptions are notably in Africa and in some countries of Latin America.

The number is more remarkable given the many compelling reasons that governments have for *not* attempting anything so difficult as to modify demographic trends. Most governments of developing countries are faced with grievous economic problems—wide-spread poverty, unemployment and under-employment, insufficient new investment, declining terms of trade, and rising external debt. In such conditions of economic contraction, tough decisions have to be made about how to allocate scarce resources. To spend some of them on a program of population control will—assuming that it is successful—show results some time in the future. But it will not make any appreciable impact on the *present* situation—although it may prevent it from getting worse—and governments, by the nature of things, are concerned first and foremost with today's problems, not those of the future. And the future results of population programs, in social and economic terms, are very difficult to quantify, thus defying cost-benefit analysis of the desirability of investing resources in this area, rather than in something else. Moreover, in the matter of population, it is particularly hard to estimate with any degree of certainty just what the future situation will prove to be. There is very little hard data, and although demographers can produce impressive calculations of population movements and profiles, the resource consumption, needs for basic services, and employment possiblilities of a generation hence, these are *projections* only, based largely on extrapolation of present trends—i.e., assumptions. Many things can happen in the course of a generation to divert population trends from the course predicted, or to change their pace. Twenty years ago, who would have foreseen that Cuba, for example, would have halved its birth rate in only 20 years, or that in a country as big as Indonesia, what had seemed an inexorable rate of growth would slow so soon? Similarly, in the expansionist years following the end of World War II, no one would have imagined the present fertility decline in the industrialized countries which so exercises their governments today. And even were the predictions to offer a reasonable basis for population

"The Politics of Population," by Margaret Wolfson, *Harvard International Review*, March 1986, pp. 4-8, 32. Courtesy of *Harvard International Review*.

## 2. POPULATION

planning, who can tell with any assurance what is the *optimum* population size for any particular nation?

There are also powerful political reasons why a government might well hesitate before embarking on a policy to reduce the nation's fertility. In countries plagued by problems of factionalism, whether from political, religious, or ethnic groups, an anti-natalist policy on the part of the government will almost certainly be interpreted by the minority groups as an attempt to limit their numbers and enhance the position of the ruling group. The fear of "genocide" is ever-present. Thus Sanjay Ghandi's sterilization campaign in the mid-1970's led to rioting in Old Delhi by the Muslim population who saw in it a Hindu ploy for domination. So acute is the "minority syndrome," and so sensitive the matter of relative numerical strength, that in some countries of Africa even census-taking has provoked violence.

Even in those countries where ethnic and/or religious differences pose no particular problem—and their number would seem to be getting fewer all the time—a government policy to control fertility is unlikely to be widely popular. At the very least it implies government interference in the most private and personal of human relations, an invasion of human rights, and very often, a disturbance of the traditional patterns of society and behavior.

Given this formidable battery of reasons for caution, why have so many developing countries decided nevertheless to go ahead and declare an official policy to reduce fertility? The answer is simple—they have done so under pressure of events, which have already made it plain that doing nothing would be more dangerous.

Which means, of course, that for many of the countries which are pursuing a policy to limit population growth, the decision has been taken only *after* the grievous consequences of not having such a policy have already become manifest. An increasingly impoverished countryside that becomes less and less able to support its growing population, the mounting numbers of unemployed and under-employed, galloping urbanization, worsening poverty, and income inequalities are pressures that no government can afford to ignore indefinitely. In countries where 40 percent or more of the population is under the age of 15, an increasingly embittered and radicalized younger generation presents a potentially dangerous political threat to the government in power. "The prime recruiting grounds for such destabilizing movements are capital city slums, where the legions of unemployed and underemployed are concentrated, where the surplus population gathers with nothing to do, and where abandoned street children are looking for adventure and diversion. It can be short march from there to the national palace." The quotation comes from an analysis of the situation in Latin America (Howard and Ieda Siquiera Warda's article "Population and Internal Unrest"). It can be applied, almost unchanged, to other regions of the developing world.

Governments confronted directly with civil unrest are not likely to respond with action to control the birth rate, but rather with political repression. The critical question, therefore, is how *soon* a government will make the connection **among** political disobedience, economic and social distress, and the population explosion, and adopt a population policy. Not only is the question critical for the internal stability of the countries concerned, but it may also have an important geopolitical dimension, since unrest—particularly if it leads to large-scale displacement of populations—offers other coun-

tries the occasion for an international response.

The view is frequently heard that the policies eventually adopted by the governments of developing countries to control their population growth tend to be too little and too late. Certainly, some governments would seem to be almost willfully tardy about recognizing the hard logic of the situation— notably those in Africa, and in some of the countries in Latin America. Others have made the connection surprisingly early; India has since 1952, Sri Lanka since 1954, and Tunisia since the early 1960's, albeit with varying degrees of effectiveness. The case of Mexico is particularly interesting, since in 1974, the President had the courage not only to reverse a pronatalist tradition going back to pre-conquest times, as well as his own frequently-stated commitment to it, but also to back it with the full force of the government authority at his command, once the new policy had been announced.

President Echeverria of Mexico had taken the precaution of preparing the ground carefully in advance, and had either secured the support or at least neutralized the opposition of the leading opinion and interest groups in the country. A stable and secure government is certainly better placed to introduce a national policy to control the country's fertility than one more vulnerable to hostile opinion. But no government, even the most arbitrary, is totally immune to the opinions and pressures of other power groups within the country. The army, for example, is likely to be of particular importance. Concerned, by its nature, with problems of order, efficiency, and international competitiveness, the army is normally quick to recognize the connection between civil unrest and a population that is growing too fast. Thus we find that not only governments headed by soldier-politicians (Bangladesh, Indonesia, Thailand, and Pakistan), but also countries where the military is a strong force behind a civilian government (as in Turkey), have strong policies of population control, some of them of many years standing.

### More is better: Pro-Natalist Policies and the Influence of Ideological and Religious Beliefs

In some countries, the government has made a deliberate appraisal of the nation's demographic perspective and has decided not to curb population growth but to encourage it instead. Indeed, this might be held to be a natural first reflex of government policy; expanding populations having been historically associated with periods of economic and political expansion (such as during Elizabethan England and the colonial era). Even today there is a lingering belief that a large population means power—economic, political, and military, despite the countervailing evidence of modern sophisticated weaponry (viz present—day Iran, for example).

It is understandable—if not wholly rational—that countries would take confidence in numbers, or fear that their lack of numbers might make them tempting prey for hostile or predatory neighbours. But population would seem to be an area where rationality has strangely little to do with reality. Why do the countries of Western Europe, for example, find the prospect of a population decline so distressing? What is at issue here is not the practical consequence of a shrinking domestic market or the problem of paying social security to increasing numbers of the aged, but rather, national prestige. Thus Jacques Chirac, speaking of the French legislation liberalizing abortion, proclaims that he does not "want our descendants to be able to say, 100 years from now, that we were irresponsible; that we deliberately sacrificed our country's future." It is honor that is at stake.

Developing countries might be expected to feel the same way. Moreover, they often have additional historical reasons for an emotional identification of national assertiveness with an increasing population. The memory of the slave trade in Africa and the excesses of colonialization is still a potent political reality. The cry of "neo-colonialism" from leaders in developing countries reached its high point at the Bucharest World Population Conference in 1974, after a decade of Western encouragement of family planning efforts. The now-famous slogan "Development is the best contraceptive," neatly brought together their resentment of the more opulent West, the desire for a more equitable share of the world's resources, and left wing philosophy, which saw birth control as a distraction from development.

The number of developing countries that have officially proclaimed a strongly pro-natalist population policy is relatively small. Of these, many have Marxist governments (e.g., Angola, Burkina Faso, the Yemen Arab Republic, and Kampuchea). Some have additional and non-ideological reasons: the fear of encirclement (Bolivia) and very low population density (Cameroon). What is surprising is not that they should have decided that their nation needs more people, but that some governments which have followed the opposite policy with considerable success have now totally reversed their position. Thus, Cuba, after achieving an astonishingly rapid population decline, has now decided that it wants a larger population. Malaysia, which has had a national population policy since 1966, has recently announced a long-term plan to raise its population five fold by the year 2100. The case of the Malaysian government is particularly interesting, since the motive seems to be the desire to preserve the pre-eminence of the *majority* group within the country, the opposite of the "minority syndrome."

In principle, resistance to fertility control is a cherished tenet of both Marxist belief and the Catholic Church. (One of the many surprises of the Bucharest Conference was the spectacle of the Vatican and the People's Republic of China making common cause on the issue.) In practice, however, it would seem that the influence of the Church has generally been the less potent of the two. The strongly conservative line of the Encyclical Humanae Vitae and subsequent papal statements has undoubtedly given a new edge to traditionalism among the devout and seems to have given pause to some Latin American governments that have not yet taken a stand on the matter of their country's exuberant population growth. (But in Latin America, the opposition to family planning comes not only from the extreme right, but from the extreme left as well.) On the other hand, the possibility of opposition from the Church leaders in such strongly Catholic countries as the Philippines and Mexico did not deter those governments from adopting policies to limit the birth rate, nor, in either case, did the Church even make significant efforts to try to do so.

Clearly, the influence of established or traditional religion in a country will depend on the particular setting. Normally, the force of religion tends to diminish with modernization. The evidence seems to suggest that if the position held by the religious leaders of a country is not in line with majority public opinion, public opinion usually prevails—c.f. the response in Italy and Spain on the matter of birth control and divorce. A critical question for a government, therefore, is to gauge the degree of popular support that the Church establishment really commands.

The experience of the Islamic countries that have official fertility control polices is particularly interesting. The Koran makes no definitive statement on the subject of fertility and contraception, thus leaving the way open to a variety of interpretations. In many Moslem countries, in fact, the religious hierarchy has been persuaded actively to support the government's population program. In Indonesia, for example, the powerful Muhammediyah movement has been co-opted to help promote the national Family Planning and Population Programme.

Today, however, a new religious influence is at work, threatening with a wholly unexpected force the attempts of governments and individuals to limit fertility. The swift rise of religious fundamentalism within the past few years is something for which the modern world seems to have been totally unprepared. Common to the Christian, Muslim and Judaic religions, its threat is greater because it defies rationalism. Beginning with a fierce defense of the sanctity of human life, it has gone on to wage war not only on abortion, sterilization and any program thought to include coercion, but eventually on the whole principle of contraception, condemning measures to limit procreation as interference with God's will. It has a powerful mystique and seems to appeal to growing numbers of people in developed and developing countries alike.

### The Role of International Agencies and Foreign Governments

The view is sometimes heard—notably in left-wing circles—that the idea of population control for developing countries is an invention of the Western world. Even dismissing the cruder Marxist "anti-imperialist" edge to this charge, one has to recognize that since the mid-1960's, Western opinion-leaders have been increasingly loud and insistent in their warnings to developing countries that failure to curb population growth would frustrate their plans for development.

This "neo-Malthusianism" has had two thrusts—the global "doomsday" approach of the Club of Rome, for example, which stressed the pressure of an inexorably mounting population on natural resources world wide, and the national approach, which pointed to the danger for *individual countries*. Of the two, it was this second approach that was likely to get the better hearing, particularly if offers of Western funding for population programs went along with it.

There can be little doubt that the international agencies and Western donors of aid succeeded in making many governments of developing countries aware of their population problem and persuaded a number of them to adopt population policies and to launch national population programs *earlier* than they would have done otherwise. In accepting the anti-natalist premise, the motives of such governments were probably mixed, as motives usually are. Among them might be the attraction of the foreign exchange that would accrue with population assistance, the desire for international support and good-will, the desire to make the country appear as a secure bet for foreign investment, as well as a genuine concern to varying degrees, depending on the case. There can be little doubt that for some countries, the prime consideration was to please international opinion, the source of foreign capital. In these countries, not only was the real conviction lacking, but so was the political commitment. The result in such cases—not surprisingly—has been a low level of program achievement, as in Kenya, for example. The Kenyan population program was devised largely as a result of Western initiative, but despite massive injections of foreign assistance, it has so dismally failed, that today the birth rate has reached an unparalleled 4.1 percent a year. It would seem that by now the Kenyan authorities recognize the necessity to take the situation more seriously; in Mexico in 1984, the Vice-President of Kenya not only forcefully repeated his Government's policy of population control, but added that no population program could succeed without a *strong political commitment* at all levels of government.

It is now recognized that in the early days of population assistance, the voice of international opinion leaders and aid agencies was sometimes over-insistent, ill-informed and insensitive. But aid agencies, like everyone else, have matured with experience and now perceive their earlier errors of exuberance. Certainly, their approach today is lower-key, better-founded, and considerably more realistic.

Leaving aside their warnings and exhortations, it is easy to overestimate the influence of international opinion in shaping third-world population policy. Foreign aid has not accounted for more than one-tenth of total expenditure on population programs in developing countries, although within individual countries, the proportion varies greatly according to the maturity of the program and the circumstances of the country. In India, for example, barely 10 percent of the program is now financed by foreign aid, whereas in Bangladesh, it accounts for about 90 percent. The international agencies and bilateral donors of aid that have been in the forefront of aid for population are emphatic about the continuing and indeed increasing need for massive population assistance. The President of the World Bank has called for a four-fold increase in assistance. And now that China has been added to the countries receiving population assistance, the overall need would indeed seem to be larger than ever.

So speaks the "population establishment." But, as already mentioned, a new challenge has arisen lately in the right-to-life movement, which is gathering momentum in the Western world as well as in developing countries. Abortion is a life-and-death issue about which many people feel passionately. Its very considerable political significance today is due to the fact that it has been joined by the (also growing) movement of right-wing populism, and together, they constitute a threat to all family planning efforts. When in 1984, the US government announced to an astonished world that its prescription for population problems had changed from that of population control to economic growth, spear headed by private enterprise, and that it would henceforth refuse US assistance to programs which included abortion or any element of coercion, the common assumption was that this was probably a temporary position, taken in response to US internal pressures in the period preceding the presidential election. This has not proved to be the case, and far from being abandoned, the position has been further hardened and extended.

The danger now is two-fold: first, starting with withdrawal of support to certain types of family planning activity, the US may be led to diminish its assistance overall. Second, these attitudes may have a spill-over effect on other population assistance agencies. The latter may already be happening. A number of bilateral donors of population assistance have indicated reservations similar to those of the US regarding the content of the programs that they will henceforward be willing to support. Their contributions to international and private agencies providing population assistance may be reduced in consequence.

The explanation may be in part that a wave of conservative fundamentalism is sweeping through our earlier rational and progress-oriented world. As a rejection of modernization and materialism, it has a powerful appeal in a world that is growing disillusioned with both. But this phenomenon is coinciding with a certain "donor fatigue" on the whole issue of population—a sense that it has been overplayed and that the crisis of a population "explosion", if indeed it ever existed, is now past. It is true, of course, that taken globally, the figures for population growth have passed their peak and, except for Africa, are now beginning to decline. A new spirit of complacency is accordingly gaining ground.

The irony is that this attitude is spreading among Western opinion just at the time that the developing countries are showing a greater understanding of the inter-relationship of "population" and "development" than ever before. The consensus on this subject at the Mexico City Conference showed a remarkable evolution from the angry controversy about population *versus* development at Bucharest ten years earlier. Many developing countries now have the knowledge and the financial resources to pursue the population policies appropriate to their situation without much outside help. But others are not yet there and will continue to need aid for this purpose for many years to come.

### Policies and Practice

Governments that adopt national policies to control fertility in either direction do so for societal ends. But the people, who are expected to implement these polices by making changes in their personal behavior are not likely to be greatly influenced by these societal reasons, as a rule. Instead, they are concerned with the implications for them as individuals and for their families. Most governments include both the societal and the personal approach in education, stressing the relationship between population, natural resources, and employment, and the possibilities of a better quality of life for the individual and the family. The proportions of these two approaches in any particular case says a lot about the nature of the government and society.

Today, it is the communist countries, with their society-based ideology, that have the directness to present their programs as a societal imperative alone. They also offer a national "mystique" which transcends the individual citizen's concern with the material and personal matters (Nazi Germany and Fascist Italy made a similar appeal). The extreme example is, of course, China, where the authorities have never pretended that their rigorous policy of population control has as its purpose the greater welfare and happiness of the individual citizen of today. Communist countries with pro-natalist population policies also use the societal approach.

When population programs are based on family planning, it is difficult for a government to persuade its people to agree to have fewer children now in order to benefit the population of tomorrow, particularly if many are living in poverty. In most cases, therefore, the government finds it more prudent to suggest that family planning is in the interest of the individual family today. The emphasis of the program is acordingly placed on "welfare." In fact, over the past decade, most governments have changed the wording of the national population programs from "family planning" to "family welfare." In India, Egypt, and Pakistan, among many others, the program is officially known as the "Family Welfare Programme". What is interesting is that the change, which initially may have been largely a question of packaging, has since come to apply to the content of the program as well. In India, for example, the Family Welfare Programme now includes, in addition to family planning, a broad range of welfare services, covering health care, nutrition, education, and the status of women, for example. Other national programs show a similar evolution.

The welfare approach may thus help to make a population program more palatable. But it does not thereby make it more successful. Indeed, how to get a population program really to work is an exceptionally difficult task. The instinctive reaction of the public, as we have noted, is to resent it. Further, in many cases, people have their own ideas about the number of children that they want and will thus resist the government's attempts to impose different norms. But even in the absence of an especially strong countervailing tradition, a population program is particularly difficult to implement for purely administrative reasons. It seeks to provide a personal service to be delivered nation wide to very large numberrs of individuals, often living in widely dispersed and remote areas. It thus requires an enormous number of workers, many at low administrative and technical levels, who have to be trained, organized, supervised, and regularly given supplies. For any country, such an administration-intensive activity will represent a formidable challenge. For a developing country, the burden is enormous.

When a government has only limited administrative resources, it is unreasonable to expect that it will be more effective in implementing its population program than its other social development programs (although aid agencies have not infrequently fallen into the error of hoping that it will). Even though a firmly entrenched government may be able to give stronger political backing to its population programs than a less secure one, the success of the program will eventually depend on the government's administrative and managerial capacity.

Governments have several strategies at their disposal, including improving the accessibility and the quality of the service (often the most difficult), promoting population education and family planning motivation (with the assistance of the media, folk art, and if possible, personal persuasion), and applying a judicious mixture of incentives and disincentives. The latter are the subject of a good deal of controversy. Some people argue that in a very poor community, a small monetary compensation such as for working time lost during a sterilization operation is not only morally justifiable but economically essential. Others argue that it is morally indefensible. Certainly, the dividing line between disincentives and coercion is a very tenuous one, as families exceeding the state-approved family size see their already exiguous salary and welfare benefits cut back while their family responsibilities increase.

Quite apart from the moral considertion, the *efficacy* of incentives is still more doubtful when used to support pro-

natalist policies. Experience has shown that it is possible for governments to induce people to have *fewer* children than they might otherwise have wanted by using a combination of pressure and persuasion. To get them to produce *more* children than they themselves desire is something else again. The experience of many industrialized countries, especially those in Eastern Europe, suggests that the monetary incentives such as children's allowances, tax reliefs, and maternity leave, influence only the poorer families in the community, those that are often larger in the first place.

For governments intent on reducing the nation's fertility, a policy that is backed by a major political commitment and then fails to meet its objectives is a dangerous thing. In such a situation, the natural tendency is to intensify the pressure, and to step up the disincentives for non-compliance. A program that starts off by offering its citizens voluntary family planning services can be led to become increasingly coercive. The change may not even be due to the program having *failed* in its objectives, but simply to its inability to achieve them fast enough. In China, for example, the government's astonishing program of planned births had brought down the rate of population growth with a speed and effectiveness unparalleled in history, but which was still insufficient to prevent the population from stabilizing at a figure above the country's anticipated carrying capacity. The authorities have accordingly intensified the pressure in order to achieve still speedier results, and introduced the one-child family policy that so disturbs opinion today in the Western world. The emphasis on sterilization in the Population Programme of Bangladesh, today, reflects a similar sense of urgency.

### The Next Ten Years

Some observers, mostly in the West, fear that this trend may be repeated in other countries, as governments become aware of the widening gap between the demands of their constantly expanding populations and their own ability to meet these demands. Such a prospect is not solely negative—this recognition may lead some African countries to adopt the population policies that they have hitherto stoutly resisted. But it may lead to some excesses as well, as pressures intensify and governments become alarmed. At the same time, it is not unreasonable to wonder whether some of those countries which have had policies to control their population growth and which have been successful in their application—whether a result of the policy itself or a combination of other factors—may not take fright at their very success. If Cuba and Malaysia now seek to increase their population size, is it not possible that, say, South Korea or Indonesia or Tunisia may at some point decide that it would be in their best national interest as well?

# Baby makes three – and no more

## China's one-child policy cuts population growth; but does it produce 'little emperors'?

**Julian Baum**

Staff writer of The Christian Science Monitor

**Canton, China**

How to raise up a child in the way he (or she) should go? The old question has new urgency in China. With a national policy that generally permits only one child per family, Chinese society is entering unknown social terrain.

Now 8 out of 10 first-graders are only-children. By the year 2000, most Chinese 20-year-olds will be from single-child families, writes Chinese Youth magazine.

"What will be the impact of these brotherless and sisterless people on China's development?" the magazine asked in its June issue.

Will they be more secure, better educated, and more independent, as some people hope? Or will they be self-indulgent, egocentric, and overbearing, as others think?

The questions are troubling schoolteachers and state officials in a country where being alone is an anathema. But for parents who are intent on pampering their only child, it seems they are raising a generation of "little emperors."

Cartoons in the Chinese press often point to the 4-2-1 syndrome, or the prob-

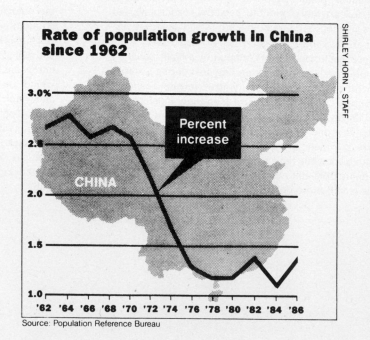

**Rate of population growth in China since 1962**

Percent increase

CHINA

3.0%

2.5

2.0

1.5

1.0

'62 '64 '66 '68 '70 '72 '74 '76 '78 '80 '82 '84 '86

Source: Population Reference Bureau

SHIRLEY HORN - STAFF

lem of four grandparents and two parents indulging one child. Children tell their own stories.

"I ride on Daddy's shoulders and ask my parents to make a circle with their arms," a schoolchild told the China Youth News recently. "Then I say, 'You're the sky and I'm the little red sun!'"

The hopeful side of China's one-child policy, begun in 1979, is that it has sharply reduced the growth rate of the world's largest country, winning praise from many international organizations concerned with population problems.

During almost three decades of rule by Mao Tse-tung, China's population grew at an average annual rate of 21 per 1,000 population. In the past 10 years, that has been reduced to an average rate of 12 per 1,000 population, though last year it slipped back up to 14 per 1,000.

China's birth-control policy has been controversial from the start. Officials are confronted with the problem of trying to enforce in a humane way a national policy that denies Chinese the

traditional pleasure and security of large families.

In the early 1980s, there were widespread reports of forced abortions and even female infanticide in rural areas. Now such reports are seldom heard and, presumably, many of the worst abuses have been curbed.

However, there has been a reversal of China's downward trend in birthrates as more and more women from the baby boom of the 1960s are marrying. Enforcement of the policy has also slackened, and more exceptions are made. Practices are especially loose in the rural areas.

"Normally, couples can have two children," said the woman responsible for family planning in a village of Guangdong Province. "Here in the rural areas the policy has always been this way. But if they have two daughters and they still want to have a son, then they can have another try. We have no way to control them."

Fines of 300 to 400 yuan ($81–$108) are sometimes levied in this village, a light penalty that can be reduced, say residents, if the couple is sufficiently "regretful."

In China's most populous province of Sichuan, stricter rules have been newly adopted. According to the People's Daily, couples in Sichuan having two or more children can be fined as much as 50 percent of their salary until the child is an adult.

Positive incentives for couples who sign a certificate pledging compliance with the one-child policy include preferential employment and access to new housing.

Family-planning officials are concerned with the recent trends, and some say that the national target of 1.2 billion people by the year 2000 will be exceeded. Although their approaches have become more sophisticated, with a strong emphasis on education and social pressure on young couples, humane enforcement is not easy.

One senior official commented bluntly that particularly in rural areas, the "measures adopted are not effective." In a candid comment last year, a senior family-planning official said: "The one-child-per-family rule is not a good policy, but we have no choice."

# Cities without limits

Rafael M. Salas

**RAFAEL M. SALAS,** *of the Philippines, is an Under-Secretary-General of the United Nations and executive director of the United Nations Fund for Population Activities, which he has headed since it became operational in 1969. A graduate of the universities of the Philippines and of Harvard (USA), he has served as a Minister and occupied other high-level posts in the Philippine Government.*

THE world has embarked on a course which will transform it into a predominantly urban planet. By the time population stabilizes at the end of the next century, truly rural populations will have become a very small minority.

More than 40 per cent of the world population currently live in urban areas. This figure will increase to more than 50 per cent shortly after the turn of the century. Developed regions have been more than 50 per cent urban since the mid-20th century. Developing countries are expected to pass the 50 per cent mark in the first quarter of the next century.

Within the less developed regions there are important differences. The developing countries of Africa and Asia are less than 30 per cent urban. Latin America, on the other hand, is nearly 70 per cent urban, reflecting the region's stage of development and the special features of its urban structure and history.

## By the year 2000: 5 'super-cities' of 15 million

Most of the world's urban population today lives in developing countries. In 1970 the total urban population of the more developed regions was almost 30 million more than in the less developed. Five years later the position was reversed

and by 1985 the difference had widened to more than 300 million. By the year 2000 the urban population of developing countries will be almost double that of the developed countries. By the year 2025 it will be almost four times as large.

At present the urban population of Africa is smaller than that of North America, but by the beginning of the next century it is expected to be substantially greater, and three times greater by the year 2025.

The proportion of the world population living·in the largest cities will almost double between 1970 and 2025, because of the growth of such cities in developing countries. By the year 2025 almost 30 per cent of the urban population in the developing regions will be living in cities of over 4 million, more than double the figure for the more developed regions. Although only a small proportion of the African population today lives in very large cities, by the end of the first quarter of the next century this proportion could be higher than that of any other continent. In developed countries, moreover, there is a trend towards deconcentration.

By the year 2000 there will be five "super-cities" of 15 million or more inhabitants, three of them in the developing regions. Two of them, in Latin America, will have populations of around 25

million. In 1970, nine of the twenty largest cities in the world were in the less developed regions; in 1985 there were ten and by the year 2000 there will be sixteen.

This change signals the end of the close relationship between large cities and economic development. Until recently such cities were because of their size centres of international political and economic networks, a situation which may now begin to change.

The urban population in developing countries is currently increasing three times more quickly than that of developed countries, at a rate of about 3.5 per cent a year, a doubling time of only twenty years.

There are important differences between the developing regions. Latin America has the lowest rates of population growth, followed by Asia. Africa, especially East Africa, has the highest. The current growth rate for Africa is 5 per cent a year, implying a doubling of the urban population every 14 years. The current figure for East Africa is above 6.5 per cent, a doubling time of little more than ten years.

## Migrants to the cities

Such extremely rapid urban growth is without precedent. It confronts the cities, especially in the developing countries,

Reproduced from the *Unesco Courier,* January 1987, pp. 10–13, 16–17, by permission.

with problems new to human experience, and presents the old problems—urban infrastructure, food, housing, employment, health, education—in new and accentuated forms.

Furthermore, despite migration to the cities, rural population in developing countries will continue to increase, at a rate of around one per cent annually.

Five important points emerge from an analysis of United Nations population figures:

• The world's rural population is now more than 2.5 thousand million;

• Rural population density is already very high in many parts of the less developed regions. Standards of living, while improving, remain low. It is doubtful whether added demographic pressure will benefit agricultural development— on the contrary it may jeopardize the development of many rural areas;

• Increasing rural population in developing countries will make it difficult to reduce the flow of migrants to the cities;

• The natural growth rate (the difference between the number of births and the number of deaths) of the rural population is higher than the one per cent rate—often more than double. The difference is due to the number of migrants to the cities;

• For most of Africa, unlike the rest of the developing world, rural populations will continue to increase until well into the next century.

Although urban fertility in developing countries tends to be lower than rural fertility, it is still at least twice as high as that in developed countries.

When natural increase in urban areas is high and migrants contribute substantially to it, the migrants' future fertility becomes an important factor. The high fertility typical of rural areas may be carried over into the urban environment; more optimistically, migrants plunging into new endeavours in a different context may adapt rather quickly to urban values, including lower fertility.

Those who consider urbanization to be a blessing hold that migration to the cities is part of a dynamic development process. Those who think that it is a burden believe that rural surplus population becomes an urban surplus, producing "over-urbanization", in which an inefficient and unproductive "informal sector" consisting of street vendors, shoeshine boys, sidewalk repair shops and other so-called marginal occupations becomes more and more important.

Urban life has its positive aspects, but they emphasize employment rather than what workers get for their labour. A city worker may earn more than a rural counterpart, but is it enough to cover the basic needs of food, health, housing and education?

Two important aspects of urban life are income distribution and the number of city-dwellers living below an acceptable and culturally adjusted "poverty line". Reliable data are lacking, but it is probably true that the distribution of incomes

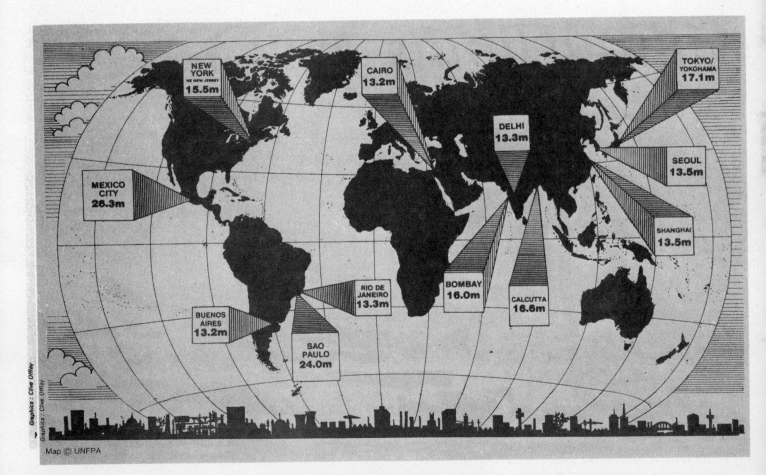

Graphics : Clive Offley

Map © UNFPA

## The rise of the cities

*By the year 2000 half of the world population will live in cities, according to the 1986* State of World Population *report from the United Nations Fund for Population Activities (UNFPA). The map above indicates the projected populations (in millions) for the* *year 2000, in the twelve largest metropolitan regions of the world.*

## 2. POPULATION

is more inequitable in urban than in rural areas, in that there are proportionally more very rich and very poor people in the cities.

This may be as much an indication of economic development in the urban areas as of the privileges enjoyed by urban élites. Rapid demographic growth among the urban masses also contributes to the inequality of income distribution and swells the numbers of the poor.

### A massive housing deficit

The most visible manifestations of the problems of rapid urban population growth are the makeshift settlements on the outskirts of every city in the developing world. They are usually in the worst parts of town as regards health and accessibility, lacking basic services and security of tenure. They are by their nature overcrowded—average occupancy rates of four to five persons per room are common.

The names given to these settlements graphically express their characteristics. In Latin America the word *callampas* (mushrooms) refers to their almost magical overnight growth. The term *bidonvilles* (tin can cities), is often used in Francophone Africa to describe their makeshift nature. There are many other labels, usually given by outsiders: those who live in these settlements might describe them differently, perhaps even considering them as starting points on the path to a higher standard of living.

There is a massive housing deficit in many large cities. The World Bank estimated in 1975 that the poorest quarter of the population in most African and Asian cities cannot afford even minimal housing. Wood and cardboard packing crates, sheets of plastic or corrugated iron, flattened tin cans, leaves, bamboo and beaten earth are the main sources of materials.

Space is also a problem. Landlords may add illegal floors to existing buildings, only to watch their dreams of wealth collapse along with the buildings and the lives of the unfortunate inhabitants. In some cities several workers will use the same "hot bed" in shifts over the twenty-four hours. In Cairo squatters have occupied a large cemetery: the tombs of the wealthy have become homes for the poor.

Colonies of squatters occupy the last areas to be settled, and may be perched on steep hillsides subject to frequent landslides, or installed by rivers or on swampy ground which is flooded regularly. In Mexico City about 1.5 million people live on the drained bed of a salt lake, bedevilled by dust storms in the dry season and floods in rainy months. In Lagos, Nigeria, the proportion of wet land to dry land settled has worsened, while the absolute area of dry land occupied has doubled.

Where squatter settlements have been established near workplaces, the inhabitants may run the risk of pollution and are exposed to dangers such as the leak of poisonous gas in Bhopal, India, or the

# The child in the city

For Third World parents the city may seem the best place to bring up a child – education and health services are usually better than in the countryside. But there are disadvantages too: the city child will spend much more of the day away from the family and at greater risk of exploitation.

## URBAN ADVANTAGES
Health and education services are easier to provide in cities. And mortality and literacy statistics do show the urban areas in a favourable light.

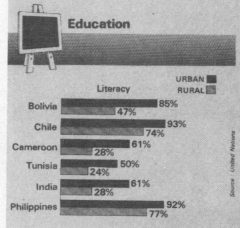

**Education**

URBAN
RURAL

Literacy

| | |
|---|---|
| Bolivia | 85% / 47% |
| Chile | 93% / 74% |
| Cameroon | 61% / 28% |
| Tunisia | 50% / 24% |
| India | 61% / 28% |
| Philippines | 92% / 77% |

*Source : United Nations*

**Health**

URBAN
RURAL

Infant deaths per thousand live births

| | |
|---|---|
| Colombia | 52 / 84 |
| Peru | 84 / 128 |
| Kenya | 91 / 110 |
| Senegal | 71 / 137 |
| Bangladesh | 115 / 137 |
| Indonesia | 60 / 96 |

*Source : World Fertility Survey*

But there will be great differences between the poorer and richer parts of each city. In Lima, Peru, for example, 19% of the children overall are malnourished but this figure rises to 36% in the poorest districts.

*Graphics : Clive Offley*

## STREET CHILDREN
Some 40 million children around the world spend their days on city streets – often working. The majority maintain contact with their families, but millions of children also live on the street.

### Why they are there
A survey in Maputo, Mozambique, asked children why there were on the street. These are the reasons they gave.

| | |
|---|---|
| Hunger and poverty in the home | 27% |
| Treated badly at home | 27% |
| Nothing else to do | 27% |
| Sent by the family | 9% |
| Abandoned by the family | 9% |
| Just following other children | 1% |

*Source : Mozambique Min. of Health*

### What they do
Many city children work (as well as going to school for part of the day). Research in Asuncion, Paraguay, asked children what their major jobs were:

| | |
|---|---|
| Selling newspapers | 27% |
| Shining shoes | 24% |
| Selling food etc. | 33% |
| Cleaning windscreens | 6% |
| Cleaning and looking after cars | 9% |
| Others | 1% |

*Source : Govt. of Paraguay*

City children also have factory jobs – often in harsh conditions. And in rich and poor countries alike street children risk falling into prostitution.

Document UNFPA

explosions at oil refineries in Mexico City.

Squatter settlements typically lack water, sewage and waste disposal facilities, electricity and paved streets. In Mexico City, 80 per cent of the population have access to tapwater, but in some squatter settlements the figure is less than 50 per cent. Water consumption in the wealthy quarters of Mexico City is at least five times as high as in the poorer areas. In Lagos, water is strictly rationed and in some parts of the city residents must walk long distances to obtain water from a few pumps which are turned on only in the early morning.

According to a study carried out in Lima, Peru, lower income groups spent three times more per month on water from vendors but consumed less than a sixth as much as those with running water at home.

It is estimated that three million inhabitants of Mexico City do not have access to the sewage system. In São Paulo, Brazil, the absence of sewage systems have turned the two main rivers into moving cesspools.

Because they occupy land owned by the government, private individuals or communal organizations, squatters are frequently subject to harassment, which increases their feeling of insecurity and the precariousness of their existence. Illegal or barely legal occupation does nothing to encourage squatters to improve or even maintain the shaky structures in which they live.

A number of schemes have been devised to give more security to squatters, but there are risks. One is that improving living conditions in the city will encourage people to move there. Another is that improvements to property will increase its value and encourage squatters to sell, while moving it out of the reach of other low-income families.

# How cities grow

**The urban population of developing countries will be almost double that of developed countries by the year 2000 – according to the 1986 'State of World Population' report from the UN Fund for Population Activities.**

## CONTINENTAL CONURBATIONS

**Latin America has some of the largest cities of the developing world – but Africa is now urbanizing at a rapid rate. The chart shows the percentage of the population living in urban areas.**

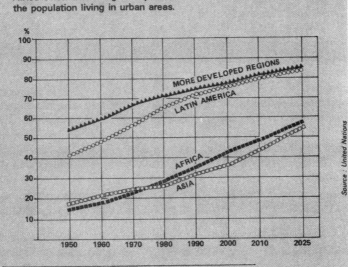

Source : United Nations

## BUILDING FROM BELOW

**The major architects of today's Third World cities are poor families building their own homes. The diagram below shows the percentage of squatters and slum dwellers in four major cities.**

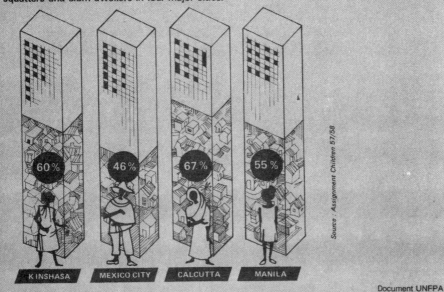

KINSHASA  60%  
MEXICO CITY  46%  
CALCUTTA  67%  
MANILA  55%

Graphics : Clive Offley

Source : Assignment Children 57/58

Document UNFPA

## Two urgent problems: child health and education

The health of the poor may be worse in urban than in rural areas. Infant mortality in the Port-au-Prince slums is three times higher than it is in the rural areas of Haiti. In some of the *favelas* of São Paulo, infant mortality is over 100 per thousand live births. The overall infant mortality rate for the slums of Delhi is 221 per thousand, twice that for some castes. In Manila infant mortality is three times higher in the slums than it is in the rest of the city. (Tuberculosis rates are nine times higher; the incidence of diarrhoea is twice as common; twice as many people are anaemic and three times as many are undernourished.) In Panama City, of 1,819 infants with diarrhoeal diseases, 45.5 per cent came from the slums and 22.5 per cent from squatter settlements. Children living in the best housing were not affected.

In most cities in developed countries, young people under 19 constitute less

## 2. POPULATION

than 30 per cent of the population. In developing countries, the proportion is typically over 40 per cent and may reach 50 per cent in cities such as Manila, Jakarta and Bogotá. If the education system breaks down under this sort of pressure, it will add immeasurably to problems of employment, delinquency and allied problems caused by the existence of "street children".

Education is probably the most pressing of urban problems. A lower rate of population growth would immeasurably help the situation, but such a decrease partly depends on the spread of education. Family planning programmes will certainly be useful, but they must be accompanied by renewed efforts to bring education to the urban masses.

### How will the cities be fed?

How will agriculture respond to the tremendous pressure of urbanization and the growth of urban population? A recent study by the United Nations Food and Agriculture Organization (FAO) and the United Nations Fund for Population Activities (UNFPA) draws attention to some of the likely effects.

First, urban populations demand cheap food. By weight of numbers they force governments to keep retail prices down. Governments may make up the difference by subsidizing farmers but experience has shown that, once established, such subsidies are difficult to withdraw.

Second, as urban populations grow and indigenous agriculture fails to keep up with demand (for lack of incentive to increase supply), more food is imported. This drains off hard currency intended for capital imports with a view to long-term development.

Third, urban population increase means that rural populations and the agricultural labour force will grow more slowly. But to meet urban needs agricultural productivity should be increasing by 17 per cent for each agricultural worker in developing countries between 1980 and the year 2000. This figure seems high, but recent experience in Asia and Latin America shows that it is possible.

For Africa, however, the increase per worker will have to be almost 25 per cent, an eventuality that seems very doubtful in view of recent events. Research in Africa has shown that lower production gains were made in countries with high rural-urban migration. This contrasts with experience in other regions, where rural-urban migration has been at least partly the consequence of higher agricultural labour productivity.

Fourth, tastes in food change under the influence of urban life-styles, as traditional staples are partly replaced by foods such as bread, meat and vegetables.

Fifth, the growth of urban population intensifies competition for land, water and energy. Cities gobble up agricultural land, often the best land because its fertility was the original attraction which stimulated urban growth. Between 1980 and the year 2000, according to one study, cities will devour four million hectares of land with the potential to feed 84 million people.

Sixth, while malnutrition may be more widespread among rural populations, the urban poor suffer more acutely. People in the lowest income groups normally have to spend more than half of their incomes on food.

### Balanced approaches to an urban planet

The transformation from a rural to an urban planet offers both great blessings and heavy burdens. The transition from agrarian to urban has always been considered a positive step, part of the process of modernization. However, the rapid growth of urban populations in societies rapidly changing in other ways is fraught with enormous tension and tremendously complex problems.

In its search for solutions to problems of urban population dynamics, UNFPA puts continuous emphasis on three fundamental objectives: economic efficiency, social equity and population balance. It recognizes that the solution for many urban problems will only come through economic efficiency and vast growth of the productive forces. Economic growth is essential to any solution of urban problems. At the same time social equity should be pursued, with emphasis on equal opportunity for all.

Neither economic efficiency nor social equity can be attained without demographic balance—balance within and between urban and rural areas, balanced population distribution and balanced population growth.

# The Global Phenomena of Immigration

*Migration today has come to mean unprecedented millions of people moving from one country or region to another. Along the way cultural and ethnic barriers have fallen and national economies and political structures have been effected worldwide.*

*Charles Keely*

*Charles Keely is a senior associate at the Center for Policy Studies of the Population Council, New York, New York.*

All over the globe people are on the move. Some are traveling long distances to find work or to share in the high wages of overseas employment, while some are seeking refuge and safe haven. Some want to build a new life altogether, but many have mixed motives.

We tend to think of overseas migration not just as the exception to the rule but as rare, unusual, and even deviant behavior. The image of a nation as a more or less culturally homogeneous and self-reproducing group of people attached to a shared history is an ideal one. Migrants are regarded as strangers who disturb the status quo and threaten the life people have come to know. Although in a statistical sense, fewer people migrate to a foreign country than live out their lives at home, migration is by no means rare. Moreover, migrants often send money home, and so those affected by migration are less rare still. In some countries, everybody is related to or knows an overseas migrant, or has seen the results of higher wages sent home.

It is impossible to enumerate the number of international migrants at any given time. Illegal or undocumented migration prohibits an easy estimate. Is a foreign student a migrant? What if he also works? Is a person on the pilgrimage to Mecca a migrant or does he only become one when he overstays his visa and gets a job? Is a Palestinian in Kuwait for 15 years still a migrant? He and his family (even if born in their adopted country) will probably never become Kuwaiti citizens nor have great hopes of a return to a home west of the Jordan River.

While practically insuperable barriers to an adequate global estimate are a reality, there are nevertheless millions of people on the move with more or less identifiable origins and destinations. These migrants change the lives and fortunes of their families, their regions, and their nations.

## Migration around the globe

One can throw a dart at a map of the world and have a good chance of hitting a country involved in large-scale migration. The postwar economic boom in Europe faced manpower shortages. "Guestworkers" were imported from southern European countries like Italy, Greece, Spain, and Portugal; from Turkey and Yugoslavia; from France's former colonies in North Africa, Algeria, Tunisia, and Morocco; from the British commonwealth; and from Finland, the poor cousin to other Scandinavian countries.

The economic miracle of postwar Europe petered out after the 1973 oil embargo and price rise. Europe has been in the economic doldrums for the last decade or so, and the labor force in most countries has been steady or has declined only slightly.

The guestworker programs had different effects on the countries that sent workers. Southern European countries bought breathing space while their economies developed. While not matching the growth of the "newly industrialized countries" (NICs) of the Far East, these latter-day entrants to the European Common Market are not just the "poor relations" any more. Italy, for example, is now a net importer of labor (much of it illegal migration) and reportedly has surpassed the British standard of living in the mid-1980s.

Turkey and Yugoslavia, on the other hand, showed no such sustained improvement. They became more dependent on the funds sent back by the workers from their European host countries to absorb their growth. The same was true of North Africa. Commonwealth nations found other outlets to replace England—Pakistan in the Middle East, and the United States for the Caribbean.

Europe stopped recruiting from outside the common market (free labor migration is permitted among the members). Workers who had residence permits have had their families join them, so the size of foreign-born concentrations has not fallen dramatically. Europe now faces what it calls its "second-generation" problem—large concentrations of foreigners whose children have been born or lived most of their lives in Europe and who have no intention of

---

# Open Immigration Legislation

President Hafez al-Assad has decreed that, in accordance with the provisions of the constitution and the decison made by the People's Assembly, Syrian Arab nationality may be granted to citizens of Arab countries by decree at the written request of the person applying for naturalization. The qualifications are that the individual must bear the nationality of an Arab country, his normal place of residence must be in Syria when his appliction is submitted, and he must be free of diseases or handicaps that prevent him from working. Additionally, he must be of good conduct and must not have been convicted of a criminal offense.

*Damascus Domestic Service, in Arabic, November 9, 1986*

---

leaving. Most of the workers have residence rights, and the hosts of the guestworkers now struggle over how to deal with what seem like de facto settlers.

## Worker flood in the Middle East

The rise in oil prices during the early and late 1970s set off a development boom in Saudi Arabia, the Gulf, and North African countries that could only have occurred with foreign workers (and companies) building roads, housing, airports, communications systems, health facilities, and a thousand other accoutrements of development. Workers are also needed to run the infrastructure, from telephone operations to teachers, from drivers to doctors.

Literally millions of workers from Arab countries and from East and South Asia did a tour or two (and not infrequently many moved) in a Middle East oil-exporting country. Korea developed a labor-export industry tied to its own companies' contracts to build. Turnkey projects, in which engineering, supplies, manpower, and labor were all part of the contract, were built on the hard work and efficiency of Korean workers. Korean projects gained a reputation for being done right, done on time, and done within budget. The reputation of Korean workers was so high that the Saudi government reportedly asked the Korean Development Institute to advise about how Saudis could be trained to work like Koreans!

Bangladesh is at the other end of the spectrum of labor-export policy. Labor is more like a commodity than an ingredient in a package-deal export strategy. Labor export is not generally tied to Bangladeshi company projects, but government efforts focus on having Bangladesh tapped for needed workers.

Most other East and South Asian countries, the Philippines, Pakistan, India, Thailand, and Sri Lan-

ka, fall in between. There has been concerted effort on the part of public or private organizations to secure contracts to build, operate, and maintain the concrete flowers of modern technology that have bloomed in the desert. Equal or greater energy, however, is spent on securing jobs for swelling labor forces.

Arab countries without large oil reserves have also joined in supplying labor. Much Arab labor is skilled or involves positions in personal service where language facility is important. Nevertheless, large numbers of Egyptians, Palestinians, Jordanians, Yemenis, and Sudanese, along with smaller numbers of Iraqis, Syrians, and North Africans were part of the high growth in the temporary labor force of the Gulf and North African capital-rich states.

In 1975, the estimate of foreign laborers in the Arab oil exporting countries was 1.6 million. The World Bank projected that foreign manpower needs for the region would be between 3.4 and 4.1 million by 1985. Knowledgeable observers estimated that the World Banks' projections were exceeded in many countries by the early 1980s. The recent downward turn in oil prices has probably led to a reduction in foreign manpower, and income sent home by workers has already shown signs of decline. Nevertheless, millions of foreign workers remain in the oil-exporting states of the Middle East and North Africa; in several, foreigners comprise a majority of the labor force.

## African immigration rampant

In West Africa, the story is repeated on a smaller scale without the exotic aura of desert sheiks with fabled wealth. There too, the poor have to travel far before earning their bread by the sweat of their brows.

Estimates in West Africa are, if anything, more hazy than elsewhere due to undocumented and illegal migration. One attempt by the World Bank staff published in 1981, put the total number at about 2.8 million in 1975 in nine West African countries (mostly former French colonies). Of these, 1.4 million were in the Ivory Coast, the principal immigration country. Every fifth person (20 percent) in the country was a foreigner.

Nigeria also has a large foreign population, much of it in the country illegally. Two recent expulsions of hundreds of thousands of Ghanaians and others were followed by quiet buildups of illegal migrants soon after. The net result, spurred by the recent decline in oil prices, is a probable decrease in Nigeria's illegal alien population.

In Southern Africa, agriculture and mines were built on the foundation of black migrant labor. Front-line states use labor as a political tool, and South Africa compounds the problem by treating all black workers as foreigners who have migrated from their tribal homeland, making an accurate count of foreigners at work in South Africa truly impossible. Estimates become a political statement in essence.

## Flocking to the New World

In the Americas, Canada and the United States

continue their historic role as recipients of a large number of immigrants. Canada plans to admit between 105,000 and 115,000 immigrants in 1986. Since Canada's 27 million population is about one-tenth of the United States' 240 million population, its immigrants are a proportionately greater share of its population than the half million immigrants legally admitted to the United States every year.

Illegal migration affects both of these North American countries. The U.S. government estimates that between 3 and 8 million migrants live or work in the United States without proper documents. Of these, perhaps 2.5 million is the estimate of those who will be eligible for legalization under the Simpson-Rodino immigration bill recently signed by President Reagan. (Those eligible for legalization have to have been in the United States illegally before January 1, 1982.)

The Census Bureau estimates that about 200,000 illegal migrants settle in the United States each year. No official estimate exists of the number of aliens that come to the United States and live or work illegally for part of a year and then return home. That shifting, seasonal group, especially along both borders, which are more like screens than dams, could be large indeed.

Other countries in the hemisphere have quite porous borders also. Venezuela has a long history of receiving large numbers of Colombians seeking some of the benefits of Venezuela's oil. From 1 to 4 million Colombians are estimated to be part of the 17 million Venezuelans. Argentina also has a tradition of unsanctioned migration with its neighbors in border provinces. Some 1.5 million or about 15 percent of

---

## And Then There Were Some

Greek military personnel stationed at Orestiás on the Maritsa River caught sight of an inflatable dinghy carrying four people from the Turkish side of the river toward Greece. The four people were Iranian refugees and represent yet another occurrence of Turks transporting political refugees from Iran. According to those who have reached Greece and have been questioned by the authorities, there are about 3,000 more refugees waiting in Turkey, where they have each paid the equivalent of $3,000 to get across the Maritsa.

*Athens News, in English, November 12, 1986*

---

Argentina's labor force comes from Chile, Bolivia, Paraguay, Uruguay, and Brazil.

This brief overview by no means includes every country that sends or receives significant numbers or proportions of their populations to find work elsewhere. Nor have refugees or those seeking political asylum been included. Those who are the personal targets of persecution plus their compatriots seeking a haven from the horror of war or from the "natural disasters" fomented or worsened by war or govern-

ment policy—like drought in East Africa—would add millions to the list of migrants in countries like Thailand, Somalia, and Mexico, not to mention Europe and North America.

### Popular wisdom versus reality

For the last two decades, the general advice from the academic analysts to labor-exporting countries has been that migration is bad for development. Nobody listened. Talking about the long term seemed irrelevant while hard currency was being sent home. Balance of payments were improved because of workers' remittances, and a whole generation grew up with food, shelter, medical care, and even an education—often without one or both parents at home. Warnings against becoming dependent on monies sent from abroad may be fine and noble unless there is no other export.

Labor exporters, like commodity exporters, are dependent on markets they do not control or even influence much. Alternatives to developing future economic strength are sparse even in good times. Keeping laborers home and idle and forgoing the income they would remit to their families was wellnigh impossible if a country had any semblance of rights and freedoms. It also made no economic sense. How could forgoing hard currency and a more balanced set of national accounts or failing to pay bills, especially for higher priced oil, possibly aid development? The trick was to maximize income from foreign sources and then to maximize savings for investment. The results have been mixed.

At the level of the national economy, remittances from migrants were a major boost in the 1970s and 1980s to flagging economies all over the globe. The amounts of money sent home by migrants that went through official channels and were counted up and reported to the International Monetary Fund was on the order of $30–35 billion dollars a year. Unrecorded money and goods are unknown but generally believed to be substantial by national bankers.

Worker remittances were the highest source of foreign currency for most major labor exporters in Asia, the Middle East, North Africa, sub-Saharan Africa, and the Western Hemisphere. Remittances are usually sent in Western currencies (dollars or pounds frequently). Many countries offer favorable exchange rates for their foreign workers. These hard currencies, when converted, become available to pay for needed imports, just like income from exported goods, as far as balancing payments in the international sphere.

Like commodity exporters, labor exporters are more or less at the mercy of the market. The decline in oil prices has reverberated upon the development plans of oil exporters who then send workers home or reduce their wages, resulting in declining remittances from oil-exporting countries.

The second macroeconomic effect is that labor-force growth has found an outlet overseas. This is not altogether a straightforward process. Emigrants are not simply the unemployed and unskilled or the newly graduated. They are more likely to be those with skills, experience, and even a job. They go abroad for the salary. How open a job market is, how quickly people can be trained, and how much upward mobility is tolerated in a given country are keys to whether excess labor can fill the vacuum left by migrants. The cycle starts again as someone else is trained, gets experience, and eventually takes off to earn higher wages elsewhere.

The benefit of labor migration for accommodating labor force growth varies. The opportunities afforded by work abroad (and in some cases the economic stimulation from remittances) allowed modest increases in standards of living for millions of families. Intelligent, energetic, and educated young people join an expanding middle class that exists beyond the borders of its country. Accountants, managers, teachers, engineers, doctors, and other young professionals are part of the international movement of labor. Like the men in grey flannel suits in the newly built suburbs in America of the 1950s, they may be far away from "home," and mobility may be an integral part of a career. Although many migrants today are women, male migrants still make up the bulk.

The term 'safety valve' is often applied to labor export. A safety valve lets off dangerous steam and is a short-term method to manage a more fundamental process. Most developing countries, including the labor exporters, face ever larger numbers of new workers entering their labor markets each year from now into the first or second decade of the next century. For some countries, the rate of that expansion is moderating, but the absolute numbers are still growing.

The oil exporters of the Middle East have absorbed about 10 percent of Pakistan's labor-force growth since 1973. At that rate, labor export is obviously no panacea for absorbing expanding groups of young adults seeking work. For other countries, particularly Arab and sub-Saharan African nations, the largest increases are yet to come.

On the macroeconomic level, then, labor export seemed like an opportunity that should not be passed up. Hard currencies, a better balance of payments, the possibility of absorption of some labor-force growth, and an incentive to develop manpower training programs were all attractive.

On the individual and family, or microeconomic, level, the effects have been no less profound. In some countries, like Jordan, it is hard to find someone who has not been affected by migration. Remittances have provided new money sources for housing, education, and medical attention, as well as increased expenditures for food and clothing. In all the labor-exporting countries mentioned, there are profound differences between the life of the young generation and that of their parents because of migration. In some smaller countries, this is generally true of the entire population. In large countries like India, it is true of the labor-exporting regions like Kerala.

Survey after survey about the use of money sent from abroad indicates that members of current migration households receiving remittances spend more on health, education, food, and shelter than their neighbors in households without a member working abroad. Debts are paid, and new houses are acquired or built. Most households "consume"—if one assumes that education and health expenditures on children are consumption and not investment in human capital with a future payoff.

Much to the dismay of some analysts and commentators, migrant families are neither otherworldly nor miserly and do not save money at a rate greater than their compatriots. Disappointed pundits berate these receivers for foolish consumption rather than investment for long-term economic development.

The expectation is ludicrous because it prescribes savings behavior that borders on the unnatural, given the circumstances. The incentives for investment are abysmally low. Information is unavailable, risk is very high, and the return would probably be so long in coming that the investor would be long dead. Land, housing, and small businesses look much better to the

---

## If They're Not Back, They're Not Coming

The presence of a Polish pope in the Vatican after centuries of Italian occupancy is attracting not only cash-laden tourists but also visitors that will cost the state some 28 billion lire ($20 million) this year alone—Polish refugees. The defection of Polish pilgrims on tours to the Holy City is reaching comic proportions. Some tours go back with only half their passengers. Airport staff at Rome's Fiumicino Airport do not bat an eyelid if the first person off the latest flight from Warsaw asks the way to the Latina refugee camp. Polish couriers ask their passengers as they step off the tour bus if they are intending to defect, purely to avoid delays on the return journey. It is not a laughing matter for the Italian government. Italy's bill for helping those who "choose freedom" is expected to rise to 31 billion lire next year, even though Italy, which grants only temporary asylum, is just a staging post for the United States, Canada, Australia, and South Africa. Four out of five requests for asylum in Italy come from Polish citizens. At the end of October, 3,697 Poles had asked for asylum in Italy this year alone. Rome's two refugee camps, the Latina and the Capoue were built to house 700 and 450 people respectively. Both currently shelter more than double their capacity —single males in dormitories, whole families in a single room. Some are put up in hotels in Rome, a solution that costs the state nearly twice as much per day as accommodation in the camps. The majority, Christian Democrats, are reluctant to close the door to fellow Roman Catholics, as West Germany, Austria, and Scandanavian countries have done, even though most refugees are seeking material rather than spiritual benefits.

*Paris AFP, in English, November 11, 1986*

small investor, after all the catch-up spending on health, housing, education, and other areas. It is no wonder that people use remittances the way they do. It is economically rational—and emotionally satisfying—to do so.

To invest significant amounts in large-scale national development projects is the equivalent of giving the money to the government under current market conditions. To ask why anyone would do that willingly and fail in his duties to family is enough of an answer to why government investment schemes have failed to attract investment of remittances.

The newfound standard of living of migrant families most probably has a price. It is too early yet to tell what the impacts have been of spousal separation and of the absence of fathers and even mothers on this generation. Some claim that extended family systems of various sorts are exactly tailored to this situation. That is not so clear. Wives and mothers who have had new responsibilities and independence may want to redefine their roles on their husbands' return. Scenarios about how children are being raised and the effects on them can as easily be sketched. We do not yet know, however, what the outcomes are, whether or not they will be more predominant, and how they will change family life, sex roles, and expectations for children. We do not know what toll migration has taken on the psyches of husbands, wives, and their children or on the texture of family relations in large parts of the developing world.

## Distant relations

Finally, the movement of so many people and so much money affects relations among states. The countries chosen to send temporary migrants, and why those countries are chosen, is an example of how migration affects and is affected by labor movements.

Saudi Arabia, for example, needed workers, wanted to maintain its political system with power highly concentrated in the ruling family, and wished to preserve its culture, including a strict interpretation of Islam and the protection of holy places. Yet, it had to acknowledge the "Arab nation" and make common cause regarding Palestinians. It also wanted influence among non-Arab, Moslem nations. Palestinians or other Arabs had to have a share of the labor market but not so great as to upset the political or religious order. Non-Arab Islamic countries like Pakistan and Bangladesh could be wooed. Non-Arabs and non-Islamic peoples like Koreans or Thais could be counted on to depart and to be controllable because they are so distinct. The same is true of Filipinos, although the Moslem discontent in the southern Philippines called for caution while providing an opportunity for Islamic leadership. Countries involved in international migration as senders or receivers face such balancing of foreign policy goals, often inter-

mixed with domestic issues and pressures.

In short, the effects of migration are both deep and broad in the many countries involved. For some, migration is life-sustaining, and remittances are the transfusion that keeps economies functioning—in some cases functioning better and in other cases allowing them to function at all.

Migration brings in hard currency to pay for imports and to pay off foreign debt; it absorbs an ever-growing labor force that in many, if not most, instances cannot be adequately accommodated. Unlike aid and government loans, it provides resources directly to the people who improve their lot economically. This wide dispersal of income is "inefficient" for large-scale investment projects, but neither governments nor migrants seem to want to stop migration to eliminate that "inefficiency."

Migration, however, is bought at a price. It is yet to be determined what the bill will be. Social change is taking place, but at what costs and what future repercussions for families and individual men, women, and children is not yet understood. The relations among nations are also affected. We do not yet understand the full impact of all these changes among so many people.

## Drawing conclusions

Why are the effects of migration so unclear, if it is so widespread and so inclusive in its impact on people and nations? The answer is that migration is a summary for millions of decisions and actions. Remittances and labor-force absorption are functions of the uncoordinated behavior of many ordinary individuals. Diplomats and political scientists usually analyze the actions of the influential. Tidal movements, like migration or population growth, or even temperature warming and desertification are not easily integrated into what they analyze or the "levers" they seek to influence events.

Economists also are not used to dealing with remittances as a major earner in a balance of payments. Economists are not even sure whether trade and labor theory is the appropriate framework to study transnational labor movements.

And there is also time and experience. Some effects of migration take a generation to show up and sometimes we do not know how to differentiate between changes due to heavy migration or to other social, economic, and cultural changes that are washing over country after country.

What is not clear is whether labor migration is now an integral part of the international economy, like the movement of capital, or whether the last twenty years were an exception that will be followed by a massive downturn in international labor migration. The lives and futures of nations and tens of millions of people are riding on the answer.

# The Future of AIDS

By the end of this century, AIDS could have
the impact of a world war, producing
recession and a stay-at-home society at the
same time that it transforms world health
and demographics.

## John Platt

John Platt is a biophysicist, general systems
theorist, and futurist who has worked on the
relations between science and society and
the rates of social change today. He taught
at the University of Chicago and has been a
visiting professor or fellow at MIT, the
University of Paris, and Harvard, among
other places. His most recent book is
*Advances in the Social Sciences, 1900-1980*.
His address is 14 Concord Avenue, #624,
Cambridge, Massachusetts 02138.

How far will the AIDS epidemic
go, and what will be its social effects?

This problem has been neglected
by many futurists, but a little analysis will show that its impact in the
1990s could be as great as a major
war unless a vaccine or cure can be
developed soon.

It is true that the death rate from
AIDS in the United States is still
less than that from auto accidents,
but AIDS has certain peculiar characteristics that make the future
ominous. For one thing, it seems
to be a new kind of disease, caused
by a "slow virus" that infects millions silently but fatally. The
number of infections today is estimated to be 30 to 50 times the
number of diagnosed cases.

Most of those infected are young
adults who do not know they are
infected, and the numbers are
doubling every year or so. In 6–10
years, half of them will have developed AIDS; death follows a year
or so after that. It is now believed
that almost all of those infected will
be contagious to others for the rest
of their lives and will eventually
die of AIDS-related diseases. No effective treatment is in sight.

The transmission of AIDS is also
deceptive. It is transmitted sexually
but with surprisingly low probability, perhaps because carriers are
only intermittently infectious. It
takes up to two years before half
of the spouses or regular sex
partners of infected persons become infected — but half of the

babies born to infected mothers are
also infected and die very young.

So far, most U.S. victims of AIDS
have been male homosexuals. But
AIDS is not a gay disease; it can be
transmitted between any two
people of any sex by the exchange
of infected blood or semen. AIDS
may simply have gotten started
most visibly here in promiscuous
gay communities.

There are also nonsexual routes
of transmission, such as the infected needles of drug users and
accidental contact with infected
blood, but these can largely be
blocked by suitable precautions.
Transmission by contact with other
bodily fluids is also theoretically
possible but has not been demonstrated and would obviously be

From *The Futurist*, November/December 1987, pp. 10–17. THE FUTURIST, published by the World Future Society, 4916 St.
Elmo Avenue, Bethesda, MD 20814.

even rarer than sexual transmission.

## The Numbers

The spread of AIDS is still small on a national scale, but it is staggering in certain "hot spots." In early 1987, the Centers for Disease Control of the U.S. Public Health Service estimated that there were about 1.5 million infections in the United States, with one in 30 men aged 30–50 being seropositive. But in New York City, which has 30% of all cases and deaths, the rates are 10 times higher, implying that about one in three men under 50 may be infected. Also, AIDS is now the leading cause of death in New York City for both men and women in their 30s. (All the estimates given here are based on public statements of health officials and are believed to be conservative.)

Drug abuse has made the problem even more severe in the black and Hispanic communities and in New York–area prisons, where the death rate from AIDS is 100 times that in the general population, according to Bureau of Prisons statistics. San Francisco and Miami are also heavily affected, and Houston and Washington, D.C., are not far behind. The general increase in the death rate will begin to reduce average life expectancy by 1988, and the total deaths of young men already infected will probably be over 1 million, more than in all our wars.

The future is even darker. A 1986 report from the Institute of Medicine–National Academy of Sciences projected a total of about 270,000 cases by 1991. Even a large error in the estimate would mean only that this number would be reached a year or so earlier or later than estimated, because the doubling time is short.

If the factor of 30 to 50 infections per diagnosed AIDS case still holds, this number of cases would imply some 10 million infections by that time. If half of those infected in turn get AIDS and die within 10 years, the death rate would reach half a million per year in the 1990s. With one more doubling, the death rate would rise high enough to make the U.S. population level off or decline after 1995 or so.

# Forecasts for AIDS Cases and Deaths

The magnitude of the AIDS epidemic in the United States is still uncertain. Estimates range from 1 to 5 million people in the United States who are presently infected with the virus.

The Centers for Disease Control (CDC) of the U.S. Public Health Service is the primary source of forecasts of deaths and new cases of AIDS up to 1991. In 1986, CDC's median forecast was for 270,000 cumulative diagnosed cases and 179,000 cumulative deaths.

The assumptions underlying their projections include:
- New infections will develop.
- Estimated median survival time after full AIDS develops is 12 months.
- Current infection trends will continue unchanged over time.

On the graph, CDC projections can be seen to be two times higher than the lowest forecast. This lowest estimate comes from the unlikely forecast of no new infections after 1985. If the transmission of AIDS had stopped by the beginning of 1986, the minimum number of cumulative cases thought possible by 1991 is 121,000 in the United States.

The lower line of the two CDC forecasts is the minimum number of cases projected; the upper line is the number thought more likely. Projected yearly deaths are illustrated by the bars.

*Editor's note: These estimates are thought to be conservative by Platt and others. Platt notes that infections in the United States could be as high as 10 million by 1991.*

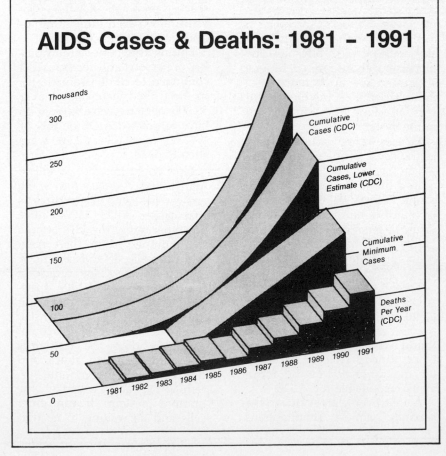

## AIDS Cases & Deaths: 1981 – 1991

Thousands

300

250

200

150

100

50

0

Cumulative Cases (CDC)

Cumulative Cases, Lower Estimate (CDC)

Cumulative Minimum Cases

Deaths Per Year (CDC)

1981 1982 1983 1984 1985 1986 1987 1988 1989 1990 1991

# "The total deaths from AIDS in the 1990s could be 50 million — more than the Black Death — [and] could wipe out some countries in 10 to 20 years."

These death rates are no higher than those from cardiovascular diseases, say, which kill a million people a year in the United States. But the concentration of AIDS deaths among young adults and the added stress on an economic system with a population no longer growing might mean a new kind of disruption for our society.

## Global Pandemic

The U.S. problem is now just one front in a much larger war. The World Health Organization (WHO) now has reports on AIDS from 113 countries; it estimates that there are 5 to 10 million infected. The number is projected to rise to 100 million by 1991.

As the Director-General of WHO said in 1986, "We stand nakedly in front of a very serious pandemic as mortal as any pandemic there has ever been. . . . All of us have been underestimating it."

AIDS has been compared to the Black Death, which swept through Europe along the trade routes from Italy to Sweden in 1347-1350, kill-

## The Source of AIDS

AIDS—a disease now known virtually everywhere—was identified only six years ago. Researchers at the Centers for Disease Control of the U.S. Public Health Service came upon it unexpectedly, noticing an unusually high incidence of previously rare conditions, particularly among young males. Among the diseases, for example, was Kaposi's sarcoma, a form of cancer that disfigures the skin with purplish blotches. The increase of these rare conditions suggested the appearance of a new disease—something that was attacking the human immune system.

Viruses were a natural suspect as the cause of the new disease, which would be named Acquired Immune Deficiency Syndrome, or AIDS. By 1983, two laboratories had isolated a retrovirus, a member of the virus family that had only recently been implicated in human disease.

Three years earlier, before AIDS was identified, Robert Gallo, a researcher at the National Cancer Institute, had found a retrovirus causing a rare blood cancer. This set the stage for the discovery of the retrovirus responsible for AIDS.

A controversy arose due to the separate, almost simultaneous discovery of the responsible virus by both a French laboratory, headed by research scientist Luc Montagnier, and an American lab in the National Cancer Institute, headed by Gallo. Both claimed credit, giving the retrovirus different names, and it took several years of wrangling before a compromise was reached on a name for the retrovirus, now called human immunodeficiency virus, or HIV.

During this period, the number of persons afflicted by AIDS continued to climb dramatically. In the United States alone, over 38,000 persons were known to have contracted AIDS by July of 1987. Of those, over 22,000 were already dead.

How could this disease kill so many so fast? At least part of the answer lies with the retrovirus that causes AIDS, HIV. Unlike any other retrovirus, HIV attacks the immune system, the system that normally defends the body against invaders. By attacking the immune system, HIV is disarming the body and making it vulnerable to a host of other diseases, such as Kaposi's sarcoma. Not only does the retrovirus have the ability to attack and destroy cells in the immune system, it can also "colonize" the immune system: It can enter cells and lie waiting to be trig-

gered and then burst forth and destroy the body's immunity.

To understand how this is possible, it is important to understand the way the HIV virus operates. The retrovirus is a microscopic package of seven genes, surrounded by an envelope made up of protein. The protein includes a receptor, a device the allows the virus to lock onto much larger human cells with matching receptors.

Once the virus is locked onto the cell—often an immune cell— it inserts itself into the cell, shedding its protein coat. The genes of the virus then migrate into the nucleus of the cell, where they become part of the human cell's genetic material. There they act as instructions, making the cell reproduce the virus. The cell, as it fills with the virus, swells and then bursts, releasing copies of the virus to go colonize other cells. Sometimes, the viral genes lie quietly in the nucleus for years, waiting for something to trigger this process of reproduction.

Even when the virus is lying dormant, the immune system will have produced antibodies— cells designed to identify and destroy an invading virus. In this case, the antibodies will prove ineffective, but their presence indicates that the virus is lurking

ing some 30 million people out of a population of 75 million in four years. AIDS probably has the same high mortality rate, but it has such slow development and low infectivity that it could be called the Black Death in Slow Motion.

Starting, perhaps, as a mutant virus in equatorial Africa in the mid-1970s, AIDS has been spread through that region for over 10 years by armies and millions of refugees. Blood tests show that 20% or more of the population in cities and along truck routes in equatorial Africa are now seropositive. Death rates are very high, and there are

reports of whole villages being abandoned.

The disease has now jumped to other countries around the world, carried by individuals ranging from tourists to immigrants to soldiers returning from overseas. The United States, except for the areas with a concentration of AIDS cases, is about four to five years behind Africa in level of infection. Europe, with one-tenth the U.S. case rate, is in turn about three to four years behind the United States — with the exception of prostitutes around U.S. military bases, who are re-

ported to be as widely infected as in New York City.

AIDS has been reported in South American nations such as Brazil and in the Caribbean Islands, most notably Haiti. The situation in the Moslem world and in Southeast Asia is uncertain. But the Soviet Union and China claim to have almost no cases of AIDS yet except for foreign visitors, and a vaccine or cure in the next few years might enable them to escape the epidemic.

With a projection of about 100 million people infected worldwide by 1991, or 2% of the world's popu-

---

in the body's cells. The blood test now commonly available in the United States reveals the presence of these antibodies and thus the potential of developing AIDS.

Based on five years of experience, researchers estimate the likelihood that those testing positive for antibodies will develop AIDS within five years is 30%–50%. The chances that the disease will develop after five years are unknown.

The HIV virus is particularly difficult to combat because, in addition to its ability to lie dormant in cells, it also is able to alter itself. One of the ways the virus changes is by reshaping the receptor, allowing it to colonize more and more cells in the body. This has become clear with the manifestation of dementia-like symptoms that are now recognized to be part of AIDS. The HIV virus is able to enter cells in the brain, ultimately disrupting the ability to think.

Not only can the HIV virus change while in the body, but it has also changed over time. While it is not understood how the change has occurred, it is known that several varieties of the virus exist. Three have been identified, two of which cause AIDS. The appearance of these mutations raises the question of

whether new strains will be found.

The virus's ability to hide in cells is also frustrating the search for an AIDS vaccine. Some vaccines work by mimicking the protein that envelopes the virus and, in the process, stimulating an immune response to the actual virus. But when HIV hides in the body's cells, it sheds its protein coating. This ability to live without the protein creates a far more complex problem for scientists searching for a vaccine.

The ability of the virus to migrate to brain cells creates another problem. The brain is protected by a mechanism described as the "blood-brain barrier," which prevents the passage of foreign substances in the bloodstream into the brain. But the "blood-brain barrier" also prevents the passage of many drugs into the brain, making it difficult to find a drug that will combat the AIDS virus in the brain as well as elsewhere in the body.

Given these characteristics peculiar to the HIV virus, the future prospects for fighting AIDS are unclear. On the dark side, the virus seems perfectly designed not only to destroy the human immune system, but to frustrate the avenues that scientists normally use to fight dis-

ease. It will not be enough to recognize and destroy the HIV virus; it will also be necessary to identify and selectively destroy those cells infected by the virus, leaving healthy cells unaffected.

There is no precedent for this type of drug or vaccine, meaning that only a scientific breakthrough will lead to an effective prevention or cure. And if a vaccine or definitive treatment were found, the HIV virus might mutate to another, not yet preventable, form.

On the bright side, however, never have so many scientists turned so quickly toward understanding and fighting a virus. The sophisticated tools of molecular biology have helped identify the genetic structure of the virus, which potentially holds clues on how to block replication of the virus. Public recognition and funding is supporting the work of some of the world's most sophisticated laboratories.

Nevertheless, the search for a prevention and cure for AIDS remains an uphill battle. Education and prevention may offer as much hope as research.

—**Jonathan Peck**

Jonathan Peck is associate director of the Institute for Alternative Futures, 1405 King Street, Alexandria, Virginia 22314.

# "The frequent assumption that AIDS may not spread far in the heterosexual community or in the smaller cities may be . . . a mistake."

lation, the total deaths from AIDS in the 1990s could be 50 million — more than the Black Death. Again, the number infected could double several more times after that, especially in the poorer countries, before vaccines or drugs could be developed. This could wipe out some countries in 10 to 20 years. If the number infected goes up to 20% of the world's population, the delayed deaths could even begin to cancel out our rapid world population growth.

## The Two Sectors

Nevertheless, it is probable that the spread of AIDS will be limited, even without a vaccine or cure, unless it changes its behavior considerably. The reason is that every society can be divided approximately into two populations. One is the "restraint sector," or R-sector, in which anyone infected will usually infect no more than one other person before he or she dies, so that the epidemic will slow to a stop. The other is the "propagation sector," or P-sector, in which the average carrier does infect more than one other person, so that the epidemic spreads in a chain reaction.

With a predominantly sexual route of transmission, the R-sector will consist of groups that are largely monogamous, with little premarital experimentation and little use of prostitutes. With systematic protection by condoms, even a regular sex partner will not usually become infected, since the time of transfer of the virus can then be lengthened to 10 to 20 years, or longer than the average additional lifespan of the initially infected person. In such groups, even occasional infections by non-sexual routes will still not spread beyond one or two people.

How large is this monogamous sector? The fringes will always be vague, with more sexual activity than parents or spouses suspect. But sex surveys indicate that 20%-30% of U.S. couples are fairly faith-

ful, and the numbers might rise quickly to double that, say to 60% or more, if tens of millions of people make radical changes in their behavior due to fear of AIDS. This R-sector of the population might then go on for generations, with AIDS having no more effect on them than any of the other sexually transmitted diseases today.

## The Possible Spread

The sector of the population with high-transmission behavior, the P-sector, may be a sizable minority, as the percentages of AIDS infections in the "hot spots" are already showing. Tens of millions of people — soldiers and sailors, family men, and conventioneers — go regularly to prostitutes, many of whom are intravenous drug users already infected. Other tens of millions of both men and women, both gay and straight, will probably go on having frequent changes in sex partners. Some 80% of all U.S. teenagers are reported to be sexually active before age 19, and only a minority use condoms.

When we add all these up — remembering that most of them will not know when they are infected and that their partners will not know either — it may be that 25 to 50 million people, perhaps 10%-20% of all Americans, is a conservative estimate for the number in the P-sector whose behavior could make them part of the chain reaction in the next few years.

It is worth noting that exponentially growing epidemics of this kind often appear to "jump" from group to group at successive times. Historically, this can be seen in the city-by-city spread of the Black Death and other plagues. The infection may rise to saturation in one group while it still seems minor in the next. This leads to misperceptions and false explanations and hopes, even among experts. Each group thinks of those caught earlier as being a wild or wicked minority, and it congratulates itself on escaping, until it is suddenly over-

whelmed in its turn. The frequent assumption that AIDS may not spread far in the heterosexual community or in the smaller cities may be just such a mistake.

How much of the population will then be infected before the disease can be leveled off? Ten percent? Twenty percent? Forty percent? No one can tell. The answer will evidently depend on factors impossible to guess at the present time, involving national psychology and politics as much as the progress of medical research or the stability of the virus.

## Society to 1991

Even with these uncertainties, though, we can make some plausible forecasts of the future impact of AIDS. They can be divided roughly into two periods: before 1991, and after 1991 if the disease continues to spread. That date is chosen because it is around the time when AIDS will have begun to add something like 10% to the total death rate and will have become conspicuous in every community. It might be a sort of break point, with a great restructuring of attitudes and actions.

Up until then, the changes will largely be in directions that are already visible and have been widely discussed. In politics, the debates over AIDS and insurance and pensions, mandatory testing and civil rights, will grow hotter. AIDS will probably be an important issue in the 1988 elections. In economics, major instability may be produced by the epidemic in Africa and the tropics, with shaky governments and defaulted loans. In medical care, hospitals and support systems will be severely stressed. It is estimated that by 1991 New York City will need 2,500 to 5,000 hospital beds for AIDS patients every day. Nationwide costs will demand federal help, perhaps even a new federal agency.

In daily life, with dozens of young community leaders dying every week, there will be a sharply

# The New Plagues

It is puzzling that at the time of our greatest achievements in technology and biomedicine, we seem to be encountering or creating a wave of new diseases or dysfunctions and a recurrence of old ones.

The new diseases are dominated by the exponential growth of the AIDS epidemic, especially in Africa, the Caribbean, and the United States. The World Health Organization calls AIDS a worldwide "pandemic as mortal as any pandemic there has ever been."

The old diseases include mumps, drug-resistant strains of tuberculosis, salmonella poisoning, yellow fever, malaria, sleeping sickness, bubonic plague, and cancers and neurological diseases.

Some of these resurgent diseases may be unrecognized or mislabeled manifestations of the protean AIDS virus or the opportunistic infections that follow it. If so, this may represent added deadly infections beyond the 10 million now estimated for AIDS by the World Health Organization or the 100 million that they project for 1991 if no vaccine has been developed before then. Other recurrences, like the drug-resistant strains, may be the result of our previous biological successes. As viruses have built up a resistance to existing drugs, we have not been able to keep up with the shifting targets of fast-changing organisms.

It is evidently time for a second wave of the Pasteurian revolution. A new level of sophistication is called for in our biomedical skills—and in our personal and social behavior—if we are to maintain or recover the freedom from death and disease that was such a glowing hope in the middle of the twentieth century.

—John Platt

rising fear of infection. Numerous precautions — many of them useless or irrational — will be taken. Antiseptic practices, with gloves and scrubbing and the covering of cuts and sores, will come back into vogue in kitchens and bathrooms, just as they were in the great campaigns of the 1920s against communicable diseases. Strangers and persons of unknown habits and associations will be avoided.

The present official campaigns for safer sex may have some effect. However, the sexually active people who make up the P-sector may simply tend to divide into two groups, the supposed noninfected and the confirmed infected, with sex about as uninhibited as before within each group. This could actually stop the epidemic if the division were perfect, but that is not likely to happen when most of those infected do not know it. But for those who do find out and who realize that they have a longer time to live than with many other dis-

eases, it will be natural to group together for support.

Like all plagues, AIDS will also produce a revival of otherworldly religions that offer personal consolation for victims and families and the assurance of life after death. Apocalyptic groups are already calling for personal and national repentance before the millennial year 2000. The modern world and science and technology will be damned, except perhaps for medicine. Revitalization movements, spread by television, will grow strong and often intolerant. Religious Purity parties will become major political powers. Yet many religious and other workers will also devote themselves to nursing and counseling AIDS victims out of love and self-sacrifice, as in the plagues of old.

## Breakdown and Opportunity

On the international scene in the next few years, national barriers and demands for blood testing will multiply, impeding immigration, tourism, student travel, and all overseas operations. In many countries, young Americans — representatives of the nation with the greatest reported number of AIDS cases — will not be welcomed. Likewise, tourists may want to avoid countries with high rates of AIDS infections. "Travel" may come to mean seeing the world by video and satellite communications, which could become the dominant international linkages.

By 1991, AIDS in Africa will have become a major world concern as it continues to spread. The human tragedy and the loss of the high hopes that followed colonialism would now seem to be irreversible. Governments will fall, and wars may be won or lost because of the impact of AIDS on leadership or morale. Gangs of looters may spread chaos, as after previous epidemics. A power vacuum in the region might lead to new unstable takeovers.

But with farseeing leadership, this great human disaster could lead to rescue and interim management by some international consortium in the name of humanity. As more countries need help, this management could become a sort of new Marshall Plan, a stepping stone to a new global order.

The international spread of disease will tend to produce the need for much stronger global cooperation on public-health measures and biomedicine. Researchers working on possible vaccines or treatments for AIDS could generate international networks of people demanding and supporting medical research. In the next few years, the challenge of coping with AIDS at all levels could give the world a new sense of planet-wide interdependence and responsibility for human survival and for the future.

### After 1991

If the AIDS epidemic in the United States does go on growing after 1991 (say until 1996 or later, with 10%-20% of the population infected and the population beginning to decline), much greater effects on society can be imagined. Fears will multiply even among R-sector individuals who are rela-

# "[AIDS] could make overpopulation, famine, environmental destruction, or the extinction of species seem like minor complaints."

tively safe, and our social behavior and arrangements will become increasingly reminiscent of life during earlier plagues.

Hospitals will be desperately overcrowded, and many AIDS patients will die at home or be abandoned. Burials will be replaced by cremation — for reasons of practicality as well as public safety. Attitudes of hopelessness and sadness will alternate with an "eat, drink, and be merry" philosophy.

Victims of AIDS may grow violent, furious with the world. A high percentage of AIDS patients may commit suicide to avoid months of suffering and enormous costs to their families. There would likely be much more religious and legal approval of suicide and euthanasia, along with medical help for suicide and abortions for AIDS-infected mothers.

The effects on daily life will multiply. Fear of AIDS will affect a broad range of activities — even those nonintimate activities where contracting AIDS would seem to be very unlikely. Food might be bought and served only in sealed packages, for example. Many people may avoid public toilets, crowds, restaurants, and even public transportation. Work, play, and education would be concentrated in the "electronic cottage," with the main connection to the outside being through the networks of a video universe.

The U.S. economy — built on consumer growth — will stagnate, with buildings and property abandoned. Travel will shrink, and oil imports will drop. For the well-off, the move away from urban life to rural areas will accelerate. We could see on the one hand survivalist camps and on the other hand large sections of great cities becoming derelict, abandoned to the poor, the sick, and the gangs.

A new New Deal will be called for to provide for those severely af-

fected by AIDS. It may be paid for by canceling other expensive projects — big science, big engineering, fusion power, the space station, the Strategic Defense Initiative — that will seem increasingly irrelevant in a world dominated by AIDS.

## The Quality of Life

Yet all is not negative. With reduced pressures of population and consumption, the environment will improve, resources per capita might increase somewhat, and life might be very good for millions who are not personally affected by infection.

The loss of top workers will accelerate automation, with machines providing the food and goods to support life. The remaining jobs will involve more communications and direct human interactions, with child care and elder care being enormous needs.

With a wider variety of jobs paying higher wages to attract a shrinking work force and with new forms of non-contact entertainment constantly being devised, work may be less constraining and leisure even more varied than today. Advances in electronic communications could make rural self-sufficiency easier to sustain.

In such a world, many families and groups of friends may also develop a new closeness across the generations, possibly in village patterns like retirement communities. In such groups, teen marriages and earlier parenting might make monogamy easier, and high birth rates could even return.

The great political danger after 1991 might be the power of new Hate Parties, with leaders promising to purge scapegoats and straighten things out. Such panaceas will have less appeal if we can begin now to work out fair and democratic ways to deal with these strange new problems. With lead-

ership, the developing crisis could be used to create a new sense of family, community, and national responsibility and to establish new political parties with a revived social concern and outreach.

## The Coming World

The continued spread of AIDS into the 1990s would transform the whole state of the world. It could make overpopulation, famine, environmental destruction, or the extinction of species seem like minor complaints — especially in the developing nations likely to be hit hardest.

AIDS may even transform the purposes of international politics. If the barriers do not become too high to communicate, the major powers will find a life-and-death interest in responding together to a mutual danger that laughs at the nation-state. Many of our nongovernmental organizations and networks, such as those interested in environmental protection, women's rights, and nuclear disarmament, could also shift their focus toward concern with AIDS and providing help across national boundaries.

Eventually, if it continues, AIDS will change the balance of power. Some countries will be destroyed by it, some badly hurt, and some almost unharmed. Those that suffer least will tend to dominate afterwards, as in previous epidemics.

Which countries are least affected will depend on cultural, behavioral, or biomedical developments impossible to foresee. But certain trends appear to be developing. For example, if the United States, which now has the largest number of AIDS cases diagnosed anywhere, has to cope with a major epidemic in the late 1990s while the Soviet Union and China are still almost untouched, power could shift toward the East.

The alternative is to create a global management system in the next few years that will integrate all our independent sovereignties and their power struggles. But the survivors, whoever they are, will determine the shape of global order for the human race for the next century and perhaps beyond.

## Alternative Futures

There are other scenarios. AIDS, like previous epidemics, may get far worse at any time because of a change in the subtypes of the virus. Or it may get milder. Or a treatment that can prevent AIDS or cure

it may be developed and produced faster than we expect.

Let us hope and push for this last possibility. Thousands of deaths could be prevented by every single day of advance in finding a vaccine or cure.

If and when a vaccine or cure for AIDS is found, many of the social changes imagined here could be reversed overnight. The sexual revolution of the 1970s might come back with a roar (though some of the constructive new paths explored might still be taken). But if a treatment is long delayed, the move-

ments toward isolation or toward religion or away from science might easily become permanent.

The question of when the AIDS epidemic levels off — whether by 1991, by 1996, or perhaps much later — is the crucial question in every forecast. If AIDS continues its present course, most of humanity will still survive, but by the year 2000 there will be new behaviors, new social structures, and new global relations in a world that even five years ago we could not have imagined.

# Natural Resources

- **International Dimensions (Articles 9-12)**
- **Raw Materials (Articles 13-15)**
- **Food and Hunger (Articles 16-19)**
- **Energy (Articles 20-23)**

In the eighteenth, nineteenth, and early twentieth centuries, the idea of the modern nation-state was developed and expanded. These legal entities were conceived of as separate, self-contained units, which independently pursued their national interests. Scholars envisioned the world as an international political community of independent units, which "bounced off" each other (a concept that has often been described as a billiard ball model).

This concept of self-contained and self-directed units, however, has undergone major rethinking in the past 15 years, primarily because of the international dimensions of the social demands being placed on natural resources. National boundaries are becoming less and less valid. The Middle East, for example, contains a majority of the world's known oil reserves; yet, Western Europe and Japan are very dependent on this source of energy. Neither this type of resource dependency nor the problems of air pollution, for example, recognize political boundaries on a map. Therefore, the concept that independent political units control their own destiny is becoming outdated. In order to understand why this is so, one must look at how the earth's natural resources are being utilized today.

The articles in the first subsection of this unit discuss the international dimensions of the uses and abuses of natural resources. The central issue has to do with whether or not human activity is bringing about basic changes in the functioning of the biosphere. In the lead article, the answer to this question is a resounding "yes." Changes in the earth's climate are traced to the greenhouse effect, which has resulted from the burning of fossil fuels. In addition, the depletion of the earth's ozone layer because of the use of modern chemicals is also described. What is central to this analysis is the fact that these problems transcend national boundaries. The problems of global changes in the climate will affect everyone and will require international efforts to respond to these changes. A single country or even a few countries cannot have a significant impact on solving these problems. The recent effort by 46 countries to limit the production of ozone-depleting chemicals is described by Thomas H. Maugh. He illustrates the problems of reaching international agreements to protect the environment.

The next two articles in this subsection examine the problems of transboundary pollution. Again, the emphasis is on the nature of problems that transcend international boundaries. The Canadian experience is described, using a variety of case studies. Next, the nuclear power plant accident at Chernobyl is reviewed in order to discover what lessons can be learned from this unprecedented event that has had profound transboundary implications.

The second subsection focuses on specific natural resource case studies. While the introductory subsection discusses the utilization of natural resources in legal and political terms, this subsection looks at specific commodities such as topsoil, fresh water, and tropical forests. These articles contain both good news and bad news. In all of them, the ecopolitical relationship is apparent. For example, in "Converting Garbage to Gold: Recycling Our Materials," the attempt to transform a "throw-away" society into one that recycles its waste products is a good illustration of how new ideas (the "meta" component) affect social structures, which, in turn, affect the natural environment.

The third subsection focuses on the most fundamental relationship between society and nature: food production and hunger. It begins with a broad overview of the dynamics of the world's food production and distribution systems. The article "The Hidden Malice of Malnutrition" then examines an often overlooked aspect of hunger, the long-term genetic effects of hunger from one generation to the next. If world hunger was solved tomorrow, the effects would linger for generations.

During the past 40 years, when the world's population almost doubled, there have been remarkable increases in agricultural output. This is known as the green revolution. Edward C. Wolf examines the potential for subsistence farmers of the new field of biotechnology. He raises some important economic concerns about whether this potential will be fulfilled given the fact that private companies, not public agencies, are doing the basic research in this area.

The final article about food production and distribution offers an interesting glimpse into the future with a Japanese case study of a fully computer-controlled "factory" for growing vegetables.

Another critical relationship between social structures and the environment is the subject of the final subsection of this unit: the production and consumption of energy. Since 1973, the fluctuations in the price and supply of energy in general and oil in particular have had a major impact on everyone. The initial price shocks of 1973 (which resulted from an Arab oil boycott of Israel's political allies) have been followed by many ups and downs. At one point, the Organization of Petroleum Exporting Countries (OPEC) was perceived to be a major new force in the international political arena. Now, in a period described as an oil glut, there are serious questions about the world oil market in general and the U.S. market in particular.

The problems of energy supply and demand are also examined from a number of other perspectives. For many people in the world, the energy crisis has nothing to do with oil, but with the daily search for firewood as described in "The World's Shrinking Forests."

While the world's demand for electricity is growing, the construction of large generating facilities often creates many new problems. In addition, many countries have been forced to reexamine their move toward nuclear power since the Chernobyl accident. What are the options and consequences if the world were to abandon nuclear energy? These and related energy issues are discussed in the articles in this subsection.

The subsection, and unit, conclude with an in-depth look at the fundamental redefinition of economic and political institutions that will be necessary for the transition away from fossil fuels to alternative sources of energy, such as solar.

Nature is not some object "out there" to be visited at a national park. It is the food we eat and the energy we consume. Human beings are joined in the most intimate of relationships with the natural world in order to survive from one day to the next. It is ironic how little time is spent thinking about this relationship. The pressures that rapidly growing numbers of people are placing on the earth's carrying capacity suggest that this oversight will not continue much longer.

### Looking Ahead: Challenge Questions

How is the availability of natural resources affected by population growth?

In what ways has the international community responded to problems of pollution and threats to the common heritage?

What is the natural resource picture going to look like 30 years from now?

How is society, in general, likely to respond to the conflicts between economic necessity and resource conservation?

How is agricultural production a function of many different aspects of a society's economic and political structure?

Are there any similarities between the global energy and food shortages?

What is the likely future of energy supplies in both the industrial world and the Third World?

What transformations will societies that are heavy users of fossil fuels have to undergo in order to meet future energy needs?

# The Heat Is On

## *Chemical wastes spewed into the air threaten the earth's climate*

At this time of year, the Cabo de Hornos Hotel in Punta Arenas (pop. 100,000) is ordinarily filled with tourists who spend their days browsing in the local tax-free shops or mounting expeditions into the rugged, mountainous countryside just out of town. But the 120 mostly American scientists and technicians who converged on Chile's southernmost city for most of August and September ignored advertisements for hunting, hiking and ski tours. Instead, each day they scanned the bulletin board in the hotel lobby for the latest information on a different sort of venture.

Thirteen times during their eight-week stay, a specially outfitted DC-8 took off from the Presidente Ibañez Airport, twelve miles northeast of Punta Arenas. Often the 40-odd scientists and support crew listed for a given flight had to leave the hotel soon after midnight to prepare the plane and its research instruments. Once airborne, the DC-8 would bank south toward Antarctica, 1,000 miles away, fighting vicious winds before set-tling into a twelve-hour round-trip flight at altitudes of up to 40,000 ft. Along the way, the instruments continuously collected data on atmospheric gases, airborne particles and solar radiation high above the frozen continent. Meantime, parallel flights took off from Ibañez to gather additional atmospheric data at nearly twice the altitude. Manned by a lone pilot, a Lockheed ER-2, the research version of the high-altitude U-2 spy plane, made twelve sorties into the lower stratosphere, cruising at nearly 70,000 ft., or more

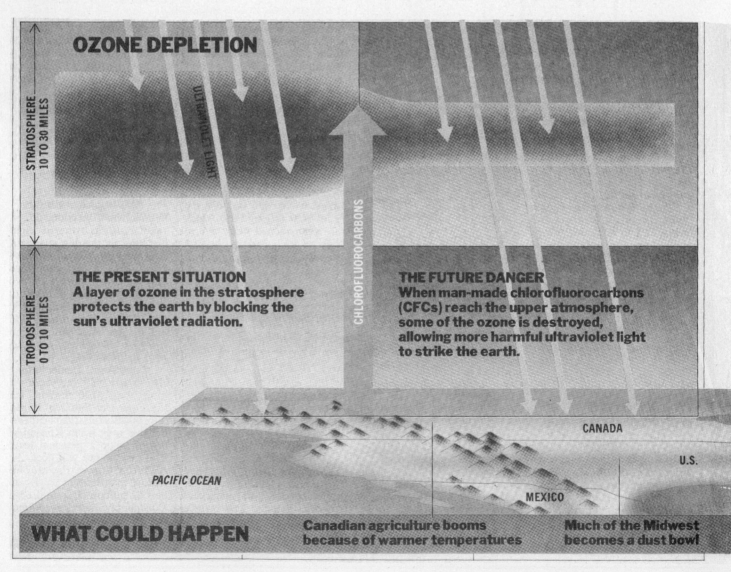

**OZONE DEPLETION**

STRATOSPHERE 10 TO 30 MILES

TROPOSPHERE 0 TO 10 MILES

ULTRAVIOLET LIGHT

CHLOROFLUOROCARBONS

**THE PRESENT SITUATION**
A layer of ozone in the stratosphere protects the earth by blocking the sun's ultraviolet radiation.

**THE FUTURE DANGER**
When man-made chlorofluorocarbons (CFCs) reach the upper atmosphere, some of the ozone is destroyed, allowing more harmful ultraviolet light to strike the earth.

CANADA

U.S.

PACIFIC OCEAN

MEXICO

**WHAT COULD HAPPEN**  Canadian agriculture booms because of warmer temperatures  Much of the Midwest becomes a dust bowl than 13 miles, for six hours at a time.

Both aircraft were part of an unprecedented, $10 million scientific mission carried out by the U.S. under the combined sponsorship of NASA, the National Oceanic and Atmospheric Administration, the National Science Foundation and the Chemical Manufacturers Association. The purpose: to find out why the layer of ozone gas in the upper atmosphere, which protects the earth's surface from lethal solar ultraviolet radiation, was badly depleted over Antarctica. The scale of the mission reflected an intensifying push to understand the detailed dynamics of potentially disastrous changes in the climate. The danger of ozone depletion is only part of the problem; scientists are also concerned about the "greenhouse effect," a long-term warming of the planet caused by chemical changes in the atmosphere.

The threat to the ozone was first discovered in 1983, when scientists with the British Antarctic Survey made the startling observation that concentrations of ozone in the stratosphere were dropping at a dramatic rate over Antarctica each austral spring, only to gradually become replenished by the end of November. At first

they speculated that the phenomenon might be the result of increased sunspot activity or the unusual weather systems of the Antarctic. It is now widely accepted that winds are partly responsible, but scientists are increasingly convinced that there is a more disturbing factor at work. The culprit: a group of man-made chemicals called chlorofluorocarbons (CFCs), which are used, among other things, as coolants in refrigerators and air conditioners, for making plastic foams, and as cleaning solvents for microelectronic circuitry. Mounting evidence has demonstrated that under certain conditions these compounds, rising from earth high into the stratosphere, set off chemical reactions that rapidly destroy ozone.

The precise chemical process is still uncertain, but the central role of CFCs is undeniable. Last month Barney Farmer, an atmospheric physicist at the Jet Propulsion Laboratory in Pasadena, Calif., announced that his ground-based observations as a member of the 1986 Antarctic National Ozone Expedition pointed directly to a CFC-ozone link. "The evidence isn't final," he said, "but it's strong enough." Earlier this month, results from

NASA's Punta Arenas project confirmed the bad news. Not only was the ozone hole more severely depleted than ever before—fully 50% of the gas had disappeared during the polar thaw, compared with the previous high of 40%, in 1985—but the CFC connection was more evident. Notes Sherwood Rowland, a chemist at the University of California at Irvine: "The measurements are cleaner this time, more detailed. They're seeing the chemical chain more clearly."

Atmospheric scientists have long known that there are broad historical cycles of global warming and cooling; most experts believe that the earth's surface gradually began warming after the last ice age peaked 18,000 years ago. But only recently has it dawned on scientists that these climatic cycles can be affected by man. Says Stephen Schneider, of the National Center for Atmospheric Research in Boulder: "Humans are altering the earth's surface and changing the atmosphere at such a rate that we have become a competitor with natural forces that maintain our climate. What is new is the potential irreversibility of the changes that are now taking place."

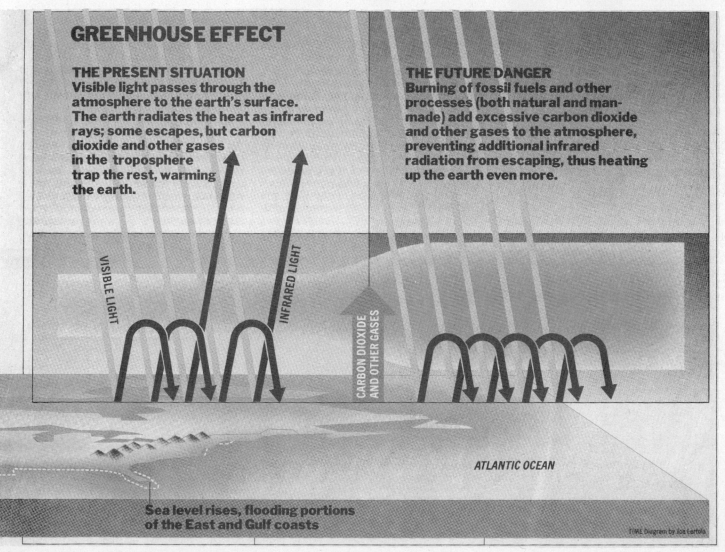

## HOW OZONE IS DESTROYED

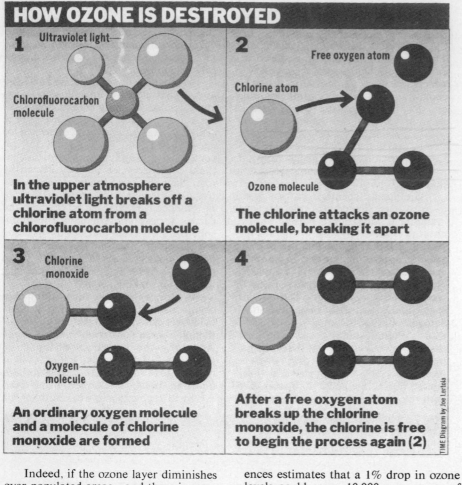

**1**

Ultraviolet light—

Chlorofluorocarbon molecule

**In the upper atmosphere ultraviolet light breaks off a chlorine atom from a chlorofluorocarbon molecule**

**2**

Free oxygen atom

Chlorine atom

Ozone molecule

**The chlorine attacks an ozone molecule, breaking it apart**

**3**

Chlorine monoxide

Oxygen molecule

**An ordinary oxygen molecule and a molecule of chlorine monoxide are formed**

**4**

**After a free oxygen atom breaks up the chlorine monoxide, the chlorine is free to begin the process again (2)**

TIME Diagram by Joe Lertola

Indeed, if the ozone layer diminishes over populated areas—and there is some evidence that it has begun to do so, although nowhere as dramatically as in the Antarctic—the consequences could be dire. Ultraviolet radiation, a form of light invisible to the human eye, causes sunburn and skin cancer; in addition, it has been linked to cataracts and weakening of the immune system. Without ozone to screen out the ultraviolet, such ills will certainly increase. The National Academy of Sciences estimates that a 1% drop in ozone levels could cause 10,000 more cases of skin cancer a year in the U.S. alone, a 2% increase. These dangers were enough to spur representatives of 24 countries, gathered at a United Nations–sponsored conference in Montreal last month, to agree in principle to a treaty that calls for limiting the production of GFCs and similar compounds that wreak havoc on the ozone.

Potentially more damaging than ozone depletion, and far harder to control, is the greenhouse effect, caused in large part by carbon dioxide ($CO_2$). The effect of $CO_2$ in the atmosphere is comparable to the glass of a greenhouse: it lets the warming rays of the sun in but keeps excess heat from reradiating back into space. Indeed, man-made contributions to the greenhouse effect, mainly $CO_2$ that is generated by the burning of fossil fuels, may be hastening a global warming trend that could raise average temperatures between 2° F and 8° F by the year 2050—or between five and ten times the rate of increase that marked the end of the ice age. And that change, notes Schneider, "completely revamped the ecological face of North America."

The relationship between $CO_2$ emissions and global warming is more than theoretical. Two weeks ago, a Soviet-French research team announced impressive evidence that $CO_2$ levels and worldwide average temperatures are intimately related. By looking at cores of Antarctic ice, the researchers showed that over the past 160,000 years, ice ages have coincided with reduced $CO_2$ levels and warmer interglacial periods have been marked by increases in production of the gas.

Although the region-by-region effects of rapid atmospheric warming are far from clear, scientists are confident of the overall trend. In the next half-century, they fear dramatically altered weather patterns, major shifts of deserts and fertile regions, intensification of tropical storms and a rise in sea level, caused mainly by the expansion of sea water as it warms up.

The arena in which such projected climatic warming will first be played out is the atmosphere, the ocean of gases that blankets the earth. It is a remarkably thin membrane: if the earth were the size of an orange, the atmosphere would be only as thick as its peel. The bottom layer of the peel, the troposphere, is essentially where all global weather takes place; it extends from the earth's surface to a height of ten miles. Because air warmed by the

# Flying High—and Hairy

**F**rom preflight preparation to landing, piloting NASA's specially equipped ER-2 high-altitude research aircraft is not for the fainthearted. The three pilots who flew the twelve solo missions through the Antarctic ozone hole found the task grueling. An hour before zooming into the stratosphere, each had to don a bright orange pressure suit and begin breathing pure oxygen to remove nitrogen from the blood and tissues, thus preventing the bends, which can result from rapid reductions in air pressure. Once airborne, "you have to have patience," says Pilot Ron Williams, who flew the first mission. "You're strapped into a seat and can't move for seven hours."

Although the pilots had been briefed by meteorologists on what to expect, they still found conditions aloft astonishingly harsh. Accustomed to clear, broad vistas at high altitudes, the pilots—who took the ER-2 as high as 68,000 ft.—were startled to encounter layers of translucent mist composed of tiny ice

LOCKHEED—CALIFORNIA CO.

**Harsh and lonely work: NASA's high-altitude ER-2 research plane**

earth's surface rises and colder air rushes down to replace it, the troposphere is constantly churning. A permanent air flow streams from the poles to the equator at low altitudes, and from the equator to the poles at higher levels. These swirling air masses, distorted by the rotation of the earth, generate prevailing winds that drive weather across the hemispheres and aid the spread of pollutants into the troposphere. Above this turmoil, the stratosphere extends upward to about 30 miles. In the lower stratosphere, however, rising air that has been growing colder at higher and higher altitudes begins to turn warmer. The reason, in a word: ozone.

Ozone ($O_3$) is a form of oxygen that rarely occurs naturally in the cool reaches of the troposphere. It is created when ordinary oxygen molecules ($O_2$) are bombarded with solar ultraviolet rays, usually in the stratosphere. This radiation shatters the oxygen molecules, and some of the free oxygen atoms recombine with $O_2$ to form $O_3$. The configuration gives it a property that two-atom oxygen does not have: it can efficiently absorb ultraviolet light. In doing so, ozone protects oxygen at lower altitudes from being broken up and keeps most of these harmful rays from penetrating to the earth's surface. The energy of the absorbed radiation heats up the ozone, creating warm layers high in the stratosphere that act as a cap on the turbulent troposphere below.

Ozone molecules are constantly being made. But they can be destroyed by any of a number of chemical processes, most of them natural. For example, the stratosphere receives regular injections of nitrogen-bearing compounds, such as nitrous oxide. Produced by microbes and fossil-fuel combustion, the gas rides the rising air currents to the top of the troposphere. Forced higher still by the tremendous upward push of tropical storms, it finally enters and percolates slowly into the stratosphere.

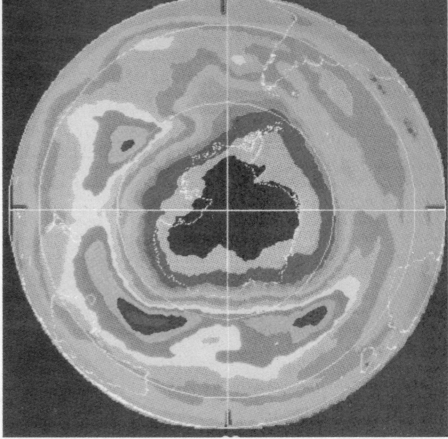

**Worse than ever: satellite image recorded Oct. 5 showing ozone hole over Antarctica**

Like most gaseous chemicals, manmade or natural, that reach the stratosphere, nitrous oxide tends to stay there. Indeed, a recent National Academy of Sciences report likened the upper atmosphere "to a city whose garbage is picked up every few years instead of daily." As long as five years after it leaves the ground, $N_2O$ may finally reach altitudes of 15 miles and above, where it is broken apart by the same ultraviolet radiation that creates ozone. The resulting fragments—called radicals—attack and destroy more ozone molecules. Another ozone killer is methane, a carbon-hydrogen compound produced by microbes in swamps, rice paddies and the intestines of sheep, cattle and termites.

For millenniums, the process of ozone production and destruction has been more or less in equilibrium. Then in 1928 a group of chemists at General Motors invented a

---

particles. "I went into clouds at 61,000 ft., and I didn't come out the whole time," says Williams of the first flight. Another surprise: temperatures did not warm when the plane soared into the stratosphere. Instead, they plummeted to −130°F, low enough to cause worries about a fuel freeze-up.

At 60,000 ft., winds as high as 150 knots buffeted the aircraft. Even so, the real difficulty came from 40-knot gusts that tossed the plane around during landings. With special scientific instruments installed in pods on its long, droopy wings, the ER-2 is "like a big albatross—it's heavy-winged," says Operations Manager James Cherbonneaux of NASA's Ames Research Center. While watching a particularly hairy approach to the runway at Punta Arenas, he recalls, "I chewed a little bit of my heart out."

Conditions aboard the DC-8 were considerably better. The plane, which carried up to 41

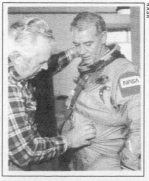

**Williams suits up for takeoff**

scientists, flew no higher than 42,000 ft. on its 13 missions, and those on board were free to move about. But heavy clouds obscured views of Antarctica most of the time, and the flights were a tedious eleven hours long. Observes Atmospheric Scientist Ed Browell, of NASA's Langley Research Center in Virginia: "I sort of likened what we were doing to taking off from the East Coast, flying to the West Coast to do our work, then flying back East to land."

To break the monotony, scientists took aboard a variety of stuffed animals, including a seal, cat and penguin, and warmed up snacks of pizza, empanadas, popcorn and hamburgers in the microwave oven. Cabin temperature was kept cool to avoid overheating the high-tech instrumentation. Says Atmospheric Physicist Geoffrey Toon, of the Jet Propulsion Laboratory in Pasadena, Calif.: "If you tried to sleep during your off hours, usually you froze."

nontoxic, inert gas (meaning that it does not easily react with other substances) that was first used as a coolant in refrigerators. By the 1960s, manufacturers were using similar compounds, generically called chlorofluorocarbons, as propellants in aerosol sprays. As industrial chemicals, they were ideal. "The propellants had to be inert," says Chemist Ralph Cicerone, of the National Center for Atmospheric Research. "You didn't want the spray in a can labeled 'blue paint' to come out red. Since then the growth of CFCs has been fabulous, and they've been pretty useful." Indeed, CFCs turned out to be a family of miracle chemicals: produced at a rate of hundreds of thousands of tons yearly, they seemed almost too good to be true.

They were. In 1972 Rowland heard a report that trace amounts of CFCs had been found in the atmosphere in both the northern and southern hemispheres. What were they doing there? The answer, as Rowland and his colleague, Mario Molina, soon found, was that there was nowhere else for them to go but into the atmosphere. CFCs in aerosol cans are sprayed directly into the air, they escape from refrigerator coils, and they evaporate quickly from liquid cleaners and slowly from plastic foams.

In the troposphere, CFCs are immune to destruction. But in the stratosphere, they break apart easily under the glare of ultraviolet light. The result: free chlorine atoms, which attack ozone to form chlorine monoxide (ClO) and $O_2$. The ClO then combines with a free oxygen atom to form $O_2$ and a chlorine atom. The chain then repeats itself. "For every chlorine atom you release," says Rowland, "100,000 molecules of ozone are removed from the atmosphere."

In 1974 Rowland and Molina announced their conclusion: CFCs were weakening the ozone layer enough to cause a marked increase in skin cancers, perhaps enough to perturb the planet's climate by rejuggling the stratosphere's temperature profile. In 1978 the U.S. banned their use in spray cans. "People assumed the problem had been solved," recalls Rowland. But the Europeans continued to use CFCs in aerosol cans; other uses of CFCs began to increase worldwide. Says Rowland: "All along, critics complained that ozone depletion was not based on real atmospheric measurements—until, that is, the ozone hole appeared. Now we're not talking about ozone losses in 2050. We're talking about losses last year."

For several years NASA's scientists failed to accept data on the Antarctic ozone hole that was before their eyes. The reason: computers prescreening data from monitoring satellites had been programmed to dismiss as suspicious presumably wild data showing a 30% or greater drop in ozone levels. After British scientists reported the deficit in 1985, NASA went back to its computer records, finally recognizing that the satellite data had been showing the hole all along.

Still, the existence of an ozone hole did not necessarily mean CFCs were to blame, and a number of alternative explanations were proposed. Among them, says Dan Albritton, director of the Federal Government's Aeronomy Laboratory in Boulder, was the notion that the "hole did not signify an ozone loss at all, just a breakdown in the distribution system." An interruption in the movement of air from the tropics, where most ozone is created, to the poles could easily result in less ozone reaching the Antarctic. Another theory: perhaps the sunspot activity that peaked around 1980 created more ozone-destroying nitrogen radicals than usual, which would be activated each spring by sunlight.

But while most scientists agree that atmospheric chemistry and dynamics are major causes, the increased scrutiny of the Antarctic atmosphere following the discovery of the hole has seriously undercut the sunspot theory. Data from Punta Arenas, says Robert Watson, a NASA scientist involved in that study, made the verdict all but final. Nitrogen and ozone levels were down, but concentrations of chlorine monoxide were 100 times as great as equivalent levels at temperate latitudes. Says Watson: "We can forget the solar theories. We can no longer debate that chlorine monoxide exists and that its abundance is high enough to destroy ozone, *if* our understanding of the catalytic cycle is correct. We need to go back to the lab and resolve the uncertainty."

That is not all. Scientists are still not completely sure why the hole remains centered on the Antarctic or why the depletion is so severe. It may have to do with the peculiar nature of Antarctic weather. In winter the stratosphere over the region is actually sealed off from the rest of the world by the strong winds that swirl around it, forming an all but impenetrable vortex. Says Cicerone: "Looking down at the South Pole is like watching fluid draining in a sink. It's like an isolated reactor tank. All kinds of mischief can occur."

One likely source of mischief making: clouds of ice particles in the polar stratosphere. Explains Rowland: "Mostly, you don't get clouds in the stratosphere because most of the water has been frozen out earlier. But if the temperature gets low enough, you start freezing out the rest." Indeed, ice may prove to be a central cause of the ozone hole, since it provides surfaces for a kind of chemistry only recently associated with reactions in the atmosphere. In a gaseous state, molecules bounce around and eventually some hit one another. But adding a surface for the molecules to collect on speeds up the reactions considerably.

It is not yet clear whether ozone depletion in the Antarctic is an isolated phenomenon or whether it is an ominous warning signal of more slowly progressing ozone destruction worldwide. Data indicate that the decline over the past eight years is 4% to 5%. Scientists estimate that natural destruction of the ozone could account for 2% of that figure. The Antarctic hole could explain an additional 1%. The remaining 1% to 2% could simply be the result of normal fluctuations. As Albritton's research team reported, "A depletion of this magnitude would be very difficult to identify against the background of poorly understood natural variation."

The same can be said for the greenhouse effect: it is too soon to tell whether unusual global warming has indeed begun. Unlike ozone depletion, the greenhouse effect is a natural phenomenon with positive consequences. Without it, points out Climate Modeler Jeff Kiehl, of the National Center for Atmospheric Research, "the earth would be uninhabitable. It is what keeps us from being an ice-frozen planet like Mars." Indeed, if gases like $CO_2$ did not trap the sun's energy, the earth's mean temperature would be 0° F, rather than the current 59°.

Still, as far back as the late 1890s, Swedish Chemist Svante Arrhenius had begun to fret that the massive burning of coal during the Industrial Revolution, which pumped unprecedented amounts of $CO_2$ into the atmosphere, might be too much of a good thing. Arrhenius made the startling prediction that a doubling of atmospheric $CO_2$ would eventually lead to a 9° F warming of the globe. Conversely, he suggested, glacial periods might be caused by diminished levels of the gas. His contemporaries scoffed. Arrhenius, however, was exactly right. In his time, the $CO_2$ concentration was about 280 to 290 parts per million—just right for a moderately warm, interglacial period. But today the count stands at some 340 p.p.m. By 2050, if the present rate of burning fossil fuels continues, that concentration will double, trapping progressively more infrared radiation in the atmosphere.

The consequences could be daunting. Says National Center for Atmospheric Research's Francis Bretherton: "Suppose it's August in New York City. The temperature is 95°; the humidity is 95%. The heat wave started on July 4 and will continue through Labor Day." While warmer temperatures might boost the fish catch in Alaska and lumber harvests in the Pacific Northwest, he says, the Great Plains could become a dust bowl; people would move north in search of food and jobs, and Canada might rival the Soviet Union as the world's most powerful nation. Bretherton admits that his scenario is speculative. But, he says, "the climate changes underlying it are consistent with what we believe may happen."

Such changes may already be under way. Climatologists have noted an increase in mean global temperature of about 1° F since the turn of the century—within the range predicted if the greenhouse effect is on the rise. But, warns Roger Revelle, of the University of California at San Diego, "climate is a complicated thing, and the changes seen so far may be due to some other cause we don't yet understand." The absence of a clear-cut

# Cloudy Crystal Balls

**C**limatologists regularly issue confident warnings about impending atmospheric disasters. The secret of their wizardry: sophisticated computer models, which are no more than mathematical representations of the world's climate and the conditions that scientists think may contribute to a specific phenomenon like, say, ozone depletion. Unfortunately, when all the variables are fed into the computer, the predictions can fail miserably to match reality.

Take the Antarctic ozone hole, for example. Before it was discovered, climate modelers trying to simulate ozone loss in the atmosphere had not yet factored in the Antarctic stratosphere. Thus their models failed to predict the existence of the ozone hole. After the hole was finally stumbled upon two years ago, Susan Solomon, a chemist at the National Oceanic and Atmospheric Administration in Boulder, and Rolando Garcia, of the National Center for Atmospheric Research, plugged more numbers into NCAR's computer model to account for the Antarctic ice clouds. Bang! The hole appeared.

Does that mean, as one critic put it, that models projecting climatic change are "just the opinion of their authors about how the world works"? Not necessarily. That the model eventually proved accurate, if only in hindsight, was a tribute to the powers of computer climate models—and a demonstration of their shortcomings. The models attempt to reduce the earth's climate to a set of grids and numbers, then manipulate the numbers based on the physical laws of motion and thermodynamics. The sheer number of calculations involved is mind-boggling. A three-dimensional model, for example, requires more than 500 billion computations to simulate the world's climate over one year.

Not surprisingly, the earliest models in the 1960s were hopelessly simplistic. The earth's surface was often reduced to one continent with one ocean, fixed cloud cover and no seasons. But as computing power grew, so did the complexity of climate modeling. Continents were added. So were mountain ranges, deeper oceans and surface reflectivity.

Even so, climate modelers admit, building a completely realistic mock earth is an impossibly tall order. "You divide the world into a bunch of little boxes," explains Michael MacCracken, an atmospheric scientist at Lawrence Livermore National Laboratory. The size of the geographic box—the degree of detail called for—limits the model. Smaller grids dramatically increase the number-crunching power required. "The state of the art would be to get down to small areas so we can say what's going to happen in Omaha," says Livermore's Stanley Grotch. "The models just aren't that good yet."

Why, then, do scientists trust them? How do they assess their accuracy? "You compare them with reality," explains Princeton Climatologist Syukuro Manabe. "How well do they reproduce the movement of the jet stream, the geographical and seasonal distribution of rainfall and temperature? You can also reproduce climate changes from the past. Eighteen thousand years ago, there was a massive continental ice sheet. Given the conditions that we know existed, can we reproduce accurately the distribution of sea-surface temperatures then? The answer is, We can do this very well. It gives you some confidence." Large-scale phenomena can be modeled more easily than those affecting small areas. So when it comes to the global warming produced by the greenhouse effect, for example, the outlines are predictable but the specifics are not. Says Manabe: "All we can say is that maybe the mid-continental U.S. becomes dryer."

A major drawback of computer models is that the various data do not necessarily behave as a system. Coaxing ocean currents to interact with the atmosphere is no small matter. For starters, oceans heat and cool far more slowly than the atmosphere. "We've had a hard time coupling the two systems," admits Manabe. "Even though the atmospheric model and ocean model work individually, when you put them together, you get crazy things happening. It's taken us 20 years to get them together, and we're still struggling."

Offsetting the obvious weaknesses of climate models, says Warren Washington, who developed the model now used at NCAR, is one significant advantage. "They are experimental tools that allow us to test our hypotheses," he says. "We can ask such questions as 'What happens when a big volcano like El Chichón goes off?' and 'How much will the earth warm up by 2030 if we continue to dump $CO_2$ into the atmosphere?' "

Models can also describe the effects of climatic phenomena that have never been seen. In 1983 a group of scientists that included Cornell's Carl Sagan calculated what would happen if the U.S. and the Soviet Union fought a nuclear war. Their conclusion: the dust and smoke from burning cities would blot out enough sunlight to plunge the land into a "nuclear winter" that would devastate crops and lead to widespread starvation.

The problem with their model was that it ignored such key factors as winds, oceans and seasons. When NCAR's Stephen Schneider and Starley Thompson ran the numbers through their agency's three-dimensional computer model, they found that the winter would be more like a "nuclear autumn." Schneider says the less dramatic conclusion does not change the fact that "nuclear autumn is not going to be a nice picnic out there on the rocks watching the leaves change color." Despite the limitations and omissions of climate models, he argues, scientists cannot afford to ignore their predictions. They are, he concedes, a "dirty crystal ball. The question is, How long do you wait to clean the glass before you act on what you see inside?"

*—By David Bjerklie.*
**Reported by J. Madeleine Nash/Chicago**

signal, however, does not disprove the theory. Scientists expect any excess greenhouse warming to be masked for quite some time by the enormous heat-absorbing capacity of the world's oceans, which have more than 40 times the absorptive capacity of the entire atmosphere.

"Right now," declares University of Chicago Atmospheric Scientist V. Ramanathan, "we've committed ourselves to a climatic warming of between one and three degrees Celsius [1.8° F to 5.4° F], but we haven't seen the effect." This extra heat, now trapped in the oceans, he says, should be released over the next 30 to 50 years—unless, of course, an event like a big volcanic eruption counteracts it. Notes Ramanathan: "By the time we know our theory is correct, it will be too late to stop the heating that has already occurred." Schneider sees no need to wait. Says he: "The greenhouse effect is the least controversial theory in atmospheric science."

Maybe. But climate is governed by an array of forces that interact in dizzyingly complex ways. The atmosphere and oceans are only two major pieces of the puzzle. Also involved: changes in the earth's movements as it orbits the sun, po-vegetable and animal life. "The feedbacks are enormously complicated," says Michael MacCracken, of the Lawrence Livermore National Laboratory in California. "It's like a Rube Goldberg machine in the sense of the number of things that interact in order to tip the world into fire or ice."

One of the most fundamental elements of the Rube Goldberg machine is the three astronomical cycles first described by Serbian Scientist Milutin Milankovitch in the 1920s. The swings, which involve long-term variations in the wobbling of the earth's axis, its tilt and the shape of its orbit around the sun, occur every 22,000, 41,000 and 100,000 years, respectively. Together they determine how much solar energy the earth receives and probably cause the earth's periodic major ice ages every 100,000 years or so, as well as shorter-term cold spells.

But Milankovitch cycles only scratch the surface of climatic change. Volcanoes, for example, send up veils of dust that reflect sunlight and act to cool the planet. Deserts, with their near white sands, also reflect sunlight, as do the polar ice caps. Tropical rain forests, however, have the opposite effect: their dark green foliage, like the dark blue of the ocean, absorbs solar radiation; both tend to warm the planet.

Clouds, which shade about half the earth's surface at any given time, are another important climatic factor. Says James Coakley of the National Center for Atmospheric Research: "If you heat up the atmosphere and pump more water in, clouds will change. But how? We don't know." Water vapor, for example, is yet another greenhouse gas, but the white-gray surfaces of clouds reflect solar energy. Which effect predominates? Answer: it depends on the cloud. The bright, low-level stratocumulus clouds reflect 60% of incoming solar rays. But long, thin monsoon clouds let solar heat in while preventing infrared radiation from escaping.

Another contributor to climatic change is the biosphere—scientific jargon for the realm of all living things on earth. And it is the biosphere that threatens to tip the balance. To be sure, many of its effects are natural and as such have long been part of the climatic equilibrium. Termites, for example, produce enormous amounts of gas as they digest woody vegetation: a single termite mound can emit five liters of methane a minute. The methane escapes into the atmosphere, where it can not only destroy ozone but also act as a greenhouse gas in its own right. "Termites," says Environmental Chemist Patrick Zimmerman, of the National Center for Atmospheric Research, "could be re-

sponsible for as much as 50% of the total atmospheric methane budget."

Actually, the biosphere becomes a problem only when humans get involved. In Brazil the Amazon rain forest, which once covered 3 million sq. mi., has been slashed by an estimated 10% to 15% as the region has been developed for mining and agriculture; an additional 20% has been seriously disturbed. When the downed trees are burned or rot, $CO_2$ and other greenhouse gases are released. The same kind of deforestation in Africa, Indonesia and the Philippines, say experts, may already be helping to make the world warmer.

To make matters worse, a host of other gases are now known to add to the greenhouse effect. In 1975, Ramanathan was amazed to discover that Freon, a widely used CFC, was an infrared absorber. "It had a very large impact," he says. "Since then, tracking down the role of other trace gases has become a cottage industry. There are dozens of them, and they are rivaling the effects of increasing $CO_2$." In fact, by the year 2030 the earth will already face the equivalent of a doubling of $CO_2$, thanks to these other rapidly increasing gases, including methane, nitrous oxide and all the CFCs. "These are the little guys," says Schneider. "But they nickel and dime you to the point where they add up to 50% of the problem."

Is there any way to slow either the greenhouse effect or the depletion of the world's ozone? The Montreal accord, agreed to last month after nearly five years of on-and-off negotiations, is a good start on ozone. It calls on most signatory countries to reduce production and consumption of CFCs by 50% by 1999. Developing nations, however, will be allowed to increase their use of the chemicals for a decade so they can catch up in basic technologies like refrigeration. The net effect, insist the treaty's advocates, will be a 35% reduction in total CFCs by the turn of the century.

Some experts do not believe the pro-

jected cutback is good enough. Says Rowland: "The Montreal agreement simply isn't sufficient to protect the ozone. We should have signed a treaty that reduced CFC production by 95%—not 50%." Nonetheless, the Environmental Protection Agency has calculated that without the accord, a staggering 131 million additional cases of skin cancer would occur among people born before 2075.

Any similar attempt to ease the greenhouse effect by imposing limits on $CO_2$ and other emissions is unlikely. John Topping, president of the Washington-based Climate Research Institute, argues that adjustments in agricultural production, like limiting the use of nitrogen-based fertilizers, would have only a slight effect. A more important step would be to protect the tropical rain forests, a move that would certainly be resisted by developers. Obviously, the most far-reaching step would be to cut back on the use of fossil fuels, a measure that would be hard to accomplish in industrialized countries without a wholesale turn to energy conservation or alternative forms of power. In developing countries, such reductions might be technologically feasible but would be all but impossible to carry out politically and economically.

Until now, the earth's climate has been a remarkably stable, self-correcting machine, letting in just the right amount and type of solar energy and providing just the right balance of temperature and moisture to sustain life. Alternating cycles of cold and warmth, as well as greater and lesser concentrations of different gases, have forced some species into extinction. The same changes have helped others evolve. The irony is that just as we have begun to decipher the climatic rhythms that have gone on for hundreds of millions of years, we may have begun to change them irrevocably. And as the unforeseen discovery of the ozone hole demonstrates, still more unexpected changes may be on the way.  —*By Michael D. Lemonick. Reported by J. Madeleine Nash/Boulder, with other bureaus*

# 46 Nations Agree on Pact to Protect Ozone Layer

## Thomas H. Maugh II

*Times Science Writer*

Representatives of 46 nations adopted a landmark treaty in Montreal on Wednesday that will lead to a 50% reduction in use of ozone-depleting chlorofluorocarbons by the end of the century. But despite its historic significance, the treaty's practical effects are likely to leave few people satisfied.

Manufacturers say that the treaty will cause a rise in the cost of CFCs, as the chemicals are called; in turn, that is likely to drive up the prices of consumer goods such as refrigerators and computers. An industry group has estimated that it will cost the United States at least $1 billion by the end of the century.

Scientists and environmental groups say the pact doesn't go nearly far enough—in part because the treaty does not place any limits on Third World countries, where the use of chlorofluorocarbons is increasing.

"The treaty is an important first step because it is a precedent for future action, but it is really only a half step in controlling the ozone problem," said David Doniger of the Washington-based Natural Resources Defense Council.

CFCs are prized by industry because they do not react with any chemials in the environment and they are nontoxic. They are widely used in refrigerators and air conditioners, as blowing agents for insulating foams and as a cleaning agent in the electronics industry. More than one million tons of the chemicals are produced worldwide each year.

But their inertness creates a danger. The chemicals remain in the atmosphere for decades and slowly rise to the stratosphere, the segment of the atmosphere extending from nine to 30 miles above the Earth's surface. There, sunlight breaks them apart, creating highly reactive chlorine atoms that destroy large amounts of ozone.

Ozone, a pollutant at ground level, is a protector in the stratosphere. Produced from oxygen by sunlight, it screens out more than 99% of the sun's harmful ultraviolet radiation. But every 1% decrease in ozone allows 2% more ultraviolet to reach the ground. Many scientists believe there has already been at least a 3% reduction in the ozone layer.

For every 1% increase in ultraviolet, scientists say, there will be as many as 30,000 extra cases of skin cancer in the United States alone. Increased ultraviolet radition can also have deleterious effects on aquatic organisms that live near the surface, on agricultural crops and on the climate.

> *"The hole changed everything. It got the governments to believe there is a problem."*

Scientists have been debating since 1972 whether CFCs damage the ozone layer, but there now seems little doubt that they do. The clincher was the discovery three years ago of a large "hole" in the ozone layer over Antarctica, according to chemist F. Sherwood Rowland of the University of California, Irvine.

The hole, a 40% decrease in ozone over an area the size of the United States, occurs every spring, and most scientists believe it is caused by CFCs. "The hole changed everything," Rowland said. "It got the governments to believe there is a problem."

The treaty adopted Wednesday calls for a freeze in CFC consumption at 1986 levels beginning July 1, 1990. The United States, Japan and the nations of the European Communities were among those that signed the treaty Wednesday.

The freeze would be followed by a 20% reduction in consumption by June 30, 1994, and another 30% reduction by June 30, 1999.

But there are several loopholes. Developing countries, such as China, India and most nations in South America and Africa, are exempted for 10 years, and the Soviet Union will be permitted to complete CFC production plants that are under construction. The Soviet Union has said it intends also to sign the treaty. India was not at the conference, and China has not yet signed.

Industrialized countries will be able to increase CFC production by 15% as long as they export to developing countries.

"The net effect is that it will really be only a 35% reduction," said Doniger of Natural Resources Defense Council.

Many scientists think more drastic action is necessary. "We have to go for a 95% cutback and soon," said Rowland. "Even if we stopped all CFC release now, the ozone-depletion would get worse for 20 years. Forty percent of the CFC that is in the atmosphere now will still be there in the year 2100."

Most scientists were pleased that the treaty has provisions for revising the cutback levels as new evidence develops. "I think that in the near future we'll have a stronger case for much more severe reductions," said chemist Mario Molina of the Jet Propulsion Laboratory in Pasadena.

But a spokeswoman for the Du Pont Co., of Wilmington, Del., which makes nearly 25% of the world's CFCs, said there is no need for treaty-imposed cutbacks because there is "no imminent hazard to humans or the environment." Cathy Forte said the company has already spent $15 million looking for alternatives, "but there is a lot of work left."

Forte said it will be five to seven years before the company can begin producing alternatives, and that they will cost two to five times as much as CFCs. An industry trade group, the Alliance for Responsible CFC Policy, says that the cost to the United States of a freeze alone would total $1 billion between 1988 and 2000.

# TRANSBOUNDARY POLLUTION and Environmental Health

## Emmanuel Somers

**EMMANUEL SOMERS** is director general of the Environmental Health Directorate of Canada's Department of National Health and Welfare. He has been a member of the Programme Advisory Committee of the International Programme on Chemical Safety since its inception and served as chairman from 1984 to 1986.

Environmental hazards show no respect for national boundaries. Canada, like the rest of the world, is subject to environmental insults from its friends and neighbors. Toxic chemicals from waste dumps or industrial activities in the United States, radioactive debris from nuclear explosions or plant accidents in the USSR, dust from natural disasters in the western United States—all can assail Canada's sovereignty. Canada, however, is not blameless. Effluents from pulp and paper mills and other industries flow into the Great Lakes basin, and when the winds are favorable, sulfur dioxide released from smelters and power plants can travel south over the border.

When we consider the effect of these environmental insults on human health, it is clear that the probability of harm rests on the extent of exposure of the population as well as on the severity of the hazard. Thus, the ultimate risk to the public will vary with the place and occasion.

Transboundary pollution could best be contained and controlled through the development of an international accord, rather in the way that international monetary policy followed the Bretton Woods Agreements. National and bilateral policy, however necessary and effective in the control of specific problems, is in the final analysis too limited to cope with the global dimensions of transboundary problems. An essential first step for any United Nations agency that would shoulder the task is a definition of the nature and scope of the insults to human health that cross national frontiers. Using the Canadian experience as an illustration, it may be instructive to look at some examples of transboundary pollution in terms of their environmental health impact to help determine the necessary elements of such an international environmental security accord.

One approach for defining environmental pollution is to classify it by source, be it chemical, physical, or biological. Sources of pollution may be natural or accidental disasters; military, industrial, or agricultural activities; consumer products; or waste dumps. Because these categories are not mutually exclusive and should be considered only as illustrative, several case histories can be used to develop the general thesis for application to an environmental security policy.

### Natural and Accidental Disasters

The eruption of Mount St. Helens in May 1980 sent volcanic gases and dusts over much of western Canada, as well as the United States, and the high-altitude plume passed over the whole of Canada from west to east. The volcanic ash led

From *Environment*, June 1987, pp. 6–9, 31–33. Reprinted with permission of the Helen Dwight Reid Educational Foundation.
Published by Heldref Publications, 4000 Albemarle St., N.W., Washington, D.C. Copyright © 1987.

# Environmental hazards show no respect for national boundaries

to appreciable crop losses in Washington State,[1] but Canadian vegetation suffered only a light dusting and no damage. This eruption was the first to be fully monitored globally, and although no direct effect on world climate was predicted by computer modeling, volcanic dust does indeed cool the Earth's surface.[2] The gases emitted were sulfurous; sulfur dioxide and hydrogen sulfide were the dominant species.[3] The total emission of such gases was roughly 10 percent of the annual human-caused Canadian release. No direct health effects from the explosion were recorded, but the potential for transboundary insult clearly existed.

The global hazards—both actual and perceived—of nuclear accidents were dramatically illustrated by the disaster at Chernobyl on April 26, 1986. This, the worst reactor accident in history, put some 100 million curies of radioactivity into the environment, the major component being xenon 133.[4] The radioactive fallout, largely of iodine 131, cesium 134, and cesium 137, was a global event; the heaviest deposition, outside the USSR, was in Western Europe, particularly in Scandanavia.[5] In Canada, the Department of National Health and Welfare, which has operated a comprehensive countrywide radiation monitoring network since 1959, first detected iodine 131 some five days after the Chernobyl accident and found measurable levels for the next two months. Although a few imported foods were removed from the market, the total dose-equivalent exposure resulting from the accident, averaged over all Canadians, amounted to no more than an increased lifetime risk of thyroid cancer of 1 in 25 million—in reality, an unmeasurable increase in risk. The impact in Europe, where the plume contamination was greater, is, of course, much more serious. The accident may ultimately be responsible for about 1,000 deaths from cancer in the European Economic Community countries alone.[6]

## Military Activities

The testing of nuclear weapons in the atmosphere in the early 1960s led to measurable contamination of the Canadian environment: gross beta-radiation activity in air samples and concentrations of cesium 137 and strontium 90 in milk have been found by Canada's program of continuing radiation monitoring.[7] In fact, caribou in the far north are still contaminated by radioactivity from the nuclear fallout, although only at levels one-sixth of those 20 years ago.[8] Caribou feed largely on lichen, which has an exceptional capacity to accumulate radioisotopes. Chernobyl as well increased the radioactivity in caribou by an average of 15 percent.

A more specific example of pollution arose in 1978 when the Soviet satellite *Cosmos 954* re-entered the atmosphere over northern Canada. Disintegration of the satellite's nuclear reactor led to widespread dissemination of radioactive fragments. An extensive search for the debris was mounted—initially in winter in the Northwest Territories.[9] A total of less than 100 kilograms of material was recovered, including some 3,000 particles, often too small to be visible, that were remnants of the nuclear fuel. The minute radioactive fragments were a potential risk if accidentally inhaled or ingested. One fragment was sufficiently radioactive to be lethal after a few hours' contact. This massive clean-up operation in the frozen north was costly. The USSR settled the compensation claim.

## Industrial Activities

Currently, the most notorious of transboundary pollutants is acid rain, or more correctly, the wet and dry acidic deposition of oxidized sulfur and nitrogen compounds. Scandinavian countries and Canada, among others, are recipients of the long-range transport of other countries' industrial emissions. The Canadian Department of the Environment estimates that more than 50 percent of the acid rain that falls on Canada comes from U.S. sources, with well-established adverse effects on our lakes, fishes, forests, and buildings.[10]

The health implications are not so clear, but the evidence is accumulating that acid rain is indeed damaging to the respiratory function.[11] A 1983 study, based on eight years of data, showed an association between increased hospital admissions for respiratory illnesses in southwestern Ontario and increased ambient levels of sulfate and ozone and higher temperatures.[12] Studies of the pulmonary function of schoolchildren living in two Canadian towns with different exposures to acid precipitation showed a small but statistically significant decrement in lung function for those in an area with high pollution.[13]

An additional, although indirect, effect of acid rain on human health lies in the acidification of water sources, which can lead to the leaching of toxic substances from mineral deposits and distribution systems; mercury, aluminum, copper, lead, cadmium, and asbestos are contaminants of major concern. Studies in the Muskoka-Haliburton region of Ontario—where acid deposition is high—showed elevated levels of copper, lead, zinc, and cadmium in tap water left standing in the pipes.[14] Flushing can solve this particular problem, but the potential for harm clearly exists. More serious is the conclusion, based on modeling studies of aluminum levels, that acid deposition is linked to changes in the water quality of subsurface, as well as surface, water supplies.[15] Aluminum levels mobilized by acid deposition could sell serve as an early warning system for the contamination of water supplies.

Common waterways may also carry hazardous chemicals across national

## Disintegration of the Soviet satellite *Cosmos 954*'s nuclear reactor caused widespread dissemination of radioactive fragments.

boundaries. From 1955 until 1980, the Reserve Mining Company of Silver Bay, Minnesota, dumped taconite waste—up to 67,000 tons of tailings daily—into Lake Superior. Asbestos fibers from these tailings were considered to have contaminated the drinking water of Duluth,[16] and transboundary migration was suspected after amphibole fibers were identified at Thunder Bay, Ontario, following the anticlockwise flow of the lake.[17] No defined effect of human health resulted, but once again the potential clearly existed.

### Agricultural Activities

Pesticides are an essential component of modern agriculture. Their usage varies from country to country, as does their regulatory control. Compounds such as endrin, dieldrin, and DDT, for example, cannot be used on food crops in Canada; they are, however, used in some other countries. Unintended chemical residues can occur on imported fruits and vegetables, requiring a system of surveillance and monitoring (administered in Canada by the Department of National Health and Welfare) to prevent the sale of foods with hazardous levels of chemicals.

Such mechanisms are common in developed countries. However, on occasion, different legislative systems can lead to different administrative actions by two countries that both accept the same scientific evidence of health risk. The use of diethylstilbestrol (DES), a recognized human carcinogen, as a growth promoter for livestock was suspended in Canada in 1972; subsequently, the sale of meat derived from

animals treated with DES was made illegal by regulation. Although similar action was taken in the United States in 1973, the ban was overruled by a court decision a year later, based on procedural factors. It was therefore necessary for the Canadian Department of Agriculture to introduce a DES certification scheme for beef imported from the United States and to analyze livers for DES residues. It was not until 1979 that the use of DES in cattle and sheep was banned by the U.S. Food and Drug Administration.

### Consumer Products

The chlorofluorocarbons (CFCs)

## Some chemicals from toxic waste dumps could pose a hazard to human health, particularly if they bioaccumulate in fish.

provide a classic example of consumer products that when misused give rise to global environmental health problems.

# The testing of nuclear weapons in the atmosphere in the early 1960s led to measurable contamination of the Canadian environment.

Although nonessential uses of CFCs in aerosols have been banned for some years in North America, their use in most of the rest of the world continues apace without, as yet, an international accord to limit their production.[18] The health danger is that these stable chemicals can migrate to the upper atmosphere where they destroy the ozone layer that serves to filter out ultraviolet radiation before it reaches the Earth's surface. Satellite data show that for the period from 1978 to 1984, the ozone layer eroded at an average annual rate of 0.5 percent and, additionally, there is alarm over the hole that recently appeared in the ozone layer over the Antarctic, although it is by no means certain that this latter effect is related simply to CFCs.[19] The U.S. Environmental Protection Agency (EPA) estimates that the lack of international control measures for CFCs could lead to an appreciable increase in the incidence of skin cancer, cataracts, and malignant melanoma in the United States.[20]

## Waste Dumps

Toxic waste is now well recognized as a national problem. In the United States alone, some 18,000 dangerous sites have been identified by EPA.[21] The proximity of a number of these dumps of potentially toxic chemicals to the Canadian border has led to great public concern and an extensive bilateral program under the auspices of the International Joint Commission. Modern analytical techniques have identified the presence of some 1,000 chemicals in the Great Lakes ecosystem.[22] At sufficiently high concentrations, some of these chemicals could pose a hazard to human health, particularly if they bioaccumulate in fish. Regulatory action has been taken in both the United States and Canada to establish guidelines for residues of PCBs and 2,3,7,8-tetrachlorodibenzo-p-dioxin in fish. Here, then, is an example of chemicals, probably released from waste dumps, contaminating a neighboring country's foodstuffs.

## Assessment and Management

The above are cases of identified hazards imported into Canada. How, then, do we assess the actual or potential risk to health? The major sources of toxicological information that determine regulatory decisions are animal tests and human epidemiological and clinical studies.[23] Supportive evidence is provided by in vitro testing and structure-activity relationships of the chemicals. Although epidemiology provides unique evidence of adverse effects on human populations, it has limitations for regulatory purposes in that it leads to reactive, rather than preventive, public health measures. In addition, the methodological problems of identifying nonspecific effects of low concentrations of ubiquitous environmental chemicals are formidable. The difficulty of determining the levels of exposure that are required for retrospective studies is also large.

The scientific community usually achieves a consensus on the estimation of risk based on knowledge of the inherent toxicity of the chemical, physical, or biological agent. The human population's susceptibility and its exposure to the agent are often less well known, making the threat to human health from traces of environmental pollutants extremely difficult to ascertain. Inevitably, governmental health agencies have to adopt prudent and cautious policies in their decision making. The ultimate political judgment, however much it relies on weighing the scientific evidence,[24] must represent the social climate of the country in which it is made.[25] Thus, nation states will invoke different cultural and economic values in their own risk assessments, so that the same scientific estimation of risk can lead to different regulatory recommendations. In a sense, the national regulatory decision represents the depth and strength of our "inarticulate major premises" in Justice Oliver Wendell Holmes's classic phrase.

### International Accord

The affronts to environmental health suffered by Canada are given only as illustrations of the world's problems. On occasion, solutions can be achieved through bilateral negotiation, as when the governments of Canada and the United States entered into the 1972 and 1978 Great Lakes Water Quality Agreements to deal with the urgent problem of pollution and eutrophication of the Great Lakes. Acting under the Boundary Waters Treaty of 1909, the two governments agreed in 1972 to initiate binational efforts to control a number of toxic substances from municipal and industrial wastes, to reduce pollution from shipping and dredging activities, and to undertake a number of major studies, including one on the significance for water quality of pollution resulting from various land uses. The resulting coordinated binational action—with municipal programs costing over $8 billion and covering industrial controls, reduction of phosphate in detergent, and massive cleanups—led to a

noticeable reduction in the eutrophication process.[26] The lakes became clearer.

The attack on specific toxic substances, however, has proved more difficult. The 1978 Great Lakes Water Quality Agreement provided for a more specific approach to the control both of toxic contamination and of various dispersed or nonpoint sources.[27] So far, the successes have been limited, largely because of the extent and complexity of the ecosystems themselves, but also because of the institutional mechanisms that must be involved in bringing about the necessary changes.

Most problems of transboundary pollution are multinational in impact and hence require international action. If we are to develop international accord on this issue, it is perhaps worthwhile to delineate some of the elements that must form the basis for such agreement, emphasizing the environmental health approach:

• *The nature and site of the pollution* should first be identified nationally and then followed by international confirmation. The international inspection program administered by the International Atomic Energy Agency under the Non-Proliferation of Nuclear Weapons Treaty may be an appropriate model for an environmental accord.

• *International consensus on the estimates of risk* could take many forms, depending on the harmful agent and the medium affected. It could be on the acceptable daily intake of a food chemical; the risk of exposure to ionizing radiation; the establishment of permissible levels of chemicals, radiation, or noise in the workplace; guidelines for contaminants in drinking water; and so forth. Under the UN aegis, a variety of expert committees and commissions have had a long and distinguished history in this field, particularly the joint committees between the World Health Organization (WHO) and the Food and Agriculture Organization and between WHO and the International Labour Organization (ILO). The International Commission on Radiological Protection provides detailed and well-constructed estimates of risk for ionizing radiation, as does the UN Scientific Committee on the Effects of Atomic Radiation.

To provide integration and coordination in the area of chemical safety, WHO administers the International Programme on Chemical Safety (IPCS), launched in 1980 as a cooperative venture of ILO, WHO, and the UN Environment Programme. At present some 20 developed and developing countries participate in the joint work. IPCS provides not just an exchange of information, valuable although that may be, but an opportunity to develop common evaluations, investigations, guidelines, and training programs. The program seeks to give international validity and cachet to the risk estimation of chemicals—essential in any international attempt to control their hazards. The main outputs of IPCS include: evaluations of the adverse effects chemicals may produce on human health (including carcinogenesis, mutagenesis, and teratogenesis); principles for establishing exposure limits for chemicals in foods, drinking water, and the working environment; guidelines for exposure assessment, toxicity testing, and epidemiology; information on chemical accidents and emergencies; and training for personnel, particularly in developing countries.

Another IPCS initiative, carried out jointly with the Scientific Committee on Problems of the Environment of the International Council of Scientific Unions, is the Scientific Group on Methodologies for the Safety Evaluation of Chemicals, which reviews advances in relevant methodology.

• *International programs for risk management* are required that, while recognizing national sovereignty, emphasize areas in which joint and common action can be taken internationally. At its recent High Level Meeting in March 1987, the Chemicals Group of the Organization for Economic Cooperation and Development (OECD) recognized the need to improve the prevention of and response to unintended releases of hazardous substances across national frontiers. The group called on OECD to intensify its efforts to address this need and, in particular, to initiate work toward establishing an international agreement.

Risk management practices do, and

always will, differ between different countries, but as we learn more of their genesis and purpose, we will be able to develop a common approach. In this context, a valuable overview of environmental health risk assessment and management practices in Europe has recently been prepared by WHO.[28] The overview noted data gaps in environmental health, particularly between environmental exposure and health assessment, as well as the necessity to use a multisectoral approach to environmental health policies.

These, then, are some suggestions as to how we can move toward an international solution to the problems of transboundary pollution. The health aspect has been underlined, but in a wider context, when we talk of pollution we talk of economics and peaceful cooperation. The UN bodies need to make a new start to address and manage these problems; environmental health and transboundary issues may provide a useful beginning. Whatever techniques we develop —and it may be argued that unless we do develop these techniques we will find the world overwhelmed by a technology out of control—they can best be developed in concert and with a common understanding. The mechanisms are available: it is the will that is required.

## NOTES

1. R. J. Cook, J. C. Barron, R. I. Papendick, and G. J. Williams III, "Impact on Agriculture of the Mount St. Helens Eruptions," *Science* 211(1981):16–22.

2. J. Gribbin, "Do Volcanoes Affect the Climate?" *New Scientist*, 21 January 1982, 150–53.

3. J. B. Pollack, "Measurements of the Volcanic Plumes of Mount St. Helens in the Stratosphere and Troposphere," *Science* 211 (1981):815–16.

4. C. Hohenemser, M. Deicher, A. Ernst, H. Hofsäss, G. Lindner, and E. Recknagel, "Chernobyl: An Early Report," *Environment*, June 1986; C. Norman and D. Dickson, "The Aftermath of Chernobyl," *Science* 233(1986):1141–42.

5. H. ApSimon and J. Wilson, "Tracking the Cloud from Chernobyl," *New Scientist*, 17 July 1986, 42–45.

6. "Chernobyl and the EEC," *Lancet*, 28 March 1987, 758.

7. E. Somers, "Environmental Monitoring and the Development of Health Standards," *Environmental Monitoring and Assessment* 1(1981):7–19.

8. "Canadian Caribou Safe to Eat, Despite Chernobyl" (News release, Health and Welfare Canada, Ottawa, 19 March 1987).

9. Atomic Energy Control Board, Canada, "Phase II of Cosmos Satellite Search Ends" (News release 78-11, Ottawa, 18 October 1978).

10. Canadian Department of the Environment, Supply and Services Canada, *The Acid Rain Story*, Cat. no. En 21-40/1984E (Ottawa: Supply and Services Canada, 1984).

11. U.S. Committee on Environment and Public Works, *Health Effects of Acid Rain Precursors*, Statement by I. Godar, 100th Cong., 1st sess., 3 February 1987 (S. Hearing 100-4).

12. D. V. Bates and R. Sizto, "Relationship Between Air Pollutant Levels and Hospital Admissions in Southern Ontario," *Canadian Journal of Public Health* 74(1983):117–22.

13. M. Raizenne, R. Burnett, B. Stern, and J. C. Méranger, "Transported Air Pollutants and Respiratory Health in Two Canadian Communities" (Abstract prepared for the Third International Conference on Environmental Lung Disease, Montreal, October 1986).

14. J. C. Méranger, T. R. Khan, C. Vairo, R. Jackson, and W. C. Li, "Lake Water Acidity and the Quality of Pumped Cottage Water in Selected Areas of Northern Ontario," *International Journal of Environmental and Analytical Chemistry* 15(1983):185–212.

15. J. C. Méranger, D. R. Gladwell, and R. E. Lett, "Acid Precipitation and Human Health," *WHO Water Quality Bulletin* 11(1986):26–33, 152–59, 179–86.

16. E. E. Sigurdson, B. S. Levy, J. Mandel, R. McHugh, L. J. Michienzi, H. Jagger, and J. Pearson, "Cancer Morbidity Investigation: Lessons from the Duluth Study of Possible Effects of Asbestos in Drinking Water," *Environmental Research* 25(1981):50–61.

17. Great Lakes Advisory Board, *Asbestos in the Great Lakes Basin*, Report to the International Joint Commission (Windsor, Ontario: IJC, 1975).

18. M. Crawford, "United States Floats Proposal to Help Prevent Global Ozone Depletion," *Science* 234(1986):927–29; M. Glenny, "America Attacks Europe over Stratospheric Ozone," *New Scientist*, 5 March 1987, 17.

19. M. Crawford, note 18 above; G. Brasseur, "The Endangered Ozone Layer: New Theories on Ozone Depletion," *Environment*, January/February 1987.

20. M. Crawford, note 18 above.

21. R. Popkin, "Hazardous Waste Cleanup and Disaster Management," *Environment*, April 1986.

22. *An Inventory of Chemical Substances Identified in the Great Lakes Ecosystem*, Report to the Great Lakes Water Quality Board, International Joint Commission (Windsor, Ontario: IJC, 1983).

23. E. Somers, "Risk Estimation for Environmental Chemicals as a Basis for Decision Making," *Regulatory Toxicology and Pharmacology* 4(1984):99–106.

24. E. Somers, "The Weight of Evidence: Regulatory Toxicology in Canada," *Regulatory Toxicology and Pharmacology* 6(1986):391–98; C. F. Wilkinson, "Risk Assessment and Regulatory Policy," *Comments on Toxicology* 1(1986):1–21.

25. Somers, note 23 above.

26. International Joint Commission, *Third Biennial Report under the Great Lakes Water Quality Agreement of 1978* (Windsor, Ontario: IJC, 1986).

27. Ibid.

28. World Health Organization, "Health and the Environment," *EURO Reports and Studies* 100 (Copenhagen: World Health Organization, 1986).

# The Lessons of Chernobyl, One Year Later

**Armand Hammer and Robert Peter Gale**

*Armand Hammer is chairman and chief executive officer of the Occidental Petroleum Corporation. Dr. Robert Peter Gale, of the University of California at Los Angeles, is working with Soviet scientists to help victims of the Chernobyl disaster.*

LOS ANGELES

Today is the first anniversary of the Chernobyl nuclear reactor accident in the Soviet Union. Chernobyl was a major tragedy for the Soviet Union—a tragedy from which it has not yet fully recovered, physically and emotionally. But Chernobyl has also influenced the Soviet Union and the rest of the world positively. Thus, this is an appropriate time to re-evaluate the lessons learned.

Chernobyl highlighted important aspects of contemporary Soviet society: the central role of modern technology in achieving socialist goals, uncertainty and debate over the free flow of information, and concern, at all levels of society, over the prospect of nuclear war.

A strong emphasis on technology has served the Soviet Union relatively well. Pre-revolutionary Russia did not experience the full impact of the Industrial Revolution, and much was accomplished rapidly in the succeeding 70 years.

Few would dispute that military parity has been achieved with the United States. But at what price? To some extent, the Soviet Union lacks the delicate balance present in our society between technological achievements and human values. In America, technological advancement proceeds against a background of ethical and moral considerations. For example, the promise of genetic engineering which is likely to save lives, is balanced against its potential dangers—eugenics, for example.

As a result of Chernobyl, this balance is developing—rapidly—in Soviet society. A poem by Andre Vosnesensky, published in Pravda, dealt with it:

" . . . Hope,
    crowned by Nobel,
like dreadful genie
woke above Chernobyl.
Forgive me, those who
shut the crack
with their bodies.
Who is to blame—
    Humanity or Science? . . .

. . . Farewell to
    planning on an easy living.
Come to your senses, world,
Before it is too late!
And if man is
    the image of God.
Is God—my image?"

The Soviet Union is beginning to realize the limitations of technology in its society. While choosing not to abandon nuclear energy—in fact, it will be increased fivefold—the Soviet Union is now more sensitive to the complex interaction between technology and man, a lesson we learned at Three Mile Island. For example, Soviet voices are being heard about radioactive waste. The Soviet Union also knows that while military technology has brought it parity, it has brought neither peace nor the high standard of living it seeks.

Chernobyl was a watershed in the evolution of glasnost—"openness." The Government's initial response was not to release information. But such a policy cannot succeed when a radioactive cloud is circling the earth, or when a satellite has an unscheduled atmospheric re-entry. After some days, Soviet policy changed, data were released, press conferences held and representatives of the International Atomic Energy Agency as well as American citizens were invited into the Soviet Union.

This new strategy proved successful and has characterized much of Soviet press coverage of controversial issues

*Moscow found it had to be more open.*

subsequently. Most significantly, America showed that it would not take advantage of this information, that it wished to help and that it considered saving lives more important than political or ideological differences.

This message was not lost on the Soviet Union. Mikhail S. Gorbachev touched upon it when both of us met him shortly after the accident, and it can only serve our mutual interests in the future.

Finally, what lesson did Chernobyl teach about the potential consequences of nuclear war? The immediate toll was 31 deaths. The projected long-term consequences are potentially more serious. These estimates range from 2,500 to 75,000 excess cancer deaths in the next 50 years, perhaps up to 1,000 excess cases of severe mental retardation in individuals exposed in utero and possibly up to 5,000 cases of severe genetic abnormalities in the next generation.

Some of these adverse consequences might be moderated if there were successful advances in cancer prevention or treatment, or in early identification of individuals at risk. Recent progress in manipulating the immune system with molecularly cloned growth factors is one such example as we move toward a cure for cancer. Undoubtedly, others would evolve were Soviet-American collaboration in cancer research to increase.

Importantly, the Soviet Union is not the only victim of Chernobyl: More than one-half of all adverse effects will occur outside that country. This means that a nuclear accident is an international event. Consider what would happen if a similar accident occurred in space—a point Mr. Gorbachev raised in our meeting with him.

The Atomic Age began with the explosion of a nuclear weapon. In these 42 years, the United States and the Soviet Union have been so preoccupied with the balance of nuclear forces that we both have forgotten the dangers of the weapons used to achieve this balance.

While mutual assured destruction may have bought us four decades without a major war, it has not bought us peace, nor peace of mind. We find ourselves with 50,000 nuclear warheads aimed at one another. If we wish to consider the consequences of even the most limited use of these weapons, we would have to multiply the effects of Chernobyl a hundredfold or thousandfold, or more.

Even in a unilateral exchange, the attacking nation would fall victim to radiation-induced cancers and other long-term effects. Clearly, there can be no winner in such a conflict.

Chernobyl also shows us that use of these weapons need not be intentional. Accidents can and will occur. Last year, it was a Soviet nuclear reactor—but why not a Soviet nuclear submarine or missile? And it is not only the Soviet Union that has technical limitations: Consider Challenger and Three Mile Island. Ironically, it is not America or the Soviet Union that may pose the greatest danger. How about nuclear power plants and weapons in developing and unstable nations?

Both superpowers must take whatever steps are necessary to reduce the likelihood of the nonpeaceful uses of nuclear energy. For some, this means an increased nuclear inventory; for others, more advanced defensive systems. Although these arguments are not without some merit, they fail to address the important issue of the limitations of technology. Clearly, the most direct cause of action is to decrease, to some reasonable level, the Soviet and American nuclear arsenals. Whether total elimination of nuclear weapons is possible remains to be determined and hinges on other complex issues such as verification and parity of conventional forces.

Americans will make a serious mistake if we confuse strength with force. Our society's strength lies in our people, our system of government, our pursuit of freedom and justice. We should not unilaterally give up our defenses, but we should not rely on them as a substitute for the responsibility of each citizen to actively participate in a democratic society.

President Reagan and General Secretary Gorbachev have taken the first steps toward a meaningful reduction in intermediate-range and perhaps short-range nuclear weapons. This process should continue since it is in the best interests of both sides.

Here is the final and most important lesson of Chernobyl: We live on a small planet. The peaceful exploration of space and peaceful uses of nuclear energy are too important and potentially too dangerous to be decided on national bases alone. The United States and the Soviet Union should search for areas of productive collaboration. Such fields could also include research on cancer and AIDS. If we can find a way to work together, surely mankind will benefit. To work against one another is an irresponsible policy in an age of international technologies.

*The Kremlin has begun to learn about the limits of technology in Soviet society.*

# State of the Earth: 1985

**Nearly five billion, and growing, we are straining earth's environment to an unprecedented degree. As human pressures build, the relationships between people and their natural support systems reach key**

thresholds, leading to breakdowns. The broad strokes of this mid–decade report often show a frightening drift in a gloomy direction. Yet some fine strokes show bright examples of moves toward a healthy, sustained balance between humans and their natural resources. Our decisions and actions (or inactions) in the remaining years of this decade will affect the fate of all life on earth in the next decade . . . and century. In concert, we will determine whether we are breaking down or breaking out.

Nowhere is the breakdown of natural systems more tragically evident than in Africa, where famine is spreading rapidly. In 1970, Africa was essentially self-sufficient in food; by 1984, however, some 140 million Africans—out of 531 million— were fed with grain from abroad. The decline in per capita food production has been attributed to drought, but the causes are more fundamental: the fastest population growth in history, widespread soil erosion, and the neglect of agriculture by African governments.

The deterioration of environmental systems can be seen in industrial and developing countries alike. Acid rain and air pollutants may be destroying the forests of central Europe even faster than the ax and the plow destroyed those of India and El Salvador. Little attention has been paid to the economy–ecosystem relationship, and our understanding of stresses on ecosystems is far from complete.

National energy policies could determine the extent and pace of a worldwide change in climate. Population policies may determine whether Africa becomes a wasteland. The scale of environmental disruptions we face lends urgency to our efforts to return to a sustainable path—to bring population growth and our economic and social systems into a long-term balance with the resource base that supports us.

*Lester R. Brown*

**Erosion of productive soils by wind and water is changing the face of**

the earth, from subsistence fields in Ethiopia's highlands to thousand-acre swaths of corn and soybeans in the Mississippi valley. One of the first scientists to assess the dimensions of world soil erosion was geologist Sheldon Judson, who estimated that the amount of river-borne soil sediment carried into the oceans had increased from 9 billion tons per year before the introduction of agriculture and grazing to 24 billion tons per year in the late twentieth century. Humans have accelerated the flow of soil to the seas.

Soil erosion is steadily speeding up and now afflicts both industrial and developing countries. Only the ninefold increase in fertilizer use and the near tripling of the world's irrigated cropland since mid-century have masked the effects of soil erosion on crop yields and harvests. Yet as of 1984, the worldwide loss of topsoil from cropland in excess of new soil formation totaled some 25 billion tons.

Topsoil is the key to productive agriculture. Rich in organic matter, it shares more characteristics with the plant life it supports above than with the mineral layers beneath. It is the medium in which roots grow, soil animals flourish, and water is stored. Although in a few regions fertile soils are yards deep, over most of the world's surface the mantle of topsoil on which agriculture depends is only six to eight inches thick. The loss of this thin layer may soon compromise economic progress and political stability.

While detailed information on soil erosion from farmers' fields is available for only a few countries, data on the sediment load of the world's major rivers and on the movement of wind-borne soil over the oceans do provide a broad-brush view of soil erosion at the continental level. Chinese scientists report that the Huang He (Yellow River) carries 1.6 billion tons of soil to the ocean each year. India's Ganga River deposits 1.5 billion tons into the Bay of Bengal. The Mississippi, the largest U.S. river, carries 300 million tons of soil into the Gulf of Mexico each year. Although less than Asia's rivers, this load is soil from the agricultural heartland and is thus a major concern of U.S. agronomists.

Scientists have recently documented that vast amounts of wind-borne soil are also being deposited in the oceans. Island-based air sampling stations in the Atlantic, along with satellite photographs, indicate clearly that plumes of soil dust are being carried out of north Africa over the Atlantic. African soil spatters cars in Miami. Researchers link the unusually high levels recorded in 1983 to Africa's severe drought. Air samples taken at Mauna Loa, Hawaii, indicate a comparable transport of soil across the Pacific from the Asian mainland. The annual peaks in the samples (in March, April, and May) coincide with periods of strong winds, low rainfall, and plowing in the semiarid regions of north Asia. Scientists at Mauna Loa can now tell when spring plowing starts in north China.

The steady growth in demand for agricultural products contributes to soil erosion in many ways. Throughout the Third World, farmers are pushed onto steeply sloping, erosive land that is rapidly losing its topsoil. In the American Midwest, many farmers have abandoned ecologically stable, long-term crop rotations in favor of the continuous row cropping of corn and soybeans, which leaves soils exposed to wind and water. In other areas, farming has extended into semiarid regions where land is vulnerable to wind erosion when plowed.

The loss of topsoil has two effects on farmers' ability to grow food: It robs the land of nutrients, and it degrades physical properties of the soil, such as its ability to absorb water. Erosion also increases the costs of food production. When farmers lose topsoil, they may increase land productivity by substituting energy in the form of fertilizer or through irrigation to offset the soil's declining water-absorptive capacity. Farmers losing topsoil may experience either a decline in their land's productivity or a rise in their costs. And when this happens, farmers can be forced to abandon their land.

The effects of erosion on harvests are not easily measured since they are usually gradual and cumulative. A survey of independent studies of soil erosion in the U.S. Corn Belt found that the loss of an inch of topsoil reduced corn yields by three to six bushels per acre. The average of these yield reductions was 6 percent. Results for wheat showed a similar relationship: Up to two and one-half bushels of wheat were lost on each eroding acre, yielding an average decline of 6 percent. At current rates, an inch of topsoil is lost from Iowa's cornfields and Montana's wheat fields every fourteen years. What are the long-term implications of erosion? One study, designed to predict the consequences of soil depletion in southern Iowa, showed that steady, uncontrolled soil loss would severely reduce yields of corn, oats, and soybeans, sacrificing as much as a third of the potential productivity of these crops.

Some governments have failed to support soil conservation enthusiastically because they do not see the link between topsoil losses and land productivity. Fortunately, new analytic tools are becoming available to scientists and policy makers. A method for calculating the ratio between actual and potential crop yields at various levels of soil loss has been developed for soils in the United States and is being tested on tropical soils in Hawaii, India, Mexico, and Nigeria. Its usefulness in estimating the global impact of erosion awaits a painstaking inventory of the world's soils.

The National Resources Inventory in the United States, conducted first in 1977 and then in 1982, is the most comprehensive national soil survey ever undertaken. Preliminary results for 1982 show that 44 percent of U.S. cropland is losing topsoil in excess of its tolerance level, a level roughly equal to the slow rate of soil formation. More than 90 percent of the soil eroding at excessive rates is on less than one-quarter of the cropland. These results attest to the need for action and point out where conservation efforts can most profitably be focused.

Two other major food-producing countries, China and India, have estimated their excessive soil loss. A study prepared for the Chinese government reports that five billion tons of soil and sand are

# Kenya: Trees and Terraces to the Rescue

Kenya may be the only Third World country to launch a successful national program to conserve its soils. A decade old, the program shows not only that conservation is compatible with small-scale farming and a large rural population but also that such improvements can boost farmers' incomes.

Kenya identified soil erosion as its most serious environmental problem when preparing for a United Nations conference in 1972. With technical and financial aid from Sweden, the Kenyan Ministry of Agriculture launched several local projects in 1974. The program encouraged farmers to plant fruit, fuel, and fodder trees and to construct simple terraces on their fields to reduce the runoff of water.

By 1983, more than 100,000 farms had enrolled in the program, and 30,000 to 35,000 more farms were being added each year. Miles of newly constructed terraces to catch moisture and cutoff drains to divert erosive flows covered a distance equal to that between Sweden and the Cape of Good Hope. This success was achieved by involving farmers in the design of the program from the outset, providing them with seedlings of valuable trees, and establishing that crop yields could be increased in the short run. Higher yields reflected not only the saving of soil but also the retention of water and nutrients behind terraces.

The Kenyan experience demonstrates that a Third World country with limited financial resources can design and carry out an effective national soil and water conservation program with a minimum of outside aid. The significance of this achievement goes far beyond Kenya, for it means that other developing countries can mount an effective response to this serious agricultural problem.—*E.C.W.*

washed into rivers each year. The government of India estimated in 1976 that soil degradation affected 370 million acres. Indian soil scientists concluded that the nation's croplands were losing a total of six billion tons of soil each year.

Despite considerable evidence of excessive soil erosion in the Soviet Union, the world's fourth major food producer, no comprehensive national survey has been undertaken. The best indirect evidence of pressures on Soviet soils is the 1984 decision to fallow more than 52 million acres of cropland, the highest level since the sixties. Despite expected grain imports of more than 50 million tons—the most by any country in history—the Soviets have decided to pull land out of production.

Although the changes in agricultural practices needed to check excessive soil erosion can be implemented only by farmers themselves, bringing erosion under control requires government involvement. Many farmers cannot easily determine whether their erosion is excessive. Measuring the gradual loss of soil requires scientific techniques and equipment; determining whether it is excessive requires information on tolerance levels for the particular cropland in question. Too, individual farmers may be unable to afford the necessary conservation practices. It may make sense for society to invest in soil conservation even if it is not profitable for the individual farmer. Only governments can calculate the long-term costs of soil erosion for a nation as a whole, including off-farm costs such as the siltation of irrigation reservoirs, hydroelectric reservoirs, and navigable rivers.

The United States unilaterally attempts to balance the world's supply and demand of agricultural commodities by withholding land from production during times of surplus. But little or no effort has been made to coordinate farm supply management programs that divert land with conservation programs designed to reduce soil erosion. Highly eroded cropland could be diverted to other uses, such as fuelwood production or grazing. This could bring the production of some grains down to a level that would reduce the need for government price supports and revive the profitability of farms.

In efforts to conserve soil, the world is faring poorly. There are few national successes, few models that other countries can emulate. The United States has the technology, the detailed information on its soil losses, and the resources to launch an exemplary soil conservation program, but it lacks committed leadership. Within the Third World, Kenya is one of the few countries to launch a successful national program to conserve its soils.

Over the past generation, many countries have, like Kenya, become unable to harvest enough to feed their people, but few have linked the shortages with the depletion of their soil by erosion. In many countries, people know that food prices are rising, but most do not know why. Understanding that lost soil means lower inherent productivity, which in turn means costlier food, is an important first step toward an international soil conservation ethic.

Uncontrolled soil erosion will eventually lead to higher food prices, hunger, and quite possibly, persistent pockets of famine. Although the world economy has weathered a severalfold increase in the price of oil over the past decade, it is not well equipped to cope with even modest rises in the price of food. The immediate effects of soil erosion are economic, but the ultimate effects are social.

*Edward C. Wolf*

# Shocking glimpses of famished drought victims dramatize water's crucial

role in meeting basic human needs in Africa. And water shortages are persistently, if less dramatically, turning up throughout the world, posing far-reaching threats to our future food supplies and to economic progress.

By virtue of a cyclic flow between the sea, air, and land, fresh water is an abundant, renewable resource. Each year, the sun's energy lifts some 500,000 cubic kilometers of water from the earth's surface—86 percent from the oceans and 14 percent from land. (One cubic kilometer equals about 264 billion gallons.) An equal amount falls back to earth as rain, sleet, or snow, but fortunately a greater share falls over the land than is evaporated from it. The net effect of this solar-powered cycle is to distill and transfer 41,000 cubic kilometers of water from the oceans to the continents each year. To complete the natural cycle, this water then makes its way back to the sea as runoff.

Viewed globally, fresh water is undeniably abundant and seems to defy notions of scarcity: The world's total renewable supply could support the material needs of five to ten times the existing world population. But these supplies are not always available where and when they are most needed. Moreover, unlike oil, metals, or wheat, water is not a global commodity—one that is easily traded internationally. If current trends continue, excessive water use in several of the world's major crop-producing regions may undermine the future capacity of the world to feed itself.

One-fifth of U.S. irrigated cropland is supported by a water supply that is diminishing. For several decades, many farmers in the High Plains have irrigated their corn, sorghum, and cotton fields by pumping water from the Ogallala Aquifer, a vast underground reservoir stretching from southern South Dakota to northwest Texas. Much of the Ogallala's water is thousands of years old and gets little replenishment from rainfall. Over the last four decades, 132 trillion gallons have been withdrawn, and hydrologists estimate that the aquifer is now half depleted beneath large portions of Texas, New Mexico, and Kansas. As water tables fall, farmers faced with rising pumping costs and diminishing well yields are taking land out of irrigation. After nearly four decades of steady growth, the total irrigated area in the six states that rely most heavily on the Ogallala is now declining. Without a concerted effort to slow it, the Ogallala's depletion will continue. Much of this water is being used to grow crops of which the nation now has a surplus. When needed to meet vital future food needs domestically or abroad, this water may not be available.

Nearly half the irrigated area in the Soviet Union is located in the central Asian republics and Kazakhstan. Water supplies for the region come primarily from two rivers, the Amu-Dar'ya and the Syr-Dar'ya, and in dry years, virtually all the available water is used. These two rivers are also the main source of inflow to the Aral'skoye More (Aral Sea), helping to replenish the water lost to evaporation. Just as falling water levels are signaling water stress in the U.S. High Plains, the shrinking Aral'skoye More testifies to the shortage pending in central Asia: Heavy irrigation withdrawals from the Amu-Dar'ya and the Syr-Dar'ya have caused the sea's level to drop 29.5 feet since 1960, and its volume may be halved by the turn of the century.

In China, also among the world's three major grain producers, a water deficit is worsening in the northern provinces. The north China plain yields 25 to 30 percent of the value of China's crop output, besides supporting the large populations of Beijing and Tianjin. Groundwater pumping in the Beijing area now exceeds the sustainable supply by one-fourth, and water tables in some areas are falling as much as three to thirteen feet per year.

Historically, when natural water supplies became inadequate to meet a region's demands, water planners and engineers built dams to capture and store runoff that would otherwise flow through the water cycle "unused," and they diverted rivers to redistribute water from areas of lesser to greater need. Engineering feats, such as Egypt's Aswan Dam and the California Aqueduct, have literally made deserts bloom. But today many countries are finding that the list of possible dam and diversion sites is growing short and that the cost of developing new supplies is rapidly increasing.

China, the Soviet Union, and the United States have each examined large schemes for diverting water from a distant river basin to increase the supplies of their water-short agricultural regions. When the U.S. Army Corps of Engineers looked at the possibility of transferring water from midwestern rivers to the High Plains, it found that the costs were far higher than farmers would be willing to pay. Tight capital and $180-billion federal deficits are now forcing to an end the long era of massive water subsidies that allowed such uneconomical projects to materialize in the past. Consequently, prospects are dim that distant water will save irrigated agriculture atop the Ogallala.

Both China and the Soviet Union are proceeding cautiously with plans for river diversions unprecedented in scale. The Chinese have apparently begun construction on a 700-mile diversion of the

## Israel: The Thrifty Irrigator

Although the history of drip irrigation goes back to experiments in Germany in the 1860s, Israel pioneered the technology's commercial development during the last three decades. A drip system typically includes an extensive network of perforated plastic piping that is installed on or below the soil surface. Because water is delivered more directly to the crop's root zone, less water evaporates and is lost from the field. Another advantage is that soluble fertilizer can be added directly to the irrigation water, thereby cutting the amount of chemicals spread over the field and lessening the chance of groundwater contamination. With plants receiving optimum amounts of water and nutrients, crop yields can increase. Experiments with drip in Israel's Negev Desert have shown per acre yield increases of 80 percent over sprinkler systems.

Israel also pioneered the development of automated irrigation, in which the timing and amount of water applied are controlled by computers. The computer not only sets the water flow; it also detects leaks, adjusts water application for wind speed and soil moisture, and optimizes fertilizer use. Motorola Israel Ltd., the main local marketer of automated systems, recently began exporting its product; by 1982 more than 100 units had been sold in the United States. Israel's overall gains in agricultural water-use efficiency, through widespread adoption of sprinkler and drip systems and optimum management practices are impressive: The average volume of water applied per acre declined by a fifth between 1967 and 1981, allowing the nation's irrigated area to expand by 39 percent while farmers' water withdrawals grew by only 13 percent.—*S.P.*

---

Chang Jiang (Yangtze) River northward to the north China plain. The Soviets are preparing detailed engineering designs for a 1,500-mile diversion of north-flowing Siberian rivers south into central Asia. A final decision as to whether to proceed with construction—estimated to cost a daunting $41 billion—is expected in 1986. Yet even this grandiose scheme will meet only one-fourth of the water deficit projected for Soviet central Asia.

Thus far, water planners have paid little attention to the demand side of the water equation. But now that the economic and environmental costs of traditional supply-side strategies are becoming prohibitive, a fundamental shift toward reducing water demand offers the best prospect for alleviating water constraints.

Since agriculture claims the bulk of most nations' water budgets—and 70 percent of water withdrawals worldwide—saving even a small fraction of this water frees a large amount to meet other needs. Raising irrigation efficiencies worldwide by just 10 percent, for example, would save enough water to supply all global residential water uses. Vast quantities of irrigation water seep through unlined canals while in transit to farmers' fields, and much more water is typically applied to crops than is necessary for them to grow. Even in a technologically advanced nation such as the United States, irrigation efficiencies are often less than 50 percent.

Most farmers irrigate their fields with gravity-flow systems, the oldest method and generally the least expensive to install. Water seeps into the soil as it flows across a gently sloping, sometimes furrowed field. Without careful management, a large share often percolates to great depths or runs off the field. Only a small portion remains in the root zone, where the crops can use it. Sprinkler systems, which come in many varieties, deliver water in a spray. They are typically more efficient than gravity systems, but since they operate under pressure,

they require much more energy. One design—the center-pivot system—was largely responsible for the rapid expansion of irrigation on the U.S. High Plains in recent decades. Drip irrigation systems release water close to the plant's roots, thereby minimizing evaporation and seepage losses. Although expensive, carefully designed and operated drip methods often use 30 to 50 percent less water than conventional gravity systems.

With the exception of countries such as Israel, which is already using 95 percent of its freshwater supplies, most governments still treat water as a limitless resource. U.S. farmers supplied with irrigation water from federal projects, for example, pay on average less than one-fifth of the real cost of supplying it. Taxpayers are burdened with the remainder, and farmers have little incentive to adopt water-conserving irrigation methods.

But at least one example worth emulating has emerged in the United States: the 1980 Arizona Groundwater Management Act. Facing a rapidly dwindling groundwater supply, Arizona is requiring its most overpumped areas—including Tucson and Phoenix—to achieve "safe yield" by the year 2025. At this level, no more groundwater is withdrawn than is recharged; the resource is thus in balance. Conservation measures will be required of all water users and all groundwater pumping will be taxed. If, by the year 2006, it appears that conservation alone will not achieve the state's goal, the government can begin buying and retiring farmland. The state's water supplies simply cannot support both a booming population and a water-thirsty farming economy for long.

Although agriculture is the biggest water consumer, conservation in cities can greatly reduce the cost of pumping and treating household water, besides delaying the need to develop more costly supplies. Several states, including California, Florida, Michigan, and New York, now have laws requiring the installation of various water-efficient appliances in new homes, apartments, and offices. A 1983 California law also requires every urban water supplier in the state to submit by the end of 1985 a management plan that explicitly evaluates efficiency measures as alternatives to developing new supplies.

In an era of growing competition for limited water sources, heightened environmental awareness, and scarce and costly capital, new water strategies are needed. Alternatives to large dam and diversion projects exist, and water crises need not occur. Failing to take steps toward a water-efficient economy is risky: Future food needs may go unmet, industrial activity may slow, and the rationing of drinking-water supplies may become more commonplace. Conservation and better management can free a large volume of water—and capital—for competing uses. Thus far, we have seen only hints of their potential.

*Sandra Postel*

# The earth's forest systems are collapsing under two different sets

of pressures; in the tropics, 76,000 acres of trees are cleared daily—an annual loss of forested area nearly the size of Pennsylvania. And in the northern tier of industrial countries, damage linked to air pollutants or acid rain affects trees covering more than 12 million acres—an area the size of New Jersey and Maryland combined.

Wooded lands of all types cover 12 billion acres, an area more than triple that in crops. Tropical America, Africa, and Asia account for 60 percent of the total, and it is in these regions that large-scale clearing of forests is taking place. Unabated population growth is causing conversion of forest to cropland as more and more rural families try to survive on increasingly marginal land. Some replacement of trees with crops is clearly essential to increase food production, but the tragedy in the tropics is that forests are often cleared either where soils are too infertile to sustain crop production over the long term or in a manner that prematurely depletes the land's productive capacity.

Shifting cultivation, which for centuries provided a sustainable agricultural system, has broken down with the population buildup of recent times. Traditionally, farmers would clear some forest, grow crops until the soil became too deficient in nutrients, and then clear a new area, returning to the original plot perhaps twenty years later. By then, the land had lain fallow long enough to restore its fertility. But in many areas, population densities no longer allow for the twenty-five to fifty acres of land per person needed to sustain this farming system. The land is overused, additional forests are cleared on soils that cannot sustain crops, and destruction spreads.

Fuelwood gathering, timber harvesting, and in Central America, conversion of forest to pasture are other forces behind deforestation. As forests dwindle, signs of scarcity grow, taking an especially large toll on the third of humanity for which firewood is the only source of cooking fuel and warmth. In many west African and Central American towns and cities, a typical family may spend one-quarter of its earnings on fuelwood and charcoal, comparable to what a family in an affluent society might spend on housing.

According to the United Nations Food and Agriculture Organization (FAO), more than 100 million people—half of them in Africa—cannot get enough fuelwood to meet their basic needs. Nearly 1.2 billion people are meeting their needs only by overcutting and depleting their forest resources, an unsustainable practice. FAO projects that by the year 2000, more than half the people of the developing world will be in one of two categories—either lacking sufficient firewood or meeting their needs by depleting the resource.

Rarely valued monetarily, the loss of the ecosystem services provided freely by a natural forest entails real economic and social costs. An intact forest moderates the water cycle, allowing rainwater to infiltrate the soil. Especially in regions subject to the extremes of a monsoon climate, deforestation and the loss of this buffering effect worsen flooding, drought, and soil erosion. The cost of repairing flood damages in India below the Himalayan watershed has recently averaged $250 million per year. In the Philippines, a government report blamed deforestation for frequent flooding, erosion, river siltation, and a loss of water supplies. Silting of the reservoir behind Ambuklao Dam has halved the hydropower plant's useful life.

Putting forestry on a sustainable footing in the Third World requires addressing deforestation's underlying causes: excessive population growth, landlessness, and the shortage of productive livelihoods for the rural poor. Recently, some projects have made forestry more responsive to people's needs. In the Indian state of Gujarat, the government has offered free seedlings to farmers, and tree farming is providing a stable source of income. Another approach, agroforestry, integrates tree and crop plantings for combined fuel and food production. In the Kordofan region of Sudan, where desertification and firewood shortages are severe, efforts have focused on restoring the traditional practice of growing nitrogen-fixing acacia trees along with food crops.

China and South Korea have each mounted national tree-planting campaigns to reclaim vast areas of degraded land. China's official goals are to increase its forest cover from 12 percent to 20 percent by the year 2000 and ultimately restore trees to one-third of its territory. South Korea had rapid success with a replanting program begun in the early seventies. In just a few years, trees were established on an area more than half that in rice, the country's food staple.

Unfortunately, the political will and commitment of resources needed to break the cycle fostered by deforestation is lacking in much of the tropical Third World. At present, only one acre of trees is planted for every ten acres cleared. The gap is greatest by far in Africa, where the ratio of tree clearing to planting is twenty-nine to one. Meeting the Third World's projected fuelwood needs by 2000 would require a thirteenfold increase in the current rate of tree planting for nonindustrial uses.

While lack of economic progress drives deforestation in the Third World, the byproducts of industrialization are threatening forests in the temperate zone. In the past decade, it has become evident that air pollutants from the combustion of fossil fuels—both oil and coal—and the smelting of metallic ores are undermining sensitive forests and soils. Many forests in Europe and North America now receive thirty times more acidity than they would if rain and snow were falling through a pristine atmosphere. Ozone levels in many rural areas of Europe and North America are now regularly in the range known to damage trees. Acting alone or together, several pollutants—including acid-forming sulfates and nitrates, gaseous sulfur dioxide, ozone, and heavy metals—are placing forests under severe stress. Needles and leaves yellow and drop prematurely from branches, tree crowns progressively thin, and ultimately, trees die. Even trees that show no visible sign of damage may be declining in growth and productivity.

In just a few years, forest damage has spread with frightening rapidity through portions of central Europe. No nation has better documented the destruction within its borders than West Germany, where forests cover roughly a third of the land area. The government's most recent survey shows that half the nation's trees are injured, and so far the destruction shows no signs of abating. (See box.) A total of 2.4 million acres are affected in Poland and Czechoslovakia. Environmental scientists have warned that by 1990 more than 7 million acres of Poland's forests may be lost if the nation proceeds with its present industrialization plans, which call for increased burning of the nation's high-sulfur brown coals.

Damage reported in other European countries, including Austria, Switzerland, the Netherlands, East Germany, Romania, and Sweden, adds to the growing evidence of unprecedented forest devastation. In the United States, from the Appalachians of Virginia and West Virginia northward to the Green Mountains and White Mountains of New England, red spruce is undergoing a serious dieback—a progressive thinning from the outer tree crown inward. Damage is most severe in the high-elevation forests of New England. By the spring of 1984, researchers had detected serious spruce damage as far south as North Carolina's Mount Mitch-

# West Germany: Death of a Fairy Tale Forest

West Germany's forests are not just sources of lumber and pulp—they helped shape the nation's cultural and literary heritage. The loss of these woodlands is a potent political and emotional issue for West Germans. *Waldsterben*—or forest death—is now a household word. A survey in the summer of 1983 showed that West Germans were more concerned about the fate of their forests than about the Pershing missiles to be placed on their land later that year.

Following a 1982 forest survey, the federal minister of food, agriculture, and forestry estimated that 8 percent of West Germany's forested area was damaged. Just a year later, a more thorough investigation found damage on more than 6.2 million acres—34 percent of the nation's forests. A third survey, conducted in the summer of 1984 and the latest to date, found that half the nation's trees are injured. Hardest hit are the heavily wooded states of Bavaria and Baden Württemberg, home of the fabled Black Forest.

Spruce, fir, and pine, which together represent two-thirds of West Germany's forests, are the most severely struck. The spruce and fir forests are typically managed in even-aged stands, with trees harvested between 80 and 130 years of age. Although damage first appeared on the older trees, spruce and fir of all ages are now affected. The value of the trees already lost exceeds $1.2 billion. Because a growing portion of the planned annual harvest consists of dying trees, the harvest may reach three times its normal level over the next few years. Although this may depress timber prices over the short term, future supplies are diminishing as sick and dying trees are harvested long before their time.

In a 1983 *Journal of Forestry* editorial, a German professor of forest policy, the president of the German Forestry Association, a Regensburg forester, and a former U.S. Fulbright visitor to West Germany joined together to note that "air pollution is now the problem that concerns West German foresters most. The results of 200 years of forest management seem to be extinguishable within the next 10 years. . . . Only a few people think about an all-too-possible scenario: central Europe without forests."—S.P.

ell—the highest peak in eastern North America—and tree deaths were expected to be identified in other areas soon thereafter.

Recent publicity about acid rain has tended to lump this forest destruction with acidifying lakes, dying fish, and other effects of acid rain. Forest damage has added impetus to calls to reduce emissions of sulfur dioxide, the primary acid rain precursor. Indeed, fifteen European countries and Canada have made formal commitments to reduce sulfur emissions by 30 percent or more by the early nineties; notably absent from this "30 percent club" are the United States and Great Britain. While putting scrubbers on smokestacks is a necessary first step to curb acid rain in the near term, a technological fix for one pollutant cannot be an ultimate solution for a multipollutant problem. Solutions are needed that will reduce levels of all threatening pollutants. Using energy more efficiently, recycling more paper and metals, and generating more power from alternative energy sources are rarely considered in strategies to control air pollutants or acid rain, but they are perhaps the most cost-effective ways that exist.

Given the rapidity with which the forest destruction has unfolded, the relevant question is no longer whether proof of damage from air pollutants or acid rain is irrefutable but whether the forests are sufficiently threatened to warrant action. West German foresters would answer with an unequivocal yes. But the real test is whether nations that so far have been spared severe losses will muster the political will to take action to avoid them.

*Sandra Postel*

# Overfishing was rare a generation ago. Now, in some regions it seems

to be a common occurrence. The world's fisheries occupy an important niche in the global ecosystem, the world economy, and the human diet. Their annual harvest—74 million tons in 1983—exceeds world beef production by a substantial margin. Yielding an average of thirty-five pounds per person worldwide, fisheries supply 23 percent of all animal protein consumed. More importantly, in many low-income countries, as well as in a few industrial ones, fish are the principal source of animal protein.

Between 1950 and 1970, the world fish catch more than tripled. The growing world population and rising per capita incomes boosted demand for animal protein. The extraordinary growth in the catch led to the feeling that the oceans contained in-

finite supplies of fish. Projections made at this time commonly indicated the catch would eventually reach 200 to 400 million tons annually. On the supply side, advances in fishing technology and the availability of cheap oil led to the development of distant-water fishing fleets that scoured the oceans in search of edible sea life.

By the early seventies, however, many signs of overfishing were appearing. Growth in the annual world fish catch slowed to less than one percent. And in per capita terms, the growth of nearly 4 percent per year during the fifties and sixties became a decline of almost one percent yearly after 1970.

The collapse of the Southeast Pacific anchovy fishery in the early seventies, caused by overfishing and ocean variability, caught the attention of many who had assumed that humanity would ultimately turn to the oceans for food. By the early eighties, eleven major oceanic fisheries—six in the Atlantic and five in the Pacific—had been depleted to the point of collapse. They range from the Peruvian anchovy, which had an estimated potential of 9 million tons, to the Alaska king crab, with a possible yield of nearly 100,000 tons. Overall, the annual harvest from oceanic fisheries has been reduced by an estimated 11 million tons because of fishery mismanagement.

Before national control was extended to 200 miles offshore, there was often no authority responsible for limiting the catch and establishing quotas for the fleets working a fishery. In some cases, overfishing resulted from a lack of information—on such things as stocks and reproductive rates—needed to manage supplies intelligently. As the biology of oceanic fisheries becomes better understood, a concern for sustainable yield is likely to dispel the myth that the oceans can provide an ever increasing supply of protein.

More than one hundred species of finfish, crustaceans, and shellfish are harvested on a commercial scale. Of this long list, some twenty-two species commonly yield 100,000 tons or more per year, and just five species—herrings, cods, jacks, redfishes, and mackerels, plus their associated relatives—account for well over half the annual catch.

The diversity of the global catch is reflected in national seafood consumption patterns. In the United States, tuna occupies a prominent position in overall seafood consumption: With tuna sandwiches and salads common fare, U.S consumption accounts for more than a third of the world tuna catch. Of the million and a half tons of squid caught yearly, most is consumed by Japan and the countries north of the Mediterranean—Spain, Portugal, and Italy. The consumption of some other abundant species is similarly concentrated in parts of the industrialized world.

Although per capita fish consumption in Third World countries is lower than in most industrial countries, fish are nonetheless a key protein source in the diet of coastal peoples. A scrap of dried fish in a rice dish can often mean the difference between a nutritionally adequate diet and one seriously deficient in protein. The worldwide decline in the per capita catch does not augur well for future nutritional improvements in developing countries.

With oceanic overfishing now commonplace, the age-old method of capturing fish by hunting and gathering is being supplemented by fish farming and ranching. In many parts of the world, fish can be raised like livestock using natural ponds or artificially flooded land. The many techniques, collectively known as aquaculture, succeed with a variety of fish and shellfish. Harvesting can be done on a small or a large scale and can often be integrated with conventional farming, using organic wastes from land to fertilize ponds and provide a food supply for fish.

Fish farming is growing at more than 7 percent each year, and cultivated fish may be the fastest-growing part of the human diet. Interest in fish farming is on the rise everywhere. China, with an estimated annual aquacultural output of just over 4 million tons, is far and away the world leader. Japan ranks second, with about a million tons—roughly one-third each of finfish, shellfish, and seaweed. Given the rapid strides in U.S. fish farming during the early eighties, a 1985 survey is likely to show the United States moving into the top ten aquacultural producers.

A growing emphasis on this approach is evident in the lending practices of such international aid agencies as the World Bank and the U.N. Food and Agriculture Organization. In the seventies, assistance that previously concentrated on investments in better boats and improved port and processing facilities shifted toward fish farming. Lenders realized that there were a limited number of offshore fisheries in which investment in additional capacity would be profitable.

Worldwide, aquaculture provides roughly one-sixth of the seafood consumed directly. Of the total finfish output of some 3.7 million tons, an estimated four-fifths is accounted for by carp, the mainstay of both the Chinese and Indian aquacultural economies. In both these countries, the aquacultural sector provides more than one-fourth of total fish consumption. In the United States, nearly all the rainbow trout, most of the catfish and crawfish, and 40 percent of the oysters are harvested from fish farms.

One of the attractions of fish farming is the high efficiency with which fish convert vegetable matter to meat. An American farmer must feed his cattle roughly 7 pounds of grain to produce a pound of beef. Pigs, by comparison, need 3.25 pounds of grain to yield a pound of pork; broilers need 2.25 pounds for a pound of chicken. Catfish, however, require only 1.7 pounds of grain to produce a pound of fish. Fish are efficient converters for two reasons. One, they are coldblooded and thus do not need to consume large amounts of energy to maintain a high and steady body temperature. And two, because they live in the water, fish do not require much energy for locomotion.

That fish farming is destined to expand seems clear; how fast it will do so is less certain. As a form of animal husbandry, it must compete with the production of beef, pork, poultry, eggs, and milk for the use of land, water, labor, fertilizer, and feedstuffs. But in a world where pressure on resources is

# Salmon at Home on the Ranch

In past times, salmon apparently thrived in streams and rivers throughout the Northern Hemisphere's higher latitudes. With modernization, however, their access to many streams and rivers was often blocked by dams, as in the U.S. Pacific Northwest and in the Baltic Sea. Some rivers—such as the Thames in England, where the salmon disappeared in the nineteenth century—became so polluted that they were no longer habitable. In other instances, merciless overfishing led to the salmon's demise.

In recent years, a better understanding of the salmon's life cycle and a strong commercial demand for this tasty fish have led to the restocking of many streams. In 1763, German biologists discovered that salmon eggs could be fertilized in captivity. This knowledge, coupled with an awareness of the salmon's homing instinct, set the stage for modern ranching. Salmon hatcheries (usually publicly supported) and commercial salmon ranching are both based on the near-legendary homing instinct of this fish. Even when released in an unfamiliar setting, salmon manage to find their way back to their nursery streams some two to five years later when it's time to breed.

The only countries with extensive salmon hatcheries and annual releases of this fish are Japan, the Soviet Union, and the United States. The Japanese now release more than a billion young salmon each year in rivers and streams on the islands of Hokkaido and Honshu. After feeding in the areas south of the Bering Sea, the Aleutian Islands, and the Gulf of Alaska, the salmon return to the rivers where they were released. In the fall of 1982, the Japanese harvested 28 million salmon—one for every four Japanese. Soviet salmon ranchers are not far behind: They are expanding the number of smolts released by roughly 100 million per year, and their goal is to release 3 billion annually by the end of the century. The Soviet salmon are released in the many small streams of Sakhalin Island and the Kamchatka Peninsula. By 1990, the USSR, Japan, and the United States are expeted to release 6 billion smolts into the North Pacific.—L.R.B.

mounting, aquaculture should also be seen as a means of tapping currently unused resources, such as low-lying land that is not suitable for crop production.

With mounting pressures on world fisheries—oceanic and domestic—fishery analysts see seafood prices rising for the rest of the century and beyond. This may annoy Western consumers for whom salmon or Alaskan king crab is a delicacy. But it will be much more than annoying for those in the Third World for whom fish is the principal source of animal protein.

*Lester R. Brown*

# Is human activity causing global climate changes? Until recently,

the question has rightly focused on fossil fuels and carbon dioxide ($CO_2$). In step with the burning of oil, coal, and natural gas, the concentration of $CO_2$ in the atmosphere has steadily climbed. Climatologists warn that increased $CO_2$ traps more of the sun's heat at the earth's surface; the implications of this "greenhouse effect" have put climate change at the center of a lively political and scientific debate.

Recently another question has emerged: Can changes in land cover, such as deforestation in the Third World, alter climate? The contribution of population growth to deforestation, overgrazing, soil erosion, and desertification in the Third World is highly visible and widely recognized. What is new is the realization that these processes may be driving climate changes in regions as diverse as the semiarid Sudan-Sahelian zone of Africa and the rain forests of the Amazon.

Natural climatic fluctuations make it difficult to separate out the possible human effects on climate. A reconstructed climatic history of the Sahel over the last 10,000 years, for example, shows extreme fluctuations, from periods of wetness to dryness. A detailed history of just the last few centuries shows that the Sahel has periodically experienced severe, prolonged drought.

Meteorologists have traditionally dismissed the notion of large-scale human-induced climate change, arguing that the natural forces driving global atmospheric circulation would override any local, human-induced alterations. Using data from other fields, such as agriculture, ecology, and hydrology, meteorologists can now piece together a plausible hypothesis that population-induced local climatic change is indeed under way in Africa, the Amazon Basin, and perhaps elsewhere as well.

The continents are watered by the oceans; therefore, any change induced by population growth must involve interfering with the mechanics of that process. Africa, for example, is watered by moisture-laden air masses from the Indian and Atlantic oceans. The Indian subcontinent receives rain from clouds moving inland from the Indian Ocean and the Bay of Bengal. The Brazilian Amazon derives almost all its water initially from the Atlantic Ocean.

Evaporation of moisture from rainfall near the coasts recharges rain clouds as they move inland. At a typical site in the central Amazon, such as one that was carefully studied near Manaus, Brazil, roughly one-fourth of the rainfall evaporates directly, and nearly one-half reenters the atmosphere in the form of transpiration from plants. Together, direct evaporation and transpiration return three-fourths of the rainfall to the atmosphere, leaving one-fourth as runoff that makes its way back to the Atlantic. Such high levels of cloud recharge have led ecologists to refer to tropical rain forests as "rain machines."

When land is deforested, however, this ratio is roughly reversed, with a quarter of the rainfall being returned to the atmosphere and three-quarters running off quickly. Rainfall in the region is accordingly reduced, as the atmosphere holds less returned moisture that can become rain later in the cycle. The more distant from the coast, the more an area depends on evaporation for the recharge of rain clouds. Even in semiarid regions, an estimated one-third to two-thirds of all rainfall comes from soil moisture evaporation.

Water first enters the Amazon area in moisture-laden air masses from the Atlantic Ocean. As these progress westward, they continually discharge moisture in the form of rain and are recharged by evaporation and transpiration. On the average, water in the Amazon that does not return to the ocean completes the cycle every 5.5 days. During this process some of the water works its way out of the evaporative cycle as runoff and begins the long trip back to the Atlantic. Moisture left in the air when it reaches the Andes moves southward into central Brazil and the Chaco/Paraguay river regions, where it becomes part of the rainfall cycle in major farming areas.

As the Amazon rain forest is converted to cropland or grassland or is cleared by logging, the share of rainfall that runs off increases. The proportion that returns to the atmosphere through evaporation falls, reducing the total amount of water in the area's hydrological cycle. The net effect is lower average rainfall, particularly in the west. Less rain in the Amazon would almost certainly reduce the amount that reaches the agriculturally important Paraguayan Chaco and central Brazilian plateau.

In Africa, northeastern Brazil, northwestern India, and northwestern China—where rapidly growing populations are generating wholesale shifts in land use—deserts are expanding. Recently the United Nations Environment Programme undertook a survey of desertification in countries in the Sudan-Sahelian region of Africa. The fourteen most populous countries in this group have a combined population of 230 million people, 43 percent of the African total. The survey focused on five manifestations of desertification—sand dune encroachment, rangeland deterioration, forest depletion, the deterioration of irrigation systems, and problems in rainfed agriculture.

Not one of the seventy indicators—five for each of the fourteen countries—showed any improvement. According to thirteen of the seventy indicators, there was no significant change during the seven years under review. Half the total measurements showed moderate deterioration. The remaining twenty-one showed serious deterioration. The three categories showing the most consistent deterioration were rangelands, forests, and rainfed agriculture. Field observers confirm the survey findings, describing them as somber but realistic.

Perhaps because of the Sahelian drought of the early seventies and the continent-wide drought experienced in Africa in 1983 and 1984, more attention has been focused on changing land-use patterns caused by population pressure and the possible effects on local climate. In addition to the evidence from agriculture and meteorology, and the desertification trends, hydrological data also suggest that Africa is "drying out." In an analysis measuring changes in river flows, J. Sircoulon observes that "the Senegal, Niger, and Chari rivers, coming from wetter regions to the south . . . have undergone a severe decrease of runoff during the last 15 years. . . . Lake Chad has shown a systematic decrease of level since 1963. At that time the lake's surface covered 23,500 square kilometers, and the volume of stored water was 105 billion cubic meters. In 1973 the surface had been divided by three and the volume by four. Since this date, the lake has been cut into two parts. The northern part dries up every year, with only a small inflow through the 'Grande Barrière.' "

Most meteorologists have been reluctant to attribute significant shifts in climate to human changes in land use. Although the evidence that can now be assembled from several fields of study is not yet conclusive, it is persuasive. Reflecting on this, Canadian meteorologist Kenneth Hare, in an analysis of desertification in Africa, has concluded that "we seem to have arrived at a critical moment in the history of mankind's relation to climate. For the first time we may be on the threshold of man-induced climatic change."

Knowing what we do about the extent of deforestation, overgrazing, and soil degradation during the past generation and about the way the hydrological cycle works, we should not be surprised by changing climate. More significantly, population growth may be driving that change in directions that will not benefit the people affected, reducing rainfall in areas where rain is needed for crop production and livestock grazing. And expanding deserts, in turn, are shrinking the land area available for growing food, grazing livestock, and producing firewood. The effectiveness—or ineffectiveness—of family planning programs may be shaping the climate of some countries for decades and possibly for centuries to come.

*Lester R. Brown*

# Treasures Among the Trees

MARK PLOTKIN

*Mark Plotkin is an ethnobotanist and director of the plant conservation program at the World Wildlife Fund. He has worked with Indians in Suriname and Brazil and has catalogued thousands of plants for medicinal and commercial uses.*

Beyond the loss of vast areas of natural beauty and timber resources, the clearing of the world's tropical rainforests will leave in its wake the extinction of thousands of species of animal and plant life – many of which provide irreplaceable medicines and essential food supplies to both local populations and the rest of the world.

The majority of the world's threatened species inhabit the tropical forests – an area which covers only 7 percent of the earth's surface but may contain well over 50 percent of the world's species. The Rio Negro in central Brazil contains more species of fish than are found in all the U.S. rivers combined. Manu National Pak in southeastern Peru is home to more species of birds than are found in the entire United States. A hectare of forest in western Amazonia may contain more than 300 species of trees.

While expeditions to the tropics, particularly the Amazon region, continue to bring back new species, destruction of the world's forests and the life systems within them is increasing at a rate much higher than the rate at which new life forms can be found and sustained. As much as 95 percent of the Atlantic Coastal Forest of eastern Brazil has already been destroyed. On the island of Madagascar, where 80 percent of the flowering plants are believed to be endemic – occurring nowhere else in the world – well over half of the original forest cover has been removed or seriously disturbed. In the Hawaiian archipelago, where the rate of endemism is higher than 90 percent, 14 percent of the flora is already believed to be extinct.

Although extinction is a natural process, biologists estimate that the present rate of global species extinctions is 400 times higher than occurs naturally – and the rate of extinction is rapidly accelerating. As populations increase in tropical countries, greater areas of forest lands will be cleared and countless more species of plants and animals will die out.

There are hidden implications to this loss of diversity. Although rainforests are often considered only for their valuable timber or the eventual crop or pasture land which remains after the timber has been extracted, they are much more valuable. Tropical ecosystems can yield a wealth of valuable non-timber materials on a renewable basis. They can, for example, significantly decrease the dependence of many Third World countries on western pharmaceutical products.

Since the Stone Age, plants have traditionally served as the world's most important weapon against disease. Only recently, with the advent of modern technology and synthetic chemistry, have developed countries been able to reduce their almost total dependence on the Plant Kingdom for medicines.

Still, almost half of all prescription drugs dispensed in the United States contain substances of natural origin – and over 50 percent of these medications contain a plant-derived principal. In 1974 alone, the United States imported $24.4 million of medicinal plants and in 1985, U.S. consumers purchased over $8 billion worth of prescriptions in which the active ingredients were extracted from plants.

Although many plant species are still unknown to scientists in the developed world, tribal people who inhabit tropical forests have understood and used this diversity for both food and medicine. A single Amazonian tribe may use over 100 species of plants for medicinal purposes alone.

Some of these tropical plants are used in the West as sources of direct therapeutic agents. The alkaloid D-tubocurarine is extracted from the South American jungle liana Chondrodendron tomentosum and is widely used as a muscle relaxant in surgery. Chemists have so far been unable to produce this drug synthetically in a form which has all the attributes of the natural product.

Harvesting of medicinal plants is often less costly than artificial drug synthesis. In 1973, less than 10 percent of the

This article is reprinted from the *Multinational Monitor,* June 1987, pp. 9, 13, 21. *Multinational Monitor* is a monthly newsmagazine published by Essential Information, P.O. Box 19405, Washington, D.C. 20036. $22 individual.

## 3. NATURAL RESOURCES: Raw Materials

76 drug compounds from plants used in U.S. prescription drugs were produced commercially by total chemical synthesis. In the mid-1970s, for example, the synthesis of reserpine, an important hypotensive agent extracted from Rauwaolfia, cost approximately $1.25 per gram while the cost of extracting it from the plant was only about $.75 per gram.

Tropical plants are used to create more complex semi-synthetic compounds as well. Saponin extracts, for example, are chemically altered to produce sapogenins necessary for the manufacture of steroidal drugs. Until recently, 95 percent of all steroids were obtained from extracts of neotropical yams.

In addition, tropical plants serve as models for new synthetic compounds. Cocaine, a product of the coca plant, has served as a model for the synthesis of a number of local anesthetics such as procaine.

Some plant species can yield a large number of beneficial derivatives. The rosy periwinkle, native to Madagascar, is the source of over 75 alkaloids, two of which are used to treat childhood leukemia and Hodgkin's disease with a very high success rate. Annual sales of these alkaloids worldwide in 1980 were estimated to reach $50 million wholesale, the retail markup is an additional 100 percent.

The potential for undiscovered plant species is enormous. One study of tropical plants found that 70 percent of the plants known to possess some kind of anti-cancer compounds are indigenous to the lowland tropics. Yet only a minute portion of tropical plant species have been screened for their anti-cancer potential. Another study concluded that 8,000 neotropical plant species probably have anti-cancer properties. And numerous species of plants in the Amazon have been used for years by forest tribes as natural contraceptives.

The value of such plants isn't limited to countries that can afford to chemically modify them. The World Health Organization has estimated that 80 percent of the people in the world rely on traditional medicine from natural sources for primary health care needs. Several African and Asian nations have begun to encourage traditional medicine as an integral component of their public health care programs. Indigenous medicines are relatively inexpensive, locally available, and usually readily accepted by the local populace. The establishment of local pharmaceutical firms could mean jobs, reduced import expenditures, and foreign exchange for the developing world. And it could spawn increased documentation of traditional ethnomedical lore. Most important, these firms – and in turn the people of the country – would have a vital stake in the conservation and sustainable use of the tropical forest.

The potential of tropical plants goes far beyond their medicinal uses. The world's food supply can be increased substantially by using the edible plants which grow in the tropics. Of the several thousand species that are known to be edible, only 150 have entered into world commerce. Today, fewer than 20 plant species produce 90 percent of the world's food. Other tropical plants have chemical properties that act as natural pesticides. Lonchocarpus, a South American plant, is the source of much of the world's rotenone, an important biodegradable pesticide. And many of the non-fuel petroleum products used in the United States can be replaced by products synthesized from tropical plants.

Unfortunately, however, knowledge of the thousands of plant species and tribal medicines may soon be lost. With the "westernization" of many native cultures, the traditions and knowledge endemic to tribal people are not being passed on to the next generation. The introduction of synthetic pharmaceutical products in many of these remote areas has encouraged native tribes to discard their tribal lore.

The situation is critical. At the current rate of environmental and cultural destruction, thousands of years of accumulated knowledge of how to use rainforest plants may disappear before the turn of the century. And without stepped up conservation efforts, the rainforests themselves may disappear shortly thereafter.

# Converting Garbage to Gold

## Recycling Our Materials

**William U. Chandler**

Recycling conserves energy, fights pollution and inflation, creates jobs, and improves the outlook for the future of materials. But converting a "throwaway" society to recycling will depend on finding good markets for waste paper and scrap metals.

Throwing away an aluminum beverage container wastes as much energy as pouring out such a can half-filled with gasoline. Failing to recycle a daily edition of the *Washington Post* or *New York Times* wastes just about as much.

Wood, iron, and aluminum are among mankind's most important materials, and they will be the basis of a sustainable future. But the future availability of these basic building blocks is clouded by the uncertain future of energy, a resource with painfully obvious constraints. Simply maintaining current levels of materials production will require prodigious quantities of energy.

Recycling saves energy and expensive raw materials, protects the environment, and cuts waste dis-

THE ALUMINUM ASSOCIATION

Heaped high, these aluminum beverage cans will be recycled using just 5% of the energy needed to make aluminum from bauxite. Recycling also reduces the environmental degradation caused by producing aluminum from ore.

From *The Futurist*, February 1984, pp. 69-75, 77. THE FUTURIST, published by the World Future Society, 4916 St. Elmo Avenue, Bethesda, MD 20814.

## "Recycling just half of world paper used today would . . . free 20 million acres of forestland from paper production."

posal costs. Despite these advantages, only about one-fourth of the world's paper, aluminum, or steel is recovered for reuse, though certain countries have made remarkable progress.

The first priority in materials recycling policy should be to establish demand for recyclable products, or "markets first, collection second." If markets are established, collection will follow, though areas that are successful in recycling have simultaneously established markets and encouraged collection with strong measures.

Iron, aluminum, and wood each requires different recycling technologies, policies, and markets; each resource—its potential for recycling and its special technical and political circumstances—will be considered in turn.

### Waste Paper Recycling

Paper recycling helps preserve forests. Paper products use about 35% of the world's annual commercial wood harvest, a share that will probably grow to 50% by the year 2000. Although a sanguine attitude regarding the state of the world's forests holds a certain following, there is little reason for complacency.

The world's tropical hardwood forests will probably decline 10% by the end of the century. The softwood forests of western Russia have long been harvested at unsustainable rates. The softwood forests of central Europe may be killed by air pollution by 1990, and the resulting decline in wood production will only shift additional pressure to other forests.

The United States produces a third of the world's commercial forest products, and its forests would be expected to take up much of this slack. But the harvest of mature softwood forests in the United States has exceeded replacement for several decades. Indus-

try-owned forests, in fact, have been cut so heavily that mature trees have been depleted at an annual rate of 1% to 2% since the early 1950s.

Paper recycling can help satisfy additional paper needs for years to come. Only 25% of the world's paper is now recycled, though no technical or economic reasons prevent doubling this share by the end of the century.

Recycling just half of world paper used today would meet almost 75% of new paper demand, and this would free 20 million acres of forestland from paper production, an area equal to about 5% of Europe's forestland. But projections for the actual future use of recycled waste paper are far less optimistic. One consulting firm specializing in paper recycling predicts that recycled paper will supply only 28% of world paper production in the year 2000.

World waste paper consumption has increased 140% since 1965. Paper consumption has doubled over the same period, however, so the share of paper recycled has changed only slightly, from 20% in 1965 to 24% in 1982. Despite the world's poor paper recycling record, certain countries have achieved much higher rates of recycling than others. Moreover, much progress has been made in only the last 10 years.

Japan, the Netherlands, Mexico, South Korea, and Portugal lead in waste paper recovery or use. Japan in 1980 collected almost half of the paper it consumed. The Netherlands recovered 44% of its paper in 1980 and has led the world for decades in paper recycling.

Why do some countries perform better than others? "Fiber rich" countries such as Canada, Norway, the United States, and Sweden have not excelled, recycling 18%, 23%, 26%, and 34%, respectively. The United States, however, is in a

category by itself. Though it recycles only one-fourth of its paper, it nevertheless leads the world in exporting waste paper.

The admirable paper recycling performance of Japan, South Korea, Mexico, the Netherlands, and Portugal, all "fiber poor" countries without substantial forests available for pulpwood harvesting, has been promoted by necessity. South Korea, Portugal, and Mexico doubly contribute to waste paper recovery: They have high national rates of waste paper recovery, and they also import waste paper.

Success in Japan and the Netherlands has been motivated by twin necessities. In addition to being "fiber poor," both are crowded, land-poor countries with populations strongly opposed to waste dumps. These factors together have driven up both the economic and the political costs of wasting paper.

Both the Dutch and the Japanese are opposed to landfill disposal of municipal waste. Since 20% to 40% of Japanese and Dutch municipal solid waste is paper, paper recycling offers a considerable reduction in waste disposal problems.

Japan's success in recycling began with the pressure of demand, since Japan is the world's second largest consumer of paper. But citizen pressure for environmental protection played a key role. Demand for waste reduction and forest protection pushed Japan into recycling as much as markets pulled it to a high rate of paper recovery.

### Trading in Waste Paper

Necessity is the mother of collection, and uneven distribution of the world's forest resources provides some of the nations with local abundance despite global scarcity. But just as wasting gasoline in an oil-rich country means lost export sales, so does waste of recyclable paper.

If properly promoted, the new international market for waste paper could supply a strong incentive to collect waste paper in all countries. The recent growth of international trade marks an important step in the waste paper market development.

International waste paper trade has grown from almost nothing in the early 1970s to about 10% of all waste paper collected, or 2% to 3% of all paper used in the world. The value of this trade totals some $600 million, depending upon volatile market prices.

The United States now dominates the international waste paper trade, accounting for 85% of net sales. The significant expansion of trade between the United States, Mexico, South Korea, and Japan during the 1970s can serve as a model for development of waste paper trade elsewhere. South Korea, in fact, produces 40% of its paper from imported waste paper.

Paper recycling can be promoted by creating or widening cost advantages for recycled paper over paper made from virgin pulp. One advantage could be provided by increasing the price of virgin wood pulp to reflect its true economic value.

In nations where mature softwood forests are harvested faster than replacement, reducing the rate of harvest would raise the price of pulp closer to its long-term economic value. Forests would thus be afforded greater protection and waste paper recycling would be encouraged. Paper and wood prices need not increase as long as additional quantities of waste paper are recovered and recycled.

The U.S. government could make a major contribution to this policy, since it owns half of all softwood forests in the country. The U.S. Forest Service significantly affects the price of pulp by leasing large areas of national forests each year regardless of market demand. The suspension or modification of this practice, coupled with setting aside more publicly-owned forests for wilderness and parkland, would reduce the environmental subsidy of the use of virgin pulp and increase the relative attractiveness of waste paper.

Higher, more stable prices would provide an incentive for commercial waste paper collection. Local zoning ordinances to reduce landfill disposal of paper wastes, along with broader regional or national laws requiring source separation and mandatory collection of waste

NATIONAL ASSOCIATION OF RECYCLING INDUSTRIES

Bales of waste paper are stacked in processor's yard awaiting shipment to a variety of consumers. Once markets are found for waste paper—for example, in "fiber poor" countries such as South Korea, which relies heavily on imported waste paper—more countries will have strong incentive to promote collection of recyclable paper, says author Chandler.

paper, will increase waste paper supplies and thus serve to prevent drastic price increases. Indeed, the greater problem will be to maintain demand for waste paper. International markets will be essential for this purpose.

Market development will remain a top priority for promoting waste paper recycling. Capital investment, advertising, procurement practices, free trade promotion, and pricing policies will all be required. But policies do not just happen. Policy implementation increasingly requires promotion by both economic interests and citizens' organizations.

### Aluminum Recycling

Aluminum plays an important role in any industrial society, and so its efficient production and use are essential. Many aspects of modern civilization, such as air travel, would be virtually impossible without affordable aluminum. Using aluminum instead of heavy steel in automobiles saves gasoline.

Using aluminum instead of glass or steel packaging saves energy in transportation and may allow easier, more efficient recycling.

Yet extracting aluminum from ore requires 20 times as much electricity as recycling the metal. Environmental degradation results from strip-mining the ore and from damming rivers to generate hydroelectric power for smelting, as well as from discarding aluminum containers. Recycling would help solve these problems.

Recycling aluminum reduces air emissions associated with aluminum production by 96%. By doubling worldwide aluminum recovery rates, more than a million tons of air pollutants—including toxic fluoride—would be eliminated.

The world is far from achieving the technical potential for aluminum recycling. Some analysts estimate that 80% of all aluminum used can be recycled. But less than 30% of world production came from recycled scrap in 1981. Even so, half of all aluminum recycled

## "Using aluminum instead of heavy steel in automobiles saves gasoline. Using aluminum instead of glass or steel packaging saves energy in transportation and may allow easier, more efficient recycling."

NATIONAL ASSOCIATION OF RECYCLING INDUSTRIES

Automobiles piled up to be shredded. Large amounts of iron and steel as well as aluminum and copper can be obtained through this process. Unfortunately, says author Chandler, the world is not recovering as much scrap as it could. The backlog of recoverable ferrous scrap in the United States has reached 680 million tons and will probably continue to grow.

came from industrial wastes—scrap produced in the smelting or cutting and fabrication of finished products—rather than from the disposal of the products themselves.

Since energy accounts for 20% of the cost of producing aluminum from virgin ore, the progress made in recycling in the 1970s can be explained in part by energy price increases. Great strides have been made in the United States, illustrating that modern society can adapt to increasing scarcity.

U.S. aluminum recycling has reduced both environmental pollution and the need to construct new power facilities, thus freeing scarce capital for use elsewhere in the economy.

The United States, the Soviet Union, Canada, Japan, and West Germany produce 60% of the world's aluminum. Adding Norway, France, Spain, Australia, China, Italy, and Great Britain brings this total to more than 75%. Italy, West Germany, and the United States have the highest rates of secondary aluminum production.

Italy produces 50% of its aluminum from scrap, while West Germany and the United States produce one-third from recycled aluminum. Italy's performance is particularly impressive because its per-capita consumption has long averaged less than half that in the United States and 60% that in West Germany.

On the other hand, the Soviet Union, the world's second largest aluminum producer, recycled and exported only 10% as much aluminum as it consumed in 1979 or 1980. Australia did only slightly better.

Norway is the world's sixth largest aluminum producer and is fourth highest in per-capita aluminum consumption. Yet it recovers only 20% of the aluminum it consumes. This poor record is probably due to Norway's abundance of inexpensive hydroelectric power.

Ten years of environmentalists' opposition to hydroelectric development in Norway have led to reduced expansion of primary aluminum production there. Similarly, opposition halted a dam designed to produce power for aluminum smelting in Tasmania. These actions, ironically, may increase the availability of affordable aluminum since they will force a more economical use of resources.

### Aluminum Scrap Trade

International trade brings a new and dynamic force to the recovery of scrap aluminum. Scrap moving across national boundaries in 1980 totaled 820,000 tons, representing more than 5% of world aluminum production. With the price of scrap at 36 cents per pound, the value of internationally traded aluminum scrap amounted to almost $600 million in 1980.

Three leading consumers of recycled aluminum—Japan, West Germany, and Italy—import large quantities of aluminum scrap. The volume of scrap imported by Japan in 1981 equaled Japan's volume of aluminum consumption 10 years earlier.

With primary production declining as a result of oil price increases, secondary production in Japan has increased 138% over the last decade, with as much as 70% of this increase made possible by scrap imports. Twenty percent of both West Germany's and Italy's total aluminum production in 1980 can be attributed to aluminum scrap imports.

European scrap smelters, nevertheless, pose a threat to the free trade of aluminum. Seeking lower scrap prices, they argue for increased trade barriers to restrict exports from their countries. But when export quotas were removed by European countries in 1981 and replaced with a less restrictive export licensing system, exports of aluminum doubled.

# Reverse Vending Machines Swallow Aluminum Cans

COURTESY OF RESOURCE RECYCLING

Can Bank, a reverse vending machine manufactured by Golden Recycling Company, a subsidiary of the Adolph Coors Co. This 24-hour machine operates outdoors, accepting small batches of aluminum cans and paying users 18 cents per pound. Although recycling centers would pay slightly more for scrap, the convenience of the reverse vending machines encourages more people to recycle their used cans rather than throw them away.

One of the most exciting innovations in aluminum can collection is the "reverse vending machine," which brings recycling operations closer to the public.

Rather than driving across town to a scrap processor or saving up large amounts of waste for periodic community recycling drives, people can bring their empty beverage cans to conveniently located vending machines that accept small amounts of scrap and dispense payment.

According to *Resource Recycling*, the Portland, Oregon, based journal of recycling, reuse, and waste reduction, reverse vending machines were invented because of the need to reduce labor costs at recycling centers. By using machines placed in supermarkets, convenience stores, parking lots, and even video game parlors, people can redeem their beverage cans while freeing the staffs of scrap centers to handle larger amounts of cans and other recyclable materials.

Several types of reverse vending machines have been developed by different manufacturers, but, according to *Resource Recycling*, the devices share five general features. First, they accept used cans—whole or flattened, singly or in small amounts. Second, they distinguish aluminum cans from other items such as bottles and steel cans. Third, the machines count or weigh the amount of aluminum deposited; they then dispense a reward in the form of coins or redeemable coupons, tokens, or chits. Finally, the machines crush the aluminum and store it until unloaded into a truck that periodically collects the scrap.

Where used, the machines are remarkably successful. In Denver, Colorado, 20 reverse vending machines paid out more than $1 million in an 18-month period. Sweden reportedly will build and install an estimated 10,000 reverse vending machines as part of an effort to recover 75% of all aluminum cans used in the country. This would save 10,000 tons of aluminum annually (50 million cans), equal to Sweden's annual aluminum imports.

For more information, write to *Resource Recycling*, P.O. Box 10540, Portland, Oregon 97210.

---

The importance of trade to the growth of recycling is clear. If the strategy for recyclers is "markets first, collection second," then that strategy will be defeated by efforts to suppress aluminum scrap prices. Such an approach has historically plagued the iron and steel scrap industry.

Growth in recycling will depend on both market development and scrap collection. International markets, especially in developing countries, could provide the impetus for increasing collection in countries with high consumption rates. Investments in secondary recovery can be encouraged by international lending agencies, by nations desiring to improve their balance of trade, by entrepreneurs, and by environmentalists.

Recycling aluminum is an environmentally sound alternative to investing time and money into additional primary aluminum production. But the switch will require campaigns to enact container deposit bills, legislation to free trade in scrap, and energy pricing policies that reflect the real economic cost of energy.

## Iron and Steel Recycling

Automobiles junked each year in the United States produce scrap equal to 4% of world steel production. World trade in ferrous scrap has become an $11 billion industry, in which the United States has the largest stake. In 1980, the United States exported more than 11 million tons of scrap worth almost $1.3 billion, for 75% of the world's net international trade in iron and steel scrap.

Countries with the best recycling records—Belgium and Luxembourg, the United Kingdom, the

United States, the Netherlands, and Japan—recycle 30% to 40% of all iron and steel consumed.

Unfortunately, worldwide iron and steel recovery has thus far failed to meet its potential. One measure of the lack of progress in iron and steel recycling is the increase in the stock of obsolete scrap available for but not being used in recycling. In 1978, the backlog of recoverable ferrous scrap in the United States alone totaled more than 600 million tons. Since then, this backlog has grown to 680 million tons and will probably continue to grow.

Norway and Sweden have been praised widely for their efforts to recycle scrap cars. In the 1970s, Sweden suffered from the blight of 400,000 abandoned car hulks littering the countryside. The government then passed a law requiring disposal of car hulks with authorized scrap dealers.

In Norway, 50,000 hulks similarly had been abandoned, with 20,000 per year being added to this total. Norway followed Sweden's example and enacted its own automobile disposal law, imposing a $100 deposit on new cars, refundable with a $50 bonus for any car properly disposed. The law resulted in the collection of 33,000 car hulks in the first eight months.

Despite their success in recycling old cars, Norway and Sweden do not rank high in overall iron and steel scrap recycling. Norway, in fact, has one of the worst records of all industrialized countries, while Sweden's record is only average. Trade policies, much more than auto deposit taxes, affect recycling rates.

### Iron and Steel Scrap Trade

History has shown that scrap exports have been and could easily again be restricted. Auto deposit and disposal laws became necessary in Norway and Sweden because of artificial constraints on the scrap market. Sweden has essentially prohibited exports of iron and steel scrap since 1927, and Norway permits export of scrap only when the would-be exporter demonstrates that no market for it exists in Norway. The result is a greatly reduced market that per-

## Collecting Recyclables: Japan Leads the Way

Japan's recycling efforts began in earnest in the mid-1960s. Now 10% of Japan's total municipal waste is recycled, and efforts are continuing to increase this proportion.

One of the first programs in Japan resulted from the efforts of an entrepreneur who in 1966 persuaded the government of Ueda City to pay him a portion of the "avoided costs" of landfilling the materials that his firm recycled. The avoided cost is the expense saved by waste reduction. The city found it cheaper to pay a small recycling incentive than to pay a larger amount for waste disposal.

The plan requires residents to separate refuse into combustible and noncombustible material. At the dump, glass is separated by hand, and ferrous metal is removed by magnet. Overall, refuse disposal has dropped by 8%.

Hiroshima has achieved stunning success: disposal of raw refuse has been reduced by 40% since 1976. The City Environmental Project Bureau helped organize participation of student clubs, parent-teacher organizations, and similar groups to teach and en-

courage citizens to sort and prepare their garbage for collection.

These organizations contract with waste haulers, who deliver the material to recyclers or to the city. Payments go to the nonprofit groups at or above market rates, with a subsidy made possible by savings from avoided landfill fees.

Citizens are urged to sort their trash into three main categories: paper, nonreturnable bottles and cans, and noncombustibles. Paper is carried to local paper collection centers located throughout the city. Other items are placed in special bins and collected separately.

The size and density of Hiroshima's population (878,000) obviously has facilitated its recycling success. However, the small, less densely populated suburban town of Mizuho, with a population of only 22,000, reported similar results. Mizuho's citizens' organizations encourage recycling, but the city government contracts for collection of refuse. Recyclables are sold, with the city keeping 40% of the revenues and paying 60% to the community groups responsible for promoting source separation.

In Fuchu City, a suburb of Tokyo with a population of 187,000, the city purchased the necessary recycling equipment and pays a company to operate it. Thus, the obstacle of an insurmountably large up-front capital requirement for the private firm was avoided.

The city gave the company further incentive for efficiency by

mits price fixing and artificially suppressed prices.

In the United States, steelmakers have consistently sought to keep scrap prices low by lobbying the government to restrict the export of scrap. Such policies seriously diminish the prospect for iron and steel recycling.

U.S. steelmakers may have legitimate complaints about unfair trade practices in some steel-producing nations. Western Europe, for example, provides extensive subsidies to steelmakers, many of which are owned in large part by governments.

These subsidies are not reflected in steel prices and therefore not only permit unfair competition but also discourage more cost-effective production such as the greater use of scrap. Just as the defense of free trade requires maintaining open borders, it requires international agreements on the regulation of unfair trading practices.

Again, market development must be the first priority for recycling's promoters. Promotion would best be accomplished by stimulating investment and by removing trade barriers. The need to conserve energy has been the allowing it to keep 20% of the revenues earned from the sale of recycled materials. In the Shiki district, the government also made the initial capital investment in equipment, but turned its operation over to a firm to which it pays no fee. Instead, the firm earns all of its revenues from sales of recyclables.

"We have to change [wasteful] culture from the very roots," asserts Muneo Matsumoto, an official in Machida, "the garbage capital of Japan." Machida boasts that its new recycling program of source separation and computerized processing recycles 90% of the city's garbage.

The grassroots information system provided by citizens and citizens' groups works well in Japan, apparently as a result of the incentives provided the groups. The Japanese make it easy to participate and difficult not to participate in paper recycling.

### The Netherlands

The approach to waste paper collection in the Netherlands has been different from that in Japan, but just as successful. As in Japan, necessity motivates national and local governments to ensure waste paper recycling: both fiber resources and land for waste disposal have been scarce.

The Netherlands has achieved the best paper-recycling record in the world, using a few key policies to make the marketplace work better. For example, the government established the world's first waste exchange, a free brokerage service to match buyers and sellers of waste.

The government has also attempted to stabilize the typical boom and bust cycles in recyclables by establishing "buffer stocks." The recycling industry is particularly vulnerable to wild cyclical swings in the market, and the recent recession has been the worst for recycling since the Great Depression.

Buffer stocks enable collectors of waste paper to sell to the government-established fund when prices drop below a predetermined level. The stock is sold when prices go up again, and the fund is thereby replenished. Some economists say this approach is costly and sometimes counterproductive. It is difficult to match its operation with the needs of the market and thus to avoid market distortions. Yet, the approach has been used both in Japan and the Netherlands, the two leading nations in paper recycling, and may merit further consideration.

The Netherlands strongly promotes source separation, though differently from Japan. Whereas Japan has relied more on awareness, information, incentives, and armies of nonprofit organizations, the Netherlands simply enacted a law requiring source separation in all municipalities that have con-tracted for collection of waste paper.

### Islip, New York

Mandatory source separation has recently been applied with success in the United States. In New York, for example, the city of Islip was sued by the state to halt landfilling, partly because its landfill was contaminating underground water and releasing vinyl chloride into the air. A court settlement required the city to initiate recycling.

In the city's mandatory program, Islip residents face a $250 fine if they fail to comply. Five inspectors patrol the collection and issue warning tickets for non-compliance. A household that fails to cooperate faces noncollection of its garbage.

The collection program has succeeded without costly investments in sophisticated engineering devices. Residents simply place recyclables in containers with glass and cans on top and paper underneath. The city sorts ferrous materials with magnets and the rest by hand, as in Ueda City, Japan.

These few examples reinforce the observation that any number of policies may be applied to effect recycling—once societies decide to do it.

—**William U. Chandler**

---

greatest impetus to the use of scrap because scrap contains great quantities of embodied energy. Eliminating subsidies for energy production and use should be a high priority for promoting iron and steel scrap recycling markets.

### Steps to a Recycling Society

Recycling has been an environmental goal for a decade now, but only a few areas of the world have made significant progress. Voluntary recycling efforts have brought some success, but progress has come about mainly in response to necessity.

Progress made in the 1970s proves recycling's practicality and worth. Nations that have moved toward recycling paper, aluminum, and iron and steel have enhanced their competitive position in international markets. Recycling will become an even more important factor in international competitiveness as energy and capital costs increase the cost of producing virgin materials.

Despite the gains, the world has fallen far short of achieving recy-cling's potential. Only about one-fourth of the paper, aluminum, and iron and steel used in the world is recovered for recycling. This rate could be doubled or tripled.

Recycling can serve society's interests as no other process can. But a series of difficult steps must be taken to collect recyclable materials and to develop additional markets for them.

Three steps will lead to a "recycling society." The first requires that consumers pay the full costs of the materials they use. For

## "Industry leaders will be forced by higher energy and raw materials prices to consider recycling or face a future in which they cannot compete."

JIM OLIVE EPA-DOCUMERICA

Young people collect litter in Arkansas. A "recycling society" can be promoted through container-deposit legislation and a wide variety of other measures.

example, additional forest reserves should be set aside to make virgin pulpwood more expensive than waste paper since the world's forests have been cut faster than they have been replaced.

A special effort must also be made to reduce energy price subsidies. No single factor has increased recycling more in the last 30 years than the energy price increases of the 1970s. Recycling saves energy, and industries adopt recycling as a way of cutting energy costs; but when the price paid by industry for energy is distorted by subsidies, industries are less motivated to recycle.

Moreover, the true cost of energy includes the cost of damage to forests from acid rain, to human health from particulates, to human and aquatic populations displaced by hydroelectric projects, and so on. Solid-waste disposal costs usu-

ally are paid in general taxes, not by persons who create waste, leaving no incentive to reduce the cost of waste. Thus, to subsidize energy consumption is to subsidize environmental degradation by the throwaway society.

The second step requires building world markets for scrap paper, aluminum, and iron and steel. Wealthy countries restrain the export of scrap iron and steel and seriously inhibit the use of imported scrap in developing countries. Such policies must be changed, for few countries needing new steel production capacity will risk reliance on imported scrap unless scrap-exporting countries remove the threat of scrap embargoes.

The final step is greater collection of wastes, which will also reduce environmental subsidies, promote international scrap trade,

and soften the impact of higher energy prices.

Container deposit legislation can dramatically increase the return of beverage containers. Incentives, information, or the threat of fines and noncollection of garbage can induce greater collection of recyclable material. A wide variety of policies, in fact, will stimulate recycling and can be applied on national or local levels.

These steps will not be taken simply because they are logical or urgently needed. Concerned citizens must insist that they be taken. Conservationists have shown too little interest in assuring market pricing for energy and free trade of scrap materials.

National and local government leaders have shown little willingness to take the difficult step of requiring collection of recyclable materials, but the rising costs of litter cleanup and landfilling waste will increasingly press them to do so. Industry leaders will be forced by higher energy and raw materials prices to consider recycling or face a future in which they cannot compete.

Materials recycling is necessary if society is to maintain current living standards. But recycling also brings the opportunity to improve the material well-being of all the world's people and to do so without great cost to the environment. In this resides the great virtue of recycling.

William U. Chandler is a senior researcher at the Worldwatch Institute, 1776 Massachusetts Avenue, N.W., Washington, D.C. 20036. He is coauthor of Energy: The Conservation Revolution and author of The Myth of TVA. This article is adapted from Worldwatch Paper 56, "Materials Recycling: The Virtue of Necessity" (October 1983, 52 pages, $2.00), which is available from the World Future Society Book Service (prepayment required; please include $1.50 for postage and handling).

## A Crisis of Many Dimensions

# Putting Food on the World's Table

## Lester R. Brown

**LESTER R. BROWN** is president of and a senior researcher with Worldwatch Institute in Washington, D.C. Formerly administrator of the International Agricultural Development Service of the United States Department of Agriculture, he is the author of several books. This article is adapted, with permission, from chapter 10 of *State of the World 1984*, a Worldwatch Institute Report on Progress Toward a Sustainable Society, W. W. Norton and Company, New York and London.

**M**easured just in terms of output, the past generation has been one of unprecedented progress in world agriculture. In 1950 the world's farmers produced 623 million tons of grain. In 1983 they produced nearly 1.5 billion tons. This increase of nearly 900 million tons was all the more remarkable because it occurred when there was little new cropland to bring under the plow.[1]

On closer examination, this 33-year span breaks into two distinct eras—before and after the 1973 oil price increase. Modern agriculture thrives on cheap energy, and the age of cheap energy came to an end in 1973. For 23 years, world food output expanded at over 3 percent per year, and, although there was concern about rapid population growth, there was a comfortable margin in the growth of food production over that of population. Since 1973, however, annual growth has been less than 2 percent, and the world's farmers have been struggling to keep pace with population.

The global increase in world food output also obscures wide variations in individual geographic regions. In North America, production has steadily outstripped demand, generating ever-larger surpluses. In the Soviet Union, output has fallen behind demand over the past decade, making the country the largest grain importer in history. And in Africa, which has a population of 512 million and which has to feed 14 million additional people each year, food production per person has fallen steadily since 1970. Despite a tripling of grain imports since then, hunger has become chronic, an enduring part of the African landscape.

The 1983 drought in North America and Africa must be considered against this backdrop. The principal effect of the precipitous decline in the North American harvest was a reduction in stocks and a rise in food and feedstuff prices. In Africa, where national food reserves are virtually nonexistent, the drought translated into widespread hunger and, in a score of countries, the threat of famine.[2]

### The Global Loss of Momentum

As the world recovered from World War II, hopes for improvement in world agriculture were high. An accumulating backlog of agricultural technologies such as hybrid corn and chemical fertilizers was waiting to be applied on a massive scale. Between 1950 and 1973, world grain production more than doubled, to nearly 1.3 billion tons. Although output expanded more rapidly in some regions than in others, all regions shared in the growth. This rising tide of food production improved nutrition throughout the world, helping to boost life expectancy in the Third World from less than 43 years in the early 1950s to over 53 years in the early 1970s.[3]

This period of broad-based gains in nutritional improvement came to an end in 1973. After the oil price hike that year, the growth in world grain output slowed. Since 1973 world grain production has expanded at less than 2 percent yearly, barely keeping pace with population (see Table 1). Although the period since the 1979 oil price hike is too short to establish a trend, $30-a-barrel oil may well slow growth further.

Since 1973, attention has focused on the impact of petroleum prices on food supply, but demand has also been affected. On the supply side, rising oil prices have increased the costs of basic agricultural inputs—fertilizer, pesticides, and fuel for tillage and irrigation—thus acting as a drag on output. On the demand side of the equation, escalating oil prices combined with ill-conceived national economic policies have contributed to a global economic slowdown so severe since 1979 that it has brought world growth in per capita income to a virtual halt.

Had incomes continued to rise at the same rate after 1973 as they did before, prices of food commodities would have been stronger, thus supporting a more vigorous growth in farm investment and output. Agricultural underinvestment in Third World countries has also contributed to the loss of momentum, but the central point is that the rise in oil prices, affecting both food supply and demand, has brought the era of robust growth in world food output to an end.

Oil is not the only resource whose questionable supply is checking the growth in food output. The loss of topsoil through erosion is now acting as a drag on efforts to produce more food. And the scarcity of water is also beginning to affect food production prospects. Since World War II, the world's irrigated area has more than doubled, but the flurry of dam building of the past generation has now subsided. With occasional exceptions, most of the remaining potential projects are more difficult, costly, and capital-intensive.[4]

In some situations, irrigated agriculture is threatened by falling water tables. The southern Great Plains, where much of the U.S. growth in irrigated area over the last two decades has occurred, provides a disturbing example. Irrigation there depends almost entirely on water from the Ogallala Aquifer, an essentially non-replenishable fossil water reserve. As the water table in this vast agricultural area begins to fall with the depletion of the aquifer, the cost of irrigation rises. Already some farmers

**Table 1**

## WORLD OIL PRICE AND GRAIN PRODUCTION TRENDS, TOTAL AND PER CAPITA, 1950–83

| PERIOD | OIL PRICE PER BARREL | GRAIN PRODUCTION | ANNUAL GROWTH POPULATION | GRAIN PRODUCTION PER PERSON |
|---|---|---|---|---|
| | *(dollars)* | | *(percent)* | |
| 1950–73 | 2 | 3.1 | 1.9 | 1.2 |
| 1973–79 | 12 | 1.9 | 1.8 | 0.1 |
| 1979–83 | 31 | 1.0[1] | 1.7 | 0.7 |

[1]Severe drought in the United States and Africa and record idling of cropland under U.S. farm programs reduced the 1983 world harvest well below trend. Thus, the slowdown in grain production is overstated.
**SOURCES:** International Monetary Fund, *Monthly Financial Statistics*, various issues; U.S. Department of Agriculture, *World Indices of Agricultural and Food Production, 1950–82* (unpublished printout) (Washington, D.C.: 1983); United Nations, *Monthly Bulletin of Statistics*, various issues.

in eastern Colorado and northern Texas are converting to dryland farming. For the 32 counties in the Texas Panhandle, the U.S. Department of Agriculture projects that irrigation will be largely phased out by 1995.[5]

A somewhat analogous situation exists in the Soviet southwest, where the excessive diversion of river water for irrigation is reducing the water level of the Aral and Caspian seas. This has many long-term negative consequences, including a diminished fish catch and the gradual retreat of the water line from coastal cities that depend on it for transportation.[6] Given the strong internal pressures within the Soviet Union to produce more food, however, the diversion is continuing.

A second major threat to irrigated agriculture is the often-intense competition for water between farming, industry, and cities. In the U.S. Southwest, the irrigated area is actually declining in states such as Arizona, where Sunbelt migration is swelling cities that are bidding water away from farmers. Nationally the net area under irrigation is projected to continue growing over the rest of the century, but at a more modest rate.

New research indicates water scarcities are also emerging in Africa. South Africa, adding 720,000 people each year, is fast running out of new irrigation sites. A 1983 report of the President's Council in South Africa identified the scarcity of fresh water as a constraint on that country's demographic carrying capacity.[7]

The worldwide loss of momentum outlined above will not be easily restored. Although agricultural mismanagement abounds, particularly in the Third World and Eastern Europe, it has not worsened appreciably over the years. Nor can the situation be explained by any farmers' loss of skills. The explanation lies in the more difficult circumstances facing farmers everywhere. In the mid-1980s it is far more difficult to raise world food output at a consistent 3 percent per year than it was during the 1950s or 60s. The cheap energy that permitted farmers to override easily the constraints imposed by the scarcity of land, soil nutrients, or water is simply no longer available.

### Population, Land, and Fertilizer

The changing relationship between world population size, cropland area, and energy supplies bears heavily on the human prospect over the remainder of this century and beyond. Increasingly, the energy used in agriculture will be in the form of chemical fertilizer. As population grows, cropland per person shrinks and fertilizer requirements climb.

And erosion that has robbed soils of nutrients is forcing farmers to use more fertilizers.

Even urbanization is raising demand, since, as people move to cities, it is harder to recycle the nutrients in human and household waste. Yet the combination of rising energy costs and diminishing returns on the use of additional fertilizer raises doubts that adequate food supplies can be produced in the future at prices the world's poor can afford.

The central importance of the population/land/fertilizer relationship is a recent phenomenon. Before 1950 increases in food output came largely from expanding the cultivated area, but with the scarcity of fertile new land and the advent of cheap chemical fertilizer this changed. Between 1950 and 1983 world fertilizer use climbed from 15 million to 114 million tons, nearly an eightfold increase within a generation.[8] In effect, as fertile land became harder to find, farmers learned to substitute energy in the form of chemical fertilizer for land. Fertilizer factories replaced new land as the principal source of growth in food production.

The hybridization of corn and the dwarfing of the wheat and rice varieties that have been at the heart of Third World agricultural advances over the last two decades figured prominently, of course, in the growth in world food output. So, too, did the doubling of irrigated area. But the effectiveness of all these practices depends heavily on the use of chemical fertilizer. Without an adequate supply of plant nutrients, high-yielding cereal varieties hold little advantage over traditional ones. Likewise, an increase in irrigation is of little consequence if the nutrients to support the higher yields are lacking.

The response of crops to the use of additional fertilzer is now diminishing, particularly in agriculturally advanced countries. Some countries, such as Argentina and India, still apply relatively little fertilizer, and so have quite high response ratios. But worldwide the return on the use of additional fertilizer is on the way

Bagging fertilizer at the Don Hercules Fertilizer Plant in Lahore, Pakistan. Fertilizer manufacturing is one of the world's major industries today, for as population grows, cropland per person shrinks and fertilizer requirements climb (World Bank photo by Tomas Sennett).

down. Although the biological constraints on fertilizer responsiveness can be pushed back with continued plant breeding, further declines seem inevitable.

Fertilizer manufacturing is one of the world's major industries. In an advanced agricultural country such as the United States, expenditures on fertilizer total some $10 billion per year.[9] Three basic nutrients—nitrogen, which is obtained from the air, and phosphate and potash, both mined from underground deposits—account for the great bulk of world chemical fertilizer production. The industrial fixing of atmospheric nitrogren in the form of ammonium nitrate, ammonium sulphate, urea, or other forms of nitrogen fertilizer is an energy-intensive process. Although natural gas is the preferred fuel and feedstock in the nitrogen fertilizer industry, oil figures prominently in the mining, processing, and transportation of phosphate and potash.

High energy prices have begun to shift nitrogen fertilizer production from the traditional industrial country producers, such as the United States and some in Western Europe, to countries with energy surpluses. Investment in this industry has been particularly attractive to oil-exporting countries that are flaring excess gas produced in conjunction with oil. To the extent that fertilizers are manufactured in countries such as Saudi

Arabia, Iran, or Kuwait with gas that would otherwise be wasted, future price increases may be curbed. The Soviet Union, in a situation similar to the gas-surplus countries in the Middle East, is also investing heavily in nitrogen fertilizer-production capacity.[10]

The distribution of phosphate rock, the principal source of phosphate fertilizer, poses a particular problem since reserves are concentrated in Florida and Morocco. With production concentrated around the Atlantic but with the world's population and future needs for phosphate mainly in Asia, high transportation costs—and thus high fertilizer prices in Asian villages—are inevitable.

With population growth projected to continue, the cropland available per person will continue to decline and the fertilizer needed to maintain consumption will continue to rise. At some point, biological constraints on crop yields will make the substitution of fertilizer for cropland increasingly difficult and costly. When this is combined with the projected long-term rise in real cost of the oil and natural gas used to manufacture, distribute, and apply chemical fertilizer, the difficulty in restoring the steady upward trend in per capita grain production of 1950–73, when it climbed from 248 kilograms in 1950 to 326 kilograms in 1973, becomes clear.

### Real Production Trends

When measuring growth, econo-mists adjust current prices for the rate of inflation in order to distill out the real gains in production. Something similar is needed in agriculture, where growth in output is inflated by agricultural practices that are not sustainable. Such an adjustment would shed light on the longer-term outlook by distinguishing between gains that are real and those that are made at the expense of future output.[11]

Similarly, adjustments should be made for the output from sloping land that was once in ecologically stable, long-term rotations of row crops with grass and hay, but that is now in row crops continuously, for topsoil loss in these situations has become excessive. If American farmers were to take the steps needed to protect their topsoil, U.S. farm output and exports would be substantially less in the short run, but they would be sustainable over the long term. Elimination of this agronomic deficit through a national soil conservation program that reintroduced the traditional practices cited above might also eliminate the troublesome short-term commodity surpluses that depress farm prices and income.

In addition to agronomic deficits, many of the world's farmers are also incurring economic deficits. Nowhere is this more evident than in the United States, where net farm income has narrowed almost to the vanishing point. Between 1973, when the world oil price began its astronomical climb, and 1982, farmers were caught in a squeeze between depressed commodity prices and the soaring costs for fuel, fertilizer, and equipment combined with high interest rates.

In 1982, many American farmers sold their products for less than they cost to produce. Between 1950 and 1982, U.S. farm output more than doubled, but net farm income in real terms (1967 dollars) fell from $19 billion in 1950 to scarcely $6 billion in 1982.[12] This precipitous decline occurred while the incomes of other Americans were rising steadily.

Farmers were able to sustain the heavy losses of the late 1970s and early 1980s only by going deeply into debt, borrowing against soaring land values. But the boom in land speculation came to an end in 1981, and land prices fell the following two years. As a result, many farmers suddenly lost their equity and faced bankruptcy.

Economic conditions fostering speculation in land have driven land values to a lofty level that bears little relationship to the land's productive capacity. Given the economics of the early 1980s, buying U.S. farmland now with the hope of paying for it from the produce would be wishful thinking.[13] Nevertheless, it was these spiraling land values that, until 1981, enabled many farmers to borrow and to stay in business.[14]

As farmers have borrowed against the soaring prices of their land and other assets, not only have they supported themselves and their families,

Men plowing a rice paddy in Sri Lanka. While a doubling of irrigated areas has figured prominently in Third World agricultural advances over the last two decades, such increases will ultimately be of little consequence if the nutrients to support the higher yields are lacking (World Bank photo by Tomas Sennett).

they have also subsidized food consumers everywhere. Borrowing against the inflated paper value of farmland has led to artificially low food prices in recent years. And just as productivity increases cannot go on forever when topsoil is being eroded, borrowing that is unrelated to the real value of the land cannot continue indefinitely—a lesson many rural banks and farmers are unfortunately learning.

If farmers are to continue to produce, prices of farm products will need to rise. Without such an increase, the more vulnerable farmers and those who have attractive employment options or who are approaching retirement will stop producing, eventually reducing output and moving prices upward to a more realistic level.

Although U.S. data might allow the conversion of current farm output to real output by adjusting for soil erosion, similar information does not exist for most countries. And it is difficult to measure the extent to which farm output has been inflated in recent years by the growing indebtedness of farmers. If these adjustments could be made, however, it seems clear that the real world food output would be far below current consumption.

### Dependence on North America

With grain, as with oil or any other basic resource, excessive world dependence on one geographic region for supplies is risky. As the North American share of world grain exports has increased, it has surpassed the Middle Eastern share of oil exports and made the world more dependent on one region for its food than ever before.

This extraordinary dependence on one geographic region for grain supplies is a historically recent phenomenon and gives North America a politically and economically strategic role in the world food economy. Many of the world's cities, particularly those in the Third World, are fed largely with U.S. and Canadian wheat. Much of the world's milk, meat, and eggs are produced with U.S. feedgrains and soybeans.

As recently as the late 1930s, Western Europe was the only grain-deficient region and Latin America was the world's leading grain supplier, exporting some nine million tons per year. North America and Eastern Europe (including the Soviet Union) each exported five million tons of grain annually. Even Asia and Africa had modest exportable surpluses.[15]

By 1950 the shift from regional grain surpluses to deficits was well under way, and the outlines of a new world grain trade pattern were beginning to emerge. Today, with North America's unchallenged dominance as a grain supplier, international grain trade bears little resemblance to that of the 1930s (see Table 2).

As North American agricultural growth gained momentum after World War II, U.S. and Canadian exports of grain climbed from 23 million tons in 1950 to 138 million tons in 1982, though they dropped back to 122 million tons in 1983 as a strong dollar and lethargic world economy weakened the buying powers of other countries. Feedgrains—principally corn, sorghum, and barley—have made up an ever larger share of the total. Today, North America is not only the world's breadbasket, but its feed bag as well.

While the United States was expanding its feedgrain exports, the shipments of soybeans grew even more rapidly. Although soybeans originated in China, they have thrived in the United States, doing far better than in their country of origin. They have also found an economic niche in the world livestock economy, with soybean meal becoming the principal protein supplement in livestock and poultry feed. Today the United States produces over 60 percent of the world's soybean crop and accounts for two-thirds of soybean exports.

The reasons for North America's emergence as the world's dominant supplier of feedgrains and feedstuffs are many. On the supply side, the United States inherited a prime piece of agricultural real estate. In contrast to Latin America, where agricultural lands are concentrated in the hands of large hacienda owners, or Eastern Europe, where state farms and collectives dominate, U.S. and Canadian agriculture are centered on the family farm. Although large by international standards, they are nonetheless family farms and have all the attendant advantages of a strong link between effort expended by those working the land and the rewards of doing so.

The restructuring of world grain trade over the last generation has resulted in part from the soil erosion problems discussed earlier and in part from differential population growth rates, as a comparison of North

### Table 2
**THE CHANGING PATTERN OF WORLD GRAIN TRADE, 1950–83[1]**

| REGION | 1950[2] | 1960 | 1970 | 1980 | 1983[3] |
|---|---|---|---|---|---|
| | | *(million metric tons)* | | | |
| North America | +23 | +39 | +56 | +131 | +122 |
| Latin America | +1 | 0 | +4 | −10 | −3 |
| Western Europe | −22 | −25 | −30 | −16 | +2 |
| E. Europe and Soviet Union | 0 | 0 | 0 | −46 | −39 |
| Africa | 0 | −2 | −5 | −15 | −20 |
| Asia | −6 | −17 | −37 | −63 | −71 |
| Australia and New Zealand | +3 | +6 | +12 | +19 | +9 |

[1] Plus sign indicates net exports; minus sign, net imports.
[2] Average for 1948–52.
[3] Preliminary.

**SOURCES:** United Nations Food and Agriculture Organization. *Production Yearbook* (Rome: various years); U.S. Department of Agriculture, *Foreign Agriculture Circular*, August 1983; author's estimates.

U.S. and Canadian agriculture are centered on the family farm. Although large by international standards, they have all the attendant advantages of a strong link between effort expended by those working the land and the rewards of doing so. Today, North America is not only the world's breadbasket, but its feed bag as well (photo by Vernon Sigl).

America and Latin America shows.[16]

Today the countries with significant exportable surpluses of grain can be counted on the fingers of one hand—the United States, Canada, Australia, Argentina, and France. Of these, the United States accounts for over half and, with Canada, covers close to 70 percent of the total.

The rest of the world's dependence on these supplies varies widely. A few countries, both industrial and developing, import more food than they produce; among these are Algeria, Belgium, Costa Rica, Japan, Lebanon, Libya, Portugal, Saudi Arabia, Switzerland, and Venezuela. Others that may shortly move into this category include Egypt, Senegal, and South Korea.[17]

This overwhelming dependence on one region, and on one country in particular, brings with it an assortment of risks. To begin with, both the United States and Canada are affected by the same climatic cycles. A poor harvest in one is often associated with a poor harvest in the other. When reserves are low, even a modest fluctuation in the region's exportable grain surplus can send price tremors through the world food economy.

An inadvertent agricultural policy miscalculation can also be costly. This was amply demonstrated in 1983 when miscalculations in the U.S. Department of Agriculture led to the idling of more cropland than had been projected, which was followed by a severe drought that further reduced harvests. Within a matter of weeks, concerned countries watched the world grain surplus change to a potential grain deficit. The U.S. corn crop was cut in half, effectively eliminating the world feedgrain surplus.[18]

When food supplies are tight, a North American grain export embargo, whether economically or politically inspired, can drive food prices upward everywhere outside the region. In 1973, for example, President Nixon embargoed soybean exports because of shortages at home. Although this helped curb food price rises within the United States, it worsened inflationary pressures elsewhere.

During the same period, American millers and bakers were pressing for restrictions on grain exports, holding out the prospect of soaring bread prices if wheat exports were not restricted. Unfortunately, the world market conditions that would lead a principal exporter to restrict outgoing supplies are precisely the conditions that are most damaging to importing countries.

In mid-July of 1975, the Canadian Wheat Board banned further exports of wheat until the size of the harvest could be ascertained. Similarly, the United States, yielding to political pressures generated by rising domestic food prices, limited grain exports to the Soviet Union and Poland in the late summer and early fall of 1975. Levied in 1972, in 1974, and again in 1975, such restrictions on exports became common when global grain supplies were tight. Perhaps more unsettling, these export controls were adopted despite the return to production of the previously idled U.S. cropland.

As with oil, exports of grain have been restricted for political purposes. In 1973, the Department of State compiled a "hit list" of Third World countries whose U.N. voting records were not compatible with U.S. interests so that they could be denied food assistance. More recently, President Carter imposed a partial embargo on exports of grain to the Soviet Union following its invasion of Afghanistan, and President Reagan delayed negotiating a new five-year grain agreement with the Soviet Union after the imposition of martial law in Poland.[19]

Countries that rely on North American food should take heed of the philosophical debate emerging within the United States about the wisdom of mining the nation's soils to meet the ever-growing world demand. Both agricultural analysts and environmentalists argue that the country should make whatever adjustments in its agricultural practices are needed to protect the resource base, even though this would reduce that exportable surplus.

Some argue that it makes little sense to sacrifice a resource that has been a source of economic strength since colonial days merely to buy a few billion barrels of oil. And some contend that the current generation of farmers has no right to engage in the agronomic equivalent of deficit financing, mortgaging the future generations to come.

The current trend is fraught with risks, both for those whose livelihoods depend on sustained land productivity and for those in countries dependent on food imports that eventually will dry up if the mining of soil continues. Even for the importers, reduced supplies in the short term and less pressure on North American soils would be better than losing the region's export capacity over the long term.

## Food Security Indicators

One of the most useful indicators of the world food situation is the food security index, which incorporates both grain carry-over stocks and the grain equivalent of idled cropland. This combines the world's two basic reserves of food and expresses them as days of consumption, a concept readily understood by policy makers everywhere.

The two components of the index differ in important ways. Carry-over stocks, the grain in storage when the new crop begins to come in, are readily accessible and require only time for shipping arrangements to be made and for transport. Idled cropland, on the other hand, can take a year or more to be converted into food by farmers.

Carry-over stocks are held for the most part by exporting countries—the United States, Canada, Australia, Argentina, and France—largely as a service to importers. Other countries, particularly large ones such as India, maintain grain stocks as well, but

Vegetable farmer in Brazil. The scenario long predicted by ecologists—that mounting population pressures in northeastern Brazil leading to deforestation and unsustainable agricultural practices would lead to a major food crises in the area—is now unfolding (World Bank photo by Yosef Hadar).

these are usually designed specifically for their own use.[20]

Maintaining adequate grain stocks is expensive not only because of the cost of grain elevators but also because stored grain represents an investment. So when interest rates are high, the cost of carrying grain is also high. And, even with the best of storage facilities, there is always some loss involved, thus adding to the cost of maintaining the reserves.

Over time, for a reserve of grain to be adequate it should expand in tandem with world consumption. In 1960, for example, world reserves of 200 million tons were more than ample, representing nearly one-fourth of world consumption. In 1983, however, the same stocks would represent

only one-eighth of world grain consumption. A level of grain reserves that was adequate in 1960 would be grossly inadequate in 1983.

The idled cropland component of the food security index consists of cropland set aside under farm programs just in the United States. Only occasionally have other countries intentionally idled cropland, and the acreages have usually been negligible. During the 1960s and early 1970s, idled U.S. cropland averaged close to 50 million acres, enough to produce an estimated 60 million tons of grain (see Table 3).

As growth in world food outputs slowed after 1973, the United States returned cropland to production from 1974 through 1977 in an attempt to rebuild stocks. Then, when grain reserves began to recover in the late 1970s, some land was taken out of production in both 1978 and 1979. With reserves beginning to drop again in 1979, all land was released for production in 1980.

The Reagan administration, wishing to reduce government intervention in the marketplace, declined to idle any cropland in 1981 and idled only a modest acreage in 1982, even though world reserves had been rebuilt following two consecutive bumper harvests in the United States and a worldwide economic recession that dampened the growth in demand. In 1983, faced with the most severe rural depression since the 1930s, the administration overreacted by devising two programs to encourage farmers to divert land to nonproductive uses.

The result was the largest diversion of acreage in U.S. history—over 70 million acres. Combined with a severe drought in the principal U.S. feedgrain- and soybean-producing areas, this led to a precipitous decline in the feedgrain harvest of over 40 percent. This in turn reduced the prospective carry-over stocks to one of the lowest levels in some years.[21]

Whenever grain stocks and the grain equivalent of idled U.S. cropland drop below 50 days of world consumption, grain prices customarily rise and become highly unstable. In 1973 and 1974, when the index dropped to 50 and 41 days, grain prices were nearly double traditional levels. The index again fell below 50 days of consumption in 1980, partly as a result of drought in the United States.

This time, however, prices were not nearly as volatile as before, perhaps in part because interest rates were at record highs, making investors less inclined to speculate in commodities. By late 1983, prices, particularly of feedgrains, began to rise, largely because of the unprecedented reduction in the U.S. grain harvest—the product of government miscalculation and drought.

The food security index measures the adequacy of food supplies at the global level and thus the broad potential for responding to national shortages, but it says nothing about conditions within individual countries. Here the best indicator, of course, is the nutritional state of a country's population. At issue is whether a growing child gets enough food to develop his or her full physical and mental potential or whether a worker gets enough food to be fully productive.

Per capita food availability for a country indicates what the national average is, but not whether an individual is adequately nourished. Assessing nutritional adequacy requires some knowledge of how the national food supply is distributed. But a lack of data on distribution makes it very difficult to estimate the extent of malnutrition, thus leaving the subject open to continuing debate.

The only time a decline in nutrition shows up officially is when it is severe enough to affect mortality. When this happens, a country is facing famine, the most obvious and severe manifestation of food insecurity. Using this criterion, inadequate though it is, developments over the past decade have not been encouraging.

From the postwar recovery years until the early 1970s, famine virtually disappeared from the world. Except in China, which now admits to a massive famine in 1960–61, when it was largely isolated, the world enjoyed a remarkable respite from famine for a quarter of a century. Whenever famine did threaten, the United States intervened with food aid, even when it required nearly one-fifth of the U.S. wheat crop two years in a row, as it did following monsoon failures in India in 1964 and 1965.[22]

By the early 1970s, however, food deficits were widening and famine was unfolding in several African countries and in the Indian subcontinent (see Table 4). Several famines claimed hundreds of thousands of lives, providing a grim reminder of the fragility of food security even in

## Table 3
### INDEX OF WORLD FOOD SECURITY, 1960–83

| YEAR | WORLD CARRY-OVER STOCKS OF GRAIN | RESERVES GRAIN EQUIV. OF IDLED U.S. CROPLAND | TOTAL | WORLD CONSUMPTION |
|---|---|---|---|---|
| | *(million metric tons)* | | | *(days)* |
| 1960 | 200 | 36 | 236 | 104 |
| 1965 | 142 | 70 | 212 | 81 |
| 1970 | 164 | 71 | 235 | 75 |
| 1971 | 183 | 46 | 229 | 71 |
| 1972 | 143 | 78 | 221 | 67 |
| 1973 | 148 | 25 | 173 | 50 |
| 1974 | 133 | 4 | 137 | 41 |
| 1975 | 141 | 3 | 144 | 43 |
| 1976 | 196 | 3 | 199 | 56 |
| 1977 | 194 | 1 | 195 | 53 |
| 1978 | 221 | 22 | 243 | 62 |
| 1979 | 197 | 16 | 213 | 54 |
| 1980 | 183 | 0 | 183 | 46 |
| 1981 | 221 | 0 | 221 | 56 |
| 1982[1] | 260 | 13 | 273 | 66 |
| 1983[2] | 191 | 92 | 283 | 68 |

[1] Preliminary.
[2] Projection.

**SOURCES:** Reserve stocks from U.S. Department of Agriculture (USDA), *Foreign Agriculture Circular*, October 1983; cropland idled in the United States data from Randy Weber, USDA, private communication, August 1983.

an age of advanced technology. Most were the product of drought and a failure of international food relief mechanisms.

During the late 1970s, world reserves were rebuilt and, except for strife-torn Kampuchea, famines subsided—only to return in 1983, a year of widespread climatic anomalies (see "El Niño and World Climate: Piecing Together the Puzzle," *Environment*, April 1984). The capacity of poor countries with falling per capita food production and deteriorating soils to withstand drought and floods has lessened. As a result, more countries than ever before face the possibility of famine in early 1984. Among the threatened countries are Bolivia and Peru in Latin America and over a score of countries in Africa. An FAO team of agronomists assessing the food situation in Africa in late 1983 identified 22 countries where crisis seemed imminent.[23]

Since all governments gather mortality data, though not equally well, it is possible to document these severe food shortages. But equally troubling is the number of people suffering from chronic malnutrition—the vast middle ground between those who are well nourished and those who are starving. Their numbers are difficult to measure and therefore easy to ignore. Indian economist Amartya Sen observes that his government "has been able to ignore this endemic hunger because that hunger has neither led to a run on the market, and chaos, nor grown into an acute famine with people dying of starvation. Persistent, orderly hunger does not upset the system."[24]

## A Crisis of Many Dimensions

There is no simple explanation of why efforts to eradicate hunger have lost momentum or why food supplies for some segments of humanity are less secure than they were, say, 15 years ago. Declines in food security involve the continuous interaction of environmental, economic, demographic, and political variables. Some analysts see the food problem almost

### Table 4
### COUNTRIES EXPERIENCING FAMINE SINCE 1950

| YEAR | LOCATION | ESTIMATED DEATHS |
|---|---|---|
| 1960–61 | China | 8,980,000 |
| 1968–69 | Nigeria (Biafra) | 1,000,000 |
| 1971–72 | Bangladesh | 430,000 |
| 1972 | India | 830,000 |
| 1973 | Sahelian Countries | 100,000 |
| 1972–74 | Ethiopia | 200,000 |
| 1974 | Bangladesh | 330,000 |
| 1979 | Kampuchea | 450,000 |
| 1983 | Ethiopia | 30,000 |

SOURCE: Worldwatch Institute estimates derived from various official and unofficial sources.

exclusively as a population issue, noting that wherever population growth rates are low, food supplies are generally adequate.

Others view it as a problem of resources—soil, water, and energy. Many economists see it almost exclusively as a result of underinvestment, while agronomists see it more as a failure to bring forth new technologies on the needed scale. Still others see it as a distribution problem. To some degree, it is all of these.

In an important sense, the food problem of the mid-1980s is the result of resource depletion. The depletion of oil reserves, the loss of topsoil through erosion, and the growing competition for fresh water are central to understanding trends in the world food economy. As world population expands, the shrinking cropland area per person and the reduction in average soil depth by erosion combine to steadily reduce per capita availability of topsoil for food production. Because the energy that farmers substitute for soil lost to erosion is becoming increasingly costly, the production costs everywhere are on the rise.

In a basic arithmetic sense, the food problem is a population problem. If world population were now growing at 1 percent instead of nearly 2 percent, there would still be an ample margin for improving diets, as

there was from 1950 to 1973. As noted, however, the annual growth in food production has unfortunately fallen from the rather comfortable 3 percent of that period to a rate that barely matches that of population.

Those who see the food problem primarily as a distribution problem argue that if all the world's food were equitably distributed among its people there would be no hunger and malnutrition. This argument is technically sound, but it represents a degree of global abstraction that is not very helpful in formulating policies. It would mean, for example, that much of the world would be even more dependent on U.S. farmers than they are today.

The only long-term solution to hunger in most Third World countries is more internal production. And improving distribution is not just a matter of a better transport system or subsidized food distribution programs. It requires dealing with fundamental sources of political conflict such as land reform and with economic policies that encourage employment.

Achieving a more satisfactory balance between the world demand and supply of food requires attention to both sides of the equation. On the demand side, the success of efforts to upgrade diets may depend on an emergency program to slow world population growth. Currently, farmers must produce enough additional food each year to feed an annual increment of 79 million people—people who must be provided for in years of good weather and bad.

Meaningful improvements in diet over the rest of the century will depend, too, on gains in per capita income, particularly in the Third World. Unfortunately those gains are narrowing or disappearing. During the 1970s, 18 countries in Africa experienced a decline in per capita income. In most instances these national declines appear to be continuing in this decade; the list of countries where incomes have fallen thus far during the present decade is far longer than it was in the last one.

## 3. NATURAL RESOURCES: Food and Hunger

Also on the demand side is the question of how available food supplies are distributed. The most vulnerable segments of society in times of food scarcity are the rural landless in Third World countries. Reducing the size of this extremely vulnerable, rapidly growing landless population will require far more vigorous family planning and land reform programs than most countries have so far been able to mount.

On the supply side, the scarcity of new cropland, the continuing loss of topsoil, the scarcity of fresh water, the end of cheap energy, and diminishing returns on chemical fertilizer combine to make expanding food production progressively more difficult. In addition, food-deficit Third World countries are now struggling with a heavy external debt load that is continuing to mount. Foreign exchange scarcities are reducing imports both of agricultural inputs and of food.

At a time when concessional food aid is needed more than ever, U.S. programs are at the lowest level of nearly a generation. From their launch in 1954 through the late 1960s, U.S. food programs expanded, reaching a high of 15.3 million tons of grain in 1966. Enough to feed 90 million people in its peak years, this aid was an important defense against hunger in many countries. Preliminary estimates for 1983, however, indicate food aid shipments had dwindled to some 4 million tons of grain.

Other assistance programs, such as the World Food Programme, have been developed and expanded, but they are small by comparison and cannot begin to offset the U.S. decline. In a modest effort to enhance food security in low-income countries, the International Monetary Fund launched a new facility in 1981 that would provide short-term supplementary financing to food-deficit Third World countries suffering from temporary rises in food import bills.[25]

In addition to the traditional problems, political conflicts are creating an instability in the Middle East, Africa, and Latin America that makes agricultural progess difficult. This new hindrance to progress is reflected in the World Food Programme's emergency relief efforts. The share of emergency food relief going to victims of human-caused disasters (refugees and displaced persons) has come to dominate the program in recent years, after starting at a relatively modest level. By 1982, less than one-third of the program's resources were devoted to helping the groups who were the principal recipients in the early years, those affected by drought or caught in sudden natural disasters such as floods or earthquakes.

Other disruptions borne of desperation are cropping up in food-deficit areas. In late 1983, reports from northeastern Brazil described hordes of hungry rural people pouring into the towns demanding food, water, and jobs. After the town of Crato was invaded on three different occasions, merchants began voluntarily distributing rations of beans, sugar, and flour to forestall sacking and looting. Merchants in another town reportedly lost some 60 tons of food to looters.[26]

Although drought and recession-induced unemployment are leading to hunger, the long-term forces converging to create these conditions in the Brazilian northeast are essentially the same as those that have led to the food crises in so many African countries: record population growth, underinvestment in agriculture, and physical deterioration in the countryside. Ecologists have for years warned that mounting population pressures in northeastern Brazil leading to deforestation and unsustainable agricultural practices would turn the area into a desert. That grim scenario is now unfolding.

Trends in Africa since 1970 are a harbinger of things to come elsewhere in the absence of some major changes in population policies and economic priorities. After rising from 1950 to 1970, per capita grain production in Africa has declined rather steadily.[27] The forces that have led to this decline in Africa are also gaining strength in the Andean countries of Latin America, in Central America,

Construction of an anti-erosion dike in Upper Volta. This agricultural project is directed primarily to increasing the production of cotton and cereals in the area (World Bank photo by Yosef Hadar).

and in the Indian subcontinent. Whether the declining food production now so painfully evident in Africa can be avoided elsewhere will be determined in the next few years.

The issue is not whether the world can produce more food. Indeed, it would be difficult to put any foreseeable limits on the amount the world's farmers can produce. The question is at what price they will be able to produce it and how this relates to the purchasing power of the poorer segments of humanity.

The environmental, demographic, and economic trends of the 1970s and early 1980s indicate that widespread improvements in human nutrition will require major course corrections. Nothing less than a wholesale reexamination and reordering of social and economic priorities—giving agriculture and family planning the emphasis they deserve—will get the world back on an economic and demographic path that will reduce hunger rather than increase it.

# NOTES

1. Food production data in this chapter are drawn primarily from U.S. Department of Agriculture (USDA), Economic Research Service (ERS), *World Indices of Agricultural and Food Production, 1950–82,* unpublished printout (Washington, D.C., 1983), and from USDA, Foreign Agricultural Service (FAS), *Foreign Agriculture Circulars,* various commodities, Washington, D.C., published monthly.

2. See, for example, Jay Ross, "Africa: The Politics of Hunger" (series), *Washington Post,* June 25-30, 1983.

3. Davidson R. Gwatkin, *Signs of Change in Developing-Country Mortality Trends: The End of an Era?* Development Paper No. 30 (Washington, D.C.: Overseas Development Council, February 1981).

4. United Nations Food and Agriculture Organization (FAO), *Production Yearbook* (Rome: annual, various years).

5. Kenneth B. Young and Jerry M. Coomer, *Effects of Natural Gas Price Increases on Texas High Plains Irrigation, 1976-2025,* Agricultural Report No. 448 (Washington, D.C.: USDA, Economics, Statistics, and Cooperatives Service, 1980).

6. Marshall I. Goldman, *The Spoils of Progress* (Cambridge, Mass.: M.I.T. Press, 1972); Dr. John Gribben, "Climatic Impact of Soviet River Diversions," *New Scientist,* December 6, 1979; Grigorii Voropaev and Aleksei Kosarev, "The Fall and Rise of the Caspian Sea," *New Scientist,* April 8, 1982.

7. Republic of South Africa, *Report of the Science Committee of the President's Council on Demographic Trends in South Africa* (Capetown: The Government Printer, 1983).

8. FAO, *FAO 1977 Annual Fertilizer Review* (Rome: 1978); Paul Andrilenas, USDA, ERS, private communication, December 9, 1982.

9. USDA, *Agricultural Statistics 1982* (Washington, D.C.: U.S. Government Printing Office, 1982).

10. USDA, ERS, "Fertilizer Outlook and Situation," Washington, D.C., December 1982.

11. For example, as farm commodity prices climbed in the mid-1970s, U.S. farmers brought land under the plow that was not suited to cultivation. By 1977 the Soil Conservation Service had identified 17 million acres of land in crops that were losing topsoil so rapidly they would eventually be stripped of all productive value. The agency recommended that farmers convert this land to grass or forests to preserve its production capacities. USDA, *Soil and Water Resources Conservation Act (RCA), Summary of Appraisal, Parts I and II, and Program Report Review Draft 1980* (Washington, D.C., 1980). To reach a figure of real, not just current, U.S. agricultural output, the yield from these 17 million acres, roughly 4 percent of the U.S. cropland total, should be subtracted from overall output.

12. *Economic Report of the President* (Washington, D.C.: U.S. Government Printing Office, 1983).

13. Say, for example, someone had invested in prime midwestern farmland at $2,000 an acre in 1981 and planted it in corn that yielded 110 bushels per acre. With a mortgage at 15 percent, the annual interest payment would be $300 an acre. Yet at the 1981 price of $2.40 a bushel, the total income from each acre would have been $264, not enough to pay the interest, much less the principal or any of the production costs.

14. While net farm income has declined markedly, farm debt has soared. As recently as 1973, net farm income exceeded $30 billion compared with a farm debt of $65 billion, a ratio of roughly one to two. By 1983, net farm income totaled $22 billion, while the farm debt had climbed to $215 billion—close to 10 times income. *Economic Report,* note 12 above.

15. Lester R. Brown, *Man, Land and Food: Looking Ahead at World Food Needs,* Foreign Agriculture Economic Report No. 11 (Washington, D.C.: USDA, ERS, 1963).

16. During the late 1930s, Latin America had a larger grain export surplus than North America, but the region's more rapid rate of population growth soon changed this. Indeed, if the regions had grown at the same rate since 1950, North America's population

in 1983 would be so large that it would consume the entire grain harvest, leaving little or none for export. And North America, too, would now be struggling to maintain food self-sufficiency.

17. USDA, FAS, "Reference Tables on Wheat, Corn and Total Coarse Grains Supply Distributions for Individual Countries," *Foreign Agriculture Circular* FG-19-83, Washington, D.C., July 1983.

18. A similar miscalculation in 1972, when record acreage of U.S. cropland was idled, contributed to the food shortages of the 1972–74 period. Figures on cropland idled in the United States are from Randy Weber, USDA, Agricultural Stabilization and Conservation Service, private communication, August 23, 1983.

19. For a discussion of manipulations of grain exports for political purposes, see Dan Morgan, *Merchants of Grain* (New York: Penguin Books, 1980).

20. India's grain stocks, typically ranging from 11-15 million tons, were drawn down to scarcely 5 million tons during 1973-75, a time of poor harvests. After this harrowing experience, India adopted a target stock level of 21-24 million tons as part of a beefed-up food security system. Bumper harvests in the late 1970s helped the government achieve its target, but after stocks were drawn down to 12-15 million tons during the 1979–80 drought, New Delhi has apparently decided for reasons of cost to maintain a more modest level of grain reserves.

21. Weber, private communication. The grain equivalent of idled cropland is calculated assuming a marginal grain yield of 3.1 metric tons per hectare.

22. For a discussion of the demographic consequences of famine in China, see H. Yuan Tien, "China: Demographic Billionaire," *Population Bulletin* (Washington, D.C.: Population Reference Bureau, 1983); U.S. food aid shipments to India are unpublished data on P.L. 480 from Dewain Rahe, USDA, FAS, private communication, August, 31, 1983.

23. Angola, Benin, Botswana, Cape Verde, Central African Republic, Chad, Ethiopia, Gambia, Ghana, Guinea, Lesotho, Mali, Mauritania, Mozambique,Sao Tome and Principe, Senegal, Somalia, Swaziland, Tanzania, Togo, Zambia, and Zimbabwe. The team of experts concluded that four million tons of emergency grain supplies would be needed to avoid starvation among the 145 million people living in these countries. Michael deCourcy Hinds, "U.S. Giving Peru and Bolivia Millions in Food Aid," *New York Times,* June 2, 1983; FAO and World Food Programme Special Task Force, "Exceptional International Assistance Required in Food Supplies, Agriculture and Animal Husbandry for African Countries in 1983/84," Rome, September 30, 1983.

24. Amartya Sen, "How Is India Doing?" *New York Review of Books,* December 16, 1982.

25. U.S. food aid shipments under P.L. 480 are from Rahe, private communication; International Monetary Fund, Washington, D.C., press release, May 21, 1981.

26. Mac Margolis, "Brazil 'dust bowl' 5 times size of Italy," *Christian Science Monitor,* August 26, 1983.

27. USDA, ERS, note 1 above.

# THE HIDDEN MALICE
# of Malnutrition

**EVEN IF WORLD hunger ended tomorrow, the long-term effects of famine would linger for more than eight generations**

PHOTOGRAPH: IRENE PEARLMAN

### Robert N. Ross

*Robert Ross is a Brookline-based freelance writer.*

Images of starving children are all too familiar: dull eyes, listless expressions, spindly limbs and protruding bellies. Images of their parents have also become commonplace: their faces similarly impassive, except perhaps for the hint of frustration and fear in their eyes.

Throughout history famine has affected young and old alike. An estimated 10 million people died in the great Bengal famine of 1769; perhaps as many as three million people died in the great Irish potato famine; and the civilian deaths during World War II

 From *Bostonia*, February/March 1987, pp. 49-57. Reprinted with permission of *Bostonia* magazine.

caused by food shortages in Russia are beyond all accurate reckoning. The count is also unknown for the famine we have witnessed most recently in the Sahel region of West Africa and in Ethiopia.

But despite the horror of famine and starvation, the effects of these disasters pale by comparison with the effects of the chronic undernutrition from which most of the world's population continually suffers. Short-term starvation, as after an earthquake or during a state of siege, is relatively easy to cure—all it takes is more food. The young are especially likely to survive and recover. The physical, mental and emotional effects of long-term malnutrition, due to an inadequate supply of nutrients, unfortunately do not all respond to short-term fixes. The simple solution of more food might remedy the initial problem, but it cannot fix the physical and physiological effects of malnutrition on future generations.

Malnutrition is more likely to occur as a chronic problem than a single devastating episode. The way of life for undernourished people of the impoverished Third World has been perpetuated for generations. In fact, recent research on the effects of undernutrition in human beings and laboratory animals shows that adults who have a condition of deficient body nutrition from an inadequate intake of food (undernutrition), bear mentally and physically weakened offspring whose newborns are likewise impaired, and so on. This pattern is closer to a downward spiral than a cycle. For surviving becomes increasingly difficult with each new generation of chronically undernourished animals — whether they are laboratory animals deliberately underfed in an experimental setting or poor people trying to get by with meager resources.

Some effects of malnutrition are painfully obvious in children. As parents are well aware, hungry infants can be irritable, restless and difficult to calm. Even trying to feed them seems to make them more irritable. Hunger and starvation, of course, are two very different states. Hunger is

a normal signal to start looking for food. Starvation (the word itself derives from the Old English word meaning to die) is all too common; but it is not natural. Although malnutrition that accompanies long-term starvation causes a variety of physical problems, it may also cause much more subtle mental and emotional difficulties. Language skills develop more slowly in malnourished children. Motor skills are retarded. Crying patterns suggest that something is not right in the central nervous system.

> "In real life, malnutrition is a chronic, long-term problem of surviving. For animals and humans alike, the process of malnutrition is intergenerational."
>
> DR. JANINA GALLER

Much of the research on malnutrition has been carried out on laboratory animals. "But starving experimental animals for short periods of time is not a realistic model of malnutrition," according to Janina R. Galler, M.D., director of the Center for Behavioral Development and Mental Retardation at Boston University School of Medicine. "In real life, malnutrition is a chronic, long-term problem of surviving. For animals and humans alike, the process of malnutrition is intergenerational."

Galler has studied the intergenerational effects of malnutrition on long-term growth and behavior of animals and human beings. In one study that has continued for 18 years, she and her co-principal investigator Dr. Frank Ramsey, Director of the National Nutrition Center in Barbados, have watched Barbadian children grow up. The most disquieting conclusions to be drawn from her Barbados study are that ongoing

under-nutrition affects long-term learning and behavior. More critical is the fact that the effects of malnutrition on learning and behavior may not disappear when the child is eventually fed a normal diet. Even after children have supposedly "recovered" from the most obvious physical effects of malnutrition, their mental and emotional growth remains impaired. Scores on tests of abstract reasoning, logical and relational thinking, language development, IQ and social relations remain well below normal. Reading and writing difficulties persist.

Low scores on achievement tests, poor grades in school, social difficulties and other problems never go away for some children.

In the Barbados study, Galler and Ramsey have been following 314 children since their first year of life. Of these children, 185 were severely malnourished in their first year of life and were later rehabilitated. The comparison group was a group of their classmates with no histories of malnutrition. The children are now grown.

"We were able to document that among the girls suffering from protein-energy malnutrition, there was a delay of about one and one-half years in menarche and sexual maturation." The girls in the study group were undernourished in the first year of their lives but were then provided with a nourishing diet. Nonetheless, as Galler says, "something went awry in the programming of their development and the girls' sexual maturation was delayed."

The delay is interesting because, surprisingly, it shows that the *brain* is severely affected by chronic undernutrition. A poorly understood "clock" in the brain is set to trigger production of hormones that stimulate changes in the reproductive organs and secondary sexual characteristics. Whatever damage the undernutrition did to the girls' brains during that first year of life must have remained dormant until, 10 or 12 years later, that part of the brain was needed to orchestrate the complex events of sexual maturation.

Many growth factors play a role in

a process as complicated as sexual maturation. One of these factors, which can be measured in the blood, is a good reflection of brain processes controlling growth and maturation. The measured substance is an insulin-like growth factor called somato-medin-C/IGF—1. Galler and her co-workers have found that in adolescents with histories of early malnutrition, levels of somatomedin-C/IGF-1 were significantly lower than one would have expected for children at that age. Lower levels of this growth factor alone did not explain the delays in sexual maturation. The abnormally low levels of the growth factor in children who had been malnourished many years earlier suggested how insidious are the long-term effects of such undernutrition.

The Barbados study has also shown that undernutrition disturbs at least one of the brain's hormonal functions. Undernutrition will also disturb how the brain processes information. In particular, undernutrition disturbs attention, even after children have been rehabilitated with a normal diet.

Galler's long-term studies have shown that a person or animal with a previous history of undernutrition has difficulty adapting to new situations. Whatever unknown neuroanatomic, neurophysiologic or neurochemical lesion is produced in the brain by undernutrition, that lesion is responsible for a wide range of subtle problems in the adult. Among the long-term consequences is attentional deficit disorder, or hyperactivity, in school-age children. A hyperactive child has a hard time settling down and is easily distracted.

And chronically malnourished children look very much like certain brain damaged children. Children with the brain condition known as attentional deficit disorder are sometimes hyperactive, impulsive, emotionally labile, subject to temper tantrums and victims of panic attacks. Some children with attentional deficit disorder have one or more of these symptoms; others may have none of them. One symptom they all share, however, is a failure to concentrate in certain settings. Not surprising, children who

cannot concentrate adequately also have learning disabilities.

"The damage to the brain does not simply occur at the time of malnutrition. Rather, there appears to be some impact on the programming of the brain," noted Galler. Even after relieving the brain, the damage continues to occur in a sequential way. "We have measured this by looking at the brain at certain periods when particular populations of cells should be developing. We are finding that certain cells that do not even appear until later in development are adversely affected by earlier malnutrition."

In the United States, these children are diagnosed as having "attentional deficit disorder." "The conditions of attentional deficit disorder and nutrition-related attentional deficits may be similar; but they are not identical." When, for instance, she compared the exploratory behaviors of malnourished animals, hyperactive animals and a comparison group, Galler found subtle but interesting differences among the groups. She found that animals experimentally made hyperactive by depleting the neurotransmitter dopamine in their brains were consistently more hyperactive than the comparison group regardless of what sort of setting they were placed in. In contrast to truly brain damaged hyperactive animals, malnourished animals were not hyperactive as long as they were in a familiar environment.

Unlike the truly brain damaged animals, the malnourished animals eventually settled down to approximately normal behavior. But when placed in a new situation, these chronically malnourished animals became hyperactive. Stress seems to be an important trigger. "If the demands are not made on the animal or the person, we may not see the behavior consequences of chronic malnutrition. When a new situation demands a new adaptive response, however, the signs of abnormal behavior are patently clear."

To understand the long-term effects of undernutrition requires carefully

controlled laboratory experiments. The body of an adult animal, including the human animal, will do everything it can to maintain a steady supply of energy to the brain. Between meals, when sugar and nutrient levels in the body normally fall, and when they rise after eating, the brain's supply of nutrients remains remarkably constant. Even in occasional times of starvation and other stresses, the adult body will sacrifice its supplies of fat, muscle, water and oxygen to keep the brain satisfied.

In babies, a lack of the critical chemical building blocks (specific nutrients) and the energy (calories) needed to fuel the biological processes of life during the critical period of the brain's growth spurt (just before birth and through infancy) is known to distort normal brain growth and development. Scientists have recognized for many years that overall brain size, the number of brain cells, the density of interconnections among the approximately one hundred billion cells in the human brain and the DNA content of those brain cells are all lower than normal in children who have been undernourished during their earliest years of life. Human beings, for instance, are highly vulnerable from the last three months of gestation through the second year of life.

To establish an experimental model of undernutrition, Galler used descendants of a colony of undernourished rats begun in the mid-1960s at the London School of Tropical Hygiene. On July 4, 1973, Galler stepped off an airplane at Logan Airport with 125 rats she had flown first-class from London to her laboratory at MIT. Using this colony as a model of chronic undernutrition typical of most impoverished human populations, Galler was able to study what happens when we stop the cycle of malnutrition and decline by providing adequate nutrition.

The logical question was whether feeding rats coming from a culture of undernutrition would reverse the deficits. According to Galler, that depends on when rehabilitation is begun, how long the animals had been undernourished, what type of malnutrition they suffered and how severe it was. Malnutrition is an insidious process. It breeds problems that make it more difficult for the succeeding generation to survive. Animals born of undernourished mothers are smaller, have a lower birth weight, have increased behavioral problems and suffer such physical problems as increased infectious diseases and a variety of failures to cope adequately with the environment. If the animals are not fed adequately, the decline continues unabated until about the eighth generation.

"At that point," says Galler, "at least as far as we can observe, generations no longer decline. The 10th generation, for example, is not observably worse off than the eighth generation."

"One of the more frightening findings," continues Galler, who followed these animals for 25 generations, "is that when we provided adequate diet after several generations of undernutrition, certain deficits persisted for as long as four generations after rehabilitation."

A person's normal mental and physical growth depends on the fine regulation of literally thousands of metabolic processes by another set of thousands of chemical regulators. In this way, the body makes itself. The genes supply the information, the blueprint that establishes the body plan and the sequence of events by which the plan will be realized. The actual substance of the body, however, comes from outside the body in the form of food.

If the nourishment is not available, the lack can disrupt the body plan as well as the sequence of events. Says Galler, "I have always marveled at how, at a certain point in time, a flower blooms or pubescence presents itself in an individual. It happens like clockwork. It is predictable. The process is set forth at the time of conception, or earlier if we consider the parental impact on the process. Malnutrition probably has the capacity to alter particular programs."

Galler's research is demonstrating conclusively that malnutrition disturbs the organism at a very basic cellular level and that these upsets endure for a long time, perhaps throughout the organism's life. This research suggests that there is no easy remedy for the effects of human malnutrition, especially for the effects of generations of undernutrition. Bringing food into an impoverished region to feed the hungry is, of course, a humanitarian gesture. It goes without saying that adequate nutrition is better than not having enough

But we now see from research like Galler's that it would be a mistake to believe that supplying adequate food will, in itself, solve the problems associated with chronic undernutrition. The Bible and Greek tragedies recognized a truth that we in the 20th century prefer to ignore: Some problems take generations to work out.

# Grains of hope

*Edward C. Wolf*

**EDWARD C. WOLF** *is a Senior Researcher with Worldwatch Institute, Washington, D.C., a non-profit research organization which was created to focus attention on global problems and is funded by private foundations and United Nations organizations. This article has been extracted from* Beyond the Green Revolution: New Approaches for Third World Agriculture, *a Worldwatch Paper published in late 1986.*

FROM 1920 to 1950, agriculture in industrial countries was dominated by mechanical technologies that dramatically increased the amount of food that could be produced per worker and per hour. Shortly after the Second World War, the mechanical age gave way to the chemical age as farmers worldwide began to adopt artificial fertilizers and synthetic chemical pesticides, which vastly expanded their harvests per acre. Biotechnologies shift the focus of research toward crop plants themselves.

So far, advances have been made in industrial countries, where public scrutiny is intense. The environmental risks posed by releasing gene-spliced microbes or plants into the environment remain poorly understood. Developing regulations and guidelines for the newly emerging technologies has led to a contentious public debate about genetic engineering. In the United States, debate has centred on proposals to release bacteria modified to retard the formation of frost on strawberry and potato plants. Because the bacteria could reproduce in the natural environment and thus spread beyond the fields where they were released, predicting environmental impacts is both more crucial and more complex a task than with many other technologies. Developing the "predictive ecology" that critics say is necessary for thorough environmental review, and drawing up regulations that guard against the uncertainties, will slow the marketing of commercial biotechnology products to farmers in industrial countries.

The genetic engineering of plants is far more complex than modifying microbes, but it is also less controversial on environmental grounds. Crops with modified traits are under a farmer's direct control, and their reproduction and spread in the environment are both slower and more predictable. Crop characteristics such as drought-tolerance, ability to withstand salty water, and pest resistance—the traits that have always concerned breeders—are a likely focus of the new technologies.

Given the ability to modify virtually any plant characteristic and to tailor plants in precisely defined ways, biotechnology would seem to offer tools well-suited to agricultural development strategies that emphasize resource efficiency and farming's internal resources. For example, it should eventually be possible to modify a plant's physiology to improve its efficiency in photosynthesis, enabling grains to produce more carbohydrate and thus higher yields. The adaptations that allow some plants to lose very little water through their leaves in transpiration, transferred to more widely grown crops, could reduce irrigation needs. Developments like these could indeed reduce pressures on marginal lands and perhaps eliminate the need for costly capital investments in water supply projects.

There is nothing in the nature of biotechnologies that renders them inherently appropriate to a strategy of efficiency and regeneration, however. Many biotechnology innovations pose trade-offs rather than clear-cut benefits. Although increasing photosynthetic efficiency could increase yields, it would also be likely to lead to accelerated depletion of soil nutrients and heavier dependence on artificial fertilizers.

The most significant factor that will affect the direction of agricultural biotechnology is the rapid shift of research from the public to the private sector. This is especially evident in the United States. For nearly a century, public agricultural experiment stations and land grant universities sponsored by the US Department of Agriculture (USDA) performed most agricultural research. Private seed companies often use the plant varieties developed by government-supported breeders. Over the last three decades, however, the private sector has assumed control of research efforts. Private companies now administer two-thirds of US agricultural research.

In biotechnology, the deck is stacked even further in favour of the private sector. USDA's Agricultural Research Service and Co-operative State Research Service support most work in agricultural biotechnology, and these two federal programmes spent less than $90 million on biotechnology research in 1984-85. Monsanto, which has the largest but by no means the only plant biotechnology research programme among private US corporations, has already invested $100 million in agricultural biotechnology development. Biotechnologies that affect agriculture in the years ahead will have a decidedly private-sector cast. With the important exceptions

**For subsistence farmers in developing countries, biotechnology has much to offer. But will the potential be fulfilled?**

Reproduced from the *Unesco Courier,* March 1987, pp. 22–24, by permission.

*Below, cassava (manioc) plants are protected from pests by ventilated bags as part of a biological pest-control project being carried out at the International Institute of Tropical Agriculture (IITA) at Ibadan (Nigeria). Some 200 million Africans rely on cassava for about 50 per cent of their calories. The IITA has developed disease-resistant cassava varieties for distribution in a number of African countries.*

Photo G. Tartagni-FAO

of mechanization and the development of hybrid corn, that has not generally been true of important innovations in agriculture.

Leaving research priorities to the marketplace may eclipse promising opportunities. Research efforts on crops will be proportional to the value of the crop and the size of the market. Because improving crops for small farmers in developing countries means producing low-cost agronomic innovations, many of which must be site-specific and thus not suitable for mass-marketing, crop improvement for the vast majority of the world's farmers offers little profit. Few private companies are likely to enter such an unpromising market. Consequently, investigations of minor crops like sorghum and millet, grown primarily by Third World subsistence farmers, will be neglected.

National research programmes and the international research centres have an obvious stake in applying biotechnology. Refinements in plant breeding, technologies for germplasm storage and for plant evaluation and propagation, and new alternatives in pest control, are exactly the kinds of innovations scientists need to extend research on developing-country

food crops. It took decades of work to produce high-yielding varieties of wheat and rice. With biotechnology, comparable improvements in millet, sorghum, cassava, or tropical legumes could come more quickly.

The private sector domination of biotechnology raises questions about the role new technologies will play in international research programmes. Private companies may become competitors with the international agricultural research centres sponsored by the Washington-based Consultative Group on International Agricultural Research (CGIAR), particularly when it comes to improvements in major, widely traded crops like wheat and rice. The full exchange of scientific information that is essential to the international centres may be curtailed if it appears to compromise proprietary corporate research. Moreover, international centres may increasingly have to purchase or license new technologies that were formerly freely available through public channels. Finally, private firms will compete with the centres for scientific talent, and the centres may be unable to match the salaries, facilities and security that corporate laboratories offer.

Uncertainties cloud the national bio-

technology programmes as well. A few developing countries, notably Indonesia, the Philippines, and Thailand, have established national programmes in agricultural biotechnology. The Philippines views its programme as the first step towards an industrialization strategy based on biological materials that can help free the country from dependence on imported oil. Philippine scientists hope to use crop residues and byproducts as raw materials to produce liquid fuels and industrial chemicals, and to develop food-processing industries with biotechnology methods. W.G. Padolina, of the National Institute of Biotechnology and Applied Microbiology at the University of the Philippines, writes, "The national strategy is to transform biomass biologically into food, fuel, fertilizers and chemicals."

Achieving these goals is certain to be costly. Few countries can afford the investment in equipment that major biotechnology programmes entail, and some countries lack sufficient numbers of trained scientists to staff such programmes. Agricultural biotechnology contrasts sharply in this regard with conventional plant breeding programmes, which require relatively modest capital investment.

# Tomatomation
## Japan's high-tech food factories

### Koichibara Hiroshi

**KOICHIBARA HIROSHI,** *Japanese economist, is a member of the Unesco secretariat.*

THE harnessing of high technology to vegetable farming may be about to trigger a new agricultural revolution in Japan, where some large manufacturers are already offering fully automatic "factories" in which vegetables are grown in a computer-controlled artificial environment. In their use of automation and high technology these facilities resemble automobile or electronics plants, but instead of automobiles or video tape recorders their mass production lines produce fresh vegetables, regardless of season or climate.

Strictly speaking, today's factory farming technology is based not on biotechnology but on applying industrial production management techniques to conventional agricultural engineering. The aim is to use artificially controlled environments to grow plants rapidly and efficiently rather than improve the adaptation of plants to natural conditions. Such ideas have already been applied to poultry farming, egg production systems, and even the production of *foie gras*. Factory farms may thus make a big impact on conventional agriculture since they provide planned cultivation regardless of weather, season, climate or soil.

The essential element in this new development is hydroponics, the cultivation of plants in nutritive solutions. Factory farms are air-conditioned, and high-pressure sodium lamps provide twenty-four-hour-a-day illumination. The density of carbon dioxide, oxygen, temperature and humidity are controlled by a computer to maintain an optimum growing environment.

The hardware used in this process is not new. It is readily available from manufacturers of electrical consumer goods, and this may be the reason why Japanese electrical conglomerates are active in this field. Companies in Denmark, the United States and Austria are also experimenting with vegetable factories but for the moment the Japanese seem to be leading the field.

In 1985, a "supertomato" plant was displayed in the Japanese government-sponsored pavilion at an international exhibition held in Japan, Tsukuba Expo. '85 (see the *Unesco Courier,* March 1985). This was a major success for a hydroponic culture system developed after many years of research by a Japanese agronomist, Nozawa Shigeo. The growth of the plant was accelerated in a nutritive solution which replaced soil and in an artificially controlled environment. As a result the plant produced more than 13,000 tomatoes during the six months of the Expo.

Daiei, Japan's biggest supermarket chain, has installed a factory farm next to its store in the Tokyo suburb of Fanabashi. This experimental facility, constructed in co-operation with Hitachi Ltd. to grow lettuce for sale in the adjoining supermarket, may be the world's first commercial factory farm using full automatic hydroponic culture technology. The system produces some 130 heads of lettuce and other green vegetables per day (some 47,000 per year) on a floor space of no more than 66 square metres. Grown from seed, the lettuce is big enough for harvesting in only five weeks, 3.5 times faster than plants cultivated using conventional methods.

In this futuristic factory, the sun is replaced by artificial twenty-four-hour lighting, soil with nutritive solution and farmers with a micro-computer. The crop is tasty and free from pesticides and herbicides, and is in great demand, regardless of the price tag, which is double that of conventionally grown lettuce.

In Mitsubishi Electric's Amagasaki laboratory, a prototype food factory assembly line succeeded in growing lettuce seedlings from 2 grams to 130 grams in 15 days—6 times faster than the natural growth rate. With specially developed fluorescent lamps, the photosynthetic ratio is said to be better than that of the sun. Sprouts cloned from the tissues of mature plants start at one end of a conveyor and move along at the rate of 20 centimetres a day.

In March 1986 Japanese National Railways (JNR) built two experimental vegetable factories, each with a size of 50 square metres and a construction cost of $60,000. Since May, each factory has been producing 120 heads of lettuce a day. Experiments are being carried out on the cultivation of other vegetables such as tomatoes, cabbage, asparagus, melon and green peppers. In the case of JNR, electric power supplied by its own power plants can be efficiently used at night when demand is low, and open spaces beneath the overhead railway or abandoned tunnels can be utilized as sites.

Artificial lighting and computers are not essential elements in factory farming. Hydroponic food factories can be installed in developing countries where food factories may be most needed. Matsushita Electric has, for example, installed a vegetable factory with minimal automation in the Maldives. The system, which has a plastic roof that keeps out harmful sunlight rays, produces 50 tonnes of vegetables a year, using about one-fifth of the water needed by field-grown plants.

Vegetable factories can offer various advantages: planned production, quality control, low labour costs, clean products. They use space efficiently and provide stable production regardless of climatic and seasonal variations. However, high electricity costs are a severe drawback. Artificial lighting is said to account for 90 per cent of the Mitsubishi system's operating costs.

On the other hand, there can be no doubt that research will continue in the search for breakthroughs in the development of energy-efficient lighting systems, the achievement of a higher photosynthetic ratio than in the natural environment, and in the applications of biotechnologies to factory farming.

It is to be hoped that food factory technology will not be monopolized by a group of industrialized countries and that it will be applied in those countries which need it most.

Reproduced from the *Unesco Courier,* March 1987, pp. 17–19, by permission.

Rethinking Energy Security

# New Directions for Oil Policy

## Robert W. Fri

**ROBERT W. FRI** is President and Senior Fellow of Resources for the Future in Washington, D.C. This article is adapted from a paper presented at a seminar at the Oklahoma State University Center for Energy Research in Stillwater on November 11, 1986.

In the headlines and on Capitol Hill, the scent of energy crisis is in the air. Oil imports are rising, and the Organization of Petroleum Exporting Countries (OPEC) is talking like a cartel again. Brave experts are once more forecasting oil prices, a hazardous occupation at best. The supply of domestic oil is down, but the supply of energy conferences is growing. There is even a major new government energy study giving rise to the unsettling prospect of a renewed energy policy debate. It seems in many ways like old times.

But times, in fact, have changed. Now the oil and gas industry is in despair, calling for higher oil prices with almost the vigor once applied to opposing price controls. On the other hand, consumers are happier now, preferring cheap gasoline to gas lines. Policymakers are talking profoundly of energy security, not of the energy independence of yesteryear.

So which is it? Are these good times or bad? Are oil prices too low or just right? Is the oil patch disintegrating or

only adjusting to a new reality? Is it time to act or—given the record of past energy policy—should we instead pray for inaction?

This article is an attempt to sort out these issues—if not to resolve them, then at least to help think about them usefully. In order to guide future policy, we must both remember what we learned about managing energy problems in times past and understand how times have changed. Accordingly, this discussion begins by examining what we know about oil markets and the players in those markets. It then assesses the implications of this knowledge for national energy security, and suggests some directions for energy policy. The concentration on oil is intended, and other energy sources are dealt with to a much lesser extent.

### Fundamental Forces at Work

Predicting the course of energy is a notoriously chancy business. The subject is large and complex, and there is

much we do not know about it. Nevertheless, there are a few fundamentals we do understand. Before attempting an educated guess at how our energy future will unfold, it is important to review the fundamental forces that will shape it.

*The world's principal reserves of low-cost oil are concentrated in OPEC, and this concentration is increasing.* In 1985 over three-quarters of proven reserves in the non-Communist world were in the hands of OPEC (see Table 1). The cost of producing the oil from these reserves has been the lowest in the world—oil from U.S. reserves, for example, is comparatively costly. Moreover, the non-Communist world outside OPEC is using up its oil reserves faster than is OPEC. Barring any major new discoveries, reserves will increasingly be concentrated within OPEC.

There are also concentrations of oil reserves within OPEC itself. Eighty percent of OPEC's reserves are in the six countries that have the longest reserve life—time that reserves will produce at capacity (see Table 2). It is interesting to note that in 1985 the other OPEC countries were producing their reserves faster than these six nations. This situation, if it persists, could further concentrate OPEC reserves.

The concentration of large, low-cost oil reserves in a few countries is the fundamental fact about oil, and it is not likely to change any time soon. The inescapable physical reason for this conclusion is that 26 of the 37 supergiant (greater than 5 billion barrels) oil fields ever discovered are found in OPEC countries. Big fields mean big, low-cost reserves, especially when they have already been found.

*Non-OPEC countries have and will continue to find smaller, higher-cost oil reserves.* In contrast to the situation in OPEC, the United States has more-limited oil reserves. In 1985 proven U.S. reserves of around 30 billion barrels produced about 9 million barrels per day. In 1986 alone production dropped about 7 percent, much of it lost forever in marginal, "stripper wells" that have been closed down. By the end of the century, these existing reserves will support only 1 or 2 million barrels per day of production, even at relatively high market prices. New production must come mainly from new discoveries and improved recovery techniques.

The United States does have substantial potential crude oil resources still to be discovered and tapped, although even these do not match the proven, commercially producible reserves of OPEC. In addition to the 30 billion barrels of proven U.S. reserves, approximately 100 billion barrels of undiscovered oil remain to be found in the United States, and about 220 billion barrels of oil are available through enhanced oil recovery (EOR) technologies.[1] This total of 320 billion barrels of potential resources compares to OPEC's proven reserves of 500 billion barrels and to the reserves of the six key OPEC countries of 400 billion barrels.

Although it is encouraging that potential U.S. oil resources are relatively large, they are likely to be costly to produce. Most of the 100 billion barrels of undiscovered resources lie in small fields.[2] These fields will generally be smaller than 25 million barrels, and two-

**TABLE 1**

## OIL SUPPLIES IN THE NON-COMMUNIST WORLD, 1985

| REGION | RESERVES (percent) | PRODUCTION (percent) |
|---|---|---|
| OPEC countries | 77 | 38 |
| United States | 5 | 25 |
| Other countries in non-Communist world | 18 | 37 |

SOURCE: Conoco, Inc., *World Energy Outlook Through 2000* (Wilmington, Del.: Conoco, Inc., 1986).

thirds are likely to be smaller than 10 million barrels. In contrast, two-thirds of the oil found in the United States to date lies in fields that contain more than 25 million barrels.

Access to these scattered reserves will require extensive drilling. The current finding rate for oil and gas in the United States is about 40 barrels of oil-equivalent per foot of drilling.[3] Assuming this rate holds up (and it may not), over 4 billion feet of drilling would be required to discover as much oil and gas as the first 500 million feet of drilling did in the United States. If, as is possible, the proportion of oil in the resource base is dropping relative to gas, even more drilling will be required to find this much oil.

We already know where to find over 60 percent of our oil reserves, however—it is the oil left behind in existing fields. Reclaiming this oil requires enhanced recovery techniques such as water or steam flooding and chemical treatment to loosen the remaining oil and bring it to the surface.

Because more extensive drilling and increased use of enhanced oil recovery are expensive, most new U.S. production will be at least as costly to find and develop as were the already high-cost proven reserves. Since the United States must rely on new production for most of its domestic oil, this nation will remain a high-cost producer. Conventional wisdom holds that a price above $25.00 per barrel (in 1985 dollars) will be required to sustain a significant exploration and production effort in the United States.

A similar price level seems needed to deploy current EOR technologies.

Between 1979 and 1985, non-OPEC production outside the United States grew by almost 30 percent. This was a major cause of the decline in OPEC production during that period. Unfortunately, these reserves do not appear to have much more growth potential. Most studies project that production in other non-Communist countries will be flat at best, and will possibly decline by 5 or 10 percent by the end of the century if prices stay below $25.00 per barrel. These are somewhat shaky estimates, but they are consistent with the view that remaining crude resources in the non-Communist world are remote or deep, and therefore more costly to develop. In any case, it would not seem prudent to assume that large, low-cost reserves will be found outside OPEC.

*The need for revenue largely explains OPEC behavior as a cartel.* Given the pivotal long-term role played by low-cost OPEC reserves, particularly those owned by the six key countries, it would be useful to know how OPEC will manage its affairs. No one can be sure, of course, but the need for oil revenues goes a long way in shaping OPEC's behavior.

Although all OPEC countries want oil revenue, their ability to generate it varies widely. There are orders-of-magnitude differences in oil wealth among the six key producers (see Table 3). To maximize their revenues, the less-wealthy countries want both to produce at capacity and to charge the highest possible price. Within limits, however, the Arab Gulf countries can generate adequate oil revenues at less than full-capacity production.

These wealth differences suggest the conditions under which OPEC can be an effective cartel. A true cartel is a compact of suppliers of a given commodity that endeavors to set the level of supply, to apportion sales territories, and to establish the price—in effect, it rigs the market. It can do so successfully when its members exercise control over the bulk of production, when there is little chance that output will expand outside the cartel, and when consumers will be for all practical purposes locked into

*Low oil prices have severely curtailed exploration for new oil reserves that has recently been concentrated in offshore areas. (Photo: DOE)*

haps 3 million barrels of production off the market, the market is in an oversupply situation, and consequently, the war has had little effect on oil supply or price.

*World oil markets are more efficient than before.* On balance, the cost and location of oil reserves and the forces that shape OPEC behavior have not changed very much since the late 1970s. In contrast, another fundamental factor—the structure of oil markets—has changed significantly. Three changes in the crude oil market have been of particular importance.

The creation of an active futures market has reduced speculative pressures in the market for current oil by allowing paper trading in oil to be produced at a later date. This has attenuated major price swings. As well, the panic to build up inventories when minor disruptions of worldwide oil production take place is greatly reduced by an efficient spot market in which large amounts of oil are immediately available. On the other hand, although efficient oil markets tend to moderate larger price swings, they also tend to exacerbate day-to-day price fluctuations. This result is characteristic of all commodity markets.

The overall energy market has also become more competitive. The last decade has seen considerable investment in fuel-switching capability, particularly by industry and utilities. Fuel switching enables the customer to move from one source of fuel to another (for example, from oil to gas) in response to minor price differentials. Open access to use of gas pipelines and increased competition in gas markets have put further pressure on oil prices by bringing affordable competitors into the marketplace. Even extensive bulk transfers of electric power are becoming more commonplace, and may add to the competitive pressures.

Netback pricing, in which the price paid to the producer is what is left after the various middlemen have taken their

buying the particular product at whatever price is charged.

Like most cartels, OPEC will be less effective when all its members must abide by production quotas in order to maintain high prices. In this circumstance, the poorer members tend to overproduce to maximize revenue. Quota violations lead to price instability, internal controversy, and, as was the case in early 1986, retaliatory action by the wealthy producers. So long as total OPEC production is well below capacity, this situation will persist.

Unlike the situation of some other cartels, however, capacity production by all its members is not prerequisite to OPEC's effectiveness as a price setter. Indeed, working cartel control of price is probably attainable when OPEC is producing at around 80 percent of its capacity. At this level of production, for

example, all but the three key Arab producers (Saudi Arabia, Kuwait, and the United Arab Emirates) can produce at full capacity. At $20 per barrel (in 1985 dollars), a production level of 60 percent capacity would probably provide adequate revenues for the relatively small populations of these three countries. Thus, everybody is happy, and OPEC can concentrate on being a cartel.

A second important consequence of the need for revenue is the apparent propensity to keep producing oil despite the inherent political instability in the Middle East. Press notices notwithstanding, the 1973 and 1979 events did not represent very large production disruptions. Indeed, in the last 35 years, only two events have seriously depressed production: the Iranian revolution in the early 1950s and the current Iran-Iraq war. Although the Iran-Iraq war has taken per-

## 3. NATURAL RESOURCES: Energy

### TABLE 2
### THE SIX OPEC COUNTRIES WITH LARGEST LONG-LIVED RESERVES

| COUNTRY | RESERVE LIFE AT CAPACITY PRODUCTION (years) | 1985 RESERVES (percent) | 1985 PRODUCTION (percent) |
|---|---|---|---|
| Kuwait | 123 | | |
| Saudi Arabia | 44 | | |
| United Arab Emirates | 37 | | |
| **Average** | | **58** | **33** |
| Iraq | 83 | | |
| Iran | 52 | | |
| Libya | 42 | | |
| **Average** | | **23** | **28** |
| Other OPEC countries | 8–35 | 19 | 39 |

SOURCE: Groppe, Long, & Littell (Houston, Tex.), private communication with author, fall 1986.

cut from the consumer price, closely links crude prices to product markets. As long as it lasts, netback pricing quickly carries the effect of product market competition back to crude markets, adding to short-run price volatility. This is a significant change from the more rigid markets of the 1970s, and it is no surprise that dropping netback pricing is a major OPEC goal.

*The factors that shape oil supply and demand change slowly*. It should be noted that making large changes in oil supply and demand requires large investments that take time to put in place. These long lead times have several consequences. They result in relatively low short-run elasticities in terms of demand that complicate adjustment to oil price changes. Long lead times also increase uncertainty, and uncertainty reduces the

propensity of both producers and consumers to invest in cost-saving measures. In fact, it appears that such underinvestment is now limiting future capability to adapt to higher oil prices, just as overinvestment on the supply side has helped create today's distress in the U.S. oil industry.

## Implications for Energy Security

The U.S. Department of Energy defines energy security as meaning that "adequate supplies of energy at reasonable cost are physically available to U.S. consumers from both domestic and foreign sources. It means that the Nation is less vulnerable to disruptions in energy supply and that it is better prepared to handle them if they should occur."[4] At least the first part of this statement is a

reasonable working definition, and it is useful to ask how the fundamental forces at work today in oil markets affect the price and availability of oil supplies from domestic and foreign sources. The question of vulnerability is more complex, and will be discussed later.

### Oil Prices

The fundamentals of the marketplace suggest that prices are likely to remain moderately unstable and relatively low well into the 1990s. There are two main reasons for this conclusion. First, while OPEC will try to impose production quotas on its members to increase prices, until excess worldwide oil production capacity is dried up, market forces and some OPEC countries' revenue needs will work to send prices down again. Second, competitive product markets will continue to put considerable pressure on oil prices. Netback pricing enhances this pressure, but a return to posted prices will not eliminate it.

After excess worldwide production capacity dries up, OPEC will be in at least a theoretical position to impose effective cartel control of oil prices. It is difficult to forecast how OPEC will behave and, indeed, even whether OPEC can behave effectively. However, the following conclusions seem reasonable:

- It would be in OPEC's self-interest to set prices at a level that would permit OPEC both to satisfy its own revenue needs and to maintain price stability. Such a price would be somewhere below the marginal cost of significant production elsewhere, perhaps in the neighborhood of $25 to $30 per barrel (in 1985 dollars).
- Even with this enlightened pricing policy, there would still be some price instability owing to long investment lead times in producing and consuming industries, and the consequent difficulties in fine-tuning a stable market clearing price where supply and demand are in balance.
- Greater price instability would be caused by a greedy OPEC attempting to set the price too high. This could happen if one of the revenue-requiring countries

### TABLE 3
### OIL AVAILABILITY IN THE SIX MAJOR OPEC COUNTRIES

| COUNTRY | 1985 RESERVES PER CAPITA (thousand barrels) | PRODUCTION CAPACITY PER CAPITA (barrels per year) |
|---|---|---|
| United Arab Emirates | 32 | 858 |
| Kuwait | 55 | 437 |
| Saudi Arabia | 18 | 409 |
| **Average** | **24** | **452** |
| Libya | 6.4 | 153 |
| Iraq | 3.0 | 36 |
| Iran | 1.2 | 22 |
| **Average** | **1.9** | **33** |

SOURCE: Groppe, Long, & Littell (Houston, Tex.), private communication with author, fall 1986.

(for instance, Iran) were in control of OPEC. However, an excessively high price would last no longer in the future than it did after 1979. Indeed, with the present market structure, it would probably last less long.

• In any case, so-called crises that drive up oil prices are less probable now than they were in the past. Owing to the sizable spot market that allows for efficient resource allocation, selective embargoes are simply not credible, as they seemed to be in 1973. Both the spot market and futures trading suggest that the speculative excesses and inventory panics of 1979 are much less probable than they were in the past.

## U.S. Oil Imports

The most recent studies conclude that significant levels of U.S. oil imports seem inevitable. Estimates of U.S. imports derived by four different studies making seven assumptions about price levels (see Table 4) indicate the reasons for predicting rising imports. The studies posit a domestic demand that tends to stay flat or increase somewhat over the next decade. At the same time, because the U.S. oil industry faces limited reserves and a high marginal cost of production, U.S. production levels may decline significantly through the end of the century. Thus, U.S. imports will rise to half or more of total consumption, even at quite high prices.

The consistency among the studies' figures is remarkable and, given past experience with energy forecasts, even alarming. It appears that most of these models assume demand elasticities that reflect current experience, and that they base production levels and reserve additions on current costs of finding and development. Like most forecasts, however, these studies do not incorporate technological advances that could alter basic supply-and-demand responses to price changes. Nevertheless, their consistency reflects an important consensus on baseline conditions that is hard to dismiss.

Although U.S. production will undoubtedly fall, there is still plenty of oil around. Thus, despite the strong possibility of large U.S. oil imports, the supply of oil from foreign sources is ade-

**TABLE 4**
### VARIOUS PROJECTIONS OF U.S. OIL IMPORTS BY 1995

| | PRICE PER BARREL (1985 dollars) | U.S. OIL DEMAND | U.S. CRUDE OIL PRODUCTION[a] | U.S. OIL IMPORTS | COST OF IMPORTS (billions 1985 dollars) |
|---|---|---|---|---|---|
| | | (million barrels per day) | | | |
| Aspen | 16 | 22 | 4 | 16 | 93 |
| National Petroleum Council | 17 | 19 | 6 | 11 | 84 |
| Dept. of Energy | 22 | 18 | 6 | 10 | 80 |
| Gas Research Institute | 23 | 17 | 7 | 9 | 75 |
| National Petroleum Council | 28 | 17 | 7 | 8 | 82 |
| Dept. of Energy | 28 | 17 | 7 | 8 | 82 |
| Aspen | 34 | 16 | 5 | 9 | 112 |

[a]Net of natural gas liquids

SOURCES: Aspen Institute for Humanistic Studies, *The Cost of Cheap Oil* (Queenstown, Md.: Aspen Institute, 1987); National Petroleum Council, *Factors Affecting U.S. Oil and Gas Outlook* (Washington, D.C.: National Petroleum Council, 1987); U.S. Department of Energy, *Energy Security: A Report to the President of the United States* (Washington, D.C.: Department of Energy, 1987); Gas Research Institute, *1986 Baseline Projection of U.S. Energy Supply and Demand* (Washington, D.C.: GRI Strategic Analysis and Energy Forecasting Division, 1986).

quate. Furthermore, efficient markets and ample transportation make foreign oil physically available. Without a disruption of some sort, importing oil does not by itself much degrade our energy security.

## Domestic Oil Supply

The outlook for U.S. prices does not appear especially favorable for domestic oil supply, given the outlook into the 1990s for moderately unstable and relatively low crude-oil prices. Furthermore, competition in product markets will remain intense for the marginal customer (chiefly industry) who can switch sources of energy, placing further pressure on prices. Because of this situation, the investment climate for domestic oil and gas exploration and production is poor.

Although price is important, there is an even more central implication of this outlook for domestic oil supply. The U.S. oil industry will shrink significantly from its current production of less than 9 million barrels per day to at most 6 to 7 million barrels per day by the turn of the century (see Table 4). Something in the neighborhood of 150 million feet per year of exploration drilling would be required to replace reserves at this level of production, and this level of drilling is on the low side for the industry. And, since the oil industry will re-

main in the unfavorable position of being a high-cost producer in a competitive commodity market, things are more likely to go wrong than right.

The decline in production of the U.S. oil industry since mid-1985 is in all likelihood merely the first step in the readjustment toward a smaller industry. Excessively high oil prices in the early 1980s helped make this step an unpleasantly large one. In this sense, the worst may be over, but the process is not.

## Implications for Vulnerability

The heart of the energy security matter is whether the foregoing outlook for oil price and supply makes us more or less "vulnerable." The answer is that we *are* vulnerable, and that we should be seriously considering policies to make us less so. But first we need a clear idea about what our vulnerabilities are and what causes them. Unfortunately, ideas on these subjects—especially the notion that importing oil is the root of the problems—are not always as clear as they should be for policymaking purposes.

Consider first the possibility of a supply disruption as a source of energy vulnerability. Since efficient markets make minor upsets less worrisome, consider a disruption of a magnitude and permanence that would actually make oil unavailable for essential uses in the United

States for several months or more. In today's world, such an event seems fairly remote. Given the propensity to produce that is characteristic of OPEC, such an event would require that worldwide oil production be essentially at capacity, and that a major OPEC exporter cut production significantly for an extended period. Such an action would, however, be adverse to that country's need for revenues and would probably require another country's imposing its will on the exporter.

Thus, aside from acts of God, a real supply disruption would most likely be accompanied by a political event considerably more profound than a Middle East internal revolution, war, or assassination. The U.S. policy response to such an event would go well beyond energy policy. About all that U.S. energy policy can do to avert disruption is buy insurance in the form of the Strategic Petroleum Reserve. Encouraging the development of non-OPEC reserves both to postpone the day when worldwide capacity is reached and to diversify sources of imports is also useful, but this may not be a permanent solution.

Short of a significant supply disruption, adverse economic impacts constitute the main source of vulnerability to excessive reliance on oil in our energy supply. In principle, three kinds of economic effects are important:

- *Income effects*. In paying for imported oil, we transfer wealth out of the United States to oil producers, thus reducing income available to create domestic demand.

- *Adjustment effects*. When oil prices rise, the economy has to adjust to this more costly input. The adjustment process both changes the size and composition of the gross national product (GNP) and alters the price of other inputs such as labor. If this adjustment process does not go smoothly, economic disruption can be more serious. Sharp changes in oil prices exacerbate frictions in the process and are thus to be avoided.

- *Distributional effects*. When prices rise, wealth moves from consumers to producers. This makes consumers unhappy, whether the producer is at home or abroad.

*Since U.S. oil is expensive to produce, most experts believe U.S. imports of less-expensive OPEC oil will continue to grow during the next decade. (Photo: DOE)*

Adjustment problems depend heavily on the rate of change in oil prices, while income and distributional effects involve wealth transfers that depend largely on the average price level. Price instability seems likely for the foreseeable future, and price levels may well rise significantly sometime in the mid-1990s. Thus, these economic effects are quite likely to happen and are worth worrying about. Adverse economic effects seem to be a much more important worry than does an outright supply disruption. Indeed, supply disruptions—save for the catastrophic kind—will probably play themselves out as economic disruptions triggered by price shocks caused by the supply squeeze.

In trying to control the causes of these adverse effects, policymakers should not concentrate on oil imports alone. This is because both supply disruptions and the adverse economic effects depend on three factors: worldwide oil supply and demand, total U.S. oil demand, and U.S. oil imports.

Worldwide oil supply and demand determine oil prices. And if demand is large enough to use up available production capacity, it allows OPEC to behave like an effective cartel. The United States would still suffer the consequent price (or even disruption) effects whether it imports any oil or not.

Total domestic oil demand determines the severity of the effect on the GNP. The more oil we use, imported or not, the larger our input costs become as prices rise. Distributional effects also depend on total demand, because consumers lose wealth when prices rise, no matter who gets it. Of course, if the wealth stays inside the United States, aggregate domestic demand would be less affected.

U.S. imports thus play a limited if important role, chiefly in determining the income effect. The more oil we buy, the more money we send abroad. Even here, however, gross wealth transfers depend on price as well as volume, and this has a leavening effect on aggregate wealth transfer. Price and volume effects can offset one another (see Table 4).

From a policy standpoint, the crucial factor is managing the size and composition of total domestic demand. Not only does domestic demand directly determine much of the adverse economic effect, it is also a principal determinant of the amount of U.S. oil imports and hence the worldwide supply-demand balance. Total domestic demand bears importantly on every aspect of our energy vulnerability.

A second important but unclear point is the relationship between oil market behavior and the cited adverse effects. Under what conditions, for example, does OPEC production restraint move from an oil-pricing problem into a deep and sustained supply disruption? The answer is not obvious, but is of central importance in managing our Strategic Petroleum Reserve (SPR) and similar reserve stocks in cooperating International Energy Agency countries.

More important, the impact of oil price shocks on economic performance is becoming less certain. Economic effects, after all, are perhaps the main reason for worrying about energy policy. However, recent research casts doubt on our understanding of how oil shocks produce these effects.[5]

In brief, neither energy's share of the GNP nor the slow rate at which energy consumption patterns change accounts for the sharp changes in production, productivity, unemployment, or infla-

tion that occurred in 1974 and 1979.[6] It appears that something amplifies the effect of oil price swings. Two candidates appear to be wage rigidities and capital obsolescence. Thus, economic policy could be at least as important as energy policy in mitigating the effects of oil shocks.

Further research is needed to clarify these matters. None of this work indicates that high oil prices or excessive imports are a good idea. However, the results to date do suggest that some care should be taken in developing policy responses to energy issues, especially policies that impose additional rigidities on the economy.

## Directions for Energy Policy

Even with these cautions, there appear to be several useful directions for energy policy—particularly as related to oil—and a number of possible roles for government.

First, it is important to reduce the cost of additional oil production, both in the United States and elsewhere. The lower the cost of significant new production, the lower the maximum stable price that the cartel can maintain. This new production may be located largely outside the United States, but since we live in a world oil market, that makes little difference. Indeed, diversification of for-

eign sources can further limit our vulnerability to supply disruption.

Because new oil reserves are harder to find and develop than previous production, and because enhanced oil recovery can play a major role in new production, technology will be critical in reducing the costs of new oil. Ordinarily, technology development is the province of the private sector, and will remain so. However, the oil industry is slashing research budgets, and this may cause more long-term harm than cutting back on exploration. Some government-sponsored research may thus be appropriate, especially in basic geosciences and enhanced oil recovery.

Second, the United States should continue to reduce its reliance on oil. Reducing the role of oil in our industrial output, for example, will mitigate the possible adverse effects of oil price changes on the economy. Conservation in the residential, commercial, and transportation sectors—especially transportation—reduces the exposure of consumers to wealth losses. And the overall reduction in U.S. demand helps put off the day when the OPEC cartel can become effective. Only the more efficient and productive use of energy has such a broadly favorable effect on the sources of energy vulnerability and thus its importance cannot be overemphasized.

Price is the primary motivation of

conservation, so the government role in this area may be limited. Private research groups like the Gas Research Institute and the Electric Power Research Institute seem more successful than government in developing and commercializing end-use devices that conserve energy and use less oil. Government could, however, usefully encourage progress in the transportation sector, where oil demand is greatest and inertia is highest. One step would be to continue the auto efficiency standards. Although consumers should be free to buy large cars if they wish, continued efficiency improvements in individual models are desirable. Beyond that, pressing forward on the methanol fuel and electric vehicle options seems like good insurance. In both cases, European nations have made considerable progress on which the United States can usefully build.

Third, energy security should be an important foreign policy objective. Because of the world oil market, we are all affected when developing countries build their economies on oil, when producers from non-OPEC countries collaborate with OPEC to raise prices, and when OPEC's greed for short-term gain results in more serious long-term losses. These are matters of national interest, and are properly the subject of government action.

This is not to say that the United States should try to impose its energy policy on others, or that energy is an isolated foreign policy goal. But energy is surely one of several critical aspects of national and international security that should be a permanent feature of U.S. policy. A national energy policy would be a starting point for diplomacy.

Fourth, efforts should be made for insulation against the effects of price shocks and potential disruption. The chief tool is the SPR, which could profitably be even larger than it is currently planned to be. As important as size, however, are both the need for an operating regime designed explicitly to moderate major price swings, as well as the need for more credible reserve stocks among our allies.

Of course, if the linkage between oil prices and economic activity turns out to be weak, the effectiveness of the SPR would be reduced. For the moment,

however, the nature of this linkage is uncertain and the SPR still represents a useful form of insurance. Knowledge of the relationship between oil price shocks and economic performance is a crucial gap affecting both our view of the SPR and broader economic policy.

Finally, do no harm. Energy is a long-term problem, and experience suggests that quick fixes often do more harm than good. Because the fundamentals change slowly, mistakes are not soon discovered nor soon repaired.

Consideration of the oil import fee seems appropriate in this context. To be sure, an import fee would shore up the domestic industry and reduce imports somewhat by depressing demand and possibly retarding temporarily the decline in U.S. production.[7] But the import fee could be seriously at odds with other goals of energy policy. In particular, it might prove to be a self-inflicted wound in producing adverse distributional and output effects. It is also reasonable to expect that the oil import fee would be followed by reregulation of oil markets, imposing rigidities that would simply make the problem worse. Moreover, just as price controls in the 1970s distorted market signals to consumers, so could price supports in the 1980s distort signals to a producing sector that is undergoing significant consolidation

and readjustment. It would probably be wise to let this process go forward unattended by excessive market intervention.

There are alternatives to the import fee that may be more promising. For example, a gasoline tax would yield comparable demand reduction without some of the adverse side effects. And if the oil industry is really hurting, direct subsidies outside the market have much to commend them. But these are all heroic measures. For now, we might content ourselves with the more modest proposals outlined above.

**NOTES**

1. William L. Fisher, "The Aggressive Pursuit of Marginal Resources" (Presidential Address to the American Association of Petroleum Geologists, Atlanta, 16 June 1986).

2. Ibid.

3. Ibid. This rate includes both oil and gas discoveries, stated in terms of British-thermal-unit-equivalent barrels of oil.

4. Department of Energy, *National Energy Policy Plan*, # DOE/S-0040 (Washington, D.C.: Department of Energy, 1985).

5. Douglas R. Bohi, "Energy and Economic Performance: How Important Are Oil Price Shocks?" (Washington, D.C.: Resources for the Future, 1986).

6. Ibid.

7. For another view, see Robert L. Hirsch, "Impending United States Energy Crisis," *Science* 235 (1987):1467–73.

*The Strategic Petroleum Reserve, the U.S. stockpiling program designed to blunt the impact of a major oil supply disruption, is seen as useful insurance. (Photo: DOE)*

# The world's shrinking forests

**David Winder**
Staff writer of The Christian Science Monitor

As twilight slipped into New Delhi, hundreds of small wood fires flickered into life. The city's homeless families were spreading out their mats and sacking and preparing their evening meal at the side of a busy road.

In the rapidly advancing darkness, scores of Indian women, bangles jangling on their thin arms, broke into a run because of the late hour, even though their heads were stacked with piles of firewood.

Every day, throughout India and the rest of Asia as well as Africa and Latin America, women ransack the countryside to find enough firewood to cook their evening meals and keep their families warm.

But as vegetation gets scarcer, they must set out earlier and travel farther to find their wood, the principal source of fuel for up to 90 percent of the developing world.

While energy comes as instantaneously as the flick of a switch in the Western world, the women of the Ivory Coast in West Africa spend four to six hours, three days a week, scouring the countryside to find fuel, according to Worldwatch Institute, an organization that focuses on global problems.

In Haiti, it is almost not worth the struggle. Between 1950 and 1980, as much as 90 percent of all forests in Haiti were cut down to provide shelter or fuel. According to the Pan-American Development Foundation, trees cover only 8 percent of all the land.

A World Bank official reports that the fuel-wood shortage is so acute in the mountainous Himalayan kingdom of Nepal that children miss three days of school a week because they have to hunt for firewood.

But the problem of deforestation is not peculiar to these three countries.

The United Nations Food and Agriculture Organization estimates that half the world's forests have disappeared since 1950. FAO says Latin America has lost 37 percent of its tropical forests, Central America 66 percent, Southeast Asia 38 percent, and Central Africa 52 percent.

Trees are being felled at such a rate that Cultural Survival, an organization of social scientists, predicts that if present trends continue, by the year 2000 only two giant forests will remain: one in western Brazil, the other in Central Africa. Some biologists think it more accurate to say that by the turn of the century there will be hardly any *undisturbed* forest left.

The World Bank has redoubled its reforestation efforts in recent years and now has some 48 ongoing reforestation and forestry-

In Old Delhi, India, many women cook whenever they can find firewood

GORDON N. CONVERSE – CHIEF PHOTOGRAPHER

Wood gathering in Ethiopia: In some parts of Africa, women spend up to 18 hours a week scouring the countryside for fuel, and children are let out of school to help

related projects around the world.

But sources within the bank feel replenishment is taking place at only 20 percent of the rate that it should be. Environmentalists and world institutions blamed the slow pace on lack of motivation in host countries, rather than on inadequate funding. Schools, dams, bridges, and roads seem more attractive and provide a faster return than the more time-consuming business of planting trees.

### Coming to grips with deforestation

Dr. Jay Savage, chairman of the biology department at the University of Miami, recently served as chairman of a National Academy of Sciences/Natural Research Council committee studying the impact of economic development on the rain forests of Central America. He says of reforestation efforts: "We're slipping behind all the time. It's a pretty pessimistic outlook."

At the same time, there are isolated, yet conspicuous examples — in China, South Korea, and India — where strong community involvement has resulted in the greening of tree-denuded landscapes — often with trees that are faster-growing and more commercially productive than those that had been felled.

A recent survey of some 2,700 rural households in Malawi in Africa, conducted by the Malawi government in conjunction with an FAO/World Bank joint project, revealed that 39 percent of those households had voluntarily planted trees because of the scarcity of trees and the rising prices of fuel wood.

A World Bank official indicated, however, that Malawi's experience was more the exception than the rule. In his view, the problem of deforestation had to be viewed in the context of two different climactic zones:

1. The tropical high forests or jungles of such lush areas as the Amazon, Central America, West and Central Africa, Indonesia, and the Philippines. The scare raised a few years ago — that at the present rate the world may lose practically all its forest cover by the year 2000 — is now seen to be unnecessarily alarmist.

But at the same time, the World Bank spokesman was careful not to minimize the problem. The felling of forests, he said, "is a serious situation" and "is still going on at an alarming rate."

The Global 2000 Report to the President, a special environmental report prepared for the Carter administration, termed deforestation the most serious environmental problem confronting the globe. The report said that at the present rate, the developing world would lose up to 40 percent of its forests by the turn of the century.

2. Wooded areas outside the tropics. These areas include Nepal, Bangladesh, and India as well as such arid regions of Africa as the Sahel and the Horn. The World Bank official called the fuel-wood situation in these nontropical forest areas "terribly serious." He added, "In some places it is reaching crisis proportions."

The problem is especially acute for the urban poor who do not have access to the countryside. They pay as much as 30 percent of their meager incomes on fuel.

Not all the trees are felled for firewood. Poor countries, hungry for foreign exchange, export tropical hardwoods to the industrialized West. The FAO reports that exports of tropical hardwoods went up nearly 15-fold between 1950 and 1980.

And as stands of trees fall to logging companies, new settlers move in and speed the deforestation process. Many of these areas are cleared of their trees to provide

Ecuador's forests are dotted with exotic foliage

Finding firewood for heat and cooking is a huge challenge for millions in the third world. While some nations are trying to grow trees, deforestation is the third world's most serious environmental problem.

new pastureland for herds of cattle. North America's appetite for hamburgers means that more and more forests are being converted to grazing to meet the growing demands of fast-food outlets for cheap beef.

But these lands soon become overgrazed and unproductive. The demand, then, is to chop down still more forests to provide more grazing land.

Peter Raven, director of the Missouri Botanical Garden and a world authority on the ecology of rain forests, says it is the population explosion that makes the problem of deforestation so daunting.

Dr. Raven, who has served as chairman of the National Research Council's committee on research priorities in tropical biology, points out that with the world population doubling every 39 years, the pressure on the land right now is "absolutely unprecedented."

The population overload is most graphically represented in the world's tropical-forest regions, where as much as 52 percent of the world's population is settled. That percentage is expected to rise to 60 percent by the year 2000. Currently 2.4 billion people, one-third of them living in absolute poverty, inhabit these tropical regions.

Dr. Raven says demographics are a critical factor in the deforestation equation: "If there are too many people in a given area," he says, "forests cannot recover."

The crush of expanding populations often impels governments to carve out new human settlements in previously forested areas. Narinder Aggarwala, regional information officer for Asia and the Pacific for the UN Development Fund, was recently in Indonesia. He cites the case of Rimbo Bujang, West Sumatra.

Rimbo Bujang, he says, was wild country 15 years ago. "Tropical hardwood forests shrouded this equatorial region. It was inhabited only by tigers, wild boars, and *kubus*, primitive tribesmen, living off berries and hunting with bows and arrows."

Today it is home to 50,000 people. It is one of a series of communities set up by the Indonesian government, which has embarked on one of the world's largest transmigration programs. Millions of Indonesians have moved to the outer islands of their archipelago as a result of the massive population dispersal program.

After initial agricultural successes, productivity in the West Sumatran settlement of Rimbo Bujang is down. Mr. Aggarwala, citing conservation experts, says the deterioration is due to erosion, leaching, and deforestation — "all attributable directly to the massive, organized human intrusion in hitherto uninhabited regions."

### Expanding deserts

While forests are declining, deserts are expanding. Deforestation, overgrazing, and overplowing mean desert-like conditions are spreading in Africa, the Middle East, Iran, Afghanistan, and northwest India. The Sahara Desert is advancing not only southward, but also northward. The encroaching desert is pushing the peoples of North Africa, once the granary of the Roman Empire, against the Mediterranean Sea.

Because desertification is viewed by environmentalists as largely a man-made process, the solution requires human adjustments.

A UN official involved in combatting desertification in the Sudano-Sahelian region of Africa says: "You can't tell people to stop grazing. They need to do this for their survival. You have to give them other economic activities which would pose less pressure on the land."

In Senegal and Gambia, where peanuts are the main export, leftover peanut shells are converted to charcoal as a way of relieving the energy crisis. African states are being encouraged to grow such drought resistant vegetation as *Acacia senegal*, which not only produces gum arabic, an exportable commodity, but also provides fodder and wood and enriches the soil with nitrogen.

Interest has also been aroused in another drought resistant crop, Jojoba (pronounced ho-HO-ba), which produces a very fine oil that rivals that of the sperm whale. It can also be used for pharmaceuticals, in shampoo and hair conditioners, and in wax paper. Although the crop has commercial possibilities, it hasn't yet taken off.

Another solution, encouraging the use of more efficient wood stoves, has not made a big impact on villagers. Either money runs out soon after an experimental project ends, or cooking habits in the world's developing villages die hard.

But at least in China and South Korea — countries with vastly different political systems — Johnny Appleseeds are working with alacrity to replace trees as fast as they fall. Both countries are cited as major success stories in reforestation.

According to the environmental organization Earthscan, China has been able to double its forested area in just 30 years — "a phenomenal afforestation rate of 1.5 million hectares [3.7 million acres] a year."

### China's success story

In just two seasons of one of the world's most prodigious tree-growing programs, 700,000 farmers in northwest China established a 930-mile-long, 40-foot-wide shelterbelt of trees to screen crops, land, and livestock from hot, drying winds. Despite this conspicuous success, deforestation remains a serious problem in China.

By involving villagers, South Korea has been planting 40,000 hectares (100,000 acres) a year, or three-quarters of China's rate on a per-capita basis.

Elsewhere, there is a growing recognition that the felling of trees can set off a chain reaction of incalculable harm. Forests act like sponges, retaining moisture during periods of drought and absorbing water during floods. Remove the forest cover and the runoff increases dramatically. Sediment that is washed down deforested hillsides fills dams and rivers, causing them to silt up, overflow, and flood the neighboring countryside.

According to Lester Anderson of Cultural Survival, the flood plains of India are expanding precisely because the destruction of trees high up on the mountainsides of Nepal increases runoff in the plains below. In 1979, India suffered $2 billion in property damage and lost hundreds of lives in the Ganges Valley because of deforestation in northern India and Nepal.

In a recent publication, "Deforestation: The Human Costs," Cultural Survival put the responsibility for the rescue effort squarely on the third world.

"Until the majority of the population in the third world begins to see the connection between their own future and healthy forests, and acts either to protect or replant it," he says, "massive deforestation will continue, and only dangers will grow in the place of trees."

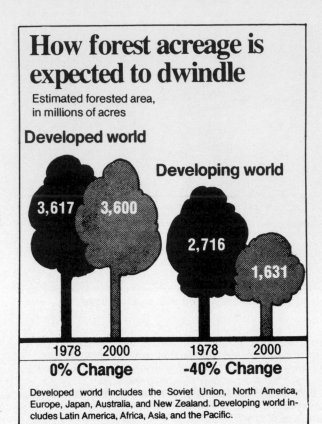

**How forest acreage is expected to dwindle**

Estimated forested area, in millions of acres

**Developed world**

**Developing world**

3,617    3,600

2,716

1,631

1978    2000          1978    2000
**0% Change**          **-40% Change**

Developed world includes the Soviet Union, North America, Europe, Japan, Australia, and New Zealand. Developing world includes Latin America, Africa, Asia, and the Pacific.

Source: Council on Environmental Quality Global 2000 Report.

# Power without nuclear

Nuclear power is good at producing large quantities of electricity. Barring a big change in the world's pattern of energy consumption, that is the kind of energy that will be most in demand if economic growth is to remain rapid. This brief looks at the options facing the world if it abandons nuclear power.

Be clear first about the scale of nuclear's contribution to the world's energy supplies: significant, and growing, but still quite small. At the end of 1985, according to the International Atomic Energy Agency (IAEA), 374 nuclear reactors were connected to the electricity-supply networks in 26 countries. These nuclear power er stations had a generating capacity of 248,000 megawatts and produced about 15% of the world's electricity.

Electricity is only part (though a growing part) of the world energy mix. About 35% of the energy which countries consume each year is committed to generating electricity. Nuclear power accounts for only around 5% of total energy use, and, because of the heat lost in power generation, 2-3% of the energy delivered to end users. Some countries, though, are much more dependent on nuclear power: like France with 65% of its energy coming from nuclear reactors (see chart).

Even by the end of the century those proportions will barely double on the nuclear industry's current plans. Hydroelectric power provides the world with 70% more energy each year than nuclear. So the world is by no means irreversibly committed to nuclear energy.

In the mid-1970s, most governments thought nuclear capacity would—and would need to—expand to 1m megawatts (four times existing capacity) by the year 2000, and to maybe five times as much again by the second quarter of the next century. Then conventional nuclear power stations would be replaced by fast breeder reactors, which breed their own plutonium fuel.

Since then, recession, greater-than-expected progress in conservation and political opposition have wrought their effects. The end-of-century nuclear capacity will probably be barely half what was predicted ten years ago, although double what it is today. If nuclear power were phased out, that would leave a lot of energy, and electricity, to be produced in other ways.

The actual size of that gap will depend partly on energy conservation. If the world can continue to conserve energy at the rate it has done since the first oil crisis in 1973, it will have no trouble in making up any shortfall in nuclear power, at least this century. But can it? Since 1974, the amount of energy used per unit of gross domestic product in the non-communist world has fallen by 13%.

It is not all conservation: structural changes in recession-afflicted economies (away from energy-intensive heavy industries) have also played a part. And there are wide differences between individual countries: the energy-inefficient United States uses twice as much energy per unit of GDP, and more than twice as much energy per head of population, as efficient Japan. Developing countries, on the other hand, because they are developing basic energy-intensive industries, increase their energy use at a faster rate than their economies grow.

But maintaining progress is going to be harder than before: since 1984 the energy-GDP ratio has risen marginally. Many of the

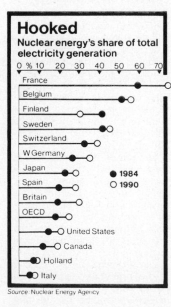

## Hooked
**Nuclear energy's share of total electricity generation**

0 % 10   20   30   40   50   60   70

France
Belgium
Finland
Sweden
Switzerland
W Germany
Japan
Spain
Britain
OECD

● 1984
○ 1990

United States
Canada
Holland
Italy

*Source: Nuclear Energy Agency*

easiest and cheapest conservation measures (eg, insulating houses) have been taken, and as energy prices fall, so too will the incentive to save on fuel bills. Many future conservation measures will require hefty capital investment, with longer payback periods. When energy costs fall below 10% of a firm's total costs, interest in conservation appears to wane sharply.

The size of the energy gap will also depend on the efficiency of power stations. Fossil-fuel power stations generate electricity by burning fuel to boil water into steam, which drives turbines. For a long time, the conversion efficiency of this method of power generation has been stuck at 35%—ie, only 35% of the energy in the fuel comes out as electricity.

Enter the fuel cell. At its best, it converts about 85% of the energy released by the oxidation of hydrogen gas into electric current and usable heat. It was used to provide on-board power and water (its only waste product when fuelled with hydrogen) for the *Apollo* spacecraft.

A fuel cell works by stripping hydrogen, methane or methanol of electrons at one electrode and giving them back, together with oxygen, at another. The net result—oxidation—is exactly the same as when the fuel is burned, but the electrons, travelling between the electrodes, can be used as electric current. Compared with turbines, fuel cells would be quiet, cool and compact.

The snag is cost. At the moment, even running on natural gas (let alone on methanol expensively made from coal or oil, or on hydrogen, expensively bred by bugs), a fuel cell cannot compete with a turbine generator. But the electricity industry is watching prototype fuel cells with interest. America's United Technologies has built several 40-kilowatt ones, while Japan has built a 4.5-megawatt one and has plans for 35,000 megawatts-worth by 2005.

● **Oil**. It remains the world's most popular fuel (see chart). But there are three reasons for not burning it in power stations. One is that oil is indispensable as the fuel for things that move about—half the oil used today powers transport. Another is that burning more oil would soon deliver consumers back into the hands of OPEC. To produce the amount of electricity that the world's nuclear power stations generated in 1984, world consumption of oil would have had to be 10% higher than it was. By the year 2000, another 500m tonnes—equiva-lent to nearly two-thirds of OPEC's output this year—would be needed.

The third reason is that oil is a finite resource. Even at today's production rates, the world's proven oil reserves will be depleted in roughly 35 years. Of course, more oil will be discovered, while a rising price will enable producers to develop smaller fields and squeeze more out of them. Even so, nobody doubts that oil is finite.

● **Coal**. For 30 years after the second world war, most countries tried to move away from their dependence on coal. But just over 40% of the world's electricity comes from coal-fired generating plants; more than 60% of the coal consumed is still burnt in power stations.

Coal is dirty and dangerous to mine; expensive to transport; and bad for the atmosphere. A large coal-fired power station produces enough ash in a year to cover an acre of ground to the height of a six-storey building. It also pumps out carbon dioxide, which turns the atmosphere into a green-

house, and sulphur dioxide and nitrogen oxides, which turn rain to acid.

Coal could easily replace nuclear power. Known coal reserves will last 200-300 years at today's consumption rates. But to use more coal, the world must either accept more pollution, or pay more to clean up coal. Fluidised-bed combustion will give fewer pollutants and up to 20% more power per tonne of coal, but not before the mid-1990s.

Synthetic fuel from coal is no answer: the cost of producing a barrel of synthetic oil from coal (and from other more promising sources such as the tar sands of North America) has stayed stubbornly above the oil price, even when that reached $35 a barrel in 1980. Synthetic crude oil production will probably not exceed 650,000 barrels a day (less than 2% of world output) in 1990.

The earth is brimming with energy. It arrives from the sun at the rate of 178 billion megawatts, 20,000 times as much as world demand for energy. Fossil fuels are merely stored supplies of that solar energy, trapped by ancient plants. So why not short-cut the storage process and use the energy as it arrives?

## Renewable energy

Renewable sources of energy cannot run out, and they do not pollute, blow up or melt down. After the first oil shock, some optimists claimed that they could eventually meet all demand for energy. That optimism is fading. The money spent by governments on research and development into renewable energy has halved from its 1980 peak of $1.2 billion.

The reason is that the renewables have two inherent drawbacks: they are diffuse and they are intermittent. The diffuseness means that a 1,000-megawatt solar farm might occupy about 5,000 acres, compared with less than 150 acres for a similar-capacity nuclear power station. A 1,000-megawatt wind farm would be several times larger still. A wave-power station generating 1,000-megawatts might be 30 miles long. If crops were grown for conversion to oil or gas by digestion, 1,000-megawatts-worth would occupy 200 square miles.

Because renewable energy is intermittent, it is also unreliable. Although the wind often blows strongest when most power is needed, it cannot be relied on to do so, nor—as any Briton will agree—can the sun be relied on to shine. Any renewable supply must therefore be attached to an

efficient means of storing energy for the lean times. Energy storage—by using big batteries, or by pumping water uphill or air into underground caverns—is getting more efficient but still wastes at least one-fifth of the energy.

Despite these problems, renewable energy is already contributing to electricity grids in various parts of the world:

● **Geothermal energy** is not strictly renewable, in that the earth's rocks eventually cool down. Nor is it new: the Italians have been running a power station fuelled by hydrothermal power (steam and hot water) on and off since 1913. Some 3,400 megawatts of geothermal energy are being used by those countries lucky enough to have geysers—New Zealand (11% of final energy consumption), the United States, Japan and Iceland. There is a lot of heat in the earth to be tapped (it comes out at a rate of 32m megawatts) but larger-scale use of geothermal power is probably still decades away. Many of the most obvious geothermal sources have already been tapped, and drilling to find new ones is expensive, since the wells have to be deep.

● **Wind**. This is the most promising of the renewables, for the obvious mechanical reason that windmills can turn turbines directly and do not need an intermediate stage of heating water. But attempts to reap economies of scale by building large windmills—those that generate more than one megawatt—have been bogged down in technical problems for some time. Capital costs have remained obstinately above $1,500 a kilowatt. At present much of the world's wind-generating capacity is in California, which has a system of tax breaks for windmill owners: nearly 9,000 turbines are producing more than 500 megawatts. In the 1990s, capacity could increase to as much as 21,000 megawatts.

● **Thermal solar power**. At least four types of plants use the sun's rays to heat water and so drive a turbine. They vary from the experimental five-megawatt solar pond operating in Israel to the 14 megawatts of installed parabolic troughs in California. The problem common to all is the high capital cost—at least $2,000 a kilowatt of capacity—for expensive items like polished mirrors that can track the sun. Do not expect more than 200 megawatts of capacity world-wide by 1995.

● **Photovoltaic cells**. Semi-conductors have the useful property of turning sunlight directly into electric current. It is a trick that is being put to commercial use in all

sorts of applications: solar-powered calculators, refrigerators, and, of course, satellites. But photovoltaics are just too expensive for large-scale power generation. Developers face a dilemma. They cannot make their cells cheap without losing conversion efficiency and vice versa.

Some 19 megawatts of photovoltaic capacity have been connected to the American grid. By 1995, that figure could have risen to 5,000 megawatts. But the big opportunity lies in the developing world. Photovoltaics, being self-sufficient and as small as needed, come into their own in remote areas that are expensive to connect to grids.

● **The sea**. Three methods for extracting energy from the ocean have been looked at seriously: wave power, ocean thermal energy conversion and tidal power. The first aims to harness the motion of the waves, using a variety of often comically named devices (eg, the Salter duck, the Lancaster flexible bag), the second to exploit the temperature differences between the warm surface layer and the cold deep waters of the oceans. Both could generate sizeable amounts of electricity (perhaps 30,000 megawatts of capacity for an ocean-bound country like Britain). But neither has yet been demonstrat-

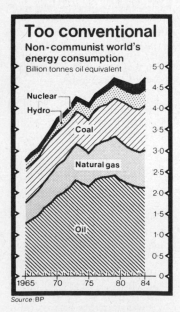

**Too conventional**
Non-communist world's energy consumption
Billion tonnes oil equivalent

Nuclear
Hydro
Coal
Natural gas
Oil

1965 70 75 80 84

*Source: BP*

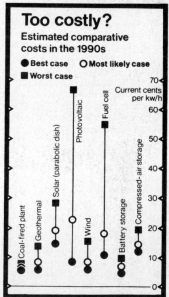

**Too costly?**
**Estimated comparative costs in the 1990s**

● Best case　○ Most likely case
■ Worst case

Current cents per kw/h

Coal-fired plant
Geothermal
Solar (parabolic dish)
Photovoltaic
Wind
Fuel cell
Battery storage
Compressed-air storage

*Source: Office of Technology Assessment*

ed beyond an experimental stage, and most big countries have scaled down their research.

The third method, tidal power, is (like hydroelectric power) limited by geography. It needs long, tapering bays that drive the tide into a large bore as it moves along the channel. The incoming tide can then be trapped behind a barrage and used to drive turbines on the way out again. There are probably fewer than 25 sites, like the Bay of Fundy in Canada and the Severn Estuary in Britain, that are suitable. If all were developed, they would yield 15,000 megawatts or so.

● **Biomass**. The most common renewable source of energy is plant matter. Most poor countries depend on wood for energy. Nearly half of India's and about 94% of Malawi's total energy consumption is of wood. In India, another tenth of the total energy consumption comes from animal dung and crop waste. But this is a precarious resource. Already, 1.3 billion people are using trees faster than they are being replanted, while, in burning dung, farmers deprive their fields of nutrients—and so reduce the amount of crops that can be grown and fed to cattle to produce more dung.

The answer, many believe, is biogas. Digesters would use the dung to make gas and yield a residue that is good fertiliser. Already China is producing the equivalent of 20m tonnes of coal a year in about 7m such digesters.

Plants may have a modest future in replacing the oil used as fuel for vehicles. Brazil's near self-sufficiency in ethanol from sugar cane is the biggest such programme, though some sceptics think that it uses more energy in purification than it generates. Elsewhere, vehicles are running experimentally on coconut oil in the Philippines and gopherweed in Arizona. In Florida, sewage-fed water hyacinths are being turned into gas. In Japan, bugs are eating rice waste to make hydrogen.

## Adding up

So what would fill the gap? By the year 2000, even on conservative estimates of economic growth, OECD countries would be generating 25% of their electricity from nuclear power. Total nuclear capacity would be about 400,000 megawatts. That is the size of the gap that would have to be filled.

These are the least-bad guesses, though they are still rough. The rate of economic growth and the progress of conservation both depend partly on the price of energy—and the price of energy depends on the speed and extent of any nuclear phase-out. But if nuclear power stations were shut overnight, power cuts would be impossible to avoid in several countries and electricity-generating costs would soar. Only oil, gas and coal could fill the gap. Consumption of either oil or coal would have to rise by 10%.

Replacing nuclear power over say 20 years would be less disruptive, but still costly. Some new sources—oil from tar sands and shale, more hydroelectric power, perhaps fuel cells—would fill the gap. But they would not prevent energy prices from rising to at least double their present levels in real terms. Indeed, they would require such a rise, because without it they would make no commercial sense.

# SHAPES OF A RENEWABLE SOCIETY

## RENEWABLE ENERGY HAS TOO LONG LANGUISHED IN THE LENGTHENING SHADOWS OF OPEC, JAMES WATT, AND OTHERS. IT'S TIME IT FLOURISHED IN THE SUNLIGHT.

## Daniel Deudney and Christopher Flavin

*Daniel Deudney and Christopher Flavin are senior researchers at Worldwatch Institute. Mr. Deudney's research deals with renewable energy technologies and issues relating to the "global commons." Mr. Flavin researches energy and resource issues. They are coauthors of* Renewable Energy: The Power to Choose.

Ever since people conceived the idea of harnessing the power of the waters, sun, winds, and earth, they have also speculated on the shape of a solar society. Today's economies and societies have been shaped as much by the availability of inexpensive oil as by any other force. But this dominance is now slowly ending, and, whatever our future energy sources, changes are inevitable.

To rely increasingly on coal and nuclear power is to narrow societies' future options and to present numerous problems. Environmental damage would limit the areas where people can live comfortably. A "security state" mentality would become pervasive as societies sought to protect thousands of central power plants from extremist groups. The power of a small elite over energy technologies would necessarily be strengthened, wrested away from ordinary people. Massive reliance on coal and nuclear power would mean that societies would increasingly have to sacrifice their other priorities to energy production.

Renewable energy, on the other hand, can preserve rather than reduce options. Harnessed by centralized or household technologies, renewable energy could boost employment, bring new life to declining rural areas, and enhance local and regional self-reliance.

### NEW LANDSCAPES

"Buy land," advised American humorist Will Rogers, "they're not making any more of it." Behind the visible constraints of water, energy, food, and housing lie the more basic limits of land. Although there are still many

 This article first appeared in *The Humanist*, issue of May/June 1983, pp. 26–32 and is reprinted by permission.

empty deserts and uninhabited expanses of tundra, productive, livable land is already in short supply. Greater use of renewable energy technology can actually help moderate rising conflicts over land use.

Because solar energy is so diffuse that large areas of collectors—whether plants, wind turbines, or solar panels—are necessary to capture significant quantities of energy, tomorrow's landscape will be far different from today's. However, the important question is not how much land a given energy system takes but whether an energy system uses land not otherwise useful or whether it can piggy-back without displacing existing uses. Some renewable energy systems, most notably large fuel plantations that displace food or fiber crops from prime farmland or hydropower projects that flood rich river-bottom land, crowd out other valuable land uses, thus limiting the physical potential of land. But a greater number of renewable energy technologies will either make use of marginal land or intensify existing land use.

The ultimate in such dovetailing, of course, is the use of passive dwellings that turn roofs, windows, and structural supports into heat collectors and regulators. With the building itself serving as a solar collector and solar water heaters and photovoltaic systems built into the roofs of houses, no additional land is needed for energy. Contrary to the image of "solar sprawl" stemming from the widespread use of solar collectors, most electricity and heat requirements of urban areas can be met from unused roof space. Some idea of this potential is provided by a

University of California study of several U.S. cities. Using detailed aerial photographs of Denver and Baltimore, the researchers found that the cities as a whole could come close to meeting their land requirements for energy; surpluses from the warehouse district would make up for deficits in the central business district.

Fast growing trees planted along roads and streams, between houses, and under power lines will also collect solar energy. Besides providing energy on a cheap, maintenance-free basis, .urban trees moderate temperatures, absorb noise, and clean the air. In a harbinger of this multi-purpose land use, the town of Hagerstown, Maryland, is planting trees on five hundred acres of marginal land. The trees will be fertilized with sludge from the town's sewage-treatment plant and will be gasified to power the plant. Soon to be firewood or a feedstock for fuel to power farm machinery and water pumps, trees planted along field borders in rural areas will provide wind breaks and moderate the local climate.

The blurring of artifice and nature will extend to lands today largely untouched by human hands. Solar ponds can turn otherwise unused desert salt flats or brine lakes into energy collectors. Taming rivers far from cities will prevent the flooding of farmland. Large windmills in mountain passes or along coastal areas can intrude on ocean and mountain vistas, so some care is needed to keep the earth's wild places wild. Harnessing the natural energies of the wilderness—Siberia, the great salt deserts of the American Southwest, the Amazon Val-

ley—may make sense in the calculus of material need but not in the deeper logic of the human spirit. Our species's ancient dream of subjecting wild spaces to human control will, without care, become the nightmare of a totally fabricated planet. Today's conflicts over the siting of oil, coal, or nuclear facilities in wild areas center around ecological and health threats, but controversies in the future could pit more benign renewable energy systems against aesthetic or spiritual values. Ultimately, only population control, improved energy efficiency, and restrained material appetites can ensure that energy complexes do not literally cover the earth.

The intensification of land use to meet energy needs will slowly erase the line between energy production and other endeavors. The "energy sector" may lose its definition, as farmers, homeowners, waste recyclers, and city governments become part of the system without devoting their full-time attention to it. Energy use and production will begin to merge with other activities. As localities, individuals, and countries pursue their own solutions, energy and energy policies could become increasingly sterile abstractions, largely irrelevant to practical living. Energy may not be an easily definable part of either the physical or the intellectual landscape in societies reliant on renewable sources.

## RENEWABLE JOBS

Too often neglected is the impact that different energy alternatives have on employment. A basic measure of economic and psychological

well-being, employment is an essential standard against which renewable energy's viability should be measured and toward which renewable energy development should be directed.

The substitution of energy and capital to perform tasks once done with human hands has been a century-

Our species's ancient dream of subjecting wild spaces to human control will, without care, become the nightmare of a totally fabricated planet.

long trend that has helped boost the worldwide production of goods and services and freed millions from drudgery. Today, however, rising energy prices and rising unemployment call into question the simple formula that worked so well in the past. Already, high energy prices have contributed to unemployment in the automobile, chemical, and steel industries, and, with thirty-six million people entering the global work force each year, technologies must be judged by their ability to create jobs as well as to supply energy.

Studies conducted in the past several years show that developing one energy source rather than another creates very different numbers and types of jobs. Each approach results not only in direct jobs —for example, in drilling oil wells, manufacturing wind machines, or building solar homes—but also in a certain number of indirect jobs in related industries and services. Moreover, some energy sources create mainly unskilled jobs, while others create only those that require specialized training. Some create jobs in urban communities, some in rural areas, and others in remote regions that often become fast-fading boom-towns.

Evidence gathered so far suggests that renewable energy development will create

> Solar energy alone was found to create nine times as many jobs per unit of energy produced as nuclear power, and overall the alternative strategy yielded nearly three times as many jobs and two times as much usable energy as would the nuclear plants.

more jobs than would the same amount of energy obtained from oil, natural gas, coal, or nuclear power. The most detailed case study, conducted by the Council on Economic Priorities, compared the job-creation potential of a solar-conservation strategy and two proposed nuclear power plants on Long Island. Solar energy alone was found to create nine times as many jobs per unit of energy produced as nuclear power, and overall the alternative strategy yielded nearly three times as many jobs and two times as much usable energy as would the nuclear plants. Studies sponsored by

the state of California indicate that active solar systems create more than twice as many jobs as either nuclear power or liquified natural gas. And according to the U.S. Office of Technology Assessment, deriving energy from forestry residues is one-and-one-half to three times as labor-intensive as using coal.

The types of jobs created in renewable energy development span the gamut. Such technologies as solar collectors, wind generators, and wood gasifiers are likely to be manufactured on assembly lines that will be partly automated but still require numerous semiskilled workers. Installing most of these decentralized devices will also create jobs, some of them quite similar to existing jobs in construction, plumbing, and the installation of appliances. Renewable energy development also creates a demand for a wide array of more technical jobs in such fields as resource assessment, advanced research in photovoltaics and other technologies, and systems engineering.

Perhaps the most labor-intensive of renewable energy sources are the various forms of biomass. Fuelwood plantations, methanol plants, and biogas digesters all use less capital and more labor—most of it rural—than do conventional energy sources. Polycultures of mixed food and energy crops will require even more labor since they are less amenable to mechanization than are monocultures.

An intriguing aspect of the employment-creating potential of "renewables" is the flexibility they allow. Each requires a different amount of labor. Each can be developed in more than one way. The variables are local priorities

and resource availability. Some industrial countries, the United States and Sweden among them, are seeking to mechanize the harvest of likely energy crops, while in the Philippines capital shortages and surplus inexpensive labor are bringing about a revival of traditional manual axes and pruning hooks.

Renewable energy alone cannot resolve the world's immense employment problems. Yet, it can take us beyond the boom-and-bust cycles that have for too long characterized energy development's impact on employment.

## RISING SELF-RELIANCE

As renewable energy becomes more important in the world energy budget, patterns of international energy trade will shift, with far-reaching consequences for the global economy and the security of nations. No form of renewable energy (or, for that matter, nonpetroleum fossil fuel) is likely to ever replace petroleum as the driving force in global trade patterns. As the world shifts to renewable energy, this global energy trade will be gradually replaced by regional self-sufficiency and local self-reliance. For the next several decades, the most important energy supply opportunities will be within nations or between neighboring countries, rather than between distant trading partners.

The years since World War II have seen an unprecedented growth in long-distance international trade. The engine of this globalization of economic exchange has been oil. Between 1950

and 1980, oil's share of total international trade ballooned from 1.5 to 19 percent. In 1980, the value of oil traded on the international market was twice the value of the second largest good, food. Even more sobering, one oil-importing country after another was forced during the 1970s to reshape—and often distort—its economy to produce for export. This chain reaction reaches deep into economies: America plows up marginal farmland to produce exportable food; Japan strives to sell high quality industrial goods; Tanzania plants fields with tobacco rather than food.

There are no Saudi Arabias of renewable energy. Most everywhere on earth has a varying abundance of strong wind, intense sunlight, rich plant growth, heavy rainfall, or geothermal heat. Moreover, neither these energy sources nor the electricity or gas that will be generated from them can be cheaply carried across the oceans. While laying electric transmission cables under bodies of water the size of the English channel or Lake Erie is feasible and could grow as nations exploit regional energy trade opportunities, transmission of electricity under the oceans or for distances over one thousand miles is unlikely because of both power losses and high costs. Building gas pipelines under large bodies of water is infeasible, and liquification and regasification is prohibitively expensive and dangerous.

Localities will be much more energy self-reliant in a world where renewable energy is dominant. David Morris of the Institute for Local Self-Reliance observes that today "a dollar spent on energy is the worst expenditure in terms of its impact on the local economy—eighty-five cents on a dollar leaves the economy." However, with renewable energy, much of the money now leaving one nation for the purchase of fuel from another will be spent on locally gathered supplies. Heat for buildings in North America will come from the rooftops, not the Middle East. Villagers in India will light their houses with electricity gathered from their surrounding environment instead of kerosene from Indonesia's outer continental shelf. As the distance between users and suppliers of most energy supplies shrinks, self-reliant communities will be ever less subject to sudden price hikes, supply interruptions, or sabotage. Energy production will thus reinforce rather than undermine local economies and local autonomy.

As energy becomes harder and harder to distinguish from real property such as farmland, buildings, or waste treatment plants, political attempts to redistribute it will be less feasible than in a world where oil is almost as convertible to other goods as money itself. Taxation of energy flows by central governments will be more difficult as an increasing share of energy used never enters the marketplace or is provided in forms not readily comparable to energy used in other communities. And attempts to redistribute international wealth by redistributing resources will find energy less and less transferable.

Localities may achieve increased self-reliance, but only larger regions will approach self-sufficiency. Energy in the form of methane, methanol, or electricity will be exchanged within regions to supplement locally produced energy. Regional trade may gradually supplant global trade. Thus, Germany will rely upon imported Danish wind power rather than Persian Gulf oil; New England on hydropower from Quebec rather than oil from Venezuela; India on electricity from Nepal rather than oil from Indonesia.

The replacement of global by regional interdependency will be powerfully reinforced by basin-wide river development projects. The large dams rising on the Parana, for example, will forge strong links between the economies of Paraguay, Brazil, and Argentina. By allowing navigation far up river and by providing power for new industries, these dams will draw these economies closer, in the same manner in which the St. Lawrence River projects affected the United States and Canada. Economies in both Southeast Asia and the Indian subcontinent will grow intertwined as the Mekong and the Ganges are harnessed. The need for all nations sharing a river basin to protect dams from sedimentation will give new impetus to regional reforestation and cropland protection. River valley inhabitants will take keen interest in the well-being and land-use practices of their highland neighbors. The easing of poverty in the uplands will be an act of regional self-interest rather than global charity.

The use of regional interdependence will make peaceful accommodation between neighboring countries more important than ever. Where deep cultural, religious, or political cleavages exist between regional neighbors, resources may remain undeveloped or rivalries may intensify as nations struggle for control over common resources. Increased reliance on large dams will affect regional politics by creating "mutual hostage" relations among neighboring countries. Yet, large-scale hydroelectric development can bind former enemies together if their leaders cooperate to reach common goals.

## SHIFTING POWER

Writing over a century ago, an early solar pioneer, John Ericsson, prophesized: "The time will come when Europe must stop her mills for want of coal. Upper Egypt, then, with her never-ceasing sun power, will invite the European manufacturers to erect his mills . . . along the sides of the Nile." While Ericsson's vision has not materialized, the use of renewable energy has already shaped the location of industry and the relative power of nations. These patterns are most visible for the renewable source of energy thus far harnessed most extensively: hydropower.

Throughout history the availability of hydropower resources has been a key to the location of industry and cities and the relative power of nations. When waterwheels were the dominant hydropower technology, factories were small and dispersed throughout the countryside. Water's influence on urban location can best be seen in the eastern United States: dozens of cities—from Springfield, Massachusetts, to Augusta, Georgia—cluster on the fall line where rivers drop from the Appalachian Piedmont to the coastal plain.

Historians rank northern Europe's abundant hydropower resources as an important reason for the eclipse of the drier Mediterranean countries over the past few centuries.

Quebec provides a dramatic contemporary example of a region's rise to prominence due to its water resources. Launched ten years ago, La Grande Complex in northern Quebec will soon produce 11,400 megawatts, enough power to double the province's installed electrical capacity. Further additions on other rivers could bring the total to 27,500 megawatts. Using cheap power shipped south on giant 735 kilovolt transmission lines, Quebec hopes to revitalize its economy by attracting new industries. Electrification of oil-using economic sectors and exports of power to the United States will reduce the area's burden of costly imported oil and provide a permanent source of foreign exchange. In a pattern of dependence certain to grow, New York City by 1984 will receive 12 percent of its power from Quebec. This ambitious hydro program will give the French-speaking province new prominence within a Canada whose Western provinces now dominate in energy and will give new leverage to Quebec's battle for greater autonomy and cultural independence.

The development of hydropower in remote areas of the world will also have repercussions on the international economic system as important energy-intensive industries relocate near water resources. The most dramatic shift is occurring in the aluminum industry. Aluminum smelting requires prodigious amounts of electrical energy. In regions where hydropower is plentiful, aluminum smelting is often the major user of electricity. Aluminum smelters cluster around major dams on every continent.

Large wind machines, ocean thermal energy plants, and solar ponds will also affect the balance of industrial and political power. Those remote regions of the world where strong winds blow or where the sun shines intensely may one day attract energy-intensive industry. The steady gale force winds howling off the Antarctic ice shelf are a far denser concentration of energy than the most sun-drenched equatorial desert. One day, they may be a valuable enough lode of energy to lure humans to adapt to that forbidding climate. The salt-rich deserts of the world are also an early candidate for colonization by human energy systems. It is, however, doubtful that large population centers will grow up along-side such large-scale energy development. Extremes of climate, lack of water, and forbidding transportation distances all stand in the way. More likely, such areas will export products such as electricity, ammonia, hydrogen, or smelted metals, all of which require intensive energy for production. Those nations containing such energy-rich but inhospitable provinces will reap the benefits. The wastelands of central Australia, southwest North America, and the great desert stretching from Morocco to the Great Wall of China will change from blank spaces on the map into economic assets. Deserts that long served as buffer zones between nations may become objects of rivalry

between them, adding a new dimension to international politics. Those energy resources which don't belong to any country—the winds of Antarctica or the thermal gradients of the ocean, for instance—could become subject to protracted Law of the Sea type negotiations.

## NEW EQUALITIES

Societies relying on renewable energy will have more balance: between the rich and the poor, between nations, and between generations. The adequacy of energy supplies is determined not by the absolute amounts available but by how they are distributed and by whether individuals can afford the energy they need. Limousine owners in London have all the gasoline they need even during "shortages," while inadequate fuelwood or kerosene is a grim but accepted reality in the mountain villages of Peru. Similarly, heating costs are hardly significant to apartment dwellers in Manhattan, while in the nearby South Bronx huddling around open ovens is the only way of keeping warm in the winter.

As the equity question underscores, the major frontier today in most renewable energy technologies is mass production, which lowers the costs of solar collectors, bio-gas digesters, wind pumps, and even passive solar homes, bringing them within reach of low-income groups. If the initial capital costs are reduced and some subsidies are provided for the least wealthy, renewable energy could help narrow the gap in living standards. And once installed, renewable energy

technologies are immune to fuel-price inflation, affording low-income people some protection from economic shocks and supply disruptions.

One successful example of renewable energy being harnessed by low-income people is in the large but isolated San Luis Valley in Colorado. There several communities with a total population of forty thousand—half of them with incomes below the poverty line—have galvanized to solve their energy problems. Since the late seventies, 15 percent of the valley's homes have been "solarized," and solar collectors, green houses, and crop dryers are now a common sight. Many of the systems are home-built at less than half the cost of comparable commercial equipment. Residents of the San Luis Valley are still not as well-off as those in other areas, but many of their energy needs are met at an affordable price.

Renewable energy can also help narrow the enormous inequalities between rich and poor nations. While some countries obviously have more abundant renewable energy sources than others, the gap between the best and least well-endowed is not great compared to the inequalities of fossil fuel ownership. Indeed, some of the richest lodes of renewable energy are found in some of the poorest countries. For the more than fifty developing countries that are plagued by both extreme poverty and a complete lack of fossil fuels, renewable energy could represent the energy base needed to create wealth. Central America, for example, currently suffers from widespread poverty and staggering oil bills but could fuel sub-

stantial economic growth by tapping abundant hydropower, geothermal, and biomass resources.

In energy terms, all nations are "developing." To be sure, some countries have advantages over others, but all the world's countries face a common need for a fundamental transition to new energy sources. Although lack of capital and scientific infrastructure will impede renewable energy and development in many countries, the lack of previous investment in large fossil fuel and nuclear systems could be an asset. Third World nations could enjoy some of the advantages that West Germany and Japan had after World War II, since they will not be burdened with outmoded equipment. It could, for example, be easier for the Philippines to build cities and industries around geothermal sites than for California to rebuild its economy around new energy sources.

After decades of developing greater dependency by importing technologies from the North, some countries of the South are—haltingly and in diverse ways—beginning to devise patterns of energy development appropriate to their own resources and circumstances. Using wood charcoal for steel-making, hydropower for cities and industries, and alcohol for automobiles, Brazil is building a modern industrial society relying heavily on renewable energy—something no major country in the North is near achieving. Israel is pioneering in solar pond development, and the Philippines in geothermal development—two areas in which the industrial nations are less developed by comparison.

Renewable energy can also restore generation-to-generation balance. Perhaps a quarter of all the petroleum that will ever be used on earth has been burned since World War II; in one generation a trove of energy accumulated in the earth over aeons has been consumed. Fossil fuels—particularly oil and gas—will continue to play a unique role in petrochemical production and in some forms of transportation; it is our responsibility to ensure that many of our descendants have at least small amounts available. The more rapidly renewable energy is developed, the more likely that legacy. With nuclear power, the present generation goes a step further, burdening the earth's inheritors with highly toxic wastes that will last millenia.

In contrast, the self-renewing energies of the sun and the earth can be harnassed by the living without diminishing the supply of energy available for the unborn. Properly executed renewable energy development bequeaths no legacy of environmental destruction and instead creates wealth for future generations. Some renewable energy technologies, such as solar collectors, small wind machines, or wood stoves, rest so lightly on the earth that the future may see no sign of their use. Other, more enduring changes, such as dam building or forestation, are assets bequeathed to the future by an otherwise profligate generation. Because the physical evidence—rotted or recycled—is gone from sight, we find it easy to forget that the early northern Europeans ran their factories with waterwheels or that southern Floridians heated their water from the sun in the 1930s.

Renewable energy development is surely the most conservative and innovative energy course to follow. At our present crossroads, we cannot maintain what we cherish unless we change the energy systems on which we rely. Only with renewable energy can our children at a reasonable cost enjoy the benefits we have enjoyed. Only with renewable energy development can we raise the living standards of the great majority.

The power needed to make these choices is at hand.

# Development

- **Nonindustrial Nations (Articles 24-30)**
- **Industrial Nations (Articles 31-35)**

One of the terms most frequently used to describe the world today is "development." Television talk shows, scholarly publications, political speeches, and countless other forums echo this term. Yet, gather together a group of experts, and it would soon be apparent that each one uses the word "development" in a somewhat different manner. For some, development means becoming industrialized—like the United States or Japan, for example. To others, development means having a growing economy; this is usually measured in terms of the expansion of Gross National Product (GNP). To others, development is primarily a political phenomenon. They question how a society can change its economy if it cannot establish collective goals and successfully administer their implementation. To yet others, development means attaining a certain quality of life—one with adequate health care, leisure time, and a system of public education, among other things. It is obvious, then, that the term must be defined before a discussion of the issue of development can begin.

Because this book includes both industrial and nonindustrial countries in its discussion of development, a broad definition will be used. Development will mean improvement in the basic aspects of life: lower infant mortality rates, greater life expectancy, lower disease rates, higher rates of literacy, healthier diets, and improved sanitation. While it is obvious that, judged by these standards, some groups of people are more developed than others, the process is an ongoing one for all nations. This unit, therefore, is divided into two parts. It looks first at the development process in nonindustrial countries, then focuses on the industrial countries of North America, Japan, and the Soviet Union. Although the Soviet Union and its economic associates are not the consumer-oriented economies of the West, as industrial nations they, like the others, are in the midst of social and economic transformations.

*Nonindustrial Nations.* What would it be like to live in a village? The traditions of village life are part of humanity's common past. In China today, 80 percent of the population resides in the countryside. In Asia, home of over half of the world's population, most of the people could be classified as peasants. In Africa, Central America, much of the Soviet Union, and elsewhere, the rural village is the dominant life-style. In the opening article of this subsection, Prafulla Mohanti, an Indian author, describes what life is like in the village where he grew up.

A dominant theme in the Third World development literature deals with the economic relationship between

industrial and nonindustrial nations. One line of argument states that this relationship is designed to transfer wealth from the Third World to the First (Western Europe, the United States, and Japan). Ali A. Mazrui develops this argument by focusing on economic and technological issues.

In the articles that follow, development issues facing the nonindustrial nations are explored in greater detail, focusing on specific issue areas and case studies. The problem of Third World debt is described in "Dance of Debt Isn't Over Yet," and attempts to creatively deal with this situation are illustrated. Following this general discussion is an analysis by Curtis Skinner of the economic situation in Mexico, one of the principle debtor nations in the world.

The social exclusion of women and the exploitation of child labor are two issues that give the problems of development a human character. The value system that supports these practices is considered, along with examples from many different settings.

Finally, this subsection concludes with a discussion of the changes brought about by economic reform in China. In particular, the improvement in the quality of life in rural China is described. The result has been changes in the management of agricultural resources and rural industrialization. This success story concludes this subsection, which began with a description of life in a village.

*Industrial Nations.* Only a few years ago, industrialization was considered by many to be the end point of the development process. Industrialization, however, is not necessarily synonymous with improvement in the quality of life. When the industrial sector of the West's economy was thrown into deep recession after the oil price shocks of the 1970s, many experts joined the growing chorus of those calling for the development of industrial societies into a new, postindustrial structure, where knowledge, information, and space-age technologies would take over. Others believed the "greening" of society, rather than a high-tech future, should become the new goal of development. This second group of people maintained that new, clean energy resources and an appreciation of the fragile nature of the environment will lead to a decentralized economy. As yet, neither of these visions (nor any other) has come to pass. The industrial countries, like the nonindustrial countries, are in the midst of a development process, with no single blueprint to guide them.

One of the dominant themes found in discussions of the problems facing the industrial nations is the interdependency of their economies. Raj Aggarwal's article focuses on newly industrialized countries and examines the recent emergence of a genuine global economy and how new technologies are impacting on traditional ways of doing business.

The next article focuses on Japan, the world's leading creditor nation. Japan's very success is forcing that country to establish new economic policies to deal with the huge trade surplus it has developed with its trading partners. However, there are many entrenched economic interests that oppose the reforms that are being proposed.

One international agreement designed to manage the economic relations between the industrial countries is discussed in "Dismantling the 49th Parallel," which describes the recent proposal between the United States and Canada to create a free-trade pact.

The final two articles take a look at the Soviet Union and some of the reforms that have been proposed for the Soviet economy. The article by Martin Walker considers the impact of these reforms on the Soviet welfare system. The other compares the Soviet and U.S. space programs and illustrates the importance of technological innovation to economic prosperity.

Industrial nations, like their nonindustrial counterparts, are in a period of transition. Many forces are at work, and as yet there is no widely accepted vision of where this is all going to lead. While so much divides the First and Third Worlds, uncertainty about the future and a lack of consensus about the policies necessary to improve the quality of life are two dimensions they ironically have in common.

## Looking Ahead: Challenge Questions

How are the social structures of traditional societies different from those of the consumer-oriented societies of the West?

How are the Third World countries dependent on the First World?

What are some of the barriers that make it difficult for nonindustrial countries to develop?

How has the role of the United States in the international economy changed in recent years?

The international economic system is faced with unprecedented problems. What are these, and what are some of the proposals for solving these problems?

How are the United States, Japan, the Soviet Union, and other industrial countries trying to alter their economies to meet new economic challenges? Are they likely to succeed?

# A village called Nanpur

## Prafulla Mohanti

**PRAFULLA MOHANTI** *was born and brought up in Nanpur, the Indian village he describes in this article. He won a scholarship to study architecture in Bombay and from there went to England in 1960 to work as an architect. He is now a painter and writer. His paintings have been shown in many parts of the world, including Europe, the US and Japan, as well as India. He is the author of* My Village, My Life, *a portrait of his village which has been translated into Japanese, Norwegian and Danish. His film,* My Village, My Life, *was shown on BBC TV during the 1982 Festival of India in the UK.*

THE name of my village is Nanpur. It is one of India's 500,000 villages and stands on the bank of the river Birupa in the Cuttack district of Orissa. It is part of a group of villages with a central market place at Balichandrapur, three kilometres away, where there is now a bank, a police station and a post office. The village is connected by road with Cuttack, 48 kilometres south-west, the commercial centre of the State.

Nanpur has a population of about 3,000 living in six settlements separated by mango groves and paddy fields. Each settlement is inhabited by one particular caste. Caste is the most important feature. It defines a person's place in the village and the work he is expected to do. One is born into a caste and it cannot be changed.

Traditionally there are four castes— Brahmins, the priests; Kshatriyas, the warriors; Vaishyas, the businessmen; and Sudras, the servant caste. But over the years there have been many sub-castes relating to professions. There are Brahmins, Karans—the administrators—farmers, barbers, astrologers and Harijans, formerly

Photo © Claude Sauvageot, Paris

**Rice is the main crop in this traditional Indian village of the Punjab. In foreground, one of the humped brahman or Zebu cattle which are common in this region. They are considered sacred by the Hindus.**

called Untouchables. The villagers are mainly farmers and craftsmen. Each craft is the property of a particular caste and together they form the village community.

The villagers of Nanpur are Hindus. They are religious. They believe in God and his many incarnations. For them He is everywhere, in a man, in a tree, in a stone. According to Arjun Satpathi, the village Brahmin, God is light and energy, like the electric current. To him there is no difference between the gods of the Hindus, Muslims and Christians. Only the names are different.

Every village has a local deity. In Nanpur it is a piece of stone in the shape of a shiva lingam. He is called Mahlia Buddha. He sits under the ancient *varuna* tree protecting the village. Kanhai Barik, the village barber, is the attendant to the deity. Kanhai, before starting his daily work, washes the deity, decorates it with vermilion and flowers and offers food given by the villagers. Clay animals are presented. It is believed that the deity rides them during the night and goes from place to place guarding the village. Mahlia Buddha was donated to the village by the barber's great-great-great-grandmother, so only his family has the right to attend to the deity. In the old days Mahlia Buddha had a special power to cure smallpox and cholera. Now, although modern medicines have brought the epidemics under control, the power of the deity has not diminished. People believe in him and worship him for everything, even for modern medicines to be effective.

Religious festivals provide entertainment. There is one almost every month. The most enjoyable is the Spring festival of Holi when people throw coloured powder and water on each other as an expression of love. As the cuckoo sings, hidden among the mango blossoms, the villagers carry Gopinath (Krishna) in a palanquin around the village accompanied by musicians.

There is no television, but some villagers have radios. Listening to film music is popular. Snake charmers, acrobats, puppeteers and wandering singers come visiting during the dry season. A wave of excitement goes through the children when they arrive.

Every villager has a *jatak* (horoscope) which is also the birth certificate inscribed on a palm leaf by Dharani Naik, the village astrologer. He is consulted for everything—if the planets are favourable and the auspicious days for starting a journey. There is a saying in Oriya, "Tuesday night, Wednesday morning, wherever you go you receive good luck".

People believe in *karma* (fate) and the cycle of rebirth. This helps them to accept their situation. Padan is the only dwarf in the village and is popular, despite his disability. He is twenty-seven and runs a tea stall in the market place. He recently married another dwarf from a distant village. Padan believes he is a dwarf in this life because of his actions in a previous incarnation.

The houses are built of mud walls and thatched roofs with a central courtyard which is private and provides shelter from the sun. Every house has an altar with a *tulashi* plant (sacred basil). This herb is so valuable for its medicinal properties that it is worshipped as a goddess.

The villagers decorate the walls and floors of their houses with rice paste for festivals and ceremonies. The lotus is the main symbol. At the harvest festival it is painted with stylized footprints to welcome Lakshmi, the Goddess of Wealth.

Marriages are arranged by parents and the bride and bridegroom must belong to the same caste. The horoscopes are shown to the astrologer, who draws diagrams and forecasts their compatibility. The girl's father has to give a dowry, although it is forbidden by law. The bride must be a virgin.

The role of a woman in Nanpur is that of a mother. A house is not a home without a child. People live in joint families and family life is strong. She has the responsibility of managing the household. If she does it well and brings prosperity, she is compared with Lakshmi, but if she destroys its unity she is compared to Kali, the Goddess of Destruction. But her duty is not complete until she has produced a son, essential for the family to continue.

The women in Nanpur worship Satyapir, a Hindu-Muslim god, to bless them with sons. "Satya" is the Hindu part meaning "truth", and "pir" in Islam means "prophet". It was a deliberate attempt to bring the two communities together through religion. There is a large Muslim settlement three kilometres from Nanpur and in a village on the other side of the river a single Muslim family lives surrounded by Brahmins. In spite of Hindu-Muslim tensions in other parts of India, the atmosphere around the village has remained peaceful.

A woman without a husband has no place

Photo © Prafulla Mohanti, Nanpur, India

**The market place in Nanpur.**

**Curved contours of a grain silo dwarf nearby buildings in Bihar State, India, near the border with Nepal.**

Photo © Claude Sauvageot, Paris

in the village. Widows are not allowed to re-marry. They lead very austere lives. When their husbands die they break their glass bangles and stop wearing the vermilion spot on their foreheads. The attitude of the other women makes them feel isolated. They are not invited to take part in auspicious ceremonies as it is considered they may bring bad luck.

There is a great respect for education. Children start going to school at the age of four. This begins at the *chatshali*, the nursery school, which is run by a villager on his verandah. I remember my first day. I took a plate containing rice, a coconut and money and presented it to the teacher. He blessed me by gently stroking my out-stretched hands with his cane. Then he took my hand and with a piece of clay chalk helped me to draw three circles on the mud floor. They are Brahma, Vishnu and Maheswar, the Hindu Trinity. Brahma, the Creator, Vishnu the Preserver and Maheswar, the Destroyer. The Oriya script is round and practising these circles helps to develop good handwriting. The children are told stories to form their character—to be kind, noble and hospitable.

In my childhood there was no primary school in Nanpur and I walked to the ad-joining village of Kusupur, over a mile away. Now the villagers have built one themselves without any government help. The school starts with a prayer acknowledg-ing the presence of God in nature. The children sing, "Why should I be afraid of telling the truth? Even if I have to die, I must tell the truth. O God, please teach me this. I need nothing else."

The villagers also built a high school at Kusupur and the children took part in the construction of the building. A private col-lege has started in Balichandrapur.

The aim of education is to get an office job, to work as a clerk sitting comfortably under a fan. The system goes back to the days of the British Raj. There is no guidance for the choice of a career and there is no social welfare scheme in India. Several highly-educated young men sit at home do-ing nothing and become a burden to their families.

The dignity of labour is not understood. The educated feel it is inferior to do manual work. A typical example is Rabi Jena, the young son of a Harijan. His father has no land and worked hard as a tenant farmer to educate him. But he was unable to pass his matriculation exam. He was desperately in search of a job and a friend offered him one

at an officers' club in the steel town of Rourkela. He worked as an attendant and at times was required to clean dishes and serve tea. He refused and left as he con-sidered it beneath his dignity. He is looking for another job but there is mass unemploy-ment everywhere.

The staple food for the villagers is rice. The poor eat it with spinach and the better-off with dal, vegetables and fish, caught in the local rivers and ponds. Occasionally goat meat is eaten but it is a luxury. Eating beef is unthinkable for a Hindu as cattle are considered sacred. The cow is called "cow mother" because the children drink her milk, and the bull is holy because Lord Shiva rides on him. Only oxen are used for ploughing the fields and pulling carts.

The main crop is paddy (rice). It is planted in June, just before the monsoon and takes four months to grow. It is harvested in November. A successful crop brings happiness to the village.

There is no hospital in the village and the nearest health centre is four miles away. There is no ambulance service and patients have to be carried there, whatever their con-dition. The consultation is free, but the villagers have to buy their own medicines, which are expensive. People complain that they have to spend half a day to get only a piece of paper, the prescription.

Young doctors are reluctant to work in the villages because there is no money. But Basant Jena is an exception. He is from Nanpur and after qualifying as a doctor opened a surgery at Balichandrapur. He is overwhelmed with the problems. He treats hundreds of patients daily but feels helpless. The illnesses are caused by pover-ty, which cannot be cured by medicines.

Many villagers turn to the quacks, who combine modern medicines with homeopathy and herbal remedies. Anyone with a little knowledge can practise as a doc-tor and modern drugs are freely available without prescription.

In my childhood the village was totally isolated. It took one whole day to reach Cuttack, the nearest town. One had to walk 20 kilometres to the railway station and there were two rivers to cross by boat. With only two trains a day, if you missed one there was a wait of twelve hours for the next. But in 1968 a motor road cut across the village to carry iron ore to the port of Paradip, 96 kilometres away. For the first time travel was made easy and the village was connected with the outside world. But the road has brought noise and pollution. I am amazed how the villagers have got used to it. When I was a child there was no noise apart from the barking of a dog or the howling of a jackal at night. The only other noise was produced by the rhythmic pounding of rice. That worried me when I was preparing for my matriculation exams. I told my mother and the pounding of the rice stopped in my part of the village so that I could concentrate on my studies.

Out of my twenty childhood friends, two died of cholera, one died of typhoid, three were disfigured by smallpox, five girls got married and left the village, six boys went to towns to find work. Only three stayed in the village; one is unemployed and the other two work as farmers.

I wanted to be a doctor to help the village but could not get into medical school. By chance I won a scholarship to study architecture in Bombay. That changed my life.

The village has also changed. Electricity has come. Epidemics are under control, but there is no proper water supply or sanitation. Education has helped to break down caste barriers. The member of parliament for my village is a Harijan. Family sizes have increased but food production has not kept pace with it. Floods, droughts and cyclones occur every year, causing suffering and malnutrition. This year all three have occurred in succession and the people who were able to smile only last year have turned into skeletons.

But in spite of poverty and suffering there is a strong desire to survive and the villagers have a natural dignity. Although they feel a part of nature they know they have no control over it. Acceptance brings contentment.

Once I leave the village I want to go back to it, its love, beauty and simplicity. Often I wonder what will happen to it.

**Lotus symbol with stylized foot-prints. At harvest time the villagers of Nanpur in eastern India paint such designs to welcome Lakshmi, the Goddess of Wealth.**

Drawing © Prafulla Mohanti, Nanpur, India

# international stratification and Third World solidarity:

# a dual strategy for change

## Ali A. Mazrui

Dr Ali A. Mazrui, *a native of Kenya, is Research Professor at the University of Jos in Nigeria and Professor of Political Science and of Afroamerican and African Studies at the University of Mighigan, Ann Arbor. His books include* Toward a Pax Africana *(1967),* Violence and Thought *(1969),* Cultural Engineering and Nation-Building *(1972),* Soldiers and Kinsmen in Uganda *(1975), and a novel,* The Trial of Christopher Okigbe *(1971).*

Two forms of solidarity are critical for the Third World if the global system is to change in favour of the disadvantaged. Organic solidarity concerns South-South links designed to increase mutual dependence between and among Third World countries themselves. Strategic solidarity concerns cooperation among Third World countries in their struggle to extract concessions from the industrialized Northern world. Organic solidarity concerns the aspiration to promote greater integration between Third World economies. Strategic solidarity aspires to decrease the South's dependent integration into Northern economies. The main focus of organic solidarity is a South-South economic marriage. That of strategic solidarity is a North-South divorce, a new marriage settlement, or a new social contract between North and South. The terms of the North-South bond have to be renegotiated.

We start also from the additional basic observation that economic flows are in any case far deeper between North and South than between South and South. On the whole, Southerners do far more trade with the North than with one another and have more extensive relations of production with industrialized states than with fellow developing countries.

Those economic relations between North and South are distorted by a tradition of dependency involving unequal partnership. The structural links give the advantage and leverage to the North and leave the South vulnerable and exploitable.

What is the way out? How can these two forms of solidarity help to ameliorate the Third World's predicament of dependency and its persistent economic vulnerability?

One of the more neglected areas of co-operation is manpower and manpower training. While a start has been made in manpower exchange and training across Third World boundaries, the importance of this area has been grossly underestimated.

It is not often realized that the most obstinate line of demarcation between North and South is not income (criteria of wealth) but technology (criteria of skill). The entire international system of stratification has come to be based *not* on who owns what but on who *knows* what. Kuwait and Saudi Arabia may have a higher per caput income than some of the members of the European Economic Community, but the Gulf States are well below Western Europe in skills of production and economic organization. Indeed, members of the Organization of Petroleum Exporting Countries (OPEC) do not even have the skills to drill their own oil.

Nowhere is this demonstrated more clearly than in southern Africa and the Near East. Fewer than five million whites in South Africa have been able to hold to ransom 10 times as many blacks. They have held neighbouring blacks to ransom both economically and militarily. The main explanation is not simply that South Africa is rich, but that that wealth has been extracted by African labour and *European* expertise. South Africa's neighbours have African labour too.

Some of them are also rich in minerals What the blacks have lacked indigenously is the superior technology of production and the accompanying culture of efficient organization.

**Skill over income**. The Near East is a clearer and more staggering illustration of the power of skill over income. At least since the 1970s, much of the Arab world has become significantly richer than Israel in sheer income. Indeed, the Israeli economy would have suffered complete collapse but for the infusion of billions of dollars from the United States and the Jewish community worldwide. Nevertheless, the outnumbered and less wealthy Israelis have retained the upper hand militarily against the Arabs. The supremacy of skill over income and numbers has been dramatically illustrated.

If then the ultimate basis of international stratification is indeed skill rather than income, what is the Third World to do in order to undo the consequences of its technological underdevelopment?

The obvious answer is for the Third World to obtain the know-how from the Northern Hemisphere as quickly as possible. But there are difficulties. Countries of the Northern Hemisphere are often all too eager to transfer certain forms of technology, especially through transnational corporations, but the South's need for certain technological transfers only helps to deepen relationships of dependency between the two hemispheres.

On the other hand, there are other areas of technology which the North is not at all keen to transfer. Pre-eminent among the taboos is the transfer of certain branches of nuclear

 Reprinted from *Ceres*, January/February 1985, pp. 16-20. CERES, the FAO review on agriculture and development.

physics and technology. The computer is part of the phenomenon of dependency through technology transfer; the nuclear plant or reactor is a symbol of dependency through technological monopoly by the North. Transnational corporations are often instruments of Northern penetration of the South through technology transfer; nuclear power, on the other hand, is a symbol of Northern hegemony through technological monopoly.

**Learn and share**. The dual strategy for Third World countries (including China) is both to learn from the North and to share expertise among themselves. Those aspects of technology being freely transferred by the North should be "decolonized" and stripped of their dependency implications as fast as possible. Those aspects of technology which are deliberately monopolized by the North should be subjected to Southern industrial espionage in a bid to break the monopoly. Pakistani scientists have been on the right track in their reported efforts to subject the Northern nuclear monopoly to Southern industrial spying.

That is one reason why the brain drain from the South is *not* an unmitigated disaster. What would be a catastrophe is a complete stoppage of the brain drain. It is vital that the South should counterpenetrate the citadels of technological and economic power. The counterpenetration can take the form of Southern engineers, teachers, and professors, medical doctors and consultants, businessmen and scientists working in the North. The North needs to be more sensitized to Southern needs not only by the speeches of Southern statesmen and ambassadors but also by the influence and leverage of Southerners resident in the North.

In any case, there is no law of gravity which says expertise can only flow from the North to the South. There is no gravitational logic which says that European teachers teaching African children is natural but African teachers teaching European children is not. The structure of scientific

*Ghana: the Akosombo Dam, Volta River. The struggle for African integration has had many setbacks*

stratification in the world should rapidly cease to be a rigid caste system—and allow for social mobility in both directions. Of course, too great a brain drain from the South northward could deeply hurt the South—but the trouble with the present level of the drain is not that it is too great, but that it is grossly underutilized by the South itself. Professor Edward S. Ayensu, a Ghanaian Research Director at the Smithsonian Institution in Washington, DC, has argued that there is large potential pool of Third World experts resident in the Northern Hemisphere who would be only too glad to serve for a year or two in developing societies if only their services were solicited. What is more, the Northern institutions where they work would, according to Professor Ayensu, be sympathetically inclined toward facilitating such exchanges from time to time if requested by Third World authorities. [1]

**Triangular flow**. If that were to happen, it would be a case of tapping the brain drain on the basis of a triangular formula. The flow of expertise would be first from South to

North, then North to South, and then South to South—often involving the same Southern experts or their equivalents, sharing their know-how across hemispheres.

This sharing of Southern experts by both North and South would be a more realistic formula than the tax on the brain drain which Professor Jagdish Bhagwati of the Massachusetts Institute of Technology has often recommended as a method of compensation by the North to the South for manpower transfer.

Unfortunately, while the North may indeed be willing to share with the South some of its newly acquired Southern experts, the South itself has shown more enthusiasm for borrowing "pure" Northern experts than for borrowing Southern experts resident in the North. The psychological dependency of the South is less likely to be impressed by an Indian or Nigerian expert coming from the United States than by an American expert with far less understanding of the Third World. The American is regarded as "the real thing" in expertise—while the Indian statistician or Nigerian engineer is deemed to be a

*Solar energy. Technology should be "decolonized" in order to flow freely between North and South*

mere Southern "carbon copy".

Fortunately, all is not bleak. There is some movement of expertise between Third World countries. Dr Boutros Boutros-Ghali, the Minister of State for Foreign Affairs of Egypt, assured me in an interview in Cairo in 1983 that Egypt had "two million experts" working in other countries, mainly in Africa and the Near East. South Asia also exports a considerable body of expertise to other parts of the Third World.

Some of the traffic in expertise across Third World frontiers is caused by political instability and economic problems at home. Qualified Ugandans are scattered in almost all the four corners of the Third World, as well as in the North. So are qualified Lebanese, Palestinians, southern Africans, Ethiopians, and others.

Then there is the intra-Third World traffic of experts caused by the magnetism of petro-wealth. The Gulf states have a particularly impressive variety of human power from different lands. Two Ghanaian scholars who visited the University of Petroleum and Minerals in Dhahran in the Kingdom of Saudi Arabia in the

summer of 1984 were impressed by the Ghanaian presence in the research complex of the university. They were also surprised to learn about "24 highly qualified Ghanaian medical officers working in and around this University town of Dhahran". [2]

**"Push" and "pull"**. To summarize, there is a "push factor" in some of the less fortunate Third World countries which forces out many of the native experts in search of alternative opportunities in other countries. But there is also a "pull factor" in the wealthier Third World societies which magnetically attracts workers and specialists from other lands. Together the two forces are helping to lay down some of the foundations of organic solidarity within the Third World in the field of know-how.

What is lacking is an adequate linkage between organic and strategic solidarity in this field of evolving Third World expertise. A systematic programme which would enable the South to borrow some of the Southern experts now resident in the North could become an important stage in the evolution of a merger between

organic and strategic solidarity.

Behind it all is the realization that the ultimate foundations of international stratification are not income differences, military gadgets, or demographic variations. Ultimate power resides neither in the barrel of the gun nor in the barrel of oil, but in the technology which can produce and utilize both effectively. A new international economic order would be void without a new international technological order. The South needs strategies of solidarity to realize both.

But although the *power of skill* is at the moment overwhelmingly in the hands of the North, there are other areas of power which the South possesses but has underutilized. OPEC is an illustration of *producer power*. From 1973 to 1983 OPEC grossly underutilized its leverage. Instead of using that golden decade to put pressure on the North for fundamental adjustments in the patterns and rules of the world economy, OPEC concentrated almost exclusively on the price game, a game of short-term maximization of returns.

There is a crying need for other producer cartels, no matter how weak in the short run. Cobalt has more promise as a mineral of leverage than copper and would involve fewer countries. Experimentation in a cobalt cartel could pay off if Zaire asserted itself a little more decisively as an independent power. After all, Zaire could become the Saudi Arabia of cobalt when the market improves in the years ahead.

The Third World has also underutilized its *consumer power*, regionally specific and patchy as it is. The Near East is especially important as a consumer of western civil and military hardware, technology, and household products. Occasionally individual Near East countries flex their muscles and threaten to cancel trade contracts or to refuse to renew them, but usually for relatively minor issues—like protesting the television film "Death of a Princess" or when an Arab delegation is snubbed by a Western power. The consumer power of the Near East could be used as leverage for more fundamental changes in the exchange patterns between North and South.

The fourth form of power currently underutilized by the South is *debtor power*. President Julius Nyerere of Tanzania, upon being elected Chairman of the Organization of African Unity in November 1984, identified development, debt, and drought as the three leading concerns of the current African condition. Of course African debts are modest compared with those of Latin America, but Nyerere identified debt as a source of power and not merely as a source of weakness. At his press conference after his election he lamented that the Third World was not more efficiently using the threat of default to induce Western banks to make more fundamental concessions to the indebted. [3]

It is indeed true that if I owe my local bank a few thousand dollars, I am vulnerable, but if I owe the bank millions of dollars, the bank is vulnerable. But Nyerere virtually declared that if he owed as much as some of the leading African debtor countries owed, he would simply refuse to pay. (Africa's leading debtor nations are Nigeria, Egypt, and Zaire.)

**Solidarity of the indebted.** In reality Tanzania would still be vulnerable unless there was substantial strategic solidarity among both African and Latin American countries. The utilization of debtor power requires considerable consensus among the indebted. The Western banks have evolved a kind of organic solidarity of their own as well as mechanisms of almost continuous consultation. The creditors of the North are united but the debtors of the South are in disarray. Africa and Latin America need to explore the possibility of creating a strategic solidarity of the dispossessed and the indebted to induce the North to make concessions on such issues as rates of interest, schedule of payment, methods of payment, and the conditions for a moratorium where needed.

Fundamental as all these areas of strategic solidarity are, they are no substitute for organic solidarity in terms of greater trade, investment, and other interactions among Third World countries themselves. Here the less developed countries (LDCs) are caught up in several contradictions. In their relations with the North, the LDCs need to diversify their economies. But in their relations with one another, the LDCs need to specialize in order to increase mutual complementarity. Uganda could revive its cotton industry and sell the fibre to Kenya to process into a textile industry. This specialization would help the two countries develop in the direction of complementary specialization. But the imperatives of Uganda's relations with the world economy as a whole dictate diversification of Uganda's industry rather than specialization. This is an acute dilemma which Third World countries need to resolve as a matter of urgency. They need to find a suitable balance between diversification for North-South relations and specialization in South-South trade.

Related to this is the imperative of finding alternative methods of payment in South-South trade. The principle of using Northern currencies for South-South trade has been very stressful. The bogey of "foreign exchange" has bedevilled Southern economies. Tanzania, Zambia, and Zimbabwe have been exploring possibilities of reviving barter as a basis of at least aspects of their economic relations. The new detente between Kenya and Tanzania also envisages areas of barter trade between the two countries in the years ahead. And if Uganda's cotton did feed Kenya's textile industry more systematically in the future, it would not be unrealistic for Kenya to pay back Uganda in shirts and processed military uniforms rather than in hard foreign exchange.

Another area of organic solidarity among Third World countries concerns the issue of sharing energy. There have been years when Kenya has needed to get a third of its electricity from the dam at Janja in Uganda. Uganda is still a major supplier of power to Kenya.

The Akasombo Dam on the Volta River in Ghana was also designed to be a major regional supplier of electricity in West Africa. Unfortunately the level of water has been so low that far from supplying power to neighbours, Ghana has periodically had to ration power domestically. Ghana has sometimes needed electrical cooperation from the Ivory Coast.

Southern African dams like Kariba have had more successful regional roles. They all symbolize a kind of pan-Africanism of energy, organic solidarity through interlocking structures of hydroelectric power.

An integrated European steel complex once served as midwife to the birth of the European Economic Community. Indeed, the integrated steel industry was envisioned as an insurance against any future fratricidal war in Europe. If European steel production was interlocked, industrial interdependence was at hand and separate military aggression in the future would therefore be less likely.

In the same spirit, interlocking electrical systems between Third World countries should deepen mutual dependence—and create incentives for cooperation in other areas.

The struggle for a more integrated Africa has encountered many setbacks—from the collapse of the East African Community of Kenya, Uganda, and Tanzania to the drying up of the Akosombo Dam.

The struggle for a more integrated South East Asia is more of a success story—as the Association of South East Asian Nations (ASEAN) has emerged as a major economic and diplomatic force in the affairs of the region.

The struggle for a more integrated Arab world is a mixed story—ranging from the positive promise of the Gulf Cooperation Council to the negative internecine squabbles of Arab politics.

In Latin America, regional integration is also a mixed record. Central America is tense under the clouds of war. On the other hand, Chile and Argentina—through the mediation of the Vatican—have diffused the sensitive issue of the Beagle canal.

## 4. DEVELOPMENT: Nonindustrial Nations

Economic cooperation has had its ups and downs throughout the region, but the ideal of greater integration is still a live flame.

The Northern hemisphere as a whole is divided between two economic blocs which coincide with the ideological divide. The split is, of course, between the socialist world of COMECON and the capitalist world of the North Atlantic.

The South, on the other hand, is still in multiple fragments. It is now in search of the elusive secret of putting the fragments together. It is in search of the secret genius of cohesion.

1. Edward S. Ayensu, "Natural and Applied Sciences and National Development", lecture delivered at the silver jubilee celebration of the Ghana Academy of Sciences (Accra), 22 November, 1984.
2. The two Ghanaian visitors were Professor Alexander Kwapong, Vice-Rector of the United Nations University in Japan, and Professor Edward Ayensu of the Smithsonian Institution in the United States.
3. The Voice of America's African Service broadcast a recording of Nyerere's speech and press conference.

# Dance of debt isn't over yet

**JAMES S. HENRY**

James S. Henry is a New York-based economist and journalist who has written extensively about Third World debt problems and the flight of capital.

Five years to the month after Mexico touched off the great Third World debt crisis by defaulting on loans, a deceptive calm is settling in. Argentina is getting new terms for its more than $50 billion in foreign debt. Five of the six largest debtor countries—including the Philippines and Mexico—have worked out new repayment schedules since last year, with only Brazil a holdout. And fears of economic collapse in the U.S. and Latin America have given way to the idea that even though the $750 billion Third World debt may be chronic, it can be managed.

Indeed, from the standpoint of avoiding disasters, the debt problem has been managed rather well so far. Former Chairman Paul Volcker of the Federal Reserve Board adroitly managed several negotiations, especially those with Mexico and Brazil. Treasury Secretary James Baker played a key role with his 1985 offer of new loans to debtors if they would move to revamp their economies. For a while, this encouraged the mistaken belief that a solution could be found without major writeoffs by the banks.

More recently the banks have behaved as if they have lost faith in the Baker plan, but no one is panicking. Since May, 1987, over $18 billion of new loan-loss reserves have been set aside by Citicorp and 60 other American banks. Major British and Canadian banks have followed suit. Aided by special tax incentives, Japanese banks have begun to transfer $62 billion of Third World loans to a new company in the Cayman Islands. Oddly enough, such measures have only reinforced the complacency. Many observers have concluded that the industrial countries, or at least their banking systems, are now thoroughly insulated against any future Third World defaults.

Besides, the new bank reserves are fostering a large market in so-called debt-equity swaps, which will supposedly make a significant dent in debt levels by enabling lenders to exchange loans made to Third World countries for investments in businesses. (See box

**People are breathing a little easier about the Third World's debts these days, but basic troubles won't go away**

next page.) Citicorp gave swaps a major push when it said recently that it wants to exchange up to $5 billion of its $15 billion portfolio of country loans over the next five years.

**Premature complacency?**

True, cassandras have been wailing about the debt crisis for years, but now a crop of new concerns is emerging that, if nothing else, merits vigilance:

■ **The Baker plan has lost most of its vital signs.**

Secretary Baker's October, 1985, plan called for a minimum of $29 billion of new loans to 15 key debtor countries from 1986 to 1988, including $20 billion from private banks and at least $9 billion from institutions like the World Bank, in return for economic reforms by the strapped countries. Since then, however, debtors, banks and official lending institutions have all failed to meet Baker's targets.

Most of the major debtor countries have fallen behind on their commitments to economic reform. In the cases of Brazil, Venezuela and Argentina, debt burdens have continued to rise, payments deficits have worsened and only a modest amount of capital that fled the countries has returned. Mexico's balance of payments has improved but at the expense of a sharp recession. Everywhere, efforts to trim bloated state enterprises and turn them over to private owners have been halting at best.

Meanwhile, the private banks that supplied so much capital to poor countries in the past are counting their chips and going home after having actually reduced their net loans to the 15 Baker-plan countries in the last two years.

Nor have official lenders like the World Bank, the International Monetary Fund and the Inter-American Development Bank picked up the slack.

Compared with 1983-84, their net loans to major debtors actually fell by almost 50 percent in 1985-86. For Brazil, the largest Third World debtor, the decline was even steeper: In the last two years, it has paid out nearly $3 billion more to these organizations in the form of interest and principal on past loans than it received from them.

All in all, the supply of new loans to the "Baker 15" from all sources since 1985 has averaged less than a third of its 1983-84 total.

■ **Unmet needs for new money remain serious.**

Venezuela is trying to raise nearly $2 billion in new foreign loans for 1988-89. Colombia seeks $4 billion over the next three years. Ecuador faces an annual financing gap of over $1 billion, even though it has stopped paying all interest and principal on its $8 billion foreign debt. Brazil will be seeking at least $6 billion in new foreign-bank financing for 1987-88 alone. Argentina, Mexico and the Philippines could all use more new capital.

All told, developing countries outside the Organization of Petroleum Exporting Countries could easily use at least $60 to $70 billion of new foreign funds per year. Without that kind of money, they will be hard pressed to grow, democratize further and increase trade with the United States.

■ **The banks' big increase in reserves creates new risks.**

The good news is that bank bookkeeping is now closer to economic reality. But the past year's successful debt reschedulings mask the fact that patience with the existing debt framework is growing very thin among borrowers and lenders alike. Banks are getting fed up with the endless reschedulings and the heavy pressures from U.S. government officials to get them to lend new money. They reflected the frustrations by, in effect, writing off many of their Third World loans. One senior Citibank officer says of the firm's chairman John Reed: "He was frustrated by the lack of progress on economic reform by the debtor countries and wanted to make the bank secure against default."

Meanwhile, debtors are also frustrated, because, while they have in most cases continued to pay interest, they have received very few new loans. From 1983 through 1986, Brazil, Mexico, Argentina and Venezuela paid nearly $120 billion in interest on their foreign debt, at a time when they were receiving less than $30 billion in new loans from all sources. Not for nothing do many Latin Americans feel that, in the words of one leading Brazilian congressman, "the debt has already been repaid." Sentiment for at least a partial moratorium on debt payments is now spreading.

## Who owes what

Third-world countries
with repayment problems

| | |
|---|---|
| Brazil | $109.2 bil. |
| Mexico | $100.4 bil. |
| Argentina | $53.0 bil. |
| Venezuela | $34.1 bil. |
| Philippines | $28.3 bil. |
| Nigeria | $25.2 bil. |
| Chile | $21.6 bil. |
| Yugoslavia | $21.1 bil. |
| Morocco | $15.9 bil. |
| Colombia | $15.0 bil. |
| Peru | $14.6 bil. |
| Ecuador | $9.0 bil. |
| Ivory Coast | $7.6 bil. |
| Uruguay | $5.2 bil. |
| Bolivia | $4.5 bil. |

Note: Figures are total external debt at year's end 1986.

USN&WR—Basic data: Institute of International Finance

# The brave new world of swaps

What in the world, you might well ask, is a nice Minneapolis institution such as Norwest Bank doing with a stake in a paper mill 6,000 miles away in southern Brazil? Even John Jones, the vice president in Norwest's international department who helped get the regional bank into the deal, concedes that it takes "something of a leap" at first to figure out the merits of the investment.

Welcome to the wonderful world of debt-for-equity swaps, where some U.S. bankers are buying in to firms in financially rickety Third World nations as a way of getting back part of the millions they have lent. The banks contend that, far from taking irresponsible gambles, they are making prudent moves. In point of fact, the swaps may actually be the best of a bunch of bad options for banks faced otherwise with waiting years to get their money—if ever. Whether swaps are wise or not, the Federal Reserve Board made them easier to do August 12 by letting banks acquire as much as 100 percent of nonfinancial companies in debt-plagued lands, up from 20 percent. All told, Third World countries have retired some $6 billion of debt that way.

In Norwest's case, says Jones, "the deal doesn't seem quite so incredible" when you weigh the risks against the potential gains. Last year, Norwest had $212 million in loans outstanding in Brazil and, as the bank saw it, little prospect that the loans would be paid off anytime soon. "We want more control over our destiny—and a better chance of being repaid," says Jones.

So Norwest began looking for swaps as a way out. The bankers reasoned that if Brazil's economy kept nosediving, Norwest wouldn't be any worse off owning part of a company than it would be holding a loan to the central bank. But if business blossomed, the bank figured, an investment in a good company offered a better bet for fatter profits.

Norwest got its chance when Jones heard in Rio de Janeiro that the 151-nation World Bank wanted to sell its stake in Papel e Celulose Catarinense (PCC) with its 80,000-tons-a-year paper mill in Santa Catarina province. The company was particularly attractive to Norwest because it was profitable and was run by one of Brazil's oldest and most successful dynasties. After months of negotiations, Norwest swapped $12.5 million of Brazilian loans for about 14 percent of PCC.

For all the optimism, potential pitfalls lie ahead. Major expansion will leave PCC saddled with new debt. Like any investment in Latin America, this one is vulnerable to both inflation and currency depreciation. Such swap deals also fire political emotions: Some Brazilian nationalists want to make swaps unconstitutional. At any rate, it is doubtful the swaps can make a big dent in the country's debt.

Still, Norwest likes what it has done. It is analyzing potential swaps for more of its $500 million Latin American loan portfolio.

by Pamela Sherrid

---

## TURNING POINTS

# 5 YEARS ON THE DEBT BOMB

### 1982
• **August**—Mexico announces it can't make payments on $75 billion in foreign debts.
• **December**—Brazil and major banks begin effort to restructure foreign debt of $86 billion.
• **December**—External debt of 15 Third World nations with repayment problems: **$388.9 billion.**

### 1983
• **April**—Chile, unable to meet payments on $18 billion in foreign debt, declares a 90-day moratorium on payments.
• **December**—Debt of 15 Third World countries with repayment problems: **$413.6 billion.**

### 1984
• **January**—Brazil and international banks sign a new $6.5 billion loan package.
• **June**—Eleven Latin American debtors meet in Cartagena, Colombia, but reach no firm agreement on a common approach to debts.
• **September**—Largest debt rescheduling in history as Mexico and international banks agree on new terms for $48.5 billion in public-sector loans.
• **December**—Debt of 15 Third World countries: $428.6 billion.

### 1985
• **May**—Chile announces agreement with foreign banks on rescheduling $7.25 billion debt.
• **June**—Argentine President Alfonsin offers new economic program including government-spending cuts and wage-and-price controls.
• **July**—New President Alan Garcia announces Peru will limit debt service to 10 percent of the value of its export earnings.

• **October**—U.S. Treasury Secretary Banker outlines the Baker plan, calling for $29 billion in loans to 15 countries over three years and revamping of debtors' economies.
• **December**—Debt of 15 Third World countries: $444.1 billion.

### 1986
• **July**—World oil prices plunge below $10, hitting oil-producing debtors hard.
• **September**—Mexico reaches agreement with 15 leading banks on a $6 billion loan package.
• **October**—IMF approves loans to the Philippines, opening the way to debt-rescheduling talks.
• **December**—Debt of 15 Third World countries: $464.7 billion.

### 1987
• **February**—Brazil suspends interest payments on commercial-bank loans.
• **May**—Citicorp announces that it is adding $3 billion to its loan-loss reserves because of debt problems. Other major banks follow.

Recently, finance ministers of the Philippines, Brazil, Venezuela and Argentina called for a "new approach" that would provide longer-term debt relief and new capital.

But banks are moving in the other direction. As Morgan Guaranty Trust notes in its *World Financial Markets* newsletter: "For some time to come, new bank money will be available only on a modest scale."

■ **Debt swaps are not likely to supply more than a fraction of the new capital needed by debtors.**

To date, the amount of such swaps has been modest: $6 billion for debt-equity exchanges in Latin America since 1982, compared with $375 billion in foreign debt. Indeed, the swap market will have to work hard just to offset future red ink. If Mexico's foreign debt grows as expected, $2 billion a year of Mexican swaps would be needed just to cap the debt at today's level.

■ **Slow economic growth in the world and increasing protectionism create serious hazards.**

Despite decades of efforts to become economically independent, the Third World remains tied to the industrial world, not only because of debt service but also because it depends on rich nations for investment, technology and export markets. Last year, the U.S. accounted for over 90 percent of Mexico's non-oil exports. So U.S. talk of protectionism throws an automatic scare into all debtors. Any recession soon would come on top of five years of slow growth in poor countries; the social consequences could be severe.

■ **Add to all the other gloomy signals, evidence that no one is paying much attention in high places.**

There is no obvious mediator to bridge the gap between banks and debtors, and few people seem willing to take the lead. Secretary Baker apparently has diverted his attention from the debt problem to trade and budget battles with Congress. Alan Greenspan, the new Fed chairman, is an unknown quantity in the debt battles. The World Bank is in the throes of a staff reorganization that has been disastrous to its effectiveness. The Interamerican Development Bank is fighting a prolonged battle with the Treasury over funding.

With leadership scarce, the world economy dicey, the Baker plan in disarray and debtor countries hungry for fresh cash, the situation is far riskier than many realize—one that could lead to prolonged confrontations between the banks and the debtors, more Brazils that refuse to pay up and possibly new costs for Uncle Sam. "It's a nasty world out there," said Reed, chairman of Citicorp, in an interview with the *Wall Street Journal* early this year. And it could easily get worse.

# THE NEXT EARTHQUAKE

## CURTIS SKINNER

*Curtis Skinner is a writer who specializes in Latin American affairs. He has lived for ten years in Mexico.*

The collapse in international oil prices has put the fear of the people into Mexico's De la Madrid government, and for good reason. A projected shortfall of $6 billion this year has pushed Mexico back to the brink of default on its outstanding foreign debt of $97 billion and made three years of grinding economic austerity imposed on the poor and working classes into a mere "exercise in hunger." Having colluded with the International Monetary Fund (IMF) to cut popular living standards by almost half since 1982 in order to pay the country's commercial bank creditors, President Miguel De la Madrid is extremely reluctant to take further belt-tightening measures for fear of driving a sorely-pressed population into open revolt.

To avoid a forced default by Mexico that would set a dangerous precedent for the rest of debt-strapped Latin America, the Reagan administration is arm-twisting U.S. banks to come up with at least half of the $4 billion in fresh credits Mexican finance officials say they will need in 1986.

Enter the Baker Plan, the Reagan administration's touted "growth solution" to the third-world debt problem. The plan, formulated by Treasury Secretary James Baker at last October's IMF-World Bank joint meeting in Seoul, calls for increased lending on more flexible terms by multilateral agencies and commercial banks to debtor countries who undertake "structural reforms" to promote foreign and domestic private investment and liberalize trade. The gist of the Baker scheme—which proposes an inadequate $29 billion in fresh credits to fifteen countries over the next three years, but offers no relief for existing debt burdens—is using third-world debt dependency as a wedge to dismantle nationalist barriers to United States capital and exports. Having pursued a market-oriented economic strategy for the past year, De la Madrid expressed support for the Baker initiative at last January's Mexicali meeting with President Reagan and appears willing to take further liberalizing measures consistent with the plan. This policy may win Mexico its new loans and increase export earnings, but it will do so by further sacrificing popular living standards, perpetuating the debt trap, and retreating from the country's decades-long effort to develop an independent, industrial economy.

The seeds of Mexico's debt bondage lie, ironically enough, in the country's emergence as an oil power. In the late 1970s, the Jose Lopez Portillo administration borrowed heavily in international credit markets to finance an ambitious industrial development program based on enormously expanded petroleum production. A huge chunk of this money, however—perhaps as much as half of the total—was never invested in Mexico at all, but ended up deposited in Swiss bank accounts by corrupt government functionaries or used by businessmen for secure investments and real estate purchases in the United States and Europe. The cost of servicing Mexico's variable-interest loans, meanwhile, increased substantially starting in 1979, as the United States pursued a tight monetary policy to fight inflation. In August 1982, with only $200 million remaining in its central bank, Mexico was forced to suspend commercial debt principal payments and go cup-in-hand to Washington for a $10 billion bailout. This encouraged other Latin American countries to publicly acknowledge their unserviceable debts and so touched off the world debt crisis. As part of the rescue package, the incoming De la Madrid government agreed to follow a three-year austerity program monitored by the IMF.

De la Madrid tried hard to be a good boy for the bankers. Mexico played a key role blocking the formation of a Latin American debtors' cartel in 1983-84, and the country's harsh economic retrenchment strategy served as Washington's model for the region. As is often the case with IMF "structural adjustment" programs, the austerity burden fell mainly on the poor and working classes. The government slashed vital consumer subsidy programs, allowing the prices of such food staples as rice, beans, and tortillas to increase severalfold. De la Madrid also sold off dozens of parastatal enterprises, contributing to a 40 percent unemployment rate that has thrown legions of grown men on the streets of Mexico City to sell Chiclets and eat fire for handouts. In collaboration with Mexico's quasi-official trade union organization, the Confederation of Mexican Workers (CTM), the government held wages well below annual inflation rates averaging 60 percent over the last three years, cutting the standard of living for most Mexicans almost by half. By late 1985, workers earning the minimum wage (about three dollars a day) were spending over 70 percent of their income on the basic food basket.

From *Commonweal*, July 11, 1986, pp. 397-400. Copyright © Commonweal Foundation 1986.

De la Madrid's assault on popular living standards was rewarded with a major debt rescheduling, but financial "recovery" on the IMF's terms continued to elude Mexico. A critical problem was the steady decline in international oil prices beginning in 1983. Oil exports account for 70 percent of Mexico's foreign exchange earnings and the price shortfall severely undercut government savings.

Another important factor, less often acknowledged by the political-business elite who exhorted Mexican workers to tighten their belts for the good of the country, was the headlong flight of capital from Mexico. Economists estimate that up to $60 billion left the country from 1977 to 1984, and up to $5 billion may have been siphoned out the first six months of 1985 solely through the practice of under-invoicing exports and over-invoicing imports. This capital flight—by far the largest of any debtor nation—has done enormous harm to the country by depleting foreign exchange reserves, reducing the government's tax base, drying up investment resources, and stifling economic growth. As a result, the government found itself compelled to increase its borrowing and deficit spending, consequently driving up interest rates, worsening inflation, and devaluing the peso. By September 1985, Mexico had fallen out of compliance with its IMF austerity goals and was barred from further borrowing; in October, only two months after signing a new commercial debt rescheduling agreement, Finance Minister Jesús Silva Herzog (who was ousted last month as finance minister following sharp differences within the De la Madrid cabinet) had to request from the bankers a six-month-extension on principal payments.

Consequently, the Saudi Arabian-instigated oil price plunge this year caught Mexico at its most vulnerable moment since 1982. The country's outstanding foreign debt is bigger than ever, with servicing charges estimated at $11 billion, and the total public debt service burden (foreign and domestic) accounting for almost half of Mexico's 1986 federal budget. In this desperate strait, De la Madrid has two apparent choices: to declare a unilateral debt payment moratorium or opt for the temporary relief afforded by the Baker Plan. Having ruled out the first as "irresponsible," the Mexican president is pressing ahead to open his protected economy to foreign trade and investment, as called for under the Reagan scheme. Among recent liberalizing measures, De la Madrid has revised foreign investment laws to permit majority equity by non-Mexicans in new companies; opened Mexico's internal market to the foreign-owned *maquiladora* assembly-and-export plants; lowered general import requirements; and announced Mexico's decision to join the General Agreement on Tariffs and Trade (GATT). The Baker/De la Madrid strategy for attracting business and promoting exports requires keeping wages "competitive" (low), maintaining a brutal rate of peso devaluation, and taking further steps to privatize the mixed economy and eliminate state subsidies. Consistent with this approach, De la Madrid announced another round of budget cuts and state enterprise sales in a major February 1986 speech on economic policy and the debt.

The net effect of these measures would be to strengthen foreign over domestic capital and restructure the economy to the dictates of the world market. The competitive pressures unleashed by joining GATT and dismantling protective barriers may force stronger companies to become more efficient. However, they will certainly drive many small Mexican manufacturers out of business, resulting in the loss of thousands of jobs, as will the *maquiladoras'* foray into the domestic market. Lifting equity restrictions on foreign investment also works against national industrial development. Studies in *Excelsior* and in *Statistical Abstract of Latin America* have shown that transnational corporations usually enter the market by taking over an existing Mexican firm—displacing domestic capital—and use their size and technological "know-how" to dominate the most dynamic industrial sectors, particularly capital goods. In current bilateral trade and investment negotiations, the United States is pressing Mexico to water down its provisions for technology transfer and to strengthen patent protections, which would help the transnationals maintain their technological monopoly.

Meanwhile, Mexico's policy of wage restraints, consumer subsidy cuts, and divestment of state enterprise constrains development of the domestic market. Though some of the money-losing public corporations up for sale are pure bureaucratic boondoggles, others provide subsidized goods and services to business and consumers that cannot profitably be replaced. If this strategy produces immediate fiscal savings and economic growth as a short-term distortion, in the long run it undermines the country's financial integrity by: reducing the state's internal revenue base, increasing the carrying cost of the unemployed and marginal sectors, and compelling excessive reliance on fickle foreign markets for economic security. It is a recipe for continued dependence on external borrowing and petroleum exports.

De la Madrid faces a mounting political challenge to this unpopular program. After fifty-six uninterrupted years in power, the ruling Institutional Revolutionary Party (PRI) is caught in the throes of a legitimacy crisis provoked by prolonged economic decline, the party's spectacular mismanagement of the national oil patrimony (a deeply felt issue), and recent examples of gross bureaucratic corruption and electoral fraud. The PRI's ability to co-opt and buy off disaffected social groups in time-honored fashion has been sapped by years of austerity. Now the party faces an unprecedented challenge to its authority from the political right and left as well as from a burgeoning grassroots movement. Though no rival organization is capable of competing on equal terms with the PRI's huge political machine, this popular mobilization could wrest some important social concessions from De la Madrid while laying the groundwork for political change.

On the electoral front, the rightist National Action Party (PAN) has been a thorn in the PRI's side, particularly in the important northern states of Chihuahua, Sonora, and Nuevo León. While PAN advocates a vague laissez-faire business philosophy, its appeal to many Mexicans is not ideological. Some supporters see National Action as more responsive to local interests than the highly-centralized PRI, but most votes for PAN, Mexico's largest opposition party, are votes against the government.

The PRI has responded to PAN's growing power at the polls with ham-handed fraud and repression, provoking PAN street protests that have turned violent. Ballot-box stuffing and falsified voting lists robbed PAN gubernatorial candidate Adalberto Rosas Lopez of a likely victory in the important Sonora race last July. In December and January of that election year, a rash of PAN-led mass protests broke out around the country against PRI vote-rigging in municipal elections. In the southern state of Chiapas, PAN militants occupied municipal offices in numerous towns and had to be forcibly removed by the police at the cost of seven lives. Demonstrators in the important central provincial city of San Luis Potosi torched the municipal palace on New Year's Eve and were also dispersed with bloodshed by the security forces.

Given this confrontational background, the local elections scheduled for Chihuahua this July stand as a watershed in Mexico's political history. President De la Madrid is under considerable pressure from the United States, backed by the creditor bankers, to avoid a repeat of last year's farce that would further discredit the PRI and undermine the system's long-term stability. On the other hand, PRI hardliners like CTM chief Fidel Velasquez oppose any weakening of the party's control at this time of acute economic strain. At stake is the state governorship, which PAN candidate and Ciudad Juárez mayor Francisco Barrio Berrazas stands to win in clean elections, according to the polls. The bets are that the PRI, never before having relinquished a governorship, will turn to massive fraud once again. Should this occur, there is a high potential for statewide violence since PAN controls over 60 percent of Chihuahua's municipalities, including the major cities.

Another symptom of a deep lack of confidence in the PRI and growing mass politicization is the emergence of independent self-help groups in the wake of last September's devastating earthquakes in Mexico City. The quakes—which caused $6 billion in damage, killed up to 20,000 people, and left another 130,000 homeless—have had a profound impact on the Mexican psyche, greatly adding to the prevailing climate of crisis and insecurity, but also inspiring impressive examples of popular initiative to cope with the tragedy. Rejecting government assistance, numerous volunteer groups sprang up around the city in the days following the disaster to channel private relief to the victims, known as *damnificados*. The De la Madrid administration, meanwhile, has come under strong criticism for corruption and inefficiency in aid administration, and for its failure to provide long-term relief for the *damnificados*, tens of thousands of whom are still camped out on city streets. The United Front of Earthquake Victims, a grassroots organization claiming 100,000 members, has held regular street demonstrations demanding new housing and urging that money spent repaying the foreign debt be used for earthquake reconstruction.

The key roadblock to both progressive political change and a socially responsible resolution of Mexico's debt crisis is the PRI's stranglehold on the country's major labor organizations and the weakness of the left, two aspects of the same problem. Since the "union insurgency" movement for political independence and internal democracy was crushed in the 1970s, the left, divided into eight small parties, has had a minimal presence in the mass organizations that carry decisive social weight in Mexico. However, the oil price plunge and redoubled austerity have given union bureaucrats like CTM chief Velasquez new cause for worry about restiveness in the ranks. The left wields a tremendously potent political weapon by linking De la

Madrid's wage policy to Mexico's national subjugation under the foreign debt, forced oil sales, and the Baker Plan. The Communist-led United Socialist Party of Mexico (PSUM), Trotskyist Revolutionary Workers Party (PRT), and social democratic Mexican Workers Party (PMT) have moved aggressively to exploit the issue in recent months. A left-organized Mexico City demonstration on February 6 drew 50,000 marchers from 122 workers', peasants', and political organizations to demand wage increases, a debt moratorium, and repudiation of the Baker Plan. Passing in front of the U.S. embassy, marchers shouted, "Thieving government, you're sold to the gringos."

With oil prices in a long-term decline, Mexico's foreign debt is unpayable, as even De la Madrid cabinet members privately acknowledge. The only question is whether default is managed to benefit the bankers or the Mexican people. The De la Madrid policy of continuing full interest payments with fresh credits and rolling over the accumulated principal lets the banks keep the loans formally in good standing and their profits intact. The cost to Mexico is ever-deepening debt dependency, and the banks also lose in the long run by increasing their overall exposure as they postpone the day of reckoning.

The alternative to this *de facto* default is a unilateral payment moratorium or flat-out debt annulment on Mexico's part. Mexican business sleaders and government officials have warned direly that such a step would provoke crippling economic retaliation from the United States, including a trade embargo and suspension of new credits. These fears are exaggerated. Mexico is neither Cuba nor Nicaragua. It is in fact the United States' third-largest trading partner after Canada and Japan. A $35 billion trade cut-off would have sharply negative effects for the U.S. economy, particularly in a Southwest already battered by plunging oil prices, and is not a credible policy option for the Reagan administration. As for a credit suspension, Mexico only stands to gain by halting the downward debt spiral, and in any case, could make up the loss from its payments savings.

A three-to-five-year total debt payment moratorium, with future interest payments limited to 20 percent of the total value of exports, would give Mexico vital breathing space to put its financial house in order, pursue economic development, and begin to redress workers' living standards. A more equitable, but riskier, option is simply to cancel the debt, preferably in conjunction with other Latin American debtors. As Fidel Castro noted at last summer's debt conference in Havana, repudiating the regional public debt would help compensate for the "illegitimate transfers" Latin America has made to the developed world in recent years in the form of excessively high interest rates, an overvalued dollar, deteriorating terms of trade, and capital flight. But the real point is that the working classes of poor nations like Mexico should not be held responsible for debts they neither contracted nor benefited from—especially when the creditors are the wealthiest financial institutions and governments in the world. (Citibank, Mexico's largest creditor, made *$1 billion* in 1985 profits.) For Mexico and much of the rest of the third world, progress depends on a clean break from the debt tar baby.

# Women on the sidelines

### Amadou Moustapha Diop

**AMADOU MOUSTAPHA DIOP,** *Senegalese specialist in migration problems, is engaged in research with the French Centre for the Study of International Relations. He also lectures at the National Institute of Oriental Languages and Civilizations, Paris.*

**With These Hands,** *a film produced and directed by Chris Sheppard and Claude Sauvageot, presents the stories of three women from three African countries: Kenya, Zimbabwe and Burkina Faso. One of the most surprising facts revealed by the film is that women, not men, grow 75• of Africa's food—as well as finding time for their domestic chores. Zenabou Bambara of Burkina Faso declares: "We wish the men would help. But a man is ashamed to do women's work."*

THE social exclusion of women in the countries of the Third World has its origin in patriarchal institutions whose standards, values and models are exclusively controlled by men. Ideological constructions subject women to a "constant reversal of values". According to this institutional framework, woman is negatively branded from birth. "Biologically, motherhood sets her apart; ethically, her impurity isolates her; metaphysically, her very being is guilty, and the great religions systematize her condemnation: original sin in Christianity, and reincarnation in the body of a woman as punishment for a misspent life in Hinduism".[1] Nor should we overlook Islam, which elaborately demarcates the territory of the two sexes: the interior of the house, the indoor world, is the woman's realm, and she herself is the secret domain of man; the outdoors is men's field of action and a strictly male preserve. And "any overlapping of these spaces is restricted and controlled by a host of rituals".[2]

Thus the traditional reproductive and nurturing role is one of the major obstacles to women's participation in society. This socio-biological role is a hindrance in that it forces women—imprisoned in the straitjacket of their responsibilities towards their children[3]—to put up with mere "pin money", starvation wages in the agro-industries of the Third World countries: "The international division of labour classes them as working mothers, working wives and working sisters. The profits of national and international corporations are swollen thanks to the concept of 'wives' earnings', which provides ideological justification for both the existence and the injustice of unequal pay for the two sexes."[1] The gravitation towards sub-proletarian work is caused by women's inferior position in the rural world, and by the family's assumption that domestic work is a woman's natural lot, which is treated as non-existent at national level because it is not productive work, and hence cannot feature in the statistics of the decision-makers and planners.[4] Furthermore, women are deprived of the means of production: under common law they cannot inherit land, and so their access to agriculture depends on the fulfilment of duly pre-established social conditions—a woman must be married, or at least have a recognized status in the community.

In *Femmes du tiers monde,*[1] J. Bissillat and M. Fiéloux describe one case of the total exclusion of Senegalese women

from the system of land ownership. In 1979, SAED, the body responsible for development of the middle region of the Senegal Valley, decided to organize a "village lottery for farmers, so that they might all, regardless of their status—whether formerly slaves, craftworkers or 'masters'—have a chance to win in the distribution of plots of land on the outskirts of the village where irrigation was planned. But this exercise in fair play ran into trouble. Whatever her status—as a wife, single woman or de facto head of a household—no woman was entitled to receive a plot of land in her own name. The only way around the difficulty was for the most needy among them, such as a widow with four children to support, to give a fictitious name for the head of the family, with the villagers' consent: that of a five-year-old son or a deceased relative, for example."

Even the usufruct of plots of land conceded to a woman by her husband becomes precarious with the development of cash crops, which are "increasingly taking over the best land, encroaching on areas formerly set aside for food crops". Cash crops have destroyed the former balance of duties and obligations; the old methods of sharing have fallen into disuse. Cash crops enhance the prestige and power of men. Women, although they play an active part in agricultural work, find their status radically changing; they become an over-exploited sub-proletariat—since they still continue to tend the food crops—and underpaid wage-earners. A Dioula woman (Senegal), for example, after working on her husband's groundnut plantations, is entitled to "one-twentieth of the money that he makes from the harvest".

Trapped in the labour of growing food, rural women are cut off from the economic circuits, and accordingly have no access to co-operatives or to loans. If anyone condescends to grant a woman a loan, it will be at a prohibitively high rate of interest. For example, Burkina-be women were offered "a loan access scheme. But then the paradox became starkly apparent, because they were compelled to accept a repayment rate fixed by the men, slightly higher than the official rate".

Women perform nearly 80 per cent of agricultural work in Africa, and yet as economic partners they are non-existent. For example, Wolof women (Senegal) "are kept at a safe distance from the knowledge, contacts and skills that are held in the highest esteem. No programme caters for them, whether literacy teaching or agricultural extension work".[5] When trading institutes do admit women, they train them in altogether marginal activities whose usefulness to the community is negligible. "Rather than being taught the new cultivation and management techniques which ... they are perfectly capable of learning, they are given lessons in embroidery, sewing, knitting and cookery."

Like the traditional societies of India and China, African societies obey the rules of "institutionalized subordination", under which women have internalized three types of submission: "Before marriage, obey your father. After marriage, obey your husband. After your husband dies, obey your son."[4]

This system of subordination and "androcentrism" has unfortunate implications which result in discrimination in the areas of food and health. On the subject of Indian women, ill-nourished and receiving inferior health care, it has been noted that "while there is a higher incidence of diseases caused by malnutrition among women, the hospital rate of admission and treatment of young and adult males for these diseases is larger."[4] This exclusion and deprivation of rights on "biological" grounds opens the door to other forms of marginalization, in education in particular: the number of illiterate women is increasing; when girls are not "drop-outs, push-outs and left-outs", they are to be found in "traditional, ornamental fields of education" considered to be "feminine".

In the political sphere, despite the fact that some women hold senior positions, most play very little part in politics, because they have never been properly taught and because of the social pressures whereby "unmarried girls [in India] are socially and culturally prohibited from free mingling with males ... owing to their parents' fear of a reduction of their 'value' in the marriage market".[3] Custom demands that a married woman follow her *dharma*, which is "to be subservient to her husband, take care of his needs, make him happy, bear and rear his children". After this taxing ordeal, how can a woman find time to involve herself in politics? Surely her everyday household drudgery is already the first barrier to any kind of participation in the life of the community.

1. Jeanne Bissillat and Michèle Fiéloux. *Femmes du tiers monde*, Paris, Le Sycomore, 1983.
2. Fatima Mernissi. *Sexe, idéologie, islam*, Paris, Tierce, 1983.
3. D. Radha Devi and M. Ravindran. "Women's Work in India", *International Social Science Journal*, Volume XXXV, No. 4, 1983.
4. Govind Kelkar. *Comparative analysis of Indian and Chinese experiences of institutionalization of popular participation in development (in particular for women)*, Unesco, 1979.
5. Claudine Vidal. *Les femmes wolof dans un milieu rural en mutation: marginalisation ou intégration?*, unpublished doctoral thesis, Paris, 1981.

# Children in Darkness
## The Exploitation of Innocence
## A Brutal Choice: Work or Starve

### Kristin Helmore

*Staff writer of* The Christian Science Monitor

Shadab is 9. Since he was 6, he has spent 12 hours a day, six days a week, squatting in semidarkness on damp ground, polishing little pieces of metal on a high-speed grinding wheel.

In the lock factory near New Elhi where he works, the gloom is broken only by a few narrow shafts of light entering through holes in the brick walls, and by a single light bulb. The air is visibly, palpably thick with metal dust, the temperature about 120 degrees F. The bare floor is damp with acid that sloshes from big vats onto the ground.

Shadab is a bright-eyed child with an eager smile and a quick intelligence. He is small and alarmingly thin. Though his skin is normally brown, by noon every inch of him has turned a metallic gray-black, coated with metal dust. His hair is stiff with it. His voice is hoarse with it.

All around the child, the unprotected belts that drive the grinding wheels whir. Metal pieces rasp and clang. When Shadab bends over to work, his face a few inches from his wheel, splinters of metal occasionally fly up into his eyes. He has never seen a pair of safety goggles.

Shadab says he likes his job. He likes making money – about 17 cents a day. His father is dead, and he is proud that his mother, two brothers, and sister depend on his contribution for survival.

The factory where Shadab works is in Aligarh, 80 miles southeast of New Delhi. It employs nine people, five of whom are under 12. The adults are paid more than three times as much as the children, though many of their tasks are the same.

By any Western definition, Shadab is exploited. Working 12 hours a day, he has never been to school; his is grossly underpaid; his health is in danger. Yet many people in developing countries might envy

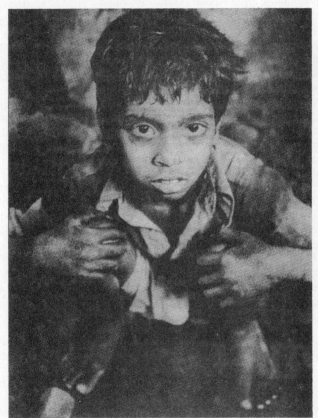

Like Shadab, this boy earns just pennies a day. He works in a brass factory in Moradabad, India.

him his job. For his family, the alternative could be starvation.

Collecting accurate data on the numbers of children working in the world today is extremely difficult, and estimates vary widely. According to the International Labor Organization (ILO), there are at least 58 million children under 16 working for wages outside their families. Most are in developing countries, though some work in industrialized countries, too. In the United States, 800,000 children are employed as migrant farm laborers.

Other calculations put the worldwide number of wage-earning children at between 100 million and 200 million. Asia has the largest number: In southern Asian nations, more than 60 percent of children are believed to be working. Some estimate the proportion in India to be even higher.

In addition to exploitation, child labor can deprive a young worker of freedom, separating him from his family and making him a virtual slave.

Deep in the jungles of Peru, an estimated 3,000 children work in gold mines. Since the government began to crack down several years ago, the children have been moved farther and farther up the remotest tributaries of the Amazon. The camps are several days' journey by boat from the nearest town, and those with the most children are defended by lookouts armed with shotguns.

Ten months ago, 13-year-old Mariel Quispe was sent by her father to work as a cook in a small mining camp in the jungle. A shy and nervous girl, she explains in a whisper that she was brought to the area by an "agent," and hopes to be taken home soon by the same man. But she has not heard from him since she arrived. Asked when he thinks Mariel will go home, a local landowner familiar with conditions here says: "Never."

The largest group of the world's child laborers work with their families in agriculture and in the home. Such work is not generally perceived to be exploitative, even though it often means the children do not go to school. According to some studies, these children, who may spend their childhood as virtual shut-ins caring for younger siblings and doing domestic chores, may not develop mentally or emotionally to their full capacity.

CHILD labor within the family is generally born of tradition and sustained by necessity. Child labor for an outside employer is born of poverty, which in turn often breeds exploitation. Children are available to work because their families need the money. Work is available for children because their labor is cheaper than that of adults and more can be demanded of them.

"Children are exploitable," says Ashok Narayan, India's joint secretary of labor. "They are more docile. They work fast and they don't get tired so easily, so more work can be extracted out of them. And even if one cheats them by paying less wages, they are not in a position to detect it. These are the reasons for child labor."

Experts point out that child labor is often most widespread in areas with the highest adult unemployment. In India's Tamil Nadu State, chronic drought has left many farmers destitute. And every day 50,000 children, some no more than five years old, are bused from their villages as early as 3 a.m. to work in the local match and fireworks factories.

Child labor also occurs in economically depressed areas where employers cannot afford to pay adult wages, or where syndicates of employers and middlemen can manipulate hiring practices in an exploitative way, drawing from a virtually inexhaustible pool of desperately poor children and adults. Researchers in India say that the owners of the match and fireworks factories in Tamil Nadu also own most of the farmland, and have deliberately withheld irrigation so that families are forced by dire necessity to send children to the factories.

In third-world countries, the potential for child exploitation is increased by the absence of unemployment insurance or welfare programs similar to those of industrialized nations. And when poor parents view children as contributors to family survival, they tend to want more children. Hence experts note that child labor can be an obstacle to population control.

The policies of the ILO specify that hazardous employment such as Shadab's should be restricted to workers 18 years old or older. India's Child Labor (Regulation) Act bans hazardous employment for workers under 15. It also calls for various safety and health measures, such as adequate lighting and ventilation and protective goggles and gloves. But government officials complain that such laws are very difficult to enforce. ILO regulations are stricter than those of many countries, and local authorities often find them unrealistic, given the present level of poverty and underdevelopment in their countries.

Many analysts say that vested interests and corruption are the reasons labor regulations are consistently ignored. Walter Fernandes, director of the Indian Social Institute in New Delhi, which studies the social impact of economic trends, charges, "Most industrialists I've interviewed said they didn't have to worry about the government machinery because they could always bribe the labor commissioners. The labor commissioners told us they dared not prosecute many industrialists because of their political clout."

One Thai government official asks, "If the police are corrupt, what do you do? This country has beautiful laws, just like any country. But they don't work!"

In Thailand, child labor is legal as of age 12, provided it is not hazardous. The Ministry of Labor officially counts 30,000

# "CHILDREN are exploitable. They are more docile. They work fast and they don't get tired so easily, so more work can be extracted out of them."

– Ashok Narayan, India's joint secretary of labor

workers between the ages of 12 and 15. But reports by nongovernmental organizations put the figure at about 2 million, with some as young as 4 or 5, and many subject to brutal, slave-like conditions.

"Looking for a servant?" said a smooth-talking young man with an ingratiating smile. He had emerged from an alley onto Bangkok's Rong Muang Road, a seedy street beside the railroad station that is lined with employment agencies handling underage workers.

"Want a young one?" the man persisted. "We have them 12, 13."

In his "office," a kind of small warehouse down the alley, he produced Dao, a shy 15-year-old who had arrived by train two days before from her village in drought-stricken northeastern Thailand.

Whoever hires Dao will pay the agency $200, and she will be bound to work for a year. The agency would not reveal how much of this sum her family receives, although her reason for coming to Bangkok is to send money home. Dao will be expected to get up every morning before her "master," work as directed until he says she can stop, and go to bed after he does. Days off will be at his discretion. And there is nothing to prevent Dao from being physically or sexually abused.

WORLDWIDE, domestic work is second only to agricultural labor as a source of child employment. In Latin America, Africa, and Asia, girls and boys, sometimes beginning at age 5 or 6, may spend their entire childhood as servants in other people's homes. Many, like Dao, come to the city from impoverished rural villages, and are considered fortunate to find work. Sometimes employers treat them as "part of the family" but most often they do grueling work for long hours, with little remuneration. Some are virtual slaves.

"These children are like objects," says Blanca Figueroa, director of a women's support organization in Lima, Peru. "They're like little animals that grow up in your home."

The forms of child labor are as varied as the economies that spawn them. Three months' travel in 11 countries turned up children under 16 working as gold miners, cooks, street vendors, maids, porters, parking attendants, seamstresses, divers in fishing operations, gas station attendants, bus ticket collectors, rag pickers, waiters, carpet weavers, brickmakers, truck mechanics, construction workers, and employees in the glass, brass, lock, and power-loom industries.

Marcelo lives on the island of Cebu, in the Philippines. He spent three years, from ages 10 through 12, on a ship in the South China Sea working as a diver for a fishing fleet. The fishing technique, called *muro-ami*, requires that as many divers as possible swim shoulder to shoulder, banging a weight tied to the end of a line against the coral on the ocean floor, to scare fish into a huge net. They must also dive as deep as 100 feet in order to secure or dislodge the net. On coming up, they frequently get caught in the net, and occasionally drown. They use no diving equipment.

"One year, three boys from my ship drowned," says Marcelo. "Sometimes we stayed down five minutes, deep in the water. Blood would come out of my ears and nose. Sometimes boys lost breath and never came up."

Children are sought after for *muro-ami* fishing partly because they take up less space, so more divers can be crammed onto each boat.

There were more than 300 boys on Marcelo's boat, along with eight pigs being raised by one of the supervisors. The boys slept on stacked shelving. Marcelo says that the filth, cramped conditions, and lack of sanitation often resulted in illness.

"THE worst was that even when we were sick they made us dive," he recalls. "If we said we were too sick to dive, they would beat us. And the younger boys, if they made a mistake, the punishment was they would be thrown in the water and held under."

Marcelo says that each year he worked he was cheated. The last year, his agreement stated he would earn $350 for 10 months' work. Instead, he received $50.

The government banned *muro-ami* fishing last December, with a "grace period" that was scheduled to expire in June of this year. But on June 4, the ban was lifted indefinitely.

Many observers see child labor as both a consequence and a cause of poverty. A child like Shadab is often physically and mentally burned out by age 14, totally unschooled and prepared for only a simple, low-paying job. And by the time he is in his teens and needs to earn more, he may face displacement by a nine-year-old willing to work for 17 cents a day.

Child labor breeds generations of illiterate adults whose health has often been undermined by their work as children, who can barely support their families, and who will, in all likelihood, have to send their own children out to work.

Nisarem has seven children, all under 15 years old. He lives in northern Pakistan.

As a boy, he worked at a bakery from 4 a.m. until 9 p.m. He says his health is poor today because of this work. "I was working near to fire, so all the time I have my chest in front of fire," Nisarem says. Today he has to take easy work in a shop, and he earns very little.

His dream has been to send his children to school and give them a better life than he has had. But so far, none of them have gone to school: Six of the seven are already working.

# RURAL INDUSTRY CHINA'S NEW ENGINE FOR DEVELOPMENT

## Tu Nan

Tu Nan, *a Chinese economist, is a senior staff member of FAO.*

Agriculture in China has made impressive progress in the past five years. Gross product value of agriculture increased at an average rate of 10 per cent per annum while in the 28 years from 1953 through 1980, it averaged only 3.5 per cent. In the Sixth Five Year Plan per caput net income of farmers more than doubled, from 190 yuan to about 400 yuan, surpassing the total gain of net income in the previous 28 years.* New policies and strategy, accumulated investment, and more input, coupled with more advanced science and technology all played an important part in the process. In the policy field, the contracted responsibility system combined with better pricing and marketing policies and decentralization all contributed to better results.

Yet in recent years, a new star is rising rapidly on the horizon and fast gaining central stage—rural industry. In the five years from 1979 to 1983, its gross product value increased an average of 17 per cent a year, surpassing the annual growth rate of national industrial development of 14 per cent. In 1984 and 1985, rural industry advanced at the astounding rate of 40 per cent and 45 per cent respectively. It is

* *1 yuan = approximately US$0.40.*

estimated that the total value of its output, at 330 billion yuan in 1986, surpassed that of agriculture, at 304 billion yuan, for the first time in history. This marked a significant new phase in China's rural development.

**The background.** The conspicuous features of the environment for China's development and modernization are the country's huge population, limited agricultural resources and a rather low starting base. China is far below world average in the use of some essential agricultural inputs. Arable land per caput is less than a third of world average. Per caput water and forest resources are only one-quarter and one-fifth of the world average respectively. Yet such limited resources have to support a huge rural population of over 800 million, 95 per cent of which is crowded into the southeastern half of continental China. Chinese peasants had long been seeking an opportunity to break out of their poverty and take part in the process of development and modernization. The family farming system introduced some eight years ago released the long pent-up enthusiasm of Chinese peasants for production and prosperity. Agricultural efficiency was thereby enormously improved, but redun-

dant labour, that which agriculture could not absorb quickly, became common in the countryside and now accounts for about half the rural labour force. It is only natural that these workers are eager for new undertakings. As the policy of invigorating the domestic economy got under way, the surplus labour force in the countryside immediately seized new opportunities to launch all kinds of rural enterprises. On the other hand, inadequate infrastructure, especially the transport bottleneck, also makes it necessary to process large amounts of additional agro-products on-site in the countryside. Rising living standards also create demand for more diversified consumer goods that the public sector cannot fully meet.

In some countries modernization has more or less followed the pattern of advanced industrial cities and backward agricultural countryside accompanied by the migration of population from the latter into the former. For a huge country like China, this is neither possible nor desirable, in either financial or physical terms. Since the founding of the People's Republic, the bulk of state investment went to cities, industry, and transport. The result has been impressive but far from satisfactory. Until eight years ago

Reprinted from *Ceres*, November/December 1986, pp. 32–38. CERES, the FAO review on agriculture and development.

differences between the cities and the countryside were actually widening. Under the old economic system one might say that the cities and the countryside of China had been running on separate tracks. In encouraging the development of rural industry and achieving admirable results, China seems to have found its own particular road to industrialization, modernization, and urbanization suited to its specific conditions.

**The miracle.** There are now 22 big cities with non-agricultural populations exceeding one million and 28 medium cities with populations between half a million and a million. The 22 megacities alone account for some 40 per cent of the urban population of China and the bulk of the country's industrial capacity, revenue base, and institutions of higher learning. On the other hand, there are over 90 000 rural towns and townships, each with a population of several thousand. It is in these towns and townships that the miracle of rural industry has taken place. The range of enterprises covers almost every trade. There are now about 370 million labourers in rural China. About 300 million of them work in agriculture at least part of their time. About 40 million are in secondary industries, mainly in manufacturing, building, and mining, representing a 74 per cent increase over 1980. About 30 million are in tertiary industries, mainly in transport, commerce, catering, and other services. Rural industry now employs about 20 per cent of the labour force of the Chinese countryside and accounts for some 25 per cent of the total industrial output value of China. In some sectors, rural enterprises have become a sizeable force in the national economy. They now produce over 80 per cent of all iron farm tools, 53 per cent of building material, around 50 per cent of garments and shoes, 43 per cent of sulphate of iron, about 25 per cent of textiles, and some 20 per cent of coal. Their products not only sell throughout the country, but have begun to enter the in-

ternational market. In 1985, they contributed US$4 billion worth of goods and services on the international market. Now over 8 000 rural enterprises are engaged in export production of some 1 500 varieties of products. Nearly 900 of them are joint enterprises with foreign capital. Their 8 million building workers represent more than 60 per cent of the national construction force. Seasonal migrant skilled workers are another feature. For instance, the province of Jiangsu alone sends 35 000 building workers to Sinjiang, in extreme west China, to work for some 10 months of the year and come home every winter. In short, rural industry is now playing an indispensable role in supplementing the deficiencies of state industries and is filling considerable gaps of every conceivable kind.

The pace of expansion of rural industry in China is really remarkable. In the six years between 1980 and 1986, the number of enterprises increased 214 times, from some 56 000 to over 12 million. Gross product value quadrupled, from 65.6 billion yuan to 330 billion yuan. The taxes paid to the state annually quintupled. In the fourth largest city of China, Shenyang, tax paid by rural enterprises accounted for 70 per cent of all local government revenue in 1985 (all Chinese cities have a number of agricultural counties under their jurisdiction). Their total profit approximately tripled in the four years from 1980 to 1984, from 6.6 billion yuan to 18.7 billion yuan. In the past five years, more than half the income increment of the rural population came from rural industry. It is now safe to say that rural industry has become the most dynamic part of the Chinese economy.

**The merits.** Rural industry in China has been developing under difficult conditions, but there are a number of positive factors that contribute to its vitality, among them:

*High flexibility.* There are various forms of partnership at varying

levels below the county. Enterprises of the county level and higher are mostly state-owned. The most popular and fastest expanding form is the family household undertaking and its alliance with some sort of collective or cooperative enterprise. These are usually centred around certain products, some kind of technology or a line of service. They are inevitably small-scale, permitting quick management decisions in fast-changing market conditions as well as specialization in the production and marketing of thousands of small commodities. About half of all the buttons in China nowadays come from a tiny township in Wenzhou in east China that has developed into the button centre of the whole country for both manufacturing and marketing. Its turnover in button trade exceeded 100 million yuan last year.

*Low cost.* Rural industry needs no investment from the state. There are no managerial staff assigned by the state with their cradle-to-grave social security cover. An elastic wage system mostly linked to performance is also highly cost saving. Where some investment is inevitable, it is much less than in a state enterprise. For instance, while large state coal pits need 200 yuan of investment to create the capacity to produce one ton of coal, small rural pits need only 20-30 yuan. Thus the 200 million tons of coal produced by rural enterprises annually saved government investment to the tune of some 3.5 billion yuan. Generally speaking, to give employment to one person in a city requires over 15 000 yuan of investment from the state, but rural enterprises need only about 10 per cent of that amount to create one job. Their circumstances dictate that their overheads have to be very small. A great many rural manufacturing enterprises subcontract the making of parts to family workshops where there might be only one or two small lathes using spare space in the family home. They are able to make optimum use of manpower; often they use marginal material or even scrap rejected by state enterprises.

*Creating employment.* The population of China, now greater than 1 billion, is expected to be between 1.2 and 1.3 billion around the turn of the century. Youngsters entering the labour market number more than 10 million a year and are expected to peak at 13 million before the year 2000. Providing jobs for them is perhaps the single most formidable task facing the Chinese Government. Rural industry, being labour-intensive by necessity, appears to be a possible solution to this problem. It absorbed 12 million additional workers in 1985, a 22 per cent increase over 1984, and is bound to provide the main outlet for 10 million-plus fresh labourers coming onstream every year in coming decades.

*Better management.* Here the picture is certainly mixed. It is generally believed that only some 30 per cent of rural enterprises are well managed, some 40 per cent are of average management standard, some 20 percent are poorly managed, barely remaining in operation, and the remaining 10 per cent are facing closure or bankruptcy. However, in some aspects, they compare favourably with state-run enterprises. In 1984 for every 100 yuan fixed asset, the output value of rural industry is more than twice the average for state enterprises. Profit, at 34 yuan, is more than three times that of the state enterprises. Tax generated at 15 yuan is nearly one and a half times as much. In a country where the science of management was once deliberately ignored, it is difficult to imagine that undereducated peasants, some still illiterate, can properly manage rural enterprises. Here the very nature of the entities in a given situation makes all the difference. In contrast to state enterprises rural enterprises link remuneration directly to performance. The quality of their management and their ability to react immediately and correctly to shifting market conditions are a matter of survival for them. Generally, only better educated and more talented peasants venture to set up such enterprises.

*Increasing revenue.* As rural industry creates much more wealth per caput than agriculture, it is fast becoming an ever more important source of revenue for the Government. In 1985, it paid over 13.7 billion yuan of tax to the state, representing 7.5 per cent of the total tax revenue and 20 per cent of new added tax income during the year. In recent years, it has been increasing at the rate of some 30 per cent a year, a rate much faster than that of other tax revenues. Besides, it paid over 30 billion yuan in the five years between 1981 and 1985 to local governments and over 8 billion yuan a year to collective welfare undertaking. Taxes paid by rural enterprises now account for over two-thirds of state revenue collected from the countryside. In Jiangsu province, some 85.5 per cent of new increased revenue came from rural industry in the past seven years.

**The problems.** Like all new ventures, rural industry in China is fraught with problems. Chief among them:

*Obsolete equipment and low technology.* There are about 1.8 million technicians in some 400 000 enterprises at the county level and above in China, but rural enterprises have extremely few, if any. Serious environmental pollution is but one aspect of this vast problem.

*Shoddy product quality.* A considerable glut of many products of inferior quality has already appeared and is forcing many rural enterprises either to improve or to be driven out of existence. But the picture is far from uniform. Some rural enterprises are turning out products of excellent quality of international standard.

*Low productivity.* This obviously depends on the method of calculation. The comparison with state enterprises can only be relative and the picture extremely mixed. While its productivity is generally higher than agriculture and could compare favourably with the less efficient part of state enterprises, it certainly lags far behind the more modern and better managed ones. It is also generally more energy-consuming.

*Shortage of raw material and energy.* This is a common problem facing many industries, but an especially acute one for some rural enterprises. Now only about a quarter of them working under contract with state enterprises or having direct links with them receive allocations of raw material at official prices under state plans. The other three-quarters have to buy their raw material on the market, where it can be several times more expensive. They get only about half their power supply from the regional grid. For the other half, they have to generate their own electricity in very expensive ways. The shortage of current compels some of them to operate only three or four days a week. A number of rural enterprises are criticized for competing with more efficient modern factories for a limited supply of certain materials.

*Shortage of capital.* Capital formation for rural enterprises relies mainly on the savings of peasants, the majority of whom are still far from prosperous. Banks and credit institutions gave some assistance, totalling nearly 48 billion yuan of loans of all kinds in 1984, but with the tightening of credit in an overheated economy, this has dwindled. Internal accumulation and the savings of employees totalled about 30 billion yuan in 1984.

*Inadequate information.* In China where commodity economy was officially recognized only recently, market information is bound to be inadequate. A few family undertakings specializing in the dissemination of market information have appeared and proved very popular, but they are far from adequate. Therefore, decisions to create new enterprises are occasionally taken on the basis of insufficient or inaccurate information.

*Declining profit.* High costs, low productivity, and excessive levies all cut into the profit margin of rural enterprises. In the five years between 1979 and 1983, their overall profit margin declined from slightly under 25 per cent to just over 15 per cent. When capital increment depends largely on the internal accumulation of an enterprise, this obviously weakens its ability to upgrade equipment and expand production.

*Irregularity and disorder*. It should not be surprising when large numbers of small enterprises based on profit incentive mushroom in an unruly manner in an underdeveloped rural society. The Government gives tax relief to new enterprises for a couple of years, but some of them change their name and brand frequently to prolong the privilege. They close down and open again too easily. In the absence of a sound land-use law, they tend to take up too much good land. Fakes and substandard products of every description have also appeared. But such practices are being subjected to regulation and are not the main stream of the development of rural industry.

*Disincentive to agriculture*. The prosperity of rural industry and the higher wages paid to its workers naturally reduces the interest of peasants in tilling the land, especially for lower-priced grain crops. The solution seems to lie in providing special favourable treatment to grain production and encouraging the development of the so-called vertically integrated farming and agro-processing as a means to achieving better economy of scale and the more even distribution of wealth.

*Polarization or equalization*. Under the new economic policies, some families become rich sooner and faster than others. But a few enterprises have grown to a sizeable scale, employing several hundred workers. Credit institutions also tend to give more credit to bigger and more profitable enterprises as there is better assurance of repayment and fewer larger loans are obviously easier to handle. Whether private enterprises of such a scale, and even larger, should be allowed to develop further in a socialist society, and whether they should be limited, raises a policy issue as well as a practical problem that has yet to be answered. But the marvellous development of rural enterprises of partnership or ownership

has so far definitely contributed to accelerate the growth of the economy and improve the living standard of the rural population.

*Uneven regional development*. As of 1984, eight relatively developed provinces and metropolitan areas along China's east coast accounted for over one-half of all the country's rural industry while eight least-developed inland provinces had only some four per cent of the total. In the highly developed province of Jiangsu, rural enterprises now employ some 10 million people. Their product value of 2.25 billion yuan in 1984 already accounted for over half of the total product value of industry and agriculture. But such uneven development is being remedied, and the less developed areas are fast catching up.

*Too much levy*. In an ambience long wedded to poverty, it is not strange for many quarters to turn to the new "rich" for all sorts of need for help. In fact, their wealthiness has been overestimated. In an underdeveloped countryside, where casual customary manners rule far more widely than strict law and order, levies of all kinds have been imposed on rural enterprises by local authorities. But such excesses have caught the attention of higher authorities and efforts are being made to curb them to lighten the burden of rural industry.[1]

**The policies.** China is now in a crucial stage of development, and economic reforms of historic significance are being implemented. The major components of a new set of more liberal policies may be summarized as:
- invigorating the domestic economy and opening up to the outside world
- reduced mandatory planning to be integrated with expanded guidance planning
- macro-economic control to be combined with micro-economic decontrol
- direct control by administrative means to be replaced by indirect control through economic leverage
- vertically controlled management to be replaced by horizontal linkages between related enterprises

- driving force of enterprises to come from within enterprises rather than from without
- enterprises are to shift from a closed pattern to an open pattern where micro-economic decision-making is decentralized.

In such a context, and in line with the official recognition of the economy as commodity-based and market-oriented, it is only logical that the main content of the Government's policy toward rural industry is to develop a sound market system in which support to the growth of rural industry is lent through such economic leverages as tax, credit, interest, subsidy, supply of raw material, and quality control. Such a market system should cover agro-products and byproducts, agricultural inputs, consumer goods, technology, information, capital and financial services, labour and jobs, and building and construction. Two aspects are being given special attention: the collection and dissemination of market information and the gradual development of a sound legal system together with the provision of legal service, as these are obviously indispensable in any effective market system. In other words, government endorsement of the development of rural industry will come mainly in the form of policy guidance with the provision of relevant information and regulation through law enforcement in a favourable economic climate. Other policy measures worth mentioning include:

*Financial assistance and resources reallocation*. It is generally believed that state enterprises still enjoy considerable advantages over rural enterprises in, for example, the supply of raw material, investment funds, planned production, marketing outlet, and energy provision. Hence it is considered necessary to give rural industry some special treatment in tax payment and credit as compensation and to ensure fair competition. It should be pointed out, however, that rural enterprises have generated as much as four times more revenue for the state than they received in favour and support from the state in recent years. But perhaps of even greater importance is the policy of using part of the revenue from rural industry to support agricultural development. It is estimated that modernization of agriculture in China at a moderate rate requires investment of 1 trillion yuan. The state would be hard-pressed to provide that amount. The bulk of it would have to come from the countryside itself. Rural industry already contributed over 10 billion yuan to agriculture accounting for 15-20 per cent of its total profit in the past five years and is destined to generate the overwhelming majority of investment capital needed by agriculture in the years to come.

*Encouraging horizontal links.* In a vast country like China, great variety in natural resources and the extent of development is a distinctive feature. Generally speaking, the coastal areas are far more developed, with much more managerial talent and technical skill, than inland provinces, which are, however, generally endowed with more natural resources, but they are also much more densely populated with an acute land shortage. Voluntary association of all kinds of partnership based on the principle of mutual benefit enables them to compensate for one another's deficiencies and give full play to the different strengths of various localities. After a long period of excessively rigid control from the central Government, the benefit of such horizontal collaboration is especially pronounced and is giving a push to rural development. In one instance, about half the rural industry near Shanghai has become subcontractors, supplying parts to large enterprises in the metropolitan centre.

*Assisting better division of work.* For historical reasons, the processing of agricultural products in China is located mostly in cities and towns rather than in the countryside. These industries are going to shift gradually back to where the raw material is produced. This would make processing much more economical. Furthermore, rural enterprises are encouraged to cover the whole line of such undertakings, including preproduction services, packaging, storage, transport, marketing, and other post-production services. In other words, rural industry, which by necessity is agriculture-based, should in turn provide a complete range of services to promote agricultural development, thus leading to the formation of local vertically integrated agro-industrial businesses. Industries not suitable for developing in cities will gradually be shifted out to the countryside.

*Technical assistance.* The Government has formulated a programme, named SPARK, designed specifically to assist the technological upgrading of rural industry in the Seventh Five Year Plan period. It consists mainly of: developing 100 complete sets of relatively advanced equipment suited to the conditions of rural China and organizing their mass production; assisting the establishment of 500 model rural enterprises for demonstration purposes and providing them with complete sets of appropriate technology, management rules, product design, and quality-control methods; training 1 million young managers every year with knowledge of appropriate technology and modern management knowhow. Some 2.3 billion yuan of investment capital has been secured so far. Bank loans and government appropriation account for only some 16 per cent of the total amount. The bulk is generated by the enterprises themselves. It is expected that this programme will add over 10 billion yuan of annual output value to the rural enterprises in a couple of years' time with an input/output ratio of nearly 1:5.[2]

**Prospects and implications.** The extraordinary pace at which rural industry is developing in China is rapidly giving it predominance in the country's rural economy and pushing agriculture into second place in the more developed parts of the country. In less advanced areas, it is rapidly catching up. The size of its employment is expected to expand by 70 per cent by 1990 to reach 120 million and further to.

220 million by 1995 or shortly thereafter. Its pace of growth in recent years is two to three times faster than the average speed of industrial development in general. Its output value is expected to reach approximately 60 per cent of the gross product value of the Chinese countryside by the end of this century. In fact, the expansion of rural industry in China accounted for around half of the net increase of gross product value of her industry in the last couple of years. But even more important is the pivotal role it played in the improvement of the structure of the rural economy by introducing extensive diversification into the countryside. Taking all factors into consideration, its productivity is expected to improve by five per cent a year in the next decade. Its share in total export is expected to account for no less than 15 per cent.

But the significance of the development of rural industry in China goes far beyond its quantitative expansion. It has important implications in finding a solution to the huge population and employment problem, in supplementing the deficiencies of the state-run industries and in narrowing the wide gap between cities and countryside. In the past 36 years, urban population in China has roughly doubled, from 100 million to 200 million, with the additional 100 million divided equally between natural growth of urban population and controlled migration of rural inhabitants into cities at very high cost to the state. It is projected that the labour force of the Chinese countryside will reach 450 million by the year 2000, but agriculture will be able to absorb no more than 220 million of them. Rural industry, labour-intensive by nature, is poised to absorb the balance. In many countries, a clearly defined way to urbanize is a problem yet to be solved. In the case of China, by one key indicator, the annual output value of an industrial worker is, at 4 500 yuan, 7.5 times that of a farmer, at 600 yuan on average. It is difficult to imagine that a modern socialist state could be built with advanced cities but a very backward countryside. The development of rural industry offers a solution to the difficult problem of narrowing the rural-urban gap; this is the gradual industrialization and modernization of the huge intermediate area between the agricultural countryside and the metropolitan centres by building large numbers of small towns and townships (the number of townships increased over 150 per cent in the past five years). Such a network of small towns and townships would form a multitude of bridges between cities and countryside through which capital, technology, managerial talent, raw material, finished and semi-finished products could flow back and forth. In another sense, it also enables China to avoid potentially dangerous antagonism between workers and peasants and between cities and the countryside which the widening differences between them would inevitably induce.

Another question of no less importance is the spiritual and cultural aspect of rural development. The significance of cultural and educational advancement and the gradual change of traditional values and social concepts cannot be over-emphasized. For rural China to move ahead from a semi-subsistence, half-closed farming society, with all its inertia and stagnation, to a modern commodity-oriented agro-industrial society, it needs all the impact of a cultural shock, which only the development of rural industry with its entrepreneurial spirit and managerial acumen can bring about. On the other hand, the material improvement of rural conditions would also con-

tribute to the rural population's cultural advancement. Some 20-30 per cent of the after-tax profit of rural industry in recent years has already been devoted to the development of education, culture, public health, sports and local government administration in the Chinese countryside.

One more lesson which China has learned in the past three decades is the limitations of state-run enterprises. The Government can take direct charge only of crucial lifelines of the economy and a limited number of key enterprises. It has to rely mainly on a whole set of policies and strategies to guide the rest of the vast economy. Rural enterprises will develop under such guidance and fill the innumerable gaps which the public sector cannot possibly take care of, especially the thousands of omnipresent small commodities.

The remarkable thing about rural industry is that it needs very little of what China is short of— investment capital—to make optimum use of what China has in surplus— manpower. By relying mainly on correct policies and strategy, it is able to tap the vast potential of the smallest economic cells of rural China in terms of both human and physical resources, thereby avoiding the biggest weakness of China in its industrialization, modernization, and urbanization and turning it to its best possible advantage. In a sense, it might be considered a sort of extension of the contracted responsibility system in agricultural production—both rely mainly on the catalytic role of policies to stimulate the initiative and enthusiasm of workers, peasants, and managers.

In another sense, it might also be likened to the early stages of the industrial revolution in the West. The main difference lies in the presence or absence of firm state guidance and/or regulation in the context of the whole social system. Past lessons in the shortcomings of excessive rigidity in economic policies and over-centralized administration in China have been well learned. The emphasis of the new approach will be the ever improved use of a gradually more finely tuned regulated market mechanism and a measured flexibility to facilitate healthy development.

The full-fledged development of rural industry in China has only a short history. All kinds of problems and defects are inevitable in the initial stage, but these are by nature relative and transitory. The objective laws governing the development of rural industry will see to it that these would be rectified in the process. China should have learned enough lessons in the past decades to realize such historical rationale and logical necessity to be able to guide rural industry to maturity.

---

[1] All these problems and difficulties have combined to drive the rate of their growth down to a more sustainable 20 per cent in 1986 and a quickening of their adjustment and restructuring, which should pave the way for more healthy further development in future.
[2] In short, the main thrust of policy orientation in the near future will be qualitative product improvement and technological upgrading rather than numerical and quantitative expansion; more local integration from upstream to downstream activities in the business cycle; and better marketin outlets to meet customer demand, with a consequent reduction of stockpile of undesirable products.

# The Strategic Challenge of the Evolving Global Economy

Raj Aggarwal

**Raj Aggarwal** is a professor of finance and international business at the University of Toledo. In September 1987 he became Mellen Professor of Finance at John Carroll University in Cleveland. In 1984 Professor Aggarwal served as the Senior Fulbright Research Scholar for Southeast Asia.

The world economy is in a period of rapid change. New market forces are emerging as the economic center of gravity continues moving westward toward the Orient. The technological revolution is likely to equal the industrial revolution in its impact on the global economy. How are industrial countries responding to these changing markets and technologies?

Driven by significant advances in technology, telecommunications, and transportation, the global economy is currently in a period of rapid change characterized by:

- Shifting strategic and commercial advantages;
- Increasing international integration; and
- The emergence of new economic power centers.

In recent years, many government and corporate managers have often been "blindsided" by these developments that begin and develop outside their normal sphere of attention.

The global economy is beginning to feel the economic and social impact of the commercialization of at least three major categories of new technologies: biotechnology, microprocessor-based information processing, and telecommunications. These new technologies, designed to supplement human intellectual and genetic abilities, are based on the creation, manipulation, and transmission of electronic and genetic information. And these technologies are likely to transform the global economy even more fundamentally than the industrial revolution, when human and animal power was supplemented by mechanical power.

The economies of most nations and regions have become more open to international influences, and their relative economic importance is shifting. Newly industrialized countries (NICs), especially those located in the Orient, are making their presence felt in global markets. International financial markets are playing a more important role than any domestic financial market.

This globalization of product and financial markets has been accompanied in most countries by a sale of nationalized enterprises to private investors. There has also been a shift to greater dependence on free-market mechanisms, even in such champions of social control as the Soviet Union and the People's Republic of China (PRC).

How significant are these trends,

From *Business Horizons*, July/August 1987, pp. 38–44. Copyright 1987 by the Foundation for the School of Business at Indiana University. Reprinted by permission.

> "Some states within the U.S. are very dependent on the international economy. For example, at least one-seventh of Ohio's manufacturing employment depends directly on exports, and more than half of all Ohio workers are employed by firms that depend to some extent on exports. Thus, for most companies there is no such thing as a *domestic* market."

and how can a business continue to compete successfully in this changed environment?

## GLOBALIZATION OF PRODUCT AND FINANCIAL MARKETS

Recent decades have witnessed significant technological advances in international communications and transportation. The availability and cost-effectiveness of these innovations have facilitated the international transmission of technology and cultural values. Thus, production and marketing are becoming increasingly global—not only for mature industrial products such as textiles, steel, farm equipment, and autos, but also for such items as consumer electronics, computers, and semiconductors.

Driven by technology and the logic of comparative advantage, world trade has grown much faster over the last few decades than has world Gross National Product (GNP). Global exports and imports were about one-fifth of global GNP in 1962. This figure had increased to about one-fourth by 1972 and to more than one-third by 1982.[1] This remarkable increase in international trade is reflected in the increased openness of almost all national economies to international influences.

As an example, the proportion of U.S. GNP accounted for by exports and imports is now more than one-fifth, double what it was two decades ago. This proportion is even higher for manufactured goods (see **Figure 1**). The U.S. Department of Commerce estimates that the U.S. exports about one-fifth of its industrial production and that about 70 percent of

all U.S. goods compete directly with foreign goods.[2]

Some states within the U.S. are even more dependent on the international economy. For example, Ohio ranks fourth in terms of manufactured exports. At least one-seventh of its manufacturing employment depends directly on exports, and more than half of all Ohio workers are employed by firms that depend to some extent on exports.[3] Thus, for most companies there is no such thing as a *domestic* market.

This increase in world trade and investment is also reflected in the recent globalization of financial markets. The external currency market, commonly known as the Eurodollar market, was at $3.6 trillion at the end of June 1986.[4] It is now larger than

any domestic financial market. Thus, companies are increasingly turning to this market for funds. For example, U.S. companies raised almost $40 billion in these external financial markets in 1985, representing about 30 percent of the funds raised.[5] Even companies and public entities that have no overseas presence are beginning to rely on this market for financing.

In addition to the rise of these external markets for funds, most national financial markets are becoming better integrated with global markets because of the rapid increase in the volume of interest rate and currency swaps ($20 billion in 1985). The foreign exchange markets have also grown rapidly. The weekly trading volume in these globally integrated

**Figure 1**
**U.S. Trade as a Share of U.S. Manufacturing Output**

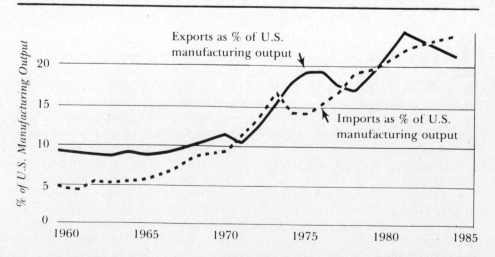

Source: U.S. Department of Labor, Bureau of Labor Statistics, 1984; Organization for Economic Cooperation and Development, 1984.
Note: For 1985, the percentages are 19 for exports and 24 for imports. Estimates for 1986 put exports at 17 percent of U.S. manufacturing output and imports at 25 percent.

markets, at about $1 trillion, now exceeds the annual trading volume on the world's securities markets.[6] Because of these changes, any financing decision now must consider conditions in global, not just domestic, financial markets.

## DECLINE OF U.S. DOMINANCE IN GLOBAL MARKETS

In addition to the globalization of product and financial markets, the relative importance and role of regional and national economies are also undergoing rapid change. As an example, the importance of the U.S. economy is declining.

While the U.S. economy created almost 19 million new jobs (a labor force increase of 23 percent) in the 1970s,

it did not keep pace with the productivity increases of its competitors. In the previous quarter-century, while per capita productivity increased at a 1.2 percent annual rate in the U.S., it increased at a 2.3 percent annual rate in the U.K., 3.4 percent in West Germany, 3.7 percent in France, 5.3 percent in South Korea, and 5.9 percent in Japan.[7]

This low rate of increase in U.S. productivity seems to be related to its low savings rate—about one-third of the Japanese rate—and a low rate of capital formation (see **Figure 2**). In recent years, the U.S. has also suffered from low expenditures on nonmilitary research and development as a percentage of GNP when compared to the percentage spent by such competitors as West Germany and Japan.

While the U.S. remains the largest economy, its share of global high-technology exports and its share of global GNP are declining (see **Table 1**). Concurrent with these changes in international trade patterns, similar changes are occurring in the global patterns of international portfolio and direct investment. As an example, both direct and portfolio investment in the U.S. have been increasing faster than U.S. investments overseas.

The declining dominance of the U.S. economy is reflected in the declining proportion of U.S. firms among the world's largest 100 industrial firms (see **Table 2**). The increased global importance of non-U.S. firms is also reflected in the fact that European and Japanese direct investment in the U.S. now exceeds U.S. direct investment in Europe and in Japan.

**Figure 2**
**International Comparison of Productivity Growth and Capital Formation, 1960-1983**

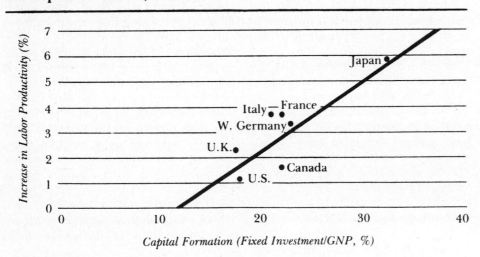

Source: U.S. Department of Commerce.

**Table 2**
**World's Largest 100 Industrials**

| Area | 1960 | 1970 | 1980 | 1985 |
|---|---|---|---|---|
| U.S. | 70 | 64 | 45 | 47 |
| Western Europe | 28 | 27 | 42 | 26 |
| Japan | 2 | 8 | 8 | 14 |
| Developing Countries | 0 | 1 | 5 | 13 |

Source: Annual lists as compiled by *Fortune*.

Just as the U.S. replaced Britain in the early part of this century, Japan is now well on its way to replacing the U.S. as the largest creditor in the world. According to the Bank for International Settlements, the Japanese now have the largest share of global banking assets.[8] For the first time since 1914, the U.S. has become a net international debtor. At the end of 1985, the U.S. had the largest foreign debt of any country in the world.[9]

## RISE OF THE NEWLY INDUSTRIALIZED COUNTRIES

One of the most significant characteristics of this changing global economy is the rise of the developing countries, especially those located in the Orient. For the past forty years, the less devel-

**Table 1**
**Global Shares of GNP**

| Region | 1960 | 1980 | Change | Annual Growth to 2000 (est.) |
|---|---|---|---|---|
| North America | 29% | 25% | −4% | 3–4% |
| Western Europe | 30% | 26% | −4% | 2–3% |
| Soviet Bloc | 19% | 17% | −2% | 4–5% |
| East Asia | 10% | 17% | +7% | 7–8% |
| Other Countries | 12% | 15% | +3% | 5–6% |

Sources: *Euro-Asia Business Review* 4 (No. 1), and *Euromoney* (October 1982).

# "Over the last quarter century, companies from the LDCs have increased their presence among the world's largest 100 industrial companies from zero to thirteen. For firms located in the U.S. and other developed countries, the LDCs represent not only growing markets but also, in many cases, a source of new competition."

oped countries (LDCs) have experienced much faster rates of economic growth and industrialization than have the developed countries. Since the 1950s, LDC GNP. has grown more than fivefold.

In the 1970s the LDCs supplied only 5 percent of the manufactured goods imported by developed countries. Now they supply more than 20 percent of their own demand for manufactured goods and more than 8 percent of the overall demand in the developed countries.[10] The ranks of the top twenty exporting nations now include such LDCs as South Korea, Taiwan, Hong Kong, Singapore, China, Mexico, and Brazil.

As Table 2 shows, over the last quarter century, companies from the LDCs have increased their presence among the world's largest 100 industrial companies from zero to thirteen. Over the same period, foreign direct investment (FDI) by these and other LDC companies grew to more than $20 billion, an annual growth rate of about 17 percent versus a growth rate of 10 percent for FDI from the developed countries.[11] In the U.S., FDI from the LDCs now accounts for more than 14 percent of the total. For firms located in the U.S. and other developed countries, the LDCs represent not only growing markets but also, in many cases, a source of new competition.

As Table 1 indicates, economic growth in the Asian Pacific region has far outpaced any other region of the world. The consensus among economists is that in the next fifteen to twenty years, the economies of the Far East are expected to grow at the highest rate (8-10 percent per annum), followed by South Asia (6-8 percent), Latin America (5-6 percent), East Bloc

(4-5 percent), North America (3-4 percent), and Western Europe (2-3 percent). These economic growth rates are reflected in trade and investment data.[12] The Pacific Rim countries now account for a higher share of world exports (38.4 percent in 1984) than do the countries of Western Europe.[13]

The volume of U.S. trade with the Asian Pacific group of countries has exceeded its trade with Europe since 1981. By 1995 U.S. trade with the Asian Pacific countries is estimated to be double that of its trade with Europe.

According to a 1985 study by the California Department of Commerce, "The Pacific Rim countries represent a $3 trillion-a-year market growing at a rate of $3 billion a week."[14] With the recent rise of the Asian Pacific economies, the global economic center of gravity is continuing its historical westward movement.

## Technology and the NICs

The growth of the newly industrializing countries (NICs) is reflected in the global activities of firms from these countries. At the top end of the technology scale, U.S. dominance in semiconductors and computers is being challenged by Japanese, Korean, and Taiwanese firms. In semiconductors, the Japanese and Koreans are now significant global competitors in memory chips, and the Japanese compete in some semicustom chips. In computers, the Japanese are major global competitors in mainframes and in personal computers (PCs), while Korean and Taiwanese firms are producing inexpensive versions for the PC market. For example, the Leading Edge (IBM PC-compatible) com-

puter, which is enjoying great success in the U.S. market, is made by Daewoo Corporation of Korea.

Japanese dominance in mature industries (for example, steel, shipbuilding, chemicals, consumer electronics, and automobiles) is being threatened by firms from Korea, Taiwan, Brazil, Mexico, and other NICs. For example, the world's largest plastics firm is now Taiwanese (Formosa Plastics), the largest petrochemical complex is in Jubail, Saudi Arabia, and the largest selling import car in Canada is Korea's Pony, made by the Hyundia Corporation. Brazil is being used by Volkswagen and others as an export base for autos, Mexico is being used by Ford as an engine manufacturing base for its North American auto operations, and all three U.S. automakers plan to supply the U.S. market with significant numbers of autos imported from Korea and Taiwan. Samsung and Tatung are now moving from being private-label suppliers to developing brand-name recognition for electronic products in the U.S. market.

There are numerous other examples of NIC manufacturers displacing advanced-country manufacturers not only in maturing global markets but also in some high-technology industries. It is, however, less well known that manufacturers in a second group of NICs at a lower level of economic development—for example, India, Thailand, Indonesia, and Mexico—are displacing manufacturers from the first group of NICs in the more mature industries, such as textiles and metal castings and fabrication. New economies seem to continually develop expertise in a technology as it matures and then to displace firms in more advanced economies.

# "Technology may reduce the role of labor costs. At least for some sectors sensitive to quality and style and in manufacturing where labor costs are a small percentage, U.S. manufacturing may once again be able to compete effectively with production bases in low-cost overseas locations."

In recent times this process of economic evolution seems to have been hastened by the decreasing costs of international transportation and communication and by the commercialization of new technologies in the highly developed countries. There is also evidence of technological leapfrogging, where some NICs acquire highly sophisticated technological capabilities. For example, China and India have developed fairly sophisticated aerospace and nuclear industries, while Brazil and Israel are exporting significant quantities of aircraft and other military hardware.

## Hope for U.S. Manufacturing

Technology may reduce the role of labor costs. With the advent of robotics and other computer-based intelligent machines, the efficiency of U.S. manufacturing seems to be improving. At least for some sectors sensitive to quality and style and in manufacturing where labor costs are a small percentage, U.S. manufacturing may once again be able to compete effectively with production bases in low-cost overseas locations.

While U.S. manufacturing has been about one-fourth of GNP since the 1950s, it may now be at the stage agriculture reached half a century ago—experiencing a steady decline in the number of workers, but poised for a large increase in output.

## NIC FIRMS IN GLOBAL MARKETS

What is the nature of the competitive challenge posed by these changes in the global economy and by the emerging firms from the NICs?

Foreign operations by firms from the NICs tend to follow certain patterns. NIC companies invest overseas to protect the markets they have developed through exports and to seek new markets for growth. They generally go overseas for risk reduction and to overcome government restrictions in their home countries. They seek reliable and lower cost sources of raw materials and technology. Their FDI is generally concentrated in countries similar in cultural characteristics, generally lower on the ladder of economic growth, and geographically nearby. However, there are important exceptions, as indicated by Korean and other NIC firm activity in U.S. markets.

NIC firms usually go overseas by means of joint ventures with local partners. Unlike U.S. companies, they hardly ever undertake wholly-owned foreign operations. Their foreign operations, again unlike U.S. companies, are not highly integrated or centrally controlled. They start by focusing on simple, standardized products, and their foreign operations may be labor intensive compared to similar local operations of firms from the developed countries. They usually start with a low-cost operation serving small markets, markets which may be considered too small and uneconomical for firms of developed economies. They generally do not engage in much product differentiation or nonprice competition. They tend to use a high proportion of local inputs and to work closely with local ethnic groups. Their relationship with the host government is usually good.

NIC firms usually operate with low levels of overhead expense. Although direct compensation and managerial benefits are low, top management often is given a significant ownership stake in the operation.

Thus, the NIC firms seem to have a well-defined niche when they engage in FDI. Although these firms share some characteristics with other multinational corporations (MNCs), they are very different in some key aspects which give them some distinct competitive advantages. FDI by these NIC firms is likely to grow rapidly in coming years and to become relatively more important as a competitive force in global markets.

## POSSIBLE RESPONSES TO NIC COMPETITION

What is the best response to this competitive threat from the NICs? In order to develop some answers to this question, it is useful to keep in mind, *first*, that the changes in the relative standing of the various economies and the globalization of product and financial markets are driven by fundamental forces such as technology and telecommunications. Thus, it may not be easy or wise to attempt to reverse or oppose these changes. Opposition is likely to be expensive, and it probably will only buy time.

*Second*, it seems that the world economy is undergoing extensive technology-driven structural changes. The relative importance of various industries and countries is changing more rapidly than in earlier times.

Companies in the U.S. and Western Europe must face up to the fact that Japanese low-cost production is being replaced by even lower cost producers from the "new Japans": Hong Kong, Korea, Singapore, and Taiwan.[15] Industries at successively higher levels of technology are facing this threat. Consequently, companies in these industries must engage in a never-ending process of moving to higher value-added operations, using ever higher levels of technology. How can this be accomplished successfully when it usually is impossible to know the exact nature of industries with emerging technologies?

Bureaucratic systems were developed in an age when change was much slower. These systems are not very good at responding to rapidly changing markets and technologies. In addition, a large, modern economy may be too complex a system to manage or even to understand. Therefore, government control or management of an economy may be an exercise in frustration.

Almost every country in the world seems to be discovering these limitations of bureaucratic systems, as evidenced by the global movement toward the privatization of government-owned and -run companies. Government companies are being sold in countries ranging from the United Kingdom and France to Turkey and Thailand. Even the PRC and other centrally planned economies are beginning to transform their economic systems to take greater advantage of systems that reward individual initiative, which is the essence of free enterprise.

To stay competitive in rapidly evolving global markets, the U.S. must depend on a system that can respond quickly and efficiently to change. A number of fields, from quantum mechanics to sociobiology, are coming to similar conclusions regarding the nature of optimal growth strategies in an uncertain environment. It seems that the most effective long-run strategy for large, complex systems to adjust to rapid environmental changes is a process of trial and error undertaken in the form of numerous random changes among the individual units.

It seems that the economic system best able to keep an economy growing and competitive in an increasingly dynamic global economy is a market-force-driven free enterprise system with appropriate, but minimal, government regulation. This is especially true for the U.S., whose role in the global economy seems to be that of developing and exploiting ever newer technologies.

Consequently, if we are to stay competitive in the global economy, the U.S. must continue to encourage innovation in our companies and economy. We should continue to emphasize corporate and social systems that encourage and reward entrepreneurship. Our tax and investment banking systems should ensure a continuing supply of venture capital and the ability to retain the rewards of taking the risks inherent in new ventures.

Similarly, companies should also develop systems to encourage and reward entrepreneurship.[16] Worker input should be valued, and employees should feel they have a stake in the success of the company. Traditional approaches to merit pay systems should be supplemented by a heavy emphasis on profit sharing and decentralized decision making to encourage individual initiative and risk taking, even in large corporations.

To avoid the problems that prevented other cultures and economies from adjusting to change, the U.S. needs to shift the focus of public policy more toward the generation of a bigger economic pie and somewhat away from the recent obsession with its distribution. It is also important that the U.S. cut government spending and reduce the growing budget deficit. Funding the deficit leaves less capital with a higher cost for business and industry. In addition, the U.S. must continue to encourage and reward a higher savings rate to fund higher levels of R&D and new capital spending.

The global economy is facing a new period of rapid change, driven at one end by the newly emerging information-processing and biological technologies and at the other by the successive emergence of countries at ever lower levels of economic development as global competitors. With the rapid rise of the Asian Pacific region, the global economic center of gravity continues its westward move toward the Orient. In response, developed countries must continue to encourage higher levels of savings and investment in new capital equipment and the development of new technology.

In view of the rapid pace of economic change, all countries must continue to develop corporate and public policies that focus on encouraging and rewarding individual initiative in responding to market signals. Government and corporate managers increasingly operate in product and financial markets that are global in nature and that are characterized by shifting competitive and technological advantages. To ignore these significant changes in the global economy is to invite disaster.

1. See C. P. Beshouri, "The Global Economy," *Federal Reserve Bank of Atlanta Economic Review*, August 1985, p. 51.

2. See the President's Commission on Industrial Competitiveness, *Global Competition: The New Reality* (Washington, D.C.: The Commission, 1985), p. 9.

3. Raj Aggarwal, "The Global Economy: Challenges of Newly Industrialized Countries," *The Ohio Economy* 2 (No. 3, Second Quarter 1986), p. 2.

4. Morgan Guaranty Trust Company, "Global Financial Change," *World Financial Markets*, December 1986, p. 15.

5. Morgan Guaranty Trust Company (note 4), p. 18.

6. See Raj Aggarwal, "Managing for Economic Growth and Global Competition: Strategic Implications of the Life Cycle of Economies," in Richard N. Farmer, ed., *Advances in International Comparative Management* (Greenwich, Conn.: JAI Press, 1986), p. 21.

7. The President's Commission on Industrial Competitiveness (note 2), p. 28.

8. See 1986 Annual Report of the Bank for International Settlements, Basel, Switzerland, p. 37.

9. Bank for International Settlements (note 8), p. 15.

10. Lionel H. Olmer, *U.S. Manufacturing at a Crossroads: Surviving and Prospering in a More Competitive Global Economy* (Washington, D.C.:

U.S. Department of Commerce, 1985), p. 23.

11. Beshouri (note 1), p. 51.

12. "Across the Globe Economic Growth Picks Up," *Euromoney*, May 1984, p. 293.

13. "Trade Winds Blowing Across the Pacific," *The Economist*, May 3, 1986, p. 79.

14. *Facts on the Pacific Rim* (Sacramento: California Department of Commerce, 1985), p. 4.

15. For details, see, for example, Aggarwal, "Managing for Economic Growth and Global Competition" (note 6), and *Global Competition: The New Reality* (note 2).

16. See Joel A. Ross, "Corporations and Entrepreneurs: Paradox and Opportunity," elsewhere in this issue.

# Japan 1987:

# A QUESTION OF COURSE

## Charles Smith

The Japanese ship of state is beginning to resemble a paddle steamer caught in a swift current with its paddles turning in opposite directions. The vessel is still very definitely afloat, and its engines appear to be churning vigorously, but there are serious doubts about the course the captain is trying to set. And there is a risk that, if nothing is done soon, external forces could inflict damage which even a more decisive captain and a hard-working crew might be unable to repair.

In the 20 months since the start of the yen's long upward climb against the US dollar, the Japanese economy had begun to adjust itself in a number of painful but potentially constructive ways to the new situation facing it in the outside world.

Yet the impression remains of an overall lack of leadership and an inability to set firm policy targets or timetables for the structural changes that are called for in almost every official document on the economy.

The increasing political weakness (and apparent lack of interest in economic issues) of Prime Minister Yasuhiro Nakasone seems to be partly to blame for this situation. Despite frequent references in his speeches to a "settlement of post-[World War II] political accounts" and to policies needed to "prepare Japan for the 21st century," Nakasone seems never fully to have grasped the historical turning point that Japan arrived at in the autumn of 1986, when the upward revaluation of the yen put paid to two decades of export-oriented growth.

More important than the personalities involved in the current policy dilemma, however, may be the system itself. Japan's consensus-based approach to decision-making—in which very little is done without the approval of all interested parties involved in any policy area—has made it extremely hard for the country to move swiftly and surely to promote domestic growth through deregulation of protected sectors, such as agriculture, or by abolishing outdated subsidies such as those which impel private salary earners to save rather than spend.

Critics of the Japanese system, who now include a handful of well-known members of the very same political and bureaucratic elite that operates it, have begun claiming during the past six months that what Japan needs in order to surmount its problems may be nothing less than to break with the 30-year tradition of rule by a single conservative ruling party in cooperation with a closed group of like-minded bureaucrats and businessmen. Failing that, the challenges facing the country should at least be used to inject some new ideas and operating procedures into the traditional decision-making machinery.

The Japanese problem, as a good many top members of the bureaucracy and the business world now perceive it, is not simply that business confidence has been badly jolted by the sharp jump in the yen exchange rate or that relations with trade partners seems to be going through one of the rougher patches in a long series of intermittent skirmishes caused by "excessive" Japanese exports.

Rather, the impression gained by talking to senior bureaucrats in Tokyo (and even more from contacts with people outside the system) is that Japan may have come to the end of a two- or even three-decade phase in its development, when it was possible for the country to export its way out of almost every external difficulty.

Japan overcame the balance-of-payments problems of the 1960s, the oil shocks of the 1970s and the global recession of the early 1980s by launching supremely successful export drives which not only paid its bills internationally but made possible high domestic growth rates and the advanced world's lowest rates of unemployment. The message of the events of the past 18 months, as perceived in Tokyo, is that all of this has ceased to be possible.

Belatedly, but sincerely, Japan's most internationally

From *Far Eastern Economic Review*, June 11, 1987. Courtesy of Charles Smith and *Far Eastern Economic Review*.

161

minded bureaucrats now seem to recognise that a chronic imbalance with the outside world of some US$50–90 billion a year must either lead to trade war or force the collapse of some of the major industrial economies on which Japan depends for the exports that are needed to maintain its own growth.

So far as the relationship between exports and growth is concerned, there has been an equally belated acceptance of the fact that a country which relies entirely on foreign demand to sustain its economic growth is headed for long-term trouble.

Yet a theoretical realisation of what is wrong may still be a far cry from actual solutions. Japan's biggest problem today would seem to be that no one can decide exactly how to start demolishing the innumerable rules and regulations that have kept the domestic economy stable but stagnant during years of dynamic overseas expansion.

A second and perhaps almost as serious handicap facing the government in its restructuring efforts is that the country's top leadership may simply not have the political clout to enact what are seen to be reasonable and desirable measures.

The ruling Liberal Democratic Party (LDP) commands a massive 100-seat majority in the lower house of parliament and is faced by four fragmented opposition groups, no combination of which seems to offer the possibility of forming an alternative government. The LDP itself, however, is essentially a loose coalition of factional groups which draw strength from the vested interest entrenched in various sectors of the domestic economy.

Given the party's background and origins, there seems to be a trade-off between political stability and continuity, on one hand, and the various measures needed to shift the emphasis of economic growth and make the country less vulnerable to external pressures, on the other.

Of the two sorts of measures which could help to refloat the domestic economy and lessen the risk of trade conflicts degenerating into total warfare, the most readily available—if not the most effective—would be a 180-degree turn in the government's fiscal policy.

For the six years between the onset of the second oil shock in 1979 and the eve of yen revaluation in 1986, Japan pursued a rigidly austere fiscal policy, freezing most types of government expenditure (except aid and defence) in the annual budget and actually cutting back (for four years running) on the public-works programmes which are often seen as one of the best means of breathing life into a flagging economy.

The justification for extreme austerity was the need to reduce dependence on borrowed funds to a "reasonable" proportion of government spending, or, more precisely, to eliminate dependence on deficit-covering bond issues as a means of financing the budget. The policy was made possible, on the other hand, by the export stimulus on which the economy relied from year to year, thanks to a low exchange rate and the willingness of trade partners to absorb Japanese exports.

With the export stimulus fading, Japan's Ministry of Finance (MoF) has come under intense pressure to abandon its zero guidelines on annual-expenditure increases, and administer some traditional Keynesian stimulus to the economy. But the hardline bureaucrats in MoF's Budget Bureau evidently think they know best.

Japan entered its 1987 fiscal year with a budget which once again reduces public-works spending by 2% from the previous year's level. A ¥5 trillion (US$35.5 billion) supplementary budget which is promised for the autumn may reverse the decline and shift fiscal policy part on the way back to the Keynesian model; but there is still a good chance that even this may be frustrated by the stubbornness and ingenuity of MoF bureaucrats.

Japanese reflationary packages have tended in the past to be paper documents, relying heavily on anticipated spending by the private sector rather than on actual government money to get the economy moving again. Unless the bureaucrats drafting the 1987 package have decided to turn over a new leaf, the ¥5 trillion-worth of extra spending promised for the autumn may turn out to be another masterpiece of window-dressing, void of any real fiscal substance.

The second, and potentially more promising, strategy which the government could pursue in its efforts to reinvigorate the domestic economy is the one known for shorthand purposes as deregulation. In contrast with most Western economies, Japan had continued to wrap large sectors of the economy in bureaucratically administered red tape, thereby protecting existing interests and ensuring stability—but also raising costs and dampening demand.

A policy of cutting through the red tape in areas ranging from retail distribution to housing and land development could do much to stimulate growth, economists argue. But some of the key areas under control are so jealously guarded that the government seems more likely to have to nibble at the problem than to be able to cut through the network of controls in a way that might be needed to produce solid results. Typical of this situation, but more important than almost any sector as a barrier to growth, is the heavily subsidised farm sector.

The prospect that the Ministry of Agriculture may actually lower its subsidy to rice producers this summer, after either raising or maintaining the subsidy every year since the mid-1950s, can be taken as a sign that the government is at last trying to turn the tables on the powerful farm lobby.

The existing ban on imports of rice, on the other

hand, seems likely to be maintained, despite US pressure for liberalisation and despite the fact that Japanese consumers now pay three times as much for this staple food as people in the US and Western Europe.

Farm liberalisation (including rice) is not officially on the agenda for the forthcoming Uruguay round of Gatt negotiations, as far as Japan is concerned, but this does not mean that the authorities are prepared to budge an inch on an issue which could lessen trade frictions besides releasing spending power for other types of consumption within the domestic economy.

Rather, the government seems to be devoting its energies to explaining why rice farming in Japan can never be exposed to international competition which might threaten the Japanese lifestyle.

Land policy is another area in which the government has inched towards during the past six months, without making any of the dramatic moves which were hinted at in earlier policy reports on economic restructuring.

A white paper on land published in mid-May by the National Land Agency talks of equalising the tax levels on housing and on agricultural land within the boundaries of big cities, thereby (it is hoped) removing the disincentives to development which have kept nearly 10% of inner Tokyo's land area out of the housing market during the past few years.

In the same document, however, nothing is said about the abolition of the antiquated "right-to-sunshine" ruling which has prevented rational use even of the limited housing space that is available in central Tokyo. The environmental lobbyists who have campaigned for right-to-sunshine in the past look less formidable than the farmers who have been able to push up rice prices year by year.

Yet the shaky Nakasone cabinet apparently feels that to take on such a lobby would pose too much of a risk to its survival prospects during its remaining five months in power. The land problem, like so many others on the LDP's domestic agenda, is, accordingly, being left for the next cabinet to solve.

Compared with the cautious approach of government to the restructuring problem, Japan's private sector seems to have tackled the challenges sparked off by the high yen and trade frictions with exemplary energy. In the first full year after the start of the yen's upward float in September 1985, there was an 84.6% rise in the value of overseas investment by the private sector, reflecting a sharp increase in the number of offshore production facilities being established by companies that could no longer afford Japanese working conditions.

Industry in Japan itself, meanwhile, began to undergo drastic rationalisation, in some cases threatening the foundations of the lifetime employment which is seen as one of the pillars of Japan's labour system.

A decision by the top five Japanese steelmakers to close a total of six blast furnaces and shift 30% of the industry's labour force out of steelmaking was one of the most dramatic moves on this front. But steelmakers are not alone in having decided to face up earlier rather than later to the changes facing Japan's economy. During 1986, the number of refineries operating in the already drastically rationalised aluminum industry shrank from six to one, as the aluminum-fabricating industry switched to using imported ingots.

The swift response of many sectors of Japanese industry to the yen shock recalls the equally drastic shrinkage of many of the older materials-processing industries after the first (1973) oil shock and is, at the very least, evidence that Japan has not lost the ability to deal effectively with purely economic threats to its survival.

But whereas the oil shocks were essentially a challenge to Japanese businessmen to find ways of making a living in a world of high energy prices, the yen revaluation and the threats of trade war that have followed look like a challenge to the entire Japanese system, addressed to the public and private sectors alike.

One, or even two years, may be too short a time to decide whether Japan can carry through the changes that seem to be needed; but it is already clear that the task now facing the government and the LDP is as tough as any since the start of the post-war era.

# Dismantling the 49th Parallel

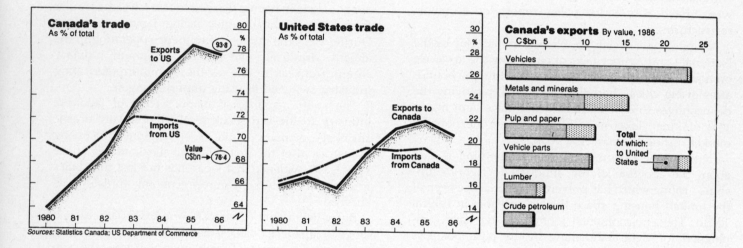

Sources: Statistics Canada; US Department of Commerce

TORONTO

**B**Y SIGNING a pioneering free-trade pact with Canada, the United States may have done a bigger favour to the cause of free trade than to its northern neighbour. The agreement was signed at midnight on October 3rd, after 16 months of talks between officials in Ottawa and Washington and a marathon final horsetrading session. It goes some way towards coming to grips with the issues which are likely to dominate the Uruguay Round of the General Agreement on Tariffs and Trade (GATT).

It takes a run at several non-tarrif barriers. For instance, both sides have promised to reduce to $25,000 the threshold for nondiscriminatory government purchases (ie, in government contracts worth more than that, protectionist favouritism for national suppliers is not permitted). At present, the threshold is $171,000, set by the GATT government-procurement code. The agreement also makes a start at liberalising trade in farm products and services.

The problem for the Canadians is that the agreement falls short of the goal set by their prime minister, Mr Brian Mulroney,

when he set the free-trade talks on the road in May 1986. His aim was to give Canadian exporters secure access to their biggest market, at a time when the mood in the American Congress was turning protectionist. The United States takes more than three-quarters of Canada's exports.

After complaining for months that the talks were not getting top-level attention in Washington, the Canadian negotiating team found a way to put the issue on the front pages and in the editorial columns of American newspapers. It broke off talks ten days before the deadline given by the Reagan administration.

The team made the break because it felt Canada was not being offered sufficient exemption from American anti-dumping levies, countervailing duties and other trade laws, which have been used several times in recent years to clamp down on Canadian timber, potash and other exports. Canada hoped to circumvent American protectionism by persuading Washington to set up a bilateral tribunal with binding powers to settle trade disputes.

Talks were resumed when the Americans made a half-concession. Canada will get its panel, but it will not be able to exempt Canadian exporters (or American ones, for that matter) from existing anti-dumping and countervailing laws. The panel will be able to overturn protectionist actions only if, in the words of the draft agreement, "either party made a decision not in accordance with its law".

Despite this disappointment, Canada has not come away empty-handed. Barriers on exports of Canadian energy products to the United States, notably enriched uranium, will be scrapped. Canadian banks operating south of the border will be given the same treatment as their American counterparts in any changes to the Glass-Steagall Act, which at present forbids commercial banks from underwriting securities. And many Canadian enterprises, which already enjoy a competitive exchange rate, expect the elimination of customs duties by the beginning of 1999 to open up big new markets in America.

Ottawa has also given a lot away. It will

From *The Economist*, October 10, 1987, pp. 61–62. © 1987, The Economist, distributed by Special Features.

lower barriers on American investment in Canada, eventually vetting only takeovers involving assets of more than C$150m ($115m). Import licences will be scrapped on wheat, barley and oats. Transport subsidies (the so-called "Crow's Nest" subsidies) will end on many farm products exported through western Canada. American banks operating north of the border, hitherto subject to curbs on assets and on shareholdings in Canadian financial institutions, will be treated in future as if they were Canadian banks. Canadian magazine publishers will lose their postal subsidies. California winegrowers will be pleased by the removal of discriminatory mark-ups on their products by Canadian liquor stores.

Free-trade enthusiasts in Canada accept the agreement, with all its warts, as a start to a more liberal trading relationship with America. Others—including some erstwhile backers of Mr Mulroney's initiative—are dismayed that they will still have to contend with the vagaries of America's trade laws. With Canadian customs duties at present twice as high on average as America's, many fear that duty-free trade will encourage American companies to close their Canadian plants, preferring to service the Canadian market from big plants south of the border.

For most American businesses, the impact will be marginal. The Canadian market is only one-tenth the size of America's. The biggest threat to the agreement, which must still be approved by both sides' legislatures comes not from protectionist Americans but from fearful Canadians.

# GATT reaction

GENEVA

TRADE officials in Geneva have mixed feelings about the United States-Canada free-trade agreement. Some think that it will inspire negotiators in the current round of GATT talks. Others, especially officials from outside Europe, are rather cross about it. They fear that yet another free-trade agreement will further undermine the basic GATT principle of non-discrimination between countries: the principle that privileges given to one trading partner should be extended to all.

GATT negotiators are interested in the way the American-Canadian agreement deals with the so-called "new issues": trade in services, foreign investment and intellectual property (such as patents and copyright). The 100-plus countries involved in the GATT talks have been floundering in a sea of abstract theorising about how GATT's fair-trade principles can sensibly be applied to "invisibles", which are often hard to measure or value.

The most annoying bits of the North American agreement are those that seem to give Canada exemption from trade controls which may be imposed on others, in the event of (say) an import surge. The America-Canada deal, like all free-trade agreements, will be vetted by GATT. It may not escape that check unchallenged, whatever America's Congress and the Canadian parliament may decree.

# Strains in the Welfare State

## Moscow raises questions about its social services

MARTIN WALKER

THE GUARDIAN

The world's biggest welfare state, perhaps the greatest pride of the Soviet system, is now officially acknowledged to be in crisis. Its key components — a nationwide free health system, old-age pensions, child care, and a massive system of food and housing subsidies — are all cracking under financial and sociological strains. Solutions that are starting to emerge suggest that various reforms are going to lead to a new kind of welfare state that bears more and more resemblance to the structures that have evolved in the mixed economies of Western Europe — with one massive difference: unemployment.

The strains on social budgets in the West have been made much worse over the past decade by long-term mass unemployment. But the Soviet constitution guarantees the right to work. And when Communist Party chief Mikhail Gorbachev recently told the central committee that automation and restructuring of the economy would eliminate the jobs of 15 million industrial workers over the next 12 years, he stressed that he was committed to finding 15 million new jobs for them. He will need the best of Russian luck.

But in the growing role of private health care, the steady dismantling of state subsidies, the acceptance of individual charity within the welfare structure, and the exploration of a national insurance system, we are seeing a convergence between the future of the Soviet and the Western European welfare states.

How did this come about? There are three main reasons: demographic, financial, and the late Party chief Leonid Brezhnev. The first two factors are common across the world: growing numbers of old-age pensioners, and increasing strains on national budgets. But the problem posed by the legacy of Brezhnev is distinctly Soviet.

Brezhnev presided over the biggest consumer boom the 280 million Soviet people have ever known. When he came

to power in 1964, one Soviet household in four had a television set. When he died in 1982, nine out of 10 households had TV sets. That period also saw a change in the national diet — a sharp drop in the traditional dependence on bread and potatoes, with the consumption of fish, eggs, and butter doubling and that of meat rising by about 50 percent.

Good for Brezhnev — except that these foodstuffs were subsidized, and those subsidies now represent about one-fifth of the national budget. The way the budget was balanced — through a dependency on alcohol sales taxes — was one of the great disasters of the Brezhnev years. The nation spent almost four times as much each year on alcohol by the time Brezhnev died as it had in Nikita Khrushchev's last year.

There was nothing symbolic or killjoy about Mikhail Gorbachev's anti-alcohol campaign, one of the first dramatic measures after he came to power. It was a matter of saving the Russian people from the threat of drastic damage. But the national budget was strongly dependent on alcohol sales. The deputy head of the state prices committee wrote this year in the Moscow daily *Izvestia* that the collapse in revenues from alcohol sales was a major cause of the current budget deficit.

Brezhnev's contribution to today's crisis of the Soviet welfare state was to finance a consumer boom through alcoholism. Reversing that process is not only a nightmare for the state budget; it has left a permanent scar on the nation's health. Thanks to *glasnost*, the Soviet press now confirms that the average life expectancy in the country began to drop in the 1970s, largely because of alcoholism.

That trend has now been reversed, but the irony of this "success" in stopping the decline in Soviet life expectancy is that it will put more pressure on the state budget. Today there are 60 million pensioners in the country. Within 12 years, there will be 70 million, all collecting pensions that Gorbachev now promises to increase.

All welfare states contain the seeds of their own crises, as vastly greater numbers of pensioners and costlier health care

From the Moscow correspondent of the daily "Guardian" of London.

By Martin Walker, *The Guardian*, London. Reprinted from *World Press Review*, October 1987, pp. 24–26. World Press Review, 230 Park Avenue, New York, N.Y. 10169.

change the balance of income and expenditure in a system that has always depended on the many subsidizing the few. As the graying of its population progresses, the Soviet Union will face the costs of demographic success.

It already is coping with inadequate hospital services. When Russians learn that they must be hospitalized, they begin preparations early. First they collect a stack of one-ruble notes. Without these small tips, the shortage of ward attendants means there will be no bedpans, and patients or their families will have to clean the floor around the bed and bring fresh towels and sheets. Patients also try to provide their own surgical equipment. Gifts and bribes to secure the services of renowned specialists are commonplace.

The new minister of health, Yevgeny Chazov, recently fulminated against the appalling quality of basic surgical equipment that forced Soviet surgeons to re-sharpen their scalpels after each operation. One of the stars of Soviet medicine, Svyatoslav Fyodorov, the pioneering eye surgeon, complains that ''we are trusting our patients' lives to absolutely unreliable technology.''

Or consider this quotation from an article by Anatoly Agranovsky, written in 1980, which could not be published in his lifetime but has recently appeared posthumously: ''I drove up to the hospital and . . . visitors with bags and bundles were stretching from the gates to the numerous buildings. They were carrying not presents and flowers to the patients, but food.''

The reason is that the planners who organize the finance of Soviet health care have refused for more than 20 years to increase the daily food allowance for patients from about 90 cents. The new health minister has just won what he described as a bruising battle with hospital administrators to begin installing kiosks where patients can buy snacks.

On paper, the Soviet health service looks magnificent, with 1.2 million qualified doctors, and 13 hospital beds for every 1,000 people — figures that seem to put Britain and the U.S. to shame. But the first thing Dr. Chazov did after being promoted from running the Kremlin's privileged health service was to run competence checks on a sample of doctors. He found that 40 percent of new graduates from medical colleges could not read X-rays or cardiograms.

The essential problem is money. The Brezhnev years saw a steady squeeze on the national health budget, from 4.1 percent of national income in 1970 to barely 4 percent today and with spending scheduled to decline to 3.9 percent by 1990. Chazov has reversed that trend and won a state commitment to double the health budget share to 8 percent of national income by the year 2000. He has also won approval for a plan to decentralize the health system, giving regional authorities a fixed budget based on the size of the local population and leaving it to them to decide where and how to spend the money, on a self-accounting, profit-and-loss basis.

He says, ''The medical institutions will now have a direct economic interest in both the quality of treatment and disease prevention, because they will have to pay for neglected cases out of their own pockets. We suggest that hospitals receive part payment some time after the discharge of the patient, and that this sum be greater or smaller depending on the quality of the treatment.''

Amid all this criticism, it is only fair to say that the Soviet health service stands as a gigantic testament to the decency of the intentions and priorities of the system, and that some

of its showcase sectors are among the best in the world. The celebrated eye clinic of Dr. Fyodorov, which he proudly says he organized in spite of the hostility and opposition of the Soviet medico-financial establishment, now has the extra political clout of being a major foreign currency earner in its own right. Intourist, the government travel agency, actually organizes eye-surgery package tours, and Fyodorov's clinic is one of the few organizations given the right to trade directly with Western companies under the recent foreign commerce reforms.

But another aspect of the Soviet welfare state emerged in a recent interview with Inspector Alekseyev, deputy head of the Moscow fraud squad, published in the trade-union daily *Trud.* ''The corruption in medicine is alarming,'' he said. ''In our famous eye microsurgery center, some doctors were taking huge bribes for an operation.''

With all of these aberrations, it is easy to forget that the concept of the welfare state was born of the industrial system of the 19th century and refined through the experience of the great depression of the 1930s — a period in which a large working class received only rudimentary health care and had a low to moderate life expectancy. It was a system designed for the many in work and in health to subsidize the minority who were not — a system tailor-made to fit the full-employment Soviet economy that Stalin created. But then we all get the welfare systems our economies deserve.

The fact that the developed nations of the West have moved on from this traditional pattern explains many of our own difficulties in adapting our welfare structure. The crisis of the Soviet welfare state lies in the essence of the Gorbachev reform program: the realization that the old industrial and economic systems will have to change. And to insure that they do, the process must be accompanied by an intensification of the political and social revolution that has been gathering momentum since Stalin died nearly 35 years ago.

The point about Gorbachev is not simply that he is an instigator of change; he also is a symbol of the change that has already happened. He is one of more than 1.5 million lawyers and economists produced in Soviet universities and institutes since 1950. In 1980, his daughter was one of more than 5 million people in full-time higher education, and she graduated to become one of the 1.2 million Soviet doctors.

The amount of human and educational investment that the Soviets have put into their welfare state and educational system has been massive. The way they have managed to pay for it was by exploiting women. About 70 percent of Russian doctors and a slightly higher percentage of teachers are women, and their salaries have been cruelly held down for the past 20 years.

The Moscow weekly *Novaya Vremya* (*New Times*) recently wrote, ''If all types of work are arranged in pyramid form of the qualifications necessary and the status attached (and that means wages or salaries), we find the following picture: Each of the layers is more densely populated by women than the one above it. The same applies more starkly to the pyramid of administrative or educational posts.''

The expansion of the Soviet welfare state has been staffed through the employment of qualified women, and then financed by holding down their salaries. Once again, like the growth of alcoholism and the falling proportion of the national income devoted to health, this is a product of the

Brezhnev era — storing up social problems that Gorbachev now has to face.

A phased pay increase for doctors and teachers is now in force. It will take years to bring them up to the salary levels of a skilled worker. This will cost money, and so will the plan to double the nation's health budget. Where will the money come from?

In theory, the answer is simple: from closing the vast system of subsidies on basic food and housing costs. It is no longer heresy for Soviet economists to attack this system. The remedy is evident: Let food prices rise to market levels, giving the farmers an incentive to grow more crops, and allowing the government to shift the money saved into the planned growth of the health and pensions budget.

This will happen, but slowly. The Kremlin knows that each of the three political crises in Poland has been sparked by price rises for basic foodstuffs. Khrushchev's price rises in 1962 led to the worst rioting the Soviet Union has known since the war and allegedly caused 70 deaths. Prices are political dynamite.

"The psychology of this change will be very hard for us," says Prof. Vladimir Groshev of the Institute of the National Economy. "I can remember as a boy in Stalin's time how every April 1 there would be an announcement of new price cuts. This was the symbol of success in building communism. And now prices will have to rise."

The economists plan to try following the Western pattern of targeting the recipients of state welfare. Rather than distort the entire economy with blanket subsidies to everybody for everything, they are going to give help directly to those who need it most.

The Soviet economy also faces the social cost of the Gorbachev drive toward automation. This means not only retraining those whose skills become redundant, but also looking after those who cannot cope with the demands and whose income and status fall.

The logic of the situation is leading not only toward a post-industrial economy like that emerging in Western Europe, but also to a similar welfare system, based upon helping the needy and letting the rest pay realistic prices. In one innovative development the state planning board has given its theoretical blessing to the opening this year of the country's first fee-charging hospital, which is supposed to make an annual profit of 15 percent.

There is a deep historical irony in the way that the Soviet Union appears to be ending the 20th century with a welfare system — and, if all goes well, an economy — markedly similar to the social democracies of Western Europe, whose politics for almost a century have been defined by the fact that they did not have a revolution in 1917.

# The Great Siberia in the Sky

MOSCOW

**Thirty years ago this Sunday, Russia put the first artificial satellite into orbit and thereby gave the West a nasty shock. Today the Soviet space programme thrives while America's flounders. Are Russia's efforts in space more successful, or just different?**

AMERICA narrowly missed its chance to be first into space when it turned down a proposal from its army to launch a test satellite in September 1957. The 84-kilogramme Sputnik soon stirred America's ambitions. In November 1958 the administration decided to go ahead with manned spaceflight, and John Glenn was sent up into orbit in February 1962. But the Russians had got there first; Yuri Gagarin had become the first man to orbit the earth.

Three decades and some $280 billion (at current prices) later, America's civil space plans are again behind and faltering. The space shuttle is out of commission for at least another nine months; there are too few rockets to launch America's satellites; and the space station planned by the National Aeronautics and Space Administration (NASA) is caught up in wrangles over its cost.

Russia's space programme is lauded by NASA's critics as a better way to do things. The truth is more prosaic. Russia seems to be ahead mainly because it can launch rockets frequently and relatively reliably. This has allowed it to spawn a host of space programmes and build up plenty of experience—not least in lengthy stays aloft by cosmonauts.

The Soviet space programme has made a virtue out of its limitations. It has stuck doggedly to what it managed to do right. America took a different tack in the early 1970s when it opted for the space shuttle and abandoned the rockets that had taken Americans to the moon: NASA was seduced by new technology and discarded the security of the old. Until recently, Russia had no new launcher technology to introduce, so it stayed with rockets that are two decades old. It now launches close to 100 of them a year, four-fifths of the world total. The rockets used by Russia to put cosmonauts in space are very similar to the rocket that sent up Sputnik. The Mir space station that Soviet cosmonauts are working in today is little changed from the Salyut modules that were first launched in 1971.

The Russians have stuck to their programme even through the failures, of which there have been quite a few. In one of the most secret phases of the Russian space programme, the Soviet Union somehow failed in its attempts to build a rocket big enough to carry a manned moon craft; one prototype may well have blown up on the ground. It abandoned its plans to put a man on the moon in the early 1970s. But the Russians maintained production of what they had. Their main workhorse rocket, known as Proton, was quite adequate for most uses, such as unmanned planetary probes. Proton rockets launched the Luna probes that brought back soil from the moon in 1970 and 1972. They have served to put Salyut and then Mir modules into orbit.

It is only now that the Russians are anywhere near to catching up with American space technology. And it is not yet clear whether they have mastered what they have developed. The Energiya heavy booster that was launched for the first time earlier in the summer at last gives the Soviet Union a rocket that is as powerful as the Saturn V which took American astronauts to the moon. Energiya uses the tricky technology of liquid hydrogen and oxygen engines that America developed more than 20 years ago. Russian scientists are also making much of

the rocket's new computerised control system and say they now have no need to pry into the technologies of the West.

Yet Russia is not overconfident. In contrast to the Khrushchev years, when the pace of Russia's space plans was forced by a desire for political prestige, the directors of the space programme are cautious. Energiya has flown only once and it failed to place its dummy payload into orbit on its first test flight. The Soviet space agency, Glavkosmos, says that Energiya may not fly again this year. Only two launches a year can be expected thereafter.

A similar circumspection surrounds the Soviet shuttle, whose existence is no longer concealed. The Challenger disaster, it is hinted, has slowed down its development. Glavkosmos now says that the craft, which Energiya will lift, is unlikely to fly before 1989. The Soviets admit that work is also under way on smaller, manned "space-planes", whose purpose may be mainly military.

Even what the Russians already have allows them more opportunity for the future than the Americans enjoy. Russia's leading space scientist, Mr Roald Sagdeyev, who is the director of the Space Research Institute, has a programme with four main objectives: radio-astronomy, x- and gamma-ray astronomy, studies of solar plasma and the earth's magnetosphere, and the exploration of Mars. Mr Sagdeyev thinks that a "sample return" mission to Mars, similar to that achieved by the Luna programme to the moon, could be achieved by Russia before the end of the century. He says that a feasibility study has indicated it would "not be terribly expensive". His budget, he says, is increasing steadily.

Next year will see the launch of two Russian Mars probes called Phobos. One reason for renewed Soviet interest in Mars is that it is a suitable eventual target for cosmonauts. It is not boiling hot like Venus, and is no colder than the chilliest of winter nights in Siberia. Russian space scientists argue that manned flight to Mars is technically feasible, but they have not yet said in public that

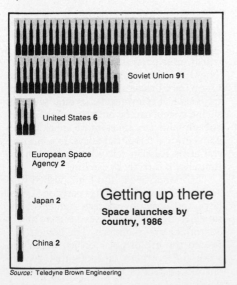

**Getting up there**

**Space launches by country, 1986**

Soviet Union 91

United States 6

European Space Agency 2

Japan 2

China 2

Source: Teledyne Brown Engineering

From *The Economist*, October 3, 1987, pp. 93–96. © 1987, The Economist, distributed by Special Features.

it is their aim. They suggest that such decisions are a couple of years away, leaving time to bring together international co-operation for such a large undertaking. The Space Research Institute has plenty of experience of working with the West—a module on the Mir space station devoted to astrophysics contains instruments from several European countries, co-ordinated by the institute. It is the obvious point of departure for such initiatives. Mr Sagdeyev wants international co-operation for all four of his pet projects for the 1990s. He hopes that the renewal this summer of a space co-operation agreement with the Americans (which was allowed to lapse in 1982 as an American protest against the imposition of martial law in Poland) will bear fruit.

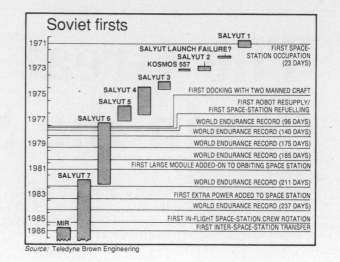

Source: Teledyne Brown Engineering

### Jobs still to do

The Russian space programme has gaps that it needs other countries to fill. Russia has so far failed to produce motors for manoeuvering spacecraft that have stood the test of time. It needs them because a return trip to Mars will be a two-year journey. Russia's communications systems are inferior to those used in American spacecraft—communication with Soviet spacecraft is intermittent, and the quality of television transmission has been poor. They may still be short of computing power and certainly lack some types of instruments for experiments.

When the reliability of Energiya is proven it will provide the launch capability for ambitous new schemes. The rocket is not just able to lift Russia's shuttle, it can also launch other things—which America's shuttle boosters cannot. It will be powerful enough to send 27 tons to Mars, or put 100 tons into a low-earth orbit. A likely cargo is modules for a large space station that Russia may have in use by the mid-1990s.

The Russians appear to be in no rush to develop their shuttle, perhaps because they have no pressing need for it. It is difficult to find a Soviet official who can say exactly what it is to be used for. Part of the American rationale for their shuttle was to make launchers re-usable. Such an approach goes against Soviet practice and an ingrained production philosophy: to produce in bulk and simply replace whatever fails to work. It is an approach with plenty of advantages in the inherently risky business of putting things into space.

It may well be that Russia decided to build a shuttle because of the same sort of insecurity that led them to imitate other prestigious, high-technology western projects. And back in the 1970s, when the Americans announced the development of their shuttle, it seemed a more efficient type of vehicle than it does now. Suspicious westerners may also wonder whether the Soviet scientists just happened to lay their hands on the design plans of America's shuttle.

The overall concept is similar, but there is no evidence that the Russians stole anything. Its long development time would suggest that they did not. When Soviet technologists copy the West's ideas, they tend to build from blueprints faster than those who drew them.

The Russians could fairly contend that their space effort owes an unusual amount to home-grown technologies—more, for instance, than their aircraft industry does. Russian pioneers designed rudimentary rockets in the nineteenth century and were testing fairly advanced ones by the 1930s. In 1945 the Russians got hold of some of the best German rocket scientists (as did the Americans). The technology of the v2 rocket proved useful, but whereas Germans—particularly Wernher von Braun—went on to become leading lights in the American space programme, it was Russians who designed the rockets that lifted Sputnik and later the first cosmonauts. The most important among them were Valentin Glushko, who in the early 1960s developed a rocket motor that was ahead of anything the Germans or Americans had built up to that point, and Sergei Korolev, the "chief designer" of Soviet history books, who has been credited with building almost everything that the Russians sent into orbit before the early 1960s.

The workhorse rockets these designers built will stay in use. They are reliable and, because they are fairly simple and built in quantity, cheap. Frequent launches, and therefore low-cost basic rockets, have been forced on the Soviet Union by the short lifespans of Russian satellites (those lifespans are now increasing) and by the sheer number of space projects.

This approach has brought considerable flexibility in the deployment of satellites. The Russians can launch reconnaissance satellites specifically to observe particular countries or military installations. America has to divert a limited number of (admittedly longer-lived) satellites.

Russia also has many civil objectives for its space programme. The great land mass of the world's largest country and its geographical features make the economic advantages of the exploitation of space greater than they are for any other nation. Mr Nicholas Johnson, an American scientist at Teledyne Brown Engineering in Colorado, who follows the Soviet space programme closely, says that the country's network of remote-sensing satellites is more versatile and developed than similar systems in the West. According to official Russian estimates, the use of satellites for oil and gas prospecting, charting routes for railways in remote regions, and predicting spring floods, among other things, benefits the economy by some 500m-600m roubles ($790m-950m at the official exchange rate) a year. But Mr Sagdeyev says that remote sensing has not been the economic boon that was once hoped, and that it has yet to "break even". He pooh-poohs some recent western speculation that the Soviet Union is working on a gargantuan project to generate power from space and beam it back to earth.

Communications from space are a clear benefit to Russia. Satellite links are ideally suited to serve sparsely populated areas—which most parts of the Soviet Union are. They have, for example, allowed Soviet television to be broadcast throughout the country, via local transmitters. Izvestia says that such a system can be built three times more cheaply and ten times more quickly than conventional terrestrial relays. In some central areas Russian television is brought to households directly by satellite.

Economic needs and logic pushed Russia into the use of satellites early on. Often large and heavy by western standards, the satellites are to western eyes a bizarre mix of Victoriana and high-tech. The Soviets pioneered the use of polar orbits, which can serve the northern latitudes that geosynchronous satellites, perched above the equator, cannot. International politics also forced some developments. In the early 1970s the Soviet Union set up Intersputnik, an almost-worldwide communications network independent of the world's main international satellite organisation, Intelsat, which is based in Washington and is strongly under the influence of America.

The rapid build-up of satellites serving the domestic American market in the early 1970s meant that America soon had more satellites than Russia in the geosynchronous arc above the equator. But in many applications there are more Russian satellites than all others put together. Military satellites, for example, account for two-thirds of the Soviet spacecraft in orbit. Russian technology appears to lag somewhat behind American technology—Soviet satellites are shorter-lived and most of them can perform fewer tasks than their American counterparts. But Russia's more frequent launches mean that the overall capability of the two countries' satellites is much the same—even in the most sophisticated eavesdropping and military-reconnaissance applications. One important technology gap, however, exists in data relay, which is crucial for keeping in constant touch with orbiting spacecraft; Russia has so far failed to make such a system work properly. Russia also used to have difficulty making high-powered solar cells, which is why it is the only country to use some nuclear-powered satellites.

Nobody in the West knows exactly how much Russia spends on space. American estimates say that it would cost America about $30 billion-35 billion a year to do what the Russians do. That is around 20% more than America currently spends.

### Don't look down

After the propaganda coup of Sputnik and Gagarin's first flight, the Russians—perhaps surprised by their own success—have pushed ahead. Practical civil and military advantages are part of the explanation. More important, perhaps, is the proof of Soviet technology—and by implication the country's economic system—that the space programme offers, which was reassuring to perennially insecure Soviet leaders.

There is no sign of space investment slackening under Mr Gorbachev. But the space programme is getting a new gloss: less emphasis on national glory and more on economically beneficial applications. Success in space, according to Mr Gorbachev in a recent speech, should be held up as a rebuke to the pervading sloppiness of other parts of the economy.

Nobody has asked the ordinary Russians what they think of their country's space programme, though they do not seem to tire of the frequently reported exploits of the nation's cosmonauts. Space seems genuinely to be popular—though because the space industry is practically a separate economy there has been no spate of non-stick samovars or other spin-offs for the Soviet consumer. Instead there are Kosmos cigarettes, Sputnik shampoo, and the like.

Space remains an important diplomatic tool. When Mr Gorbachev, Mr Ryzkov or Mr Shevardnadze go abroad they can offer to send one of their host nation's countrymen into orbit. This helps with close allies: a Syrian went up to the Mir space station in July, a Bulgarian will go up in 1988; other East Europeans have preceded him. Britain and Austria have also been offered the chance to send up an astronaut and a Frenchman, Mr Jean-Loup Chrétien, will go up for the second time next year. Russia has offered to train Chinese astronauts.

Because of falling hard-currency income from oil exports, the Russians are trying to earn some money out of space, too. Glavkosmos—which is two years old this month—is offering to launch medium-sized satellites for the West for $25m-40m on its Proton rockets. The agency reckons it costs some $17m to launch a Proton, so it could still make a handsome profit while undercutting the Western market rate of $40-50m. At the end of 1986 it extended its product range to leasing satellite capacity, or complete satellite systems. It has not had any takers, except for an Indian satellite due to be launched in the next few months (and this was agreed before Glavkosmos made its offer to the world). The main reason why there have been no takers from the West is that America is barring the transfer of Western-made high-technology components (which most Western satellites contain) from entering the Soviet Union—despite Russian offers that the satellites could be accompanied and guarded by Western technicians or soldiers.

The Russians keep pushing, and are becoming slicker salesmen. From its modest Moscow headquarters in the ground floor of what looks like a council-house block, Glavkosmos produces glossy brochures and is learning Western ways. One offer is for manufacturing and mineral processing in space. The Russians have been carrying out small-scale processing on Salyut and Mir since the beginning of the decade, though what benefits have emerged from it are not clear. Russia is also keen to sell high-resolution pictures of the earth from its satellites and the US Geological Survey, for one, wants to buy. America can get pictures that are just as good from its own spy satellites, but keeps them secret—even from some of its own governmental agencies.

# Conflict

In the international arena, governments are sometimes able to fulfill their goals by making mutually agreeable exchanges (i.e., giving up something in order to gain something they value more). This exchange process, however, often breaks down. When threats and punishments replace mutual exchanges, conflict ensues. Neither side benefits, and there are costs to both. Each side may hope the other will capitulate, but if efforts at coercion fail, the conflict may escalate into violent confrontation.

There is no scarcity of conflict in the world today. The Middle East is criss-crossed with divisions of hostility. Iran and Iraq are at war, and Israel continues to confront many of its neighbors. There are also violent conflicts in Central America, Afghanistan, and parts of Africa.

In the lead article, well-known military commentator Klaus Knorr offers a very important observation. He argues that there has been a significant trend that has shifted military conflicts to the Third World. In the two articles that follow, this hypothesis is examined in greater detail. Marc S. Miller describes a new military doctrine known as "low intensity conflict" and examines its applications by the United States in Central America. Then, the future course of terrorism is discussed by Brian Michael Jenkins.

The theme of the concluding three articles shifts to the nuclear arms race. Frank Barnaby focuses on the development and spread of nuclear arms technology in the Middle East. The next article, by Secretary of State George Shultz, describes the recent agreement reached between the United States and the Soviet Union to eliminate intermediate range weapons from Europe. Shultz places this agreement in the broader context of arms reduction talks with the Soviets and responds to critics of the agreement. In contrast to the Shultz discussion, the final article in this section points out that nuclear weapons are a symptom of deeper political problems. According to the authors, if meaningful nuclear disarmament is to take place, the sources of superpower conflicts must first be resolved.

Like all the other global issues described in this anthology, international conflict is a dynamic problem. It is important to understand that it is not a random event, but there are patterns and trends in this social phenomenon. While the superpowers contain each other with vast expenditures of money and technological know-how, the Third World increasingly has become the arena for conflict. For people in the United States, the motives of the participants in these conflicts are often difficult to understand as are the values they represent. Success at conflict management, whether it be preventing nuclear war or bringing peace to the Middle East, requires insights into cultural values and social dynamics. Like many other things in the world, insights into this arena seem to be another scarce resource.

## Looking Ahead: Challenge Questions

Is violent conflict and warfare increasing or decreasing today?

What changes have taken place in recent years in terms of the types of conflicts that occur and who participates?

How is military doctrine changing to reflect new political realities?

How do the superpowers contribute to political instability in the Third World?

What are the objectives of terrorists? Why do they seem to be so successful?

Why is the danger of nuclear confrontation increasing in the Middle East?

What are the sources of tension between the superpowers? What might be done to reduce these tensions?

# Unit 5

# On the International Uses of Military Force in the Contemporary World

## KLAUS KNORR

In this essay, Klaus Knorr rejects the proposition that military force
has lost its utility in contemporary world politics. Given the con-
stancy with which states resort to military force, Knorr concludes
that the most important trend is the shift of military conflicts to
the Third World. Author of *The Power of Nations* (1975) Knorr
is professor emeritus at the Woodrow Wilson School, Princeton
University.

In 1965, this author wrote a book (published by Princeton University Press in 1966)—*On the Uses of Military
Power in the Nuclear Age*—in which he was one of the
first to advance the thesis that the usability and usefulness
of military force in interstate relations, compared with previous historical periods, had been diminished by several
changes in underlying conditions. . . . [Now] it seems interesting to review this proposition in the light of subsequent
writings that greatly amplified it, on the one hand, and in
consideration of the actual uses of military power and the
preparations for its use that have occurred since, on the
other. Do the relevant events of the past decade or so, and
what they foreshadow, confirm or disconfirm the thesis and
the amplications it has received? . . .

This theme of the declining value of military forces has
been pushed a great deal further in more recent writings.
For the sake of economy, I will briefly sum up these opinions and the propostions without attributing them to
individual authors.

This new school of thought asserts that international relationships have recently been experiencing, and are still
undergoing, a revolutionary transformation in the following terms. First, the nuclear balance of terror, which is
assumed to be safely stable, has inhibited any large-scale
use of force between powerful states, whose leaders, as
rational actors, are completely self-deterred. Second, societies everywhere are now preoccupied with the solution
of economic and social problems on which national welfare depends. The fading of serious questions of military

security has facilitated this emphasis on domestic priorities over the previous stress on defense budgets and military
service. Third, rapidly growing international interdependence, particularly economic, has been accompanied by
the vigorous growth of transnational forces and organizations, including multinational business corporations, which
in turn have undermined the primacy of governmental
inter-state behavior in favor of that of private actors and
have greatly reduced the significance of state boundaries.
Indeed, as many see it, the classic nation-state, in which
military sovereignty reposed, is being increasingly hemmed
in and dominated by these forces and is probably on the
way out. Fourth, contemporary international affairs are
more and more devoted to problems—economic, environmental and normative—that generate negotiations in which
military power is irrelevant, which are more subject to
international economic power, and which in any case
increasingly require management by authorities and institutions that transcend national boundaries.

The world, according to this concept, is being shaped
by forces and visions that are creating new forms of "international life," in relation to which the realities and teach-
ings of the past are largely, if not wholly, irrelevant. The
extent to which the members of this new school assert the
presence of novel realities or express a vision of the future
is often unclear. They apparently believe they are addressing themselves to an international reality that is in the
process of swift and irresistible change and that is evidently escaping from the grim shackles of the premodern

From *The Global Agenda: Issues and Perspectives*, 1984, pp. 59-64. Reprinted from ORBIS 21 (Spring 1977), pp. 5-7. A Journal
of World Affairs, Foreign Policy Research Institute, Philadelphia.

world. . . . [The author next cites information on the actual behavior of governments in military matters, including the incidence of their wars, their military expenditures, their military interventions, the number of their military personnel, their arms transfers abroad, and their propensity to contribute to nuclear arms proliferation. These, in conjunction with the general absence of efforts at international arms control and the continuation of military alliances, lead Knorr to observe that there has been substantially little change in the attachment of states to military instruments of foreign policy—eds.]

. . . A firm believer in the thesis that international resort to military force has become and is becoming less useful, possible and relevant can contend that there have been no wars between major powers, that the military conflicts that have taken place have been small-scale, short-lived or both, and that the continued high level of military spending results from the lagging ability of governments to comprehend the real changes that are going on around them or from bureaucratic and special-interest-group politics.

The same evidence can be interpreted differently. . . . [P]rolonged periods without wars between major powers have occurred before, and the number of international military conflicts in recent years has certainly not been small. If many of these conflicts have been on a modest scale, this has been because many of the states involved have modest capabilities that do not permit them to wage war for very long or very far beyond their boundaries. If several of these conflicts have been of extremely short duration, this has been either because . . . the weapons supply, especially of sophisticated imported arms, was quickly exhausted—or because one belligerent proved far superior to the other and achieved quick results. In regard to the persistently high level of military expenditures, it is possible that governments do perceive serious security problems and believe scholarly assertions of a transformed world to be premature. . . .

The frequency of armed conflict in recent years, the rise in global military expenditures and manpower, and the expansion of the international trade in arms does not appear prima facie to support any thesis asserting a secular diminution in the use of force or in the expected utility of military capabilities. If there is a pronounced trend, it expresses a remarkable international shift. Military conflicts have occurred mostly in the Third World, mainly between Third World countries, and this shift is paralleled by the fact that the proportion of world military spending, manpower and weapons imports outside the developed capitalist states has sharply increased.

All this is incontrovertible. Nevertheless, it is arguable that most government behavior in these repects is lagging behind changes in underlying realities. Whether it is or is not we cannot know. But we can subject to critical analysis the components of the theses asserting a decline in the utility of force. To what extent is it true or plausible that the costs of employing force have been rising relative to the gains that may be expected from its use?

The evidence concerning the range and imputed value of expected gains is naturally very poor because motivations are involved. It does seem, though, that the notion of economic gain as a justification for the aggressive use of force is far less in evidence, at least superficially, than it was for millennia prior to World War II. . . .

It would nevertheless be imprudent to disregard or unduly belittle economic motives that might fuel military conflict in the future. Severe shortages of food and raw materials, combined with the attempt of states controlling scarce supplies to exploit such control for economic and political purposes, may well serve to preserve some potential—even if a lesser one relative to other issues—for dangerous conflict. Current moves to extend territorial control over the sea are indicative of this prospect.

The use of force to seize or control territory for reasons of military security, also a traditionally important motive, likewise seems to have lost attraction. Yet it has not disappeared altogether. . . .

. . . [T]he fading importance of some objectives does not mean that there are not other goals that may justify the use of military force. Several other traditional objectives of this kind have lost little, if any, of their urgency or legitimacy, either internationally or domestically. Deterrence of, and defense against, attacks on political or territorial integrity as well as the rescue of citizens facing organized violence abroad fall into this category. Nor is there any lack of grounds on which to justify force for the purpose of revising the status quo. Aside from the Arab-Israeli conflict, which is in some ways unique, the recent military conflicts . . . suggest the contemporary importance of three major issues capable of generating the decision to go to war. One involves disputes over established boundaries that are regarded unjust by one side or the other. A second, sometimes overlapping with the first, is the protection or liberation of ethnically related peoples; that is, ethnic unification or national reunification. The third issue, apparently the one most productive of international conflict in the world today, is intervention in civil strife, either to support or help combat incumbent regimes. The precise objective or combination of objectives no doubt varies from case to case, but ideological commitments and the desire to maintain or extend spheres of influence, or reduce the interest of a rival power, evidently play an important part. Anyhow, contemporary governments do not seem to lack incentives to consider force or to be militarily prepared for executing that option.

Turning to the cost side, the deterrent effect of the nuclear balance of terror has figured as a major reason for speculations about the declining utility of military force. The risk of a nuclear war that would destroy both sides, it is argued, keeps each side from using lesser military force against the other. So long as this balance of terror prevails, the agressive use of military force is undoubtedly curbed. But if deterrent power is needed for this purpose, that power has extremely high utility as an insurance of self-protection. Moreover, because strategic nuclear reprisal against lesser military attacks, including attacks against allies, is suicidal under these conditions, and because its threat therefore has low credibility, the maintenance of adequate conventional forces for defense also has a great deal of utility. The effective balance of both types of forces accounts for the military stability in Europe in recent decades—provided, of course, that deterrence was needed to stifle the emergence of aggressive designs. The claim that nuclear technology has engendered a decline in the utility of military force can only refer to one thing: namely, fear that a serious conflict might increase the risk of escalation to the strategic nuclear level has restrained adventurism. This consequence, however, will endure only so long as the nuclear balance of terror and that of associated defense capabilities remain solid. The future is by no means certain in this regard. New technological choices or an unreciprocated decay of the will to retaliate or to provide sufficient capabilities for deterrence and defense could upset this balance.

States without nuclear weapons are apparently little, if at all, restrained in their behavior toward states possessing nuclear arms. (The behavior of North Vietnam and North Korea toward the United States is illustrative.) This is so because a powerful moral stigma has become attached to the use of nuclear weapons, especially against a nonnuclear opponent. The magnitude of the expected moral and political costs constrains their use and reduces their utility in these relationships. The fact that states possessing nuclear weapons are thus inhibited from bringing their most effective military technology into play against the vast majority of countries is greatly to the advantage of latter. It tends to increase the utility of their military forces against the nuclear superpowers, thereby making the distribution of military deterrence and defensive power less unequal than it would otherwise be. . . .

Heightened awareness of war's destructiveness, claimed to have greatly increased in recent decades, should lead to greater reluctance to use military power. Indeed, numerous surveys in highly developed countries provide evidence that confirms this awareness of the costs of using military force. . . .

However, there is far less evidence that this sensitivity is equally developed in other parts of the world, specifically in the communist societies and the LDCs. Of course, restricted access to opinions and attitudes in these countries obstructs the assembly of relevant evidence one way or the other. Such evidence is sparse. But it would not be surprising if this awareness were more thinly spread in those societies where some of the conditions that seem to account for its development in the capitalist-democratic nations are absent or nearly so: namely, a strong sensitivity to the destructiveness of war, broad-based higher education, a huge volume of news production and dissemination under conditions of freedom of speech and press, and lively media competition.

Sensitivity to the destructiveness of war has also inspired the new normative restraints that are part of the UN Charter. . . .

The frequency of recent armed conflict in the Third World does not encourage the view that the new norm has attracted more than a shallow adherence. This is not surprising. After all, the prohibition of aggressive warfare in the UN Charter was a Western, particularly an American, idea, and it was lodged in the charter at a time when relatively few Third World states were present—at a time when decolonization had only begun. Given their historical experience, countries in the Third World are primarily anxious about aggression by great powers.

Thus, it is not difficult to be skeptical about the profound systemic transformations that, as a number of writers have proposed, governments will increasingly be compelled to adapt to, and that tend to make war less feasible and relevant. We have already dealt with the consequences believed (with inadequate justification) to stem from the evolution of nuclear arms. The thesis that contemporary societies are primarily preoccupied with solving domestic political, economic and social problems seems to be true by and large. How much of a systemic change this sense of priorities represents is problematical. Moreover, the thesis often associated with this finding—that the forementioned preoccupation has generally caused societies to turn "inward"—is implausible. The economies of the highly developed capitalist coutries are far too dependent on one another to encourage this sort of isolationism, and the vast majority of the LDCs seek the solution of their economic problems predominantly through the establishment of a new world economic order. While these are not problems that commend the use of military force as a solution, the historical record does not suggest that other pressing issues cannot come to dominate the agenda and the international behavior of states. In the past, certainly, societies have not rarely been content to devote themselves for considerable periods of time primarily to domestic problems, only to be seized by, or have forced on them, international issues that claimed priority. There are a number of countries whose structure of priorities is largely shaped by international considerations that do not rule out the use of force. . . .

The further thesis that growing international interdependence and the rise of transnational actors and institutions are threatening the demise of the nation-state, to which military sovereignty is attached, thus far has scant claim to validity. The citizens of democratic-capitalist nations have been making greatly increased demands on their national governments. In the communist states, the national governments reign supreme. The Third World is engaged in an intensive effort to establish and strengthen national government. If anything, the nation-state as an institution, long restricted to Western societies, is only now coming into its own in the rest of the world. . . .

One can only conclude, unhappily and disappointingly, that the global picture is far from clear so far as the utility of military force is concerned. The components of this picture do not encourage the prediction that the use and the usefulness of military force are definitely on the decline. What look like considerable changes in parameters are too ambiguous and have been with us for too short a time to permit confident answers to the questions we have raised. The changes on the cost side (actual, probable, possible?) certainly do not establish the disutility of force, and they could not do so even if we accepted the changes as substantial and if their impact were uniform throughout the world. Rational actors, to be sure, will not resort to force unless they expect gains to exceed costs. But aside from the circumstance that deviations from rationality are not unknown among political leaders, there is a powerful subjective element and a great deal of unavoidable guesswork in estimates of costs and gains. All we can argue is this: if cost-increasing factors persist and become less unevenly distributed, then war will become a less likely choice of action statistically speaking. This would be an important change, but such a downgrading effect would be acting only marginally on a historically high level of readiness to consider military options when vital, or seemingly vital, values are at stake. Even if the costs of using force rose substantially, rational actors would be willing to meet them when expected gains have exceeding appeal. The recent behavior of governments in regard to military conflict, both engaging in it and preparing for it, is in line with this judgment.

The conclusion I arrived at more than ten years ago did maintain that the utility of military power was on the decline, but several qualifications were attached. Among them, I noted the uneven global distribution of the relevant changes in parameters. Yet I did not then perceive their importance nearly so much as I do at this time, and I regard my overall assessment now to justify less optimism than I expressed then. The world would seem to contain plenty of state actors for whom the avoidance of violence, including international violence, is not the supreme good; and, as if in recognition of this fact, there are even more actors who still find the aura of military power attractive, if only for reasons of security. I now expect international military conflict and direct foreign intervention in civil wars to continue at a high level, and I expect, too, that the superpowers will have diminishing military influence in the Third World. . . . [T]he military relationship between the Soviet Union and the United States, both on the strategic level and in Europe, . . . depends on the ability of each to maintain solid deterrence. Conflicts in the Third World are likely to remain localized so long as this condition obtains.

It seems to me also interesting that the appreciably more optimistic analyses and predictions that have been offered in more recent years are virtually all the product of scholarship in those societies wherein the new distaste for the use of force is most highly developed. This suggests the possibility that these comforting interpretations suffer from being a bit culture-bound, unless one takes the patronizing view—which seems to be congenial in the West—that revolutionary, systemic transformations have been first generated in the West, that the rest of the world is only lagging behind, and that it is therefore only a matter of time before it catches up.

# AMBIGUOUS
# WAR

## The United States and Low-Intensity Control

## Marc S. Miller

*MARC S. MILLER is a senior editor of Tech-nology Review. He recently was part of a Wit-ness for Peace delegation to Nicaragua.*

*Conflicts in Central America reflect a new doctrine that will likely influence U.S. military operations for the rest of the century.*

Missiles, bombers, and nuclear weapons capture public attention in military debates, but a new doctrine that eschews these tech-nologies is emerging as more important in U.S. preparations to fight actual wars. Tested by U.S. forces in anti-guerrilla operations in Vietnam, the concept of low-intensity con-flict (LIC, pronounced "lick") refers to oper-ations that fall short of large-scale conventional or nuclear war. This is the "most likely form of warfare the U.S. Army will be involved in for the remainder of this century," according to that service's 1985 manual, *Operational Concept for Low Inten-sity Conflict*. And Lt. Gen. Samuel Wilson, former head of the Defense Intelligence Agency, says, "There is little likelihood of a strategic nuclear confrontation with the So-viets. . . . We live today with conflict of a different sort . . . and we had better get on with the ball game."

Officials at the highest level are advocat-ing that the United States improve its ability to engage in this kind of fighting in response to their view of international politics. "The world today is at war," Secretary of Defense Caspar Weinberger told a conference on LIC last year. "It is not global war, though it goes on around the globe. It is not war between fully mobilized armies, though it is no less destructive for all that."

The term "low-intensity" derives from the sparing use of U.S. troops and weapons. Instead, U.S. LIC operations include covert activities, non-military forces, political or-ganization, and economic and humanitarian aid, all coordinated to accomplish long-term foreign-policy goals as opposed to purely military ends. And as LIC theory becomes increasingly sophisticated, it demands spe-cialized technology to achieve this melding of political and military ends.

While the low-intensity approach to war is far from universally accepted within military and other policymaking circles—it often sparks tension between the State and Defense departments over the proper role for the armed services—the concept is a key influence on U.S. military strategy in Central America and elsewhere. LIC critic Michael Klare, professor of peace and world security studies at Hampshire College, says the doctrine, as practiced by both the United States and other countries and groups, "applies to the current fight-ing in Afghanistan, Angola, Cambodia, Lebanon, the Philippines, and Central America." Secretary of State George Shultz adds Ethiopia but leaves the Phil-ippines off when making such a list.

### Presidential Wars

Despite the name, LIC is not truly lim-ited—it is "low" only in that U.S. troops are not overtly committed. Rather, Col. John Waghelstein, commander of the ar-my's Seventh Special Forces, wrote in *Mil-itary Review*, it posits total war—"a fusion of economic, political, and military intelligence." The types of conflict under this heading vary according to who you ask. Different analysts place everything from revolutions, counterrevolutions, and "internal wars" to guerrilla wars within the LIC rubric. Allan Sabrosky, professor of politics at Catholic University, terms U.S. low-intensity activities "presidential wars" because they are fought without explicit congressional approval.

When U.S. military personnel, often called "advisors," do play an open role in LIC, the doctrine calls for "special-operations forces"—highly trained, highly mobile units such as the army's 1st Special Operations Command (SOCOM), headquartered at Fort Bragg, N.C. Such special units are trained to perform, in Secretary George Shultz's words, a "multitude of tasks," ranging from surveillance to guerrilla operations to distributing medicine for civilians. SOCOM has four departments: special forces, rangers, psychological operations, and civic affairs.

The growing U.S. emphasis on LIC is borne out by increases in the special-operations divisions of the army, navy, and air force. As of mid-1987, special-operations forces numbered 34,000, including active, reserve, and national-guard personnel. In addition, about 25,000 personnel are classified as "special-operations qualified," indicating they have undergone training but now have other assignments. By comparison, special-operations forces previously peaked during the Vietnam War at 3,700. The number fell until rebuilding began in the late 1970s.

The official status of LIC was elevated this June with the nomination of Kenneth Bergquist to be the first assistant secretary of defense for special operations and low-intensity conflict. Congress mandated that position in an amendment to the Goldwater-Nichols Department of Defense Reorganization Act of 1986. The amendment also led to the creation of an inter-service body to engage in LIC and other special operations. As the act specifies, a four-star general, James Lindsay, heads the new U.S. Special Operations Command (USSOC), activated at MacDill Air Force Base in Tampa, Fla., on June 1, 1987.

U.S. military and political leaders who advocate the LIC approach to war term it a response to similar moves by America's adversaries. Weinberger has charged that the Soviet Union uses LIC as its primary method of spreading communism and subversion, and he equates Soviet LIC with terrorism: "Any effort to improve the lot of peoples is a target. . . . [I]t is not a nation's military forces that are attacked. Instead, agricultural assistance teams are murdered, as are medical assistance teams, teachers, judges, union leaders, editors, and priests." Secretary of State Shultz also invokes terrorism, calling LIC the terrorist's "answer to our conventional and nuclear strength." He labels LIC "ambiguous war" and foresees "a wide range of ambiguous threats, in the shadow area between major war and millenial peace." One purpose of the legislation creating USSOC was to augment the U.S. capability to deal with terrorism and other LIC threats.

Yet both Shultz's and Weinberger's descriptions of LIC fit current U.S. offensive military involvements at least as much as those of other nations or groups. Events in Central America especially illustrate LIC's blending of military and political approaches. As Tom Barry, author of *Low Intensity Conflict* and critic of the doctrine, notes, Central America "is a laboratory for the current theories of low intensity conflict." Reacting to the public's post-Vietnam aversion to direct military intervention, U.S. policymakers have chosen instead to fund and guide the Nicaraguan contra forces, give military and civilian aid to friendly governments, and make wide use of covert operations rather than send in U.S. troops.

### Appropriate Weapons

Just as it redefines the role of the military, LIC's emphasis on political ends redefines the technology for waging war. Rejecting the weaponry common in large-scale battles, LIC moves surveillance and intelligence technology to center stage instead. Sam Sarkesian, a Loyola University political scientist and leading LIC proponent, notes that some U.S. military leaders have resisted the idea of low-intensity conflict for this very reason. "In the American scheme of things, war tends to be viewed as a technological and managerial conflict," he says.

Which military technology *is* appropriate is under debate in El Salvador in the low-intensity war between U.S.-supported government troops and rebel forces. In *Armed Forces Journal International*, Tammy Arbuckle—a journalist now covering Central America who formerly accompanied CIA officers working in Laos—severely criticized U.S. military aid to El Salvador because it stresses the wrong hardware. "Helicopters, fixed-wing aircraft, and artillery are inappropriate for counterinsurgency operations," he maintains. Instead, he suggests other equipment better suited to surveillance and highly mobile guerrilla operations. "Future U.S. military material support should be limited to small arms, nothing larger than heavy machine guns and mortars, plus specialized equipment such as sniper weapons, radio communications gear, lightweight canvas boots, and other items suitable to mobile warfare in a tropical climate and difficult terrain."

An intelligence technology that could contribute to the U.S. capacity to wage low-intensity conflicts is a light, armed surveillance plane. According to Jerome Klingaman, an aerospace consultant and retired air force officer, "Many, if not all, of the friendly states in Central America, South America, and Southeast Asia would benefit considerably by the addition of a cheap, yet effective, aerial surveillance, reconnaissance, and light-strike capability."

Instead of developing such a vehicle, he says, the United States provides expensive, inappropriate A-37 fighter bombers to El Salvador under the U.S. Military Assistance Program. The A-37's ability to deliver bombs is only marginally useful against the guerrillas in El Salvador, he maintains, where distinguishing between friend and foe is difficult. "Even if light armed surveillance aircraft cost $150,000 each, that cost would be no more than the replacement cost for one A-37 engine," he points out.

In Nicaragua, the United States may be selecting technology that is more appropriate for fighting a guerrilla war. According to *New York Times* reporter James LeMoyne, "The Central Intelligence Agency has turned the contras into the best equipped guerrilla force Latin American has ever seen." During a visit to the U.S.-supplied rebels, he observed Tandy computers used to decode Sandinista radio messages as well as computerized radio coding machines and Redeye anti-aircraft missiles. Moreover, as revealed in the Iran-contra hearings, Col. Oliver North supplied approximately a dozen sophisticated KL-43 encryption machines to the contras. These highly secret devices, obtained from the National Security Agency, enable users to send and receive coded messages. According to LeMoyne, "CIA agents train and advise rebel commanders" and use their intelligence capability to provide lists of targets, including electrical towers and bridges. By focusing on such targets, the United States undermines the Nicaraguan economy as much as it weakens the Sandinista military—as called for by LIC doctrine.

LIC advocates have made a number of other suggestions for developing new technology. A report by a panel on combating terrorism, convened at Georgetown University's Center for Strategic and International Studies in 1985, called for increased R&D to develop higher-tech weapons. The panel recommended that the U.S. military develop "low-profile antivehicle perimeters"—electronic fences that could surround U.S. bases and stall the engines of enemy vehicles that cross the barrier. The report also suggested that "longer-term capabilities could include remote sensing to distinguish terrorists from victims." Similarly, a 1984 conference at Maxwell Air Force Base in Alabama produced several suggestions for advanced "appropriate technologies" for LIC.

Conference participants pointed to synthetic aperture radar (SAR), a technology that the U.S. Air Force first employed in Southeast Asia, as having a potential niche in today's LIC operations. A computer in the SAR processes radar signals as a plane flies within 50 miles of its target. This technology, which provides a very high resolution image, advanced significantly with improvements in digital-processing technology in the 1970s. Because SAR works in the dark, in bad weather, and, most important, from afar, it can "image politically sensitive areas including those where overflight is not authorized or militarily advisable," according to Robert E. Lambert and Charles R. Dotson, senior program managers at Goodyear Aerospace Corp. The United States used SAR's mapping ability to plan naval mine laying in the Vietnam War, says Dotson, although he doubts it was used to aid the mining of Nicaragua's harbors in 1984.

Computer-based models and simulations for staff training and strategic analysis have recently been used in LIC special operations. In 1982 analysts at the National Defense University (NDU) at Fort McNair in Washington, D.C., developed the Strategic Unconventional Warfare Assessment Model (SUWAM)—a computer gaming model of LIC. This early model was simple and functioned only as an educational tool to make NDU students aware of LIC, but the NDU has since refined it. The result, SUWAM III, incorporates weather, terrain, equipment capabilities, and mission importance, thus approaching the complexity needed to analyze real-life situations. Sterling Hart, director of NDU's War Gaming and Simulation Center, carried SUWAM III on a Kaypro II portable computer to Hawaii and South Korea. There, according to Thomas Allen, author of *War Games*, he used it to demonstrate U.S. LIC tactics to American and Korean officials—including techniques for conducting raids and gathering intelligence in a high-risk environment.

U.S. Air Force Maj. Norman Routanen advocates using electromagnetic pulses (EMP) to "disrupt or upset target [enemy] electrical systems" during LIC operations. He notes that this type of electromagnetic warfare is "quite bloodless and, therefore, quite appealing when international opinion is considered." Other applications of EMP sound like science fiction. For example, Routanen has proposed using "very powerful microwave devices to confuse, disable, or even kill the enemy." The report by the Georgetown University panel on combating terrorism similarly proposes "techniques to impair brain functions." Navy physician Capt. Paul E. Tyler sees an opposite use for electromagnetic radiation: he suggests that exposing U.S. military personnel or their allies to electromagnetic radiation might allow them to act "with minimal rest and still maintain peak performance."

Efforts to create a super soldier are not as far-fetched as they sound, nor are they new. Members of the navy's SEALS—its elite special-forces unit—took dexedrine to stay awake for several days on missions during the Vietnam War. Since at least 1954, various Defense Department agencies have conducted hundreds of experiments on ways of enabling troops to endure extremely taxing conditions. As Gen. Frank Besson, Jr., told a 1968 conference on human factors in the military, "In a limited warfare situation, man—more than ever—is *the* weapons system."

### Central America: Lab for Total War

While advocating new technology, LIC proponents continually stress that the focus of LIC is not machinery—or even military might. Richard Shultz, professor of international relations at the Fletcher School of Law and Diplomacy, warns that the special-forces division of SOCOM has mistakenly overemphasized a military approach in opposing El Salvador's rebels. He maintains that the "social, economic, and psychological aspects of counterinsurgency are being downplayed."

Instead, as LIC supporter Sam Sarkesian says, the success of LIC depends most "upon the commitment and skill of political cadre, political organization, and psychological warfare." Col. Harry Summers, Jr., a leading analyst with the Defense Department's Strategic Studies Institute, calls President Reagan's 1984 TV address on a "communist reign of terror" in Central America an example of the use of such "political and psychological instruments of power." The address served the dual purpose of trying to convince the U.S. public to support aid to the contras and threatening Nicaragua.

Military maneuvers in Central America and the Caribbean serve as even more effective psychological weapons. Sara Miles, author of *The Real War: Low Intensity Conflict in Central America*, points out that the maneuvers force Nicaragua to respond to the real possibility of an invasion and thus devote more than half of its budget to defense. This means that the government must divert limited funds from social programs, thus opening it to the charge that it spends money on weapons instead of food. After the United States conducted its Big Pine II military maneuvers in Honduras in 1983, which included 10,000 U.S. troops and a rehearsal to invade a Central American nation, Nicaragua instituted a draft. The United States responded by distributing leaflets that encouraged Nicaraguan youth to resist the draft.

The doctrine of low-intensity warfare has led to a mushrooming role for civilian and private refugee aid and development

agencies—particularly in El Salvador, despite the continuing emphasis there on military solutions. As Army Lt. Col. James A. Taylor has written, "Humanitarian aid in a low-intensity conflict is as defense-oriented as the providing of training and technology. It is in no way soft." Describing LIC in general, Weinberger says, "Our Special Operations Forces play a role here as well, through Civic Action: the construction and restoration of infrastructure, the assisting of others in the improvement of their own lives, whether by restoring land, building roads, digging wells, or helping provide medical and educational services." Col. David Steele, head of U.S. MilGroup in El Salvador, puts this pragmatic approach to humanitarian aid more succinctly. "Civic action shows the people that the army doesn't just go in and rape."

Through both military and civilian aid programs, the United States supplies food, medicine, and other "humanitarian" supplies to the Salvadoran army. According to Robert Wolthius, the Defense Department's coordinator for humanitarian assistance, such aid has a crucial role in Central America. "I think we learned from Vietnam that contests like this are not only about military tactics, but about winning the hearts and minds of the people."

The United States also funds more strictly civilian projects through the Agency for International Development and other government and private agencies, including a literacy training program that consciously imitates the Sandinistas' literacy brigades. However, analyst Miles notes that the U.S.-sponsored brigades "were quietly shelved in late 1985," perhaps reflecting continuing ambivalence over this approach to war within U.S. policymaking circles.

More successful were U.S. attempts to temporarily curb the infamous abuses committed by El Salvador's security forces and death squads while building up José Napoleón Duarte as a legitimate alternative to the rebels. This became especially necessary in the wake of the U.S. public outcry following the 1980 murders of Archbishop Oscar Romero and four U.S. nuns. Today human-rights violations in El Salvador may again be on the rise.

### The Health Front

A key political and psychological battlefield throughout Central America is health care. As with other civic-action projects, the United States seeks both to prove that its clients can improve medical care for their citizens and to limit the enemy's ability to provide such benefits.

U.S. Medical Readiness Training Exercise (Medretes) teams have been especially active in Honduras, supplying health care to civilians during military maneuvers. According to Capt. Carol Corn, supervisor

*Advocates of LIC are quietly but consistently involving the United States in permanent war.*

of Medretes at the Palmerola Air Base in Honduras, in 1984 medical teams treated as many as 5,000 rural people a day. However, the Medretes teams mostly distributed aspirin and pulled teeth. As Corn admitted in an interview with author Tom Barry, "It's mostly public relations."

Moreover, according to public-health specialists Steven Gloyd of the University of Washington in Seattle and Paul Epstein of Harvard, the Medretes teams were "insensitive to the particular health care needs of Hondurans. Most of the treatment they gave out was inappropriate." Among other problems, the teams handed out a drug that kills parasites that affect U.S. children but that is useless against hookworm, the primary parasite affecting Honduran children. Gloyd and Epstein estimate that as many as 30 percent of the tooth extractions were unnecessary.

U.S.-supported forces have specifically targeted the health-care system in Nicaragua—which greatly expanded services between 1980 and 1983—for attack. Says Miles, "There is a conscious effort to remove successful social programs" because of the goodwill they generate for the Nicaraguan government.

Concerned about the ramifications of this policy, Columbia University researchers Richard Garfield, Thomas Frieden, and Sten Vermund have surveyed the impacts of the war on the health of noncombatants. Writing in the *American Journal of Public Health,* they note that civilians accounted for nearly a third of all war-related deaths in Nicaragua through mid-1986, including 42 health workers killed by contras. Between 1983 and 1984 the number of medical visits declined 9 percent and hospitalizations declined 10 percent. Coverage of a supplemental feeding program for malnourished children declined from 38 percent in 1983 to 28 percent in 1985.

The researchers attribute the declines to the closing of health centers—contras have completely or partially destroyed 65 clinics—and to the mobilization of over 5,000

health-care workers into the militia for up to a year each. The researchers also found that attacks on health clinics and health-care workers have contributed to recent malaria, dengue, and measles outbreaks.

A pilot study conducted by the Nicaragua Health Study Collaborative of the Harvard School of Public Health and Nicaragua's schools of medicine and public health further documents the impact on civilians of the U.S.-directed low-intensity war. The study focused on the health of women and children, comparing factors such as nutrition and access to health services in two rural towns: Acoyapa, in the center of a war zone, and El Ostional, which has not suffered any direct attacks for three years. According to collaborative member and public-health nurse Cindy Broholm, the study shows how LIC "blurs the distinction between combatants and civilians."

The study documents the physical disruption of both communities, especially Acoyapa. While the figures are preliminary, attacks on civilian targets, say the researchers, have clear public-health implications. For example, both literacy rates for women and school attendance have declined, and it has long been recognized that a mother's educational status is connected with infant mortality. The study also found that recent contra attacks near Acoyapa have forced a fifth of the people surveyed to leave agricultural production. As food shortages increase and diets become more limited, health can be expected to decline. Moreover, the most reliable indicators available suggest that only about half as many children and women have received tetanus, polio, and DPT vaccines in the war village of Acoyapa as in El Ostional. The long-term effects of LIC may be even more severe than is now obvious, since the results of factors such as malnutrition and lower rates of vaccinations may take years to appear.

### From Covert to Overt

That civilians are the victims of LIC is not surprising, since the doctrine considers them integral to the struggle to attain political goals. Says Secretary of Defense

Weinberger, "The social and economic dimensions of these conflicts are of paramount importance." However, unlike aid that is labeled humanitarian, attacks on non-combatants can be counterproductive in gaining domestic and international acceptance for such operations. Therefore, one of LIC's greatest advantages and fundamental requirements—especially given widespread opposition to Reagan administration foreign-policy goals and post-Vietnam reluctance to commit U.S. troops—is its low profile and emphasis on covert operations. Secretary of State Shultz refers to "an important new role for our military in the area of covert operations," regretting the "web of restrictions on executive action embedded in our laws" that has hindered U.S. operations since Vietnam.

J. Michael Kelly, deputy assistant secretary of the air force, believes that even though LIC doctrine calls for a great deal of secrecy, in the long term it must win the support of the U.S. public. "I think the most critical special operations mission we have today is to persuade the American people that the communists are out to get us." Similarly, Col. Waghelstein proposes that troop training for counterinsurgency missions occur in public—not just on military reservations—to get "the [U.S.] populace familiar with this type of warfare."

Public acceptance is crucial, Shultz emphasizes, because LIC requires a long-term commitment: "The safeguarding of fragile democracies and vulnerable allies against subversion, in Central America or elsewhere, will require more than brief and quickly completed uses of American power." Sam Nunn (D-Ga.), chair of the Senate Armed Services Committee, agrees: "I'd rather flex our muscles a little bit on a weekly basis than have to resort to a great display of force at some very high level of danger."

Indeed, on both sides of the aisle, LIC advocates are quietly but consistently involving the United States in permanent war. The enemy is ostensibly communist subversion, but in Central America—and wherever the United States wages low-intensity conflict—the targets and the victims are ordinary people.

# The Future Course of
# International Terrorism

## Brian Michael Jenkins

Brian Michael Jenkins, a former captain in the Green Berets, is the head of The RAND Corporation's political science department and is one of the world's leading authorities on international terrorism. His address is The RAND Corporation, 1700 Main Street, P.O. Box 2138, Santa Monica, California 90406.

This article is adapted from his chapter, "The Future Course of International Terrorism," in *Security in the Year 2000 and Beyond*, edited by Louis A. Tyska and Lawrence J. Fennelly (ETC Publications, 1987, 276 pages),

**The world will face continued growth in terrorist attacks in the next decade, and large-scale incidents involving hundreds of deaths will become more common, says an expert on international terrorism.**

International terrorism emerged as a problem in the late 1960s, and, despite increased governmental efforts to combat it, terrorism remains a serious problem in the 1980s. Will terrorism continue? Yes.

Modern theories of guerrilla warfare — which, of course, is not synonymous with terrorism but did contribute doctrinally to the use of terrorist tactics — developed from the late 1940s to the early 1960s. World War II represented the culmination of state-organized violence. Since then, there has been a long-range trend toward the "privatization" of violence.

Terrorism has become a routine way of focusing attention on a dispute, of bringing pressure on a government. New causes and new groups have emerged — Armenian terrorists, Sikh terrorists, issue-oriented groups opposed to nuclear power, abortion, technology, pollution, animal vivisection, etc. There certainly will be no lack of causes.

There are economic incentives to the use of terrorist tactics. Kidnapping and extortion based upon threats of violence have become routine means of financing revolutionary movements.

A semipermanent infrastructure of support has emerged. Behind the terrorist groups, and supporting them often without regard to ideology or cause, is an ephemeral but resilient network of connections, alliances, safe houses, arms suppliers, and provisioners of counterfeit documents and other services. This network resembles the infrastructure that supports organized crime.

States have recognized in terrorism a useful weapon and are exploiting it for their own purposes. To a certain extent, international terrorism has become institutionalized.

From *The Futurist*, July/August 1987, pp. 8-13. Published by the World Future Society, 4916 St. Elmo Avenue, Bethesda, MD 20814. Reprinted by permission.

And, increasingly, terrorism is expected and "tolerated."

All these reasons suggest that terrorism as we know it now is likely to persist as a mode of political expression for various groups and as a means of warfare among states. It will probably continue, but at what level? *Will we see more or less terrorism?* Measured by the number of incidents, terrorism has increased in volume over the last 17 years. It is a ragged increase, with peaks and valleys, but the overall trajectory is clearly upward.

Overall, the annual growth rate in the volume of terrorist activity has been approximately 10%–12%. If that rate of increase continues, we could see between 800 and 900 incidents a year by the end of the decade.

There are several other factors that suggest the likelihood of continued growth:

- The increase in the volume of terrorist activity has been matched by its geographic spread — a slow, long-term trend. The number of countries experiencing some sort of terrorist activity each year has gradually increased.

- A handful of nations — the United States, France, Israel, the United Kingdom, and Turkey — remain the favorite targets of terrorists and account for approximately half of all the victims, but the number of nations targeted by terrorists has also increased. In 1984, there were terrorist attacks directed against the citizens of 60 countries.

- Although it is difficult to monitor with any precision the appearance and disappearance of the many hundreds of groups that claim credit for terrorist actions — some of them are only fictitious banners — the level of international terrorist activity no longer appears to depend on a handful of groups. Despite the virtual destruction of some terrorist groups and the decline in operations by others, the total volume of terrorism grows.

- As international communications spread and as populations move or are pushed about — two features of the 1980s — we will probably see more local conflicts manifesting themselves at the international level through terrorist tactics.

## Will Attacks Become More Severe?

Simply killing a lot of people has seldom been a terrorist objective. Terrorists want a lot of people *watching*, not a lot of people *dead*. Terrorists operate on the principle of the minimum force necessary. They find it unnecessary to kill many, as long as killing a few suffices for their purposes.

Statistics bear this out. Only 15%–20% of all terrorist incidents involve fatalities; and of those, two-thirds involve only one death. Less than 1% of the thousands of terrorist incidents that have occurred in the last two decades involved 10 or more fatalities, and incidents of mass murder are truly rare. This suggests that it is either very hard to kill large numbers of persons or it is very rarely tried.

Unfortunately, as we have seen in recent years, things are changing. Terrorist activity over the last 20 years has escalated in volume and in bloodshed. At the beginning of the 1970s, terrorists concentrated their attacks on property. In the 1980s, according to U.S. government statistics, half of all terrorist attacks have been directed against people. The number of incidents with fatalities and multiple fatalities has increased.

A more alarming trend in the 1980s has been the growing number of incidents of large-scale, indiscriminate violence: huge car bombs detonated on city streets, bombs planted aboard trains and airliners, in airline terminals, railroad stations, and hotel lobbies, all calculated to kill in quantity. Ten major international terrorist incidents have resulted in a total of more than 1,000 deaths in the last 15 years, but more than two-thirds of these have occurred in the last three years.

There are several explanations for the escalation:

- Like soldiers in a war, terrorists who have been in the field for many years have become jaded by the long struggle. Killing becomes easier.

- As terrorism has become more commonplace, the public too has become somewhat desensitized. Terrorists can no longer obtain the same amount of publicity using the same tactics they used 10 years ago, and they may feel compelled to escalate their violence in order to keep public attention or to recover coercive power lost as governments have become more resistant to their demands.

- Terrorists have become technically more proficient, enabling them to operate at a higher level of violence.

- The composition of some terrorist groups has changed as the fainthearted who have no stomach for indiscriminate killing drop out or are shoved aside by more ruthless elements.

- The religious aspect of current conflicts in the Middle East pushes terrorists toward mass murder. As we have seen throughout history, the presumed approval of God for the killing of pagans, heathens, or infidels can permit acts of great destruction and self-destruction.

- State sponsorship has provided terrorists with the resources and technical know-how to operate at a higher, more lethal level of violence.

### Restraints Against Terrorism

At the same time, several factors work against escalation, such as self-imposed restraints and technical ceilings. Without resorting to more exotic weapons, terrorists are approaching limits to their violence. The deadliest terrorist incidents — huge bombs detonated in buildings, the bomb presumably detonated aboard an Air India jumbo jet that exploded over the Atlantic Ocean, a deliberately set fire in a crowded Teheran theater — each produced several hundred deaths, roughly equal to such accidental disasters as hotel fires, explosions, and airline crashes.

Death on a larger scale is seen only in the slaughter of great battles or in natural disasters like earthquakes and floods. The most plausible scenarios involving chemical or biological weapons in a contained environment — a hotel, a convention, a banquet — would produce deaths in the hundreds. To get above that, terrorists

# "Terrorists blow up things, kill people, or seize hostages. Every terrorist incident is merely a variation on these three activities."

would have to possess large quantities of deadly substances and solve problems of dispersal, or they would have to resort to nuclear weapons.

Another limiting factor is security. Protective measures taken in the wake of the huge car and truck bombings in the Middle East are reducing the vulnerability of the most obvious targets to this type of attack. More stringent security measures may be applied on a permanent basis to prevent a repeat of the Air India bombing. Of course, terrorists can obviate these by shifting their sights to other, still-vulnerable targets, but security measures force them to become even less discriminate.

On balance, it appears that incidents involving significant fatalities probably will become more common, with incidents resulting in hundreds of deaths remaining, for the foreseeable future, the outer limit of terrorist violence.

## New Terrorist Tactics

Terrorists operate with a fairly limited repertoire. Six basic tactics have accounted for 95% of all terrorist incidents: bombings, assassinations, armed assaults, kidnappings, hijackings, and barricade and hostage incidents. Looking at it another way: Terrorists blow up things, kill people, or seize hostages. Every terrorist incident is merely a variation on these three activities.

I don't think we will see much tactical innovation; there have been few changes over the years. Seizing embassies was a popular tactic in the 1970s. It declined as security measures made embassy takeovers more difficult, and as governments became more resistant to the demands of terrorists holding hostages and more willing to use force to end such episodes, thus increasing the hostage-takers' risk of death or capture.

This is indicative of the kind of innovation we are likely to see. Ter-

rorists innovate in an incremental way to solve specific problems created by security measures. If one tactic ceases to work, they abandon it in favor of another one or merely shift their sights to another target. Since terrorists have virtually unlimited targets, they have little need for tactical innovation.

For example, how might terrorists respond to the new security measures aimed at protecting embassies against car bombs? Conceivably, they might resort to aerial suicide attacks, which are technically and physically more demanding. Or they might resort to stand-off attacks — with mortars, rocket launchers, rocket-propelled grenades — the traditional response to strong defenses. Or they might simply detonate large bombs at other, still-vulnerable targets. Finally, there remains a potential for the use of portable precision-guided munitions, which terrorists already have employed on several occasions.

## New Targets for Terrorists

The greatest advantage that terrorists have and will continue to have is a virtually unlimited range of targets. Terrorists can attack anything, anywhere, anytime, limited only by operational considerations: Terrorists usually do not attack defended targets; they seek soft targets. If one target or set of targets is well protected, terrorists merely shift their sights to other targets that are not so well protected.

Over the years, the range of targets attacked by terrorists has expanded enormously. They now include embassies, airlines, airline terminals, ticket offices, trains, railroad stations, subways, buses, power lines, electrical transformers, mailboxes, mosques, hotels, restaurants, schools, libraries, churches, temples, newspapers, journalists, professors, diplomats, businessmen, military officials, missionaries, priests, nuns, the

Pope, men, women, and children.

With the exception of a couple of minor episodes, terrorists have not attacked nuclear reactors. Targets meant to cause disruption may be more appealing to armchair terrorists than to those who are active in today's terrorist groups. Attacks on energy infrastructures or against computer systems, for example, have been done, but they are technically demanding and produce *no immediate visible effects*. There is no drama. No lives hang in the balance. There is no bang, no blood. They do not satisfy the hostility of the terrorists.

For the most part, terrorists have

## Why Terrorism Will Persist

A number of developments may lead to increased terrorist activities over the long-term future, including:

• A rebirth of racism and growth of membership in racist groups.

• A resurgence of religious fanaticism that results in the proliferation of cults.

• Growing contempt for the criminal justice system.

• An increase in single-issue politics and in the number of narrow-interest groups.

• An unmeasured decline in police intelligence activities.

• Growing mistrust of government and corporations as incompetent, negligent, and irresponsible in protecting public health and safety.

• A sense of insecurity as a result of a growing perception that law enforcement cannot effectively protect citizens.

— **Brian Michael Jenkins**

not operated at sea. There have been no attempts to take over offshore platforms. Prior to the hijack of the *Achille Lauro*, there had been a number of bombs planted aboard ships or mines planted on their hulls. There had been several ship hijackings and attempted hijackings suggesting that the idea of taking over a large vessel had crossed the terrorists' minds.

The future targets of terrorism will be pretty much the same ones as today:

● Representatives of governments and symbols of nations — notably diplomats and airlines.

● Representatives of economic systems — corporations and corporate executives.

● Symbols of policies and presence — military officials.

● Political or other leaders. In the past 15 years, terrorists have killed, or have tried to kill, or have been reported on their way to kill Lord Louis Mountbatten, Anwar Sadat, Pope John Paul II, Indira Gandhi, and Margaret Thatcher, among others.

### Nuclear Terrorism

Will terrorists resort to weapons of mass destruction? Will they employ chemical or biological warfare? Will terrorists go nuclear?

Many people believe that nuclear terrorism of some sort — such as stolen nuclear weapons or a clandestinely fabricated nuclear explosive device to kill or threaten to kill large numbers of people — is likely and may be inevitable. I happen to think nuclear terrorism is neither imminent nor inevitable. Lesser terrorist acts are possible — the seizure or attempted sabotage of a nuclear reactor, for example or the dispersal of radioactive material, or an alarming nuclear hoax that may cause panic.

The question of nuclear terrorism involves an assessment of both capabilities and motivations. It is conceivable that someone outside of government who is familiar with the principles of nuclear weapons could design an atomic bomb. However, the ease with which people outside of government can build one, assuming they had somehow acquired the necessary nuclear material, has been

greatly exaggerated. But let's for a moment say they can. Would they want to? Terrorism has certainly escalated, but it is still a quantum jump from the kinds of things that terrorists do today to the realms of nuclear destruction. Why would terrorists take that jump?

Simply killing a lot of people is not an objective of terrorism. Terrorists could do more now, yet they don't. Why? Beyond the technical constraints, there may be self-imposed constraints that derive from moral considerations or political calculations. Some terrorists may view indiscriminate violence as immoral. The terrorists' enemy is the government, not the people. Also, terrorists pretend to be governments, and wanton murder might imperil the image.

There are political considerations as well: Terrorists fear alienating their perceived constituents. They fear provoking public revulsion. They fear unleashing government crackdowns that their groups might not survive. Certainly, in the face of a nuclear threat, the rules that now limit police authorities in most democracies would change.

Terrorists must maintain group cohesion. Attitudes toward violence vary not only from group to group but also within a group. Inevitably, there would be disagreements over mass murder, which could expose the operation and the group to betrayal.

Obviously, not all groups share the same operation code, and certain conditions or circumstances might erode these self-imposed constraints.

What about chemical or biological weapons, which are technically less demanding? Although there have been isolated incidents, neither chemical nor biological warfare seems to fit the pattern of most terrorist attacks. These attacks are generally intended to produce immediate dramatic effects. Finally, the terrorists retain control. That is quite different from initiating an event that offers no explosion but instead produces indiscriminate deaths and lingering illness, an event over which the terrorists who set it in motion would have little control. For the near-term future — say, the next five

years — we are more likely to see threats of chemical or biological contamination made by authentic lunatics or criminal extortionists.

Over the long-term future — the next 10 to 15 years — my concern is that chemical weaponry will be acquired by unstable, dangerous countries and used in warfare — such as the Iran–Iraq War. If chemical warfare becomes more commonplace, particularly in a region like the Middle East, we cannot dismiss its potential use by terrorists. The same is true of nuclear weapons, but probably over a longer time period.

### Terrorism and Future Wars

The current trend toward state sponsorship of terrorism will probably continue. Limited conventional war, classic rural guerrilla war, and international terrorism will coexist and may appear simultaneously. The Iranian revolution and its spread to Lebanon, which has involved the effective use of international terrorism as an instrument of policy, may provide a model for other Third World revolutions and revolutionary states, just as the Cuban model inspired a generation of imitators in Latin America. If it does, we are in for a lot of trouble.

We also may see international terrorism emerge as a new kind of global guerrilla warfare in which terrorist groups sally forth from the political jungles of the Third World to carry out highly publicized hit-and-run attacks — militarily insignificant but politically of great consequence — avoiding confrontations where they might run into well-equipped, well-trained, specialized anti-terrorist forces.

Terrorists now avoid seizing embassies in Western capitals. They hijack airliners, keep them on the move to evade any rescue attempt, and retreat with their hostages to sanctuaries like Teheran or Beirut. The absence of government, as in Lebanon, or the presence of a government sympathetic to the terrorist's cause, means these sanctuaries lie beyond the reach of the world regime of treaty and law.

### Future Security

The "privatization" of violence

185

# 5. CONFLICT

has been matched by the "privatization" of security, as illustrated by the tremendous growth of private-sector security expenditures. In the United States, a total of $21 billion is now spent annually for security services and hardware (compared with $14 billion spent annually on all police). The figure will reach $50 to $60 billion a year by the end of the century. Private security corporations will grow to meet the demand.

We will see the further proliferation of inner perimeters, the rings of security that now surround airline terminals, government buildings, and, increasingly, corporate offices. From this last development, however, emerges a crude counter-terrorist strategy. By protecting the most obvious symbols — terrorists' preferred targets — this security will force terrorists to become less discriminate in their attacks. That will create greater public outrage, which governments can exploit to obtain domestic support and international cooperation to crush the terrorists.

In sum:
- Terrorism will certainly persist.
- It will probably increase.
- Large-scale incidents will become more common.
- Terrorism probably won't enter the mind-boggling world of high technology or mass destruction.
- In terms of weapons and tactics, terrorism will be for the foreseeable future a continuation of the past.
- States will continue to exploit terrorism — to use it for their own purposes. We may enter a protracted worldwide guerrilla war.
- Terrorists will create crises, forcing governments and corporations to divert more and more resources toward combating them.

# The Nuclear Arsenal in the Middle East

## FRANK BARNABY

FRANK BARNABY is the former director of the Stockholm International Peace Research Institute. During the 1950s he worked as a physicist at the British government's Atomic Weapons Research Establishment. He has held appointments at University College in London, the Free University in Amsterdam, and the University of Minnesota.

NEITHER superpower is likely to start a nuclear war by attacking the other out of the blue. It is more likely that a conflict in a Third World region between client states of the superpowers would escalate to a global scale. And the region where this escalation would most probably begin is the Middle East.

The dangers of escalation stem from the superpowers' involvement in the Third World, particularly the arms trade. Most of the weapons used in conflicts in the Third World are supplied by the United States and the Soviet Union. Because modern war uses weapons, particularly missiles, at a great rate, supplies must flow continually, as was shown dramatically in the October 1973 Middle East war. Both Egypt and Israel ran short of weapons within a few days; each was saved only by massive airlifts from its respective Soviet or American supplier. The arms supplier thus becomes the guarantor of its client's survival.

Neither the United States nor the Soviet Union can readily allow a client to be beaten in war or it will lose credibility as an ally. When Egypt faced defeat in the 1973 war, President Nixon risked escalation to all-out nuclear war by putting the U.S. Strategic Air Command on high nuclear alert to deter the Soviets from sending in troops.

Escalation to nuclear world war is most likely if a client state first resorts to its own nuclear weapons, and nuclear weapons are beginning to proliferate in the Middle East. Last October the London *Sunday Times* published the revelations of Mordechai Vanunu, the 31-year-old technician who worked for 10 years at Israel's nuclear establishment in Dimona and who was later abducted to Israel. Vanunu implies that Israel has a nuclear arsenal comparable to that of China, France, or the United Kingdom. Iraq has also sought to make a nuclear weapon, and Libya and Egypt have cultivated their nuclear technologies to the point where they could well make nuclear weapons. Even a subnational group such as the Palestine Liberation Organization (PLO) might produce a nuclear weapon.

Much of the Middle East's nuclear technology was imported from developed nations, ostensibly for power plants and other peaceful purposes. Nuclear-weapons proliferation will be checked only when developed nations take into account that any nuclear technology can be adapted to military use. Such technology should not be exported without safeguards to ensure that it is used for its intended purpose. And the superpowers must reduce their own nuclear arsenals if they expect client nations in the Third World to forego acquiring such weapons.

*The developed nations are fueling a nuclear arms race in the Middle East. A spark could ignite global nuclear war.*

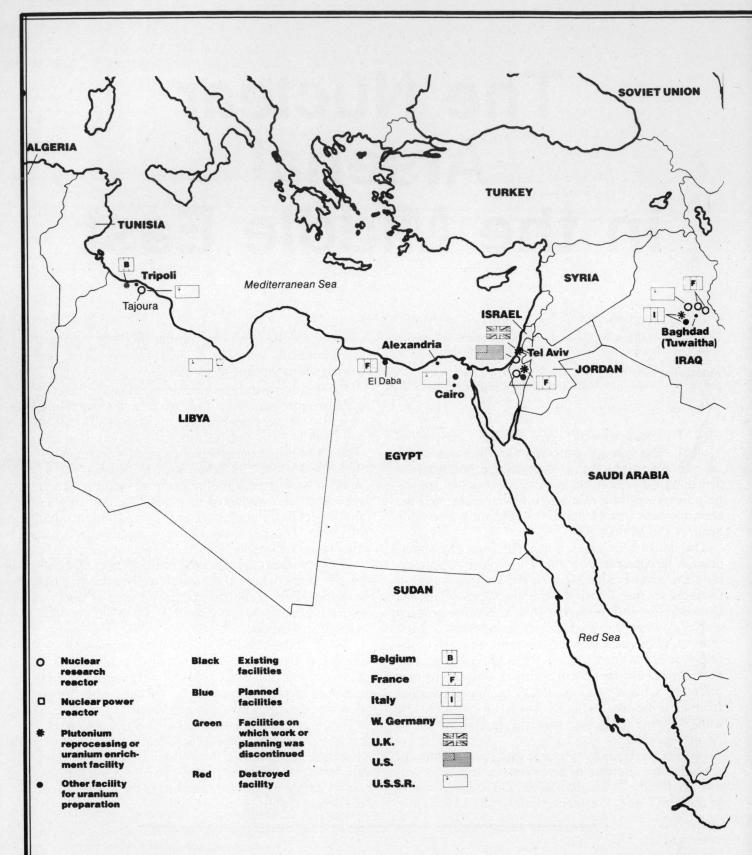

ALGERIA

TUNISIA

Tripoli

B

Tajoura

*Mediterranean Sea*

SOVIET UNION

TURKEY

SYRIA

F

ISRAEL

Tel Aviv

JORDAN

F

Baghdad
(Tuwaitha)

IRAQ

I

Alexandria

F

El Daba

Cairo

LIBYA

EGYPT

SAUDI ARABIA

SUDAN

*Red Sea*

| ○ | Nuclear research reactor | Black | Existing facilities | Belgium | B |
| ▫ | Nuclear power reactor | Blue | Planned facilities | France | F |
| ✳ | Plutonium reprocessing or uranium enrichment facility | Green | Facilities on which work or planning was discontinued | Italy | I |
| | | | | W. Germany | |
| ● | Other facility for uranium preparation | Red | Destroyed facility | U.K. | |
| | | | | U.S. | |
| | | | | U.S.S.R. | |

## Israel's Nuclear Program

International interest in Israel's nuclear arsenal has been rekindled by Vanunu's revelations. Prior information from the U.S. Central Intelligence Agency suggested that Israel might have two dozen fission bombs of the type dropped on Nagasaki. *Time* reported that during the October 1973 war, Israeli Prime Minister Golda Meir ordered nuclear warheads deployed. There has been speculation that the Soviet Union responded by sending nuclear warheads to Egypt.

Before publishing Vanunu's story, the *Sunday Times* asked me to check its technical accuracy, and I was convinced. During our interview, Vanunu showed me some 60 photographs of the nuclear operations at Dimona and various models of the bomb. One photo showed the production of lithium deuteride, a compound used almost exclusively for thermonuclear, or fusion, bombs. His descriptions of plutonium processing were accurate, although they could have been gleaned from unclassified sources. His detailed descriptions of lithium-deuteride production, however, could have been gained only firsthand. Particularly convincing was his explanation of how lithium-6, the isotope needed for thermonuclear weapons, is separated from ordinary lithium.

The fact that the Israelis lured Vanunu from London to Rome and abducted him to Israel for trial adds to his credibility. Israeli authorities would have been unlikely to mount a sophisticated intelligence operation and embarrass the Italian government if Vanunu's story were not true.

According to Vanunu, for 10 and possibly 20 years Israel has been producing about 30 kilograms of weapons-grade plutonium annually at Dimona. This means that the capacity of the reactor is about five times greater than it was previously thought to be. Vanunu also claims that about 4 kilograms of plutonium go into each Israeli nuclear weapon. Thus Israel could produce about 7 nuclear weapons a year and may now have well over 100.

Plutonium could be used to make fission weapons of the Nagasaki type. It is impractical to produce weapons of this type that will have a yield greater than 50,000 tons of TNT. (The Nagasaki bomb had a yield of about 20,000 tons of TNT.) Larger yields require thermonuclear bombs, which use fusion.

Vanunu's evidence of lithium-deuteride production at Dimona implies that Israel has thermonuclear weapons. These come in two types. In a "boosted" weapon, tritium and deuterium (isotopes of hydrogen) are put in the center of the plutonium sphere of a fission warhead. When the plutonium explodes, the tritium and deuterium fuse. Militarily usable boosted weapons have yields of 100 thousand to 200 thousand tons of TNT. In a "staged" device, the fu-

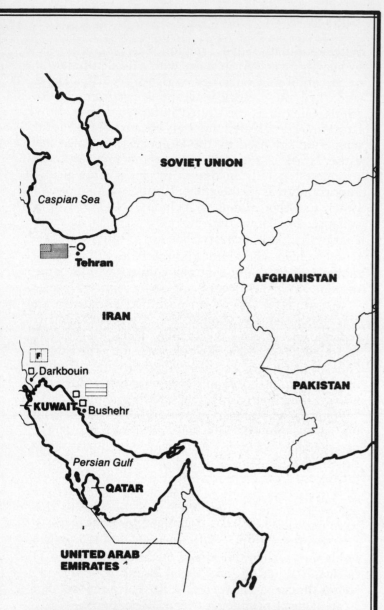

Lack of domestic demand has led nuclear industries in the developed world to seek contracts to build power plants in the Middle East. France and Italy are exporting nuclear technology to Arab countries in exchange for guaranteed oil supplies. This technology can be turned to military purposes. Two types of facilities are particularly dangerous. Uranium-enrichment plants increase the concentration of the uranium-235 isotope, needed to sustain fission in bombs as well as reactors. Plutonium-reprocessing plants separate plutonium from radioactive spent fuel. Like enriched uranium, this plutonium can be used for generating power or creating a weapon. Source (except for Egypt): Leonard Spector, Carnegie Endowment.

sion material is placed outside the plutonium sphere, forming a second stage that is triggered by the fission explosion. Lithium deuteride, a solid at normal temperatures, is typically used. There is no theoretical limit to the explosive power of such weapons. Even without testing, Israeli scientists could be confident that a boosted weapon would explode. But they would want to test a staged device. In 1979 a U.S. satellite observed an event over the Indian Ocean that, some have speculated, could have been a joint Israeli-South African nuclear test.

As a thermonuclear power with some 100 nuclear weapons, Israel is in the same league with China, France, and the United Kingdom. Each has a few hundred nuclear weapons, including some thermonuclear weapons.

In 1963 France, not greatly concerned about providing nuclear-weapons technology to a then-friendly country, secretly supplied Israel with the Dimona reactor. The reactor may be fueled with natural uranium dug from the ground, which has 0.7 percent of the U-235 isotope that most easily undergoes fission. Or it may be fueled with uranium enriched to have a slightly higher U-235 content. The spent fuel elements of a reactor contain unused uranium, radioactive fission products, and plutonium. France further helped Israel build a reprocessing facility to separate the plutonium from the rest of the used fuel, and this is the material that Israel uses for nuclear weapons. Apart from this initial assistance, Israel designed and manufactured its nuclear force indigenously.

Israel, and for that matter other Middle Eastern powers, could easily deliver nuclear weapons to targets in the region. Even a fairly crude modern nuclear weapon would probably weigh much less than 800 kilograms. It would contain a few kilograms of plutonium and some 200 kilograms of chemical high explosive that would create a shock wave to crush the plutonium, thus producing a chain reaction. Much of the remaining weight would go into a heavy metallic "tamper" around the plutonium, allowing more fissions and producing more energy. A combat aircraft such as a U.S.–supplied F-4 Phantom or an Israeli Kfir could carry several such weapons. The Israeli Jericho missile, with a range of about 200 miles, could carry one such warhead.

## Why Did Israel Acquire Its Arsenal?

With a population of 4.3 million, Israel is confronted by heavily armed Arab states with a total population of 90 million. Concerned with its security, Israel embarked on a nuclear-weapons program in the 1960s. Of course, the United States would not allow Israel to be devastated, not only because of the moral obligation imposed by the Holocaust, but also because Israel is the only true democracy and the strongest U.S. ally in one of the most strategically important areas of the globe. If America abandoned Israel, its other alliances, including NATO, would collapse. But Israel does not rely on such de facto guarantees. The memory that no country was prepared to help when Hitler murdered 6 million Jews makes Israelis doubt that any country would come to their aid if they were being pushed into the sea.

Because they depend on no other country in an emergency, Israelis want to be as self-sufficient as possible in weapons production, including nuclear weapons. This is especially true since both the United States and the Soviet Union have provided sophisticated weapons to Arab states, narrowing the technological gap between Israel and its enemies.

Some Israelis are bound to argue for improving nuclear weapons because Iraq has shown that it will use chemical weapons. Authoritative reports of the British Broadcasting Co. indicate that Iraq is producing 60 tons of mustard gas per month, as well as 4 tons per month of each of the deadly nerve agents Sarin and Tabun. Syria and Egypt may also have chemical weapons. Like nuclear bombs, these are weapons of mass destruction. NATO policy holds that a chemical attack on cities would justify nuclear retaliation, and Israel would probably respond similarly. However, the BBC also reports that Israel is itself producing chemical weapons.

Most commentators assume that Israel's nuclear weapons are intended as a last-ditch deterrent to military moves by Arab nations that would threaten Israel's existence. But this does not account for the size and quality of Israel's nuclear weapons. Israel could provide adequate deterrence by targeting ordinary fission weapons on major Arab cities—a dozen weapons the size of the Nagasaki bomb would suffice. No Arab city is big enough to "justify" a thermonuclear weapon.

*I*raq appears to be producing
*the deadly nerve agents Sarin and Tabun,*
*each at a rate of four tons a month.*

Could Israel want a tactical nuclear arsenal—to be used, for example, against an Arab tank attack—as well as a strategic deterrent? The United States produces neutron warheads—fusion weapons designed to release high-energy neutrons to irradiate and kill tank crews. But they are basically ineffective. A simple plastic cover impregnated with boron can absorb most of the neutrons and protect the tank crew. If tanks are spaced a typical 200 meters apart, only one tank on average will be caught by a neutron warhead of reasonable yield. Finally, even if tank crews have been exposed to enough radiation to kill them, they are likely to survive for at least a few hours. During that time they would probably run amok, kamikaze fashion, doing far more damage than they would otherwise. The competent Israeli military knows the limitations of neutron warheads, and would surely prefer to purchase far more cost-effective conventional antitank weapons.

It is hard to imagine any legitimate tactical use for Israeli nuclear weapons. The country is so small that fallout from any detonation of nuclear weapons in the Middle East would be a major hazard for Israeli troops and civilians.

Israel has probably produced its relatively large and sophisticated nuclear force primarily because of the technological momentum of the nuclear-weapons program. To design, develop, and produce its weapons, Israel had to form a team of nuclear scientists and technologists. Such professionals want to continue pushing forward the frontiers of their field. They may sincerely believe that national security depends upon the next advance in military R&D, while bureaucratic and economic forces add to their zeal.

Other nuclear-weapons powers follow this same pattern. There is no rationale for any country to produce high-yield thermonuclear weapons. The American nuclear-weapons scientist J. Robert Oppenheimer pointed out in the late 1950s that boosted nuclear fusion weapons are powerful enough to destroy any conceivable target. But Oppenheimer was silenced, and the U.S. nuclear-weapons community, closely followed by its Soviet counterpart, went on to produce megaton thermonuclear weapons. The United Kingdom, France, and China came next, and Israel now seems to have followed.

## Arab Nuclear Weapons

Israelis naturally differ as to the wisdom of possessing nuclear weapons, and some of their views are surprising. For example, several otherwise dovish factions of the Labor Party are pronuclear because they believe that Israel can give up the West Bank if it has the security of nuclear weapons. And some hawkish factions, headed, for example, by former Defense Minister Ariel Sharon, are antinuclear because they want to increase Israel's conventional military strength.

Israel's official policy is to keep its nuclear-weapons capabilities ambiguous. No Israeli leader has ever admitted that the country has nuclear weapons. A statement by former Minister of Defense Moshe Dayan in June 1981 is one of the most explicit to date: "We are not going to be the first ones to introduce nuclear weapons into the Middle East, but we do have the capacity to produce nuclear weapons," Dayan said. "If the Arabs are willing to introduce nuclear weapons into the Middle East, then Israel should not be too late in having nuclear weapons too." The statement did not make clear whether Israel merely had the necessary technological capacity, or whether it had components ready to assemble into warheads.

Such a policy has served Israeli purposes. Firm knowledge that Israel has a nuclear arsenal larger than needed for deterrence would encourage Arab states to acquire nuclear weapons, and would increase the likelihood of a preemptive Arab attack against Israeli facilities related to nuclear weapons. It would also prompt the Soviets to guarantee their Middle Eastern allies nuclear retaliation against an Israeli nuclear attack. And not least, proof of a sophisticated Israeli arsenal would complicate Israel's relations with the United States. In particular, Congress could become reluctant to supply Israel with sophisticated conventional weapons.

How will Arab nations react to Vanunu's statements implying that Israel's nuclear-weapons capability rivals that of France, England, or China? Even if technological momentum is the real reason for such developments, Arab states will assume that Israel seeks an overwhelming first-strike capability,

*S*everal otherwise dovish factions
of Israel's Labor Party are pronuclear, and some
hawkish factions are antinuclear.

since nations inevitably assume the worst when judging enemy intentions. Consequently, Arab states are likely to accelerate the development of their own nuclear capability. Of course, they might acquire nuclear weapons even if Israel had none.

There are relatively few obstacles to acquiring such weapons. Any Middle Eastern country could obtain natural uranium. Using materials purchased on the open market, it could clandestinely construct a small nuclear reactor fueled by natural uranium and cooled with graphite blocks. Such a reactor could produce a few kilograms of plutonium a year, enough to make a weapon the size of the Nagasaki bomb. A small reprocessing plant to remove the plutonium from the irradiated reactor fuel could also be built. Reprocessing is economically difficult on a commercial scale, but on a small scale it entails only straightforward chemistry. To make the bomb itself work, the chemical high explosives used to compress the plutonium and produce a chain reaction must be detonated with microsecond precision. This is the most difficult part of making a bomb, but a Middle East nation could succeed in doing it. The reactor, the processing plant, and an area to construct nuclear weapons of the Nagasaki type could be housed in a three-story building.

A Middle Eastern country could secretly produce such weapons, and would require only a few to destroy Israel. In fact, three nuclear weapons targeted on Tel Aviv, Haifa, and the coastal region between them would be enough to decimate Israel's main population centers and industry, and to destroy its most important military command centers.

Iraq, Egypt, and Libya have significant nuclear-energy programs that, if carried through, would enable them to construct nuclear weapons. Iraqi nuclear ambitions were set back in June 1981 when Israel bombed the French-supplied Osirak research reactor. Israel feared that Iraq could make nuclear weapons from the highly enriched uranium supplied by France to fuel the reactor or the plutonium produced in it. Israel's attack accorded with one of its main foreign-policy goals: to prevent the emergence of any new nuclear-weapons power in the Middle East.

Iraq's nuclear plans have also been hindered by the war with Iran, but after the war Iraq will presumably revitalize its program with French or Soviet assistance. Meanwhile, Iraq could use the enriched uranium fuel to make a nuclear weapon. Leonard Spector, an analyst of nuclear proliferation at the Carnegie Endowment for International Peace, has reported Iraqi attempts to buy plutonium illegally. Even one nuclear weapon could kill a large proportion of Israelis, and the fallout from a ground-level explosion could render much of the country uninhabitable.

Several facts suggest that Libya may be able to produce nuclear weapons within a decade. Libya plans to import nuclear reactors from the Soviet Union, and numerous students are receiving training abroad in nuclear science and technology. Libya operates a research reactor at Tajoura and has secretly provided Pakistan with nuclear assistance, including uranium obtained from Niger. Furthermore, Libya has agreements with Argentina and the Soviet Union to collaborate in developing nuclear technology. The agreements ostensibly pertain to peaceful uses, but the technology always has some military applicability. Libya's implacable hatred of Israel and support of international terrorism make its prospect of securing nuclear weapons fearsome.

Egypt would have little difficulty building nuclear weapons once it acquired a stock of plutonium. The country already has a cadre of nuclear scientists and engineers. By 1961 it had a research reactor and a flourishing nuclear research center. It is now considering bids for one or two reactors to be built near Alexandria, and it optimistically plans to build a total of eight reactors over the next 20 years.

Egypt has used political means to thwart Israeli acquisition of nuclear weapons. In the late 1960s, President Abdul Nassar secured Soviet promises of nuclear retaliation against a nuclear attack on Egypt. President Anwar Sadat sought similar U.S. guarantees in the early 1970s. Egypt has threatened Israel with a preemptive attack on nuclear-weapons facilities, and has said that it would respond to an Israeli nuclear arsenal by producing its own nuclear weapons. Egypt recently proposed that Israel join in establishing a nuclear-weapon-free zone in the Middle East.

This political approach makes sense only while Israel's nuclear policy remains ambiguous. Once the

*G*iven plutonium,
*even a subnational group such as the PLO
could make a nuclear explosive.*

Arab world believes that Israel has a sophisticated nuclear arsenal, the policy will no longer be credible. Will Egypt then build nuclear weapons, despite the risk that Israel would destroy the production site?

The danger of preemptive attacks against nuclear-weapons sites makes the Middle East particularly unstable. A large-scale Israeli deployment of nuclear weapons could provoke a preemptive Arab attack against production sites, arsenals, and command centers. Israel would almost certainly respond to any Arab attempt to acquire nuclear weapons with a military strike such as the one on Iraq's reactor. As it loses technological superiority in conventional weaponry, Israel will be increasingly tempted to destroy suspected Arab facilities before they can produce enough material for a nuclear weapon. A preemptive strike by either side could lead to war.

The Middle East is also home to subnational groups such as the PLO. Given weapons-grade material, even these groups could make a nuclear explosive. As the U.S. Congressional Office of Technology Assessment has concluded, "A small group of people, none of whom would ever have had access to the classified literature, could possibly design and build a crude nuclear device. . . . Only modest machine-shop facilities that could be contracted for without arousing suspicion would be required. The financial resources for acquisition of [the] necessary equipment on open markets need not exceed a fraction of a million dollars."

## What Can Be Done?

Despite the intimate relationship between the military atom and the peaceful atom, nuclear industries in the advanced countries—including the United States, France, West Germany, the United Kingdom, Italy, Japan, and the Soviet Union—are energetically trying to export nuclear power facilities to the Middle East. Except in France and the Soviet Union,

nuclear industries need export orders to survive because of the lack of domestic orders for nuclear plants. And countries like France and Italy are exporting nuclear facilities and know-how to Arab countries to obtain guaranteed oil supplies.

Developed nations should not export nuclear technology unless the recipient nation signs the 1970 Nuclear Non-Proliferation Treaty (NPT) or agrees to nuclear-facility inspections required by the treaty. Such inspections help prevent the peaceful atom from being turned to military purposes.

Unfortunately, it would be almost impossible to enforce an adequate inspection system in the Middle East. The fact that some European countries are hostages to Arab oil puts pressure on them to export nuclear facilities and material to the region without adequate safeguards. Moreover, Israel will not accede to nuclear-facility inspections or sign the NPT. Doing so would require Israel to give up its nuclear advantage just when its technological lead over Arab nations is diminishing. For the same reason, the Egyptian-Israeli negotiations to achieve a nuclear-free zone in the Middle East are almost sure to flounder.

The nuclear-weapons powers could make a significant contribution toward slowing the proliferation of nuclear weapons around the world. These powers are constantly upgrading their arsenals, showing that they believe in the political and military value of nuclear weapons. They should not be surprised when other countries follow their example and acquire their own such weapons.

The need to stop nuclear proliferation is one of the strongest arguments for arms control. The NPT obligates the Soviet Union and the United States to take significant steps toward reversing the arms race and achieving nuclear disarmament. A comprehensive test ban would be a good first step. If the superpowers wish to halt nuclear proliferation in the long run, they must follow such a ban with actual nuclear disarmament.

# Foundation Stone, Stepping Stone

## George P. Shultz

*George P. Shultz is Secretary of State.*

The signing ceremony for the treaty on intermediate-range nuclear forces was a moment filled with potential for the future. Such moments are to be savored, and then we return to the realities of the tough work still to be done.

That is what President Reagan and General Secretary Mikhail S. Gorbachev did.

Within an hour after the ceremony, they were in a deep discussion on other key arms control issues, human rights and regional problems. When the working groups meeting at the State Department convened again that afternoon, everyone seemed to feel that the conclusion of the treaty had added something new to our exchanges on these difficult issues: a sense of satisfaction that a key objective had been reached.

The completion of the treaty tells us four important and encouraging things:

1. Our defense strategy is not only fundamentally sound but effective. The treaty embodies the two basic principles of our defense doctrine: stability through strength and America's enduring commitment to allied security. What was not possible in the 1970's became possible today because we are strong and our alliance is solid.
2. Negotiations can work. Yes, past agreements have proved unsatisfactory. This agreement demonstrates we can learn from past mistakes. It is an unsparing document. Its nuts and bolts are fastened tightly.
3. The treaty has opened doors (not windows of vulnerability). It has opened new possibilities for improving international security. And it has removed concrete as well as conceptual barriers to the eventual achievement of greater strategic stability at progressively lower levels of offensive arms.
4. The arms reductions provided for in the treaty have opened a healthy debate here and in Europe. Progress always brings change and the need for readjustment. We and our allies must think together about how we can continue to assure the freedom and security of our nations while reducing strategic offensive nuclear arms.

Our North Atlantic Treaty Organization alliance fully understands that the Soviet Union continues to pose a great threat to the security of the free world and its values. Our political resolve must remain constant and our defense robust. At the same time, we and our allies know that arms and arms agreements alone do not insure our security. That can only come when the deep distrust that gives rise to conflict is removed. That is why we attach so much importance to the human rights obligations undertaken in the Helsinki Final Act.

As we look at America's broad defense strategy, we can see that the treaty is both a foundation stone and a stepping stone.

From the beginning of his Administration, President Reagan has proceeded from three basic convictions about arms control—convictions that are shared by the vast majority of the American people.

First, the nuclear era demands that we pursue an effective dialogue with the Soviet Union—one based on strength and realism. Every successful negotiated document must meet the needs of both parties. Hard common ground has been found, not a lowest common denominator. The President is under no illusions about our differences with the Soviet Union. But he has always been willing to engage in clear-eyed negotiations in areas where a more stable relationship can be pursued consistent with allied security.

The second conviction is that any negotiation with the Soviet Union must proceed from strength. It is allied strength, unity and determination that brings the other side to the table and keeps them there.

Eight years ago, in response to Soviet deployments of SS-20 intermediate-range missiles in Europe in the late 1970's, NATO decided to deploy Pershing 2 and ground-launched cruise missiles. Then, in 1981, President Reagan proposed the "zero option" to eliminate intermediate-range nuclear forces.

We and our allies hung tough with our decision. We began deployment in 1983, despite Soviet efforts at intimidation, a year-long walkout from negotiations and considerable public opposition in Europe. Our resolve brought the Soviets back to the table in 1985. Building on this successful model, if we display the same resolve and strength, there are real prospects for success in our negotiations on strategic weapons.

The third conviction that has guided negotiations is that negotiated results must not diminish our security or that of our allies but strengthen it.

No agreement—let alone the I.N.F. treaty, with its focus on one class of missiles—is a panacea for the Soviet threat. But it represents a significant first step in the direction of stabilizing arms cuts—not just caps or regulated buildups—and that is a major strategic objective of our alliance. Every step of the way, we have consulted with our friends—including Japan, Australia, and South Korea as well as NATO. Every comma and every detail of this treaty has been scrutinized by our technical experts.

The treaty has helped to strengthen the North Atlantic Treaty organization's commitment to our current strategy of collective defense and flexible response. We are continuing to work to meet our conventional and nuclear modernization requirements.

In the meantime, we have enough nuclear capability to provide NATO with nuclear options across the full spectrum of graduated response—from short-range cannon and ground-launched missile systems to intermediate-range weapons delivered by aircraft and ships—in addition to strong and modern strategic forces.

Of course, the "coupling" of the United States to the defense of Europe does not depend on the deployment of one or another type of military hardware.

It is founded on the recognition that the security and well-being of the United States and Europe are inextricably linked—and those ties remain firm on both sides of the Atlantic. There can be no stronger expression of our commitment to the defense of our allies than the continued presence of our servicemen and women on European soil.

The treaty meets the rigorous criteria originally set by the president and our alliance partners.

In accordance with their exacting standards, the agreement provides for equal rights and limits between the United States and Soviet Union.

Achieving such equality has meant Soviet acceptance of asymmetric reductions. Roughly four times as many Soviet warheads on deployed missiles will be eliminated for every American warhead—a precedent that could be valuable in future negotiations on conventional arms.

In addition, the agreement covers only American and Soviet systems (not British or French nuclear forces or the cooperative defense arrangements we maintain with our allies). The treaty in no way constrains NATO's conventional defense capability or the carrying through of improvement programs already under way.

---

## The I.N.F. treaty opens new doors.

---

Furthermore, we insisted from the outset that an I.N.F. agreement be global in scope. There can be no transfer of the threat from Europe to Asia. Again, by hanging tough we got the Soviets to go to zero in Asia, without eliminating or restricting a single American system in Asia. And because we cannot afford to rely on trust in dealing with the Soviet Union, the treaty contains the most detailed and comprehensive verification regime ever achieved in the history of arms control.

When the clock starts ticking on missile destruction, we will have multiple opportunities for inspections on Soviet territory for 13 years. First, we will take inventory of some 2,000 Soviet missiles declared to us in writing. Then we will observe their destruction by agreed methods. As each missile site is cleared of its weapons we will conduct a close-out inspection. And, throughout the three-year elimination period, as well as during the following 10 years, we will be able to carry out an annual quota of short-notice inspections at any of approximately 100 Soviet facilities to insure treaty compliance.

In addition, we will station around-the-clock inspectors at the Soviet factory where the now-banned SS-20 missile was assembled and the similar intercontinental SS-25 continues to be assembled. For the first three years verification will be improved by the requirement that the Soviets display their missiles in the open at new SS-25 bases several times a year, at times of our choosing.

In sum, the I.N.F. treaty carries positive implications far beyond its substance, but it can stand on its substance alone.

When the Senate exercises its constitutional powers of advise and consent, the treaty's intrinsic merits will argue for themselves.

I believe that the Senate will recognize a good deal when it sees one. The Administration is eager to work with the Senate to scrutinize this treaty from every angle. We are confident that the outcome in the Senate will give our allies the answer they are waiting for, reaffirm the importance of negotiations to solve tough problems and open a new chapter in the effort to strengthen global stability.

# Arms control: misplaced focus

*The authors believe that paying attention to weapons
—whether advocating increases or reductions—detracts
from the basic task of dealing with the sources of conflict and militarism.*

## William A. Schwartz and Charles Derber

*William Schwartz is a doctoral student in the Boston College sociology department, where Charles Derber teaches. This article, a project of the Boston Nuclear Study Group and excerpted from a book in progress, was written in collaboration with the group's other members: Gordon Fellman and Morris Schwartz, who teach sociology at Brandeis University; William Gamson, who teaches sociology at Boston College; and Patrick Withen, a doctoral student in sociology at Boston College.*

ALMOST EVERYONE takes for granted the importance of the nuclear arms race. Right, center, and left fiercely disagree about whether the United States should try to win it, end it, or maintain a stalemate, but underneath lies a hidden consensus that its outcome is the key to nuclear war and peace. Most of the nuclear debate consists of arguments about which weapons systems should be built, controlled, cancelled, frozen, or retired.

Short of virtually complete, multilateral nuclear disarmament, however, no change in the pace, balance, or even the direction of the arms race can make much difference in the risk of nuclear war, the damage should one occur, or the division of international political power. This includes Star Wars, the nuclear freeze, and even large cuts in or stabilization of offensive nuclear arsenals.

A better starting point for nuclear politics would be the insight that nuclear weapons have completely changed the logic of power as it has been handed down through the ages. Military force, perfected to its highest level, has invalidated itself—for in a nuclearized world, any resort to force by a nuclear power risks escalation to its ultimate level, and thus to oblivion for all. Trying to rationalize and control the ultimate force is far less realistic and important than limiting the provocation of conflict and the use of force at lower, non-nuclear levels—by the United States, its clients, and, to the extent possible, its adversaries.

WITHOUT DOUBT, the existence of nuclear weapons per se and their possession by particular nations matters a great deal. The fallacy lies in attributing great significance to the size and characteristics of the superpowers' nuclear stockpiles, and especially to the margins of each arsenal: incremental additions to or subtractions from the current force, such as the building of 100 MX missiles or the removal of cruise missiles from Europe.

With conventional military technology, such concerns —what political scientist Samuel Huntington has called "weaponitis"[1]—do make some sense, because conventional wars are largely processes of attrition. One side's weapons and soldiers must gradually neutralize those of the enemy before a threat of destruction can be posed to the enemy's inner society. The side with more or better weapons does not always win, because other factors may intervene, but it enjoys a definite edge.

The immense power of an individual atomic weapon, especially the later hydrogen weapon, changed this. A nation's armed forces do not have to be defeated before its society can be credibly threatened by such weapons, since only a single one must penetrate to destroy a city. General war was no longer to be a process of military attrition, but one of outright, mutual social devastation. After both superpowers accumulated enough nuclear weapons to destroy the other—perhaps as early as 1955, and certainly by the early 1960s—increasing the number or quality of such weapons could add little to military potential or risks.

Even the massive "overkill" in modern nuclear arsenals might not have rendered the arms race irrelevant if it had proved possible either to build effective defenses against these great arsenals, or to keep a nuclear exchange limited to a very small fraction of available warheads. But precisely because of the great power of the individual hydrogen weapon, neither can be achieved with any confidence. A meaningful defense of cities against such weapons would have to be near-perfect, which no military technology can achieve, and even small numbers of nuclear weapons could do unthinkable damage to rural areas, to the underlying ecological, economic, and social infrastructures that support human life, and perhaps even to the planetary temperature-regulation system.

Moreover, in its diverse physical effects—blast, heat, radiation, electromagnetic pulse—this weapon not only kills people and destroys property, but also disrupts the complex pathways of authority, communication, transportation, coordination, and technology that permit a society and its military system to function. After its use on anything but the most limited scale, there could be no predicting or rational planning for what will happen after hostilities break out. To assume that cities may be spared or that only a small number of missiles will be used is to presuppose a level of control that probably will not exist. All-out escalation is not inevitable, but its possibility is inherently present, and its probability is unknown.

Very simply, then, developments in the arms race do not much affect the risk of nuclear war because they cannot change the basic situation faced by national leaders: if nuclear weapons are ever again used in war, whatever the sizes and characteristics of the arsenals, this will necessarily precipitate a substantial but unknown chance of mutual annihilation.

MANY WHO understand this continue to worry about the arms race, partly because of an understandable gut-level fear that since nuclear weapons are bad, more of them must be worse. A more sophisticated concern, felt equally on both sides of the political spectrum, is that the emergence of "first strike" weapons may undermine this condition of mutual vulnerability upon which stability is thought to depend. Some fear the Soviet SS-18 and SS-19, while others think the Pentagon is seeking its own first-strike arsenal, with MX, Pershing II, Trident II, and Star Wars.

The concern is that one side may develop the ability to rob the other of its retaliatory capability and thus wage nuclear war without risking its own destruction. The "superior" side will supposedly be tempted to launch a disarming premeditated attack. And the vulnerable side will supposedly feel that it must "use or lose" its own weapons, believing that a preemptive first strike of its own, though very hazardous, is preferable to being disarmed. If, as many argue, both powers are building first-strike arsenals, then the situation is even more alarming, for both will feel the war incentives of the superior as well as the inferior position.

Despite all the worry, the simple fact remains that hydrogen warheads are too powerful, and nuclear weapons platforms too diverse and well-defended, for any existing or anticipated technology to permit one side to rob the other of its retaliatory capability. This would require the emergence of an overwhelming, near-simultaneous threat to the survivability of virtually all nuclear delivery vehicles, including submarines at sea, or even less plausibly, to warheads after launch. Even a single surviving ballistic-missile submarine or several dozen ICBMs or strategic bombers would sustain the essential risk—destruction of the attacking nation. Even were such a wildly implausible threat to become possible in principle, it could never preclude retaliation with confidence, because of the risk of malfunctions and miscalculations associated with all complex human/machine systems, especially untestable ones.

Even those who accept this view often continue, strangely, to decry the dangers of first-strike weapons. In the peace movement, for example, many insist that nuclear war cannot be won, no matter who strikes first, yet worry that these new weapons will destabilize the arms balance precisely because they may give one side the ability to strike first. The two positions are inconsistent.

Consider the most common image: some future Soviet premier is confronted with horrifying blips on a radar screen during a crisis. He could, as feared, preempt, using his missiles out of fear of losing them—thus seriously risking an exchange producing unacceptable damage to the Soviet Union, whether or not a real U.S. attack was in progress.

Or he could wait to see for certain if the suspected attack is real. If it is, the Soviet Union is destroyed, and a retaliatory blow will fall on the United States—a smaller one than if he had launched before absorbing the attack, but probably enough to destroy the United States. Preempting, then, is tantamount to suicide, while *not* preempting holds out a chance of survival: the very real chance that the radar blips are a false alarm. The strength of incentives to preempt is questionable, no matter how many first-strike weapons the United States has. The premier's goal is not, after all, to save missiles. It is to save the Soviet Union.

In any case, from the premier's standpoint the most worrisome threat is not that the blips are new counterforce missiles coming at his missile silos. Rather, it is that they are missiles, counterforce or not, coming at his nuclear command and control network—which, like its U.S. counterpart, has been at risk since the 1960s and could be easily neutralized by current offensive weapons. After such "decapitation," Moscow would probably lose the ability to choose, order, and coordinate a retaliatory response. Some form of spasmodic, uncoordinated retaliation would probably occur anyway on the initiative of local commanders, but the Soviet state would have lost any capability to conduct the war in a planned way with specific goals. The ability to control whatever weapons survive, and thus to use them to advance Soviet goals, is far more important than the number that survive, which will always be sufficient for retaliation.

While the importance of the first-strike scenario has been

highly exaggerated relative to others, such as incremental escalation from a conventional war, there is at least one circumstance in which it could become the most likely path to nuclear war—when a leader is virtually certain that the other side is about to push the button. Once war is assumed to be inevitable, a preemptive first strike may seem to offer the best chance of disrupting enemy attacks, thereby somewhat limiting damage and holding out some small chance of eliminating retaliation entirely through decapitation.

What must be avoided, then, are the extreme *political* conditions in which a Soviet or U.S. leader could actually believe that his counterpart had decided to launch World War III. The desperate feeling that the axe is about to fall one way or the other, not the size, accuracy, or speed of the axe, is the key factor. To the extent that first strike and preemption are worrisome possibilities, avoiding them depends much more upon the prevention and defusing of military confrontations and the reduction of war hysteria than either the construction or obstruction of new weapons.

P REVENTING A nuclear attack might also depend upon countering any misperception of the facts as we have described them. Weapons might matter, some argue, if only because people think they do. Leaders might mistakenly believe they could win a war on the strength of their new systems, or that they had to preempt because of the other side's new systems. Or short of this, one side might gain major political advantages on the strength of a nuclear arsenal perceived by others to be superior.

It is true that leaders on both sides decry the dangers of the opponent's nuclear weapons and constantly seek new systems of their own. In the peacetime budgetary and domestic political processes, weapons certainly matter to them. But this does not mean that leaders also *act* in the international arena on the basis of these same exaggerations of the importance of weapons.

Historical experience suggests, instead, that military and political leadership on both sides have a self-contradictory philosophy of nuclear weapons. While they do attach great importance to the weapons balance in the planning and procurement process, in real foreign policy decisions and in the handling of real crises their behavior is not substantially affected by which weapons each side has built. This does not mean that they are unwilling to run substantial risks of nuclear war—they are—but only that when they do, the details of the nuclear balance do not influence them.

In the Cuban missile crisis, for example, according to President Kennedy's senior advisers: "American nuclear superiority was not . . . a critical factor, for the fundamental and controlling reason that nuclear war, already in 1962, would have been an unexampled catastrophe for both sides. . . . No one of us ever reviewed the nuclear balance for comfort in those hard weeks."[2] A recent study of newly released documents adds: "There is no evidence that President Kennedy and his advisers counted missiles, bombers, and warheads, and decided on that basis to take a tough line. . . . No one discussed what American counterforce

capabilities were—that is, how well the United States might be able to 'limit damage' in the event of an all-out war. It was as though all the key concepts associated with the administration's formal nuclear strategy . . . in the final analysis counted for very little."[3]

Similarly, nowhere in President Nixon's extensive memoirs can one find any reference to consideration of the nuclear weapons balance in his decision to alert U.S. nuclear forces during the Middle East superpower crisis of October 1973 —despite Nixon's deep concern with weapons systems in domestic politics both before and afterward. Nixon apparently had no doubt that the Soviets saw things as he did.[4]

Other crises and foreign policy initiatives have shown the same pattern. As McGeorge Bundy has said, "There has been no Soviet action anywhere that can be plausibly attributed to the so-called window of vulnerability."[5] And no one has demonstrated that U.S. power anywhere in the world has concretely benefited since the mid-1950s from an American strategic edge. Bundy was probably correct, as well, when he said that in none of the great Suez, Berlin, and Cuban crises "would the final result have been different if the relative strategic positions of the Soviet Union and the United States had been reversed. . . . A stalemate is a stalemate either way around."[6]

In their more honest moments outside the budgetary process, military leaders on both sides have agreed that weapons hardware does not affect the basic military realities. Marshal Ogarkov, the Warsaw Pact commander in chief, said in a May 1984 interview in the Soviet press: "The deployment of U.S. intermediate-range missiles in Western Europe did not increase the possibility of a 'first strike' against the Soviet Union. Both sides fully recognize the inevitability of a retaliatory strike."[7] General David Jones, former chairman of the Joint Chiefs of Staff, has agreed: "I don't know any American officer, or any Soviet officer, who really believes either superpower can achieve a true first-strike capability, that one side could ever so disarm the other as to leave it without the ability to retaliate. . . . [Both] strongly agree that neither side can win a nuclear war in any meaningful sense."[8] Such men might well advise a leader to begin World War III someday, but not because they misperceive the importance of figures on a nuclear weapons balance sheet.

Besides, even if some consequential misperceptions about weapons do exist, we still would doubt the wisdom of pretending that weapons matter in order to assuage the fears of those who think they do. This inevitably involves one in a twisted logic that ends up reinforcing the very misperceptions one is trying to counter. Hawks frequently argue for new U.S. weapons to counter Soviet misperceptions that we have become strategically inferior. But to justify the expense to Congress and the public, they must decry glaring weaknesses in the U.S. force posture. This only adds to the undeserved image of weakness that was the reason for concern in the first place, as psychologist Steven Kull has brilliantly shown.[9] Similarly, when the peace movement works to stop "destabilizing" weapons, partly to prevent any misperception that the United States is acquiring a knock-out first-strike capability, it must urgently decry the dangers of first-strike weapons. It thus, unwittingly, adds legitimacy to the erroneous idea that in nuclear war it matters who strikes first—reinforcing the very fears it is trying to allay.

QUESTIONS MUST be raised, then, about the weapons-focused political agendas of right, center, and left—respectively, rearmament, arms control, and disarmament. In each case, the attention to hardware betrays a serious misunderstanding of the nuclear problem. But for each, "weaponitis" also serves narrower political interests by deflecting attention from the difficult political questions that a more rational nuclear debate would inevitably raise.

While U.S. military power cannot be significantly boosted by nuclear rearmament, focusing the debate on nuclear hardware helps the political right to safely channel opposition away from its more important international agenda: massive conventional military buildup, and the political and ideological shifts that will permit use of the military in emerging Third World conflicts. Similarly, nuclear arms control can do very little to prevent nuclear war, but it does provide middle-of-the-road politicians with a popular and risk-free program for addressing the nuclear problem.

As veteran arms-controller George Rathjens of the Massachusetts Institute of Technology has said, arms control "is deceptive to the point of almost being a gigantic fraud: there is the implicit suggestion that controls on weapons of the kind that have been tried will solve the problem—or at least make a big difference—when there is no real reason for so believing. . . . The negotiations have been predicated on a belief that numbers and detailed performance characteristics of weapons are important," and as a result "the importance of differences in capabilities have been exaggerated to the point where political leaders and the public have been led to believe that such differences could be exploited militarily, when almost certainly they could not be."[10]

Although mainstream arms-controllers rarely advocate this, reductions to less than one-tenth of current stockpiles might somewhat reduce the damage of a nuclear exchange. But under current political conditions it is unclear whether such reductions would increase or decrease the likelihood of an exchange, and it is unrealistic to think that they will follow naturally from the incremental reductions now being discussed. In the absence of long-term political change, near-total nuclear disarmament would pose qualitatively new and perhaps insurmountable political difficulties and verification problems.

The peace movement's strategy of opposing weapons, and even viewing progress toward disarmament as the guiding program, must also be challenged. As difficult as it may be for activists to accept, stopping the MX, killing Star Wars, or even negotiating a comprehensive nuclear weapons freeze would probably not improve the risks or consequences of nuclear war by more than a small amount. This "weapons strategy" has, however, permitted the peace movement to mobilize large segments of the population, the

media, and the Congress, for it is a way to be active on the nuclear issue without confronting the more radical and divisive issue of the links between nuclear war and U.S. foreign policy.

Activists often respond that even if working to stop the arms race cannot much reduce the risk of nuclear war, it has other virtues, such as saving the billions of dollars wasted on new systems and limiting other social and psychological costs of the arms race. These benefits may be real, and may in fact constitute the best reasons for opposing the arms race, but they should not be confused with direct progress in preventing nuclear war. It is also conceivable, as some argue, that the purely symbolic benefits of ending the nuclear arms race might improve superpower relations to the point of affecting the risk of war between them. But such benefits are speculative, do not square with the very short-lived aftereffects of past arms control agreements, and are probably small compared with the potential benefits of direct assault on the more significant causes of bad superpower relations: for example, on their mutual use of a largely mythical threat from the other to justify violent actions to maintain control within their own empires.

Activists also respond that the arms race, even if not important in itself, is an excellent vehicle for mobilizing populations around the nuclear danger generally. Once recruited to the nuclear issue by the nuclear freeze or other antiweapons campaigns, people can and often do move on to confront more important matters, such as the legitimacy of nuclear diplomacy as a tool of state.

The peace movement has done incalculable good by educating people about the consequences and danger of nuclear war. But using the "weapons strategy" to do this is questionable, for it requires giving the public misinformation: that the race in weapons is the problem and stopping the arms race is the solution, or least a major step along the way. The main reason that the weapons themselves carry such great mobilizing power is precisely that much of the public has been led to believe that halting their accumulation can materially reduce the chances that they and their families will die in a nuclear war. If activists came to accept the marginal strategic significance of the nuclear arms race and still continued this strategy, they would then be engaged in a calculated misrepresentation of the issue to the movement rank-and-file and the general public—something no democratic movement should tolerate, and no activists would support.

Nor is it obvious that the weapons strategy even works as a mobilizer in the long run. If the arms race is successfully portrayed as the problem, then a major movement victory such as the freeze—literally the end of the arms race—could well destroy public concern through complacency, even though the risk of nuclear war would be unchanged. If, more likely, major antiweapons campaigns continue to fail, the movement risks demobilization through despair, as we have recently seen in the European peace movement after the deployment of the euromissiles, and the American one after the failure to achieve the bilateral freeze or to defeat even a single new weapons system.

# 5. CONFLICT

THE NUCLEAR debate must break free from the technicism and insularity of a primarily *nuclear* discourse focused on weapons. It must, instead, highlight the endemic *conventional* violence of the world, from which nuclear war can always escalate, and the sources of this violence in domestic and international social structures, political systems, cultures, and ideologies. It must therefore be a sociopolitical debate which acknowledges the futility of seeking technical solutions to the deeply social problems of war and peace.

The central task must be to avert armed confrontation involving one or more nuclear-armed powers. This logically requires two steps: restricting the spread of nuclear weapons to states and organizations that do not now possess them, and avoiding political and military facedowns between those that do. In both cases the essential problem is the pervasive conventional militarism that has brought bloody domestic and interstate conflict to virtually every region of the world since World War II.

Like the more general nuclear debate, proliferation has traditionally been couched as a technical problem—of denying non-nuclear powers the strategic materials, technology, and knowledge to build bombs. Undoubtedly, the massive spread of nuclear technology, under the guises of the "peaceful atom" and the Non-Proliferation Treaty, have scandalously increased the dangers, and tighter controls are essential. But this process has now advanced so far that it can only be a matter of time before the capacity to make or steal nuclear warheads becomes available to any nation or major organization that seeks it.

As long as nations and other organized international groups feel threatened by aggression, or suffer grievous disenfranchisement or oppression, some will seek the ultimate weapon as a way out. This largely explains the patterns of nuclear proliferation to date, with technically advanced but nonmilitarist countries such as Switzerland, Canada, Australia, Austria, Belgium, and Yugoslavia avoiding nuclear weapons for lack of motive, while others seek them because they are embroiled in conflict.

Focusing on sources of conflict and the militarism they produce is equally the best strategy for averting confrontations involving those powers that have already built nuclear stockpiles—which, barring outright accidental launches on a large scale, will be the immediate cause of any new world war. As Noam Chomsky has sensibly put it: "If we are concerned to avert nuclear war, our primary concern should be to lessen tensions and conflicts at the points where war engaging the superpowers is likely to erupt."[11] Europe has traditionally received the most attention, especially around the possible escalation of an uprising in Eastern Europe. But despite recent Administration "rollback" rhetoric, Europe remains far more stable and controllable than many points in the Third World. Conflicts there—especially those involving our own nation, whose policies Americans stand the most chance of affecting and have the most responsibility for monitoring—must therefore assume a central role.

Technical approaches such as crisis management, while not without value, are inadequate. Keeping major crises limited is extremely difficult and uncertain at best. Making basic changes in the foreign policies which enflame regional conflicts and bring about crises in the first place is much more important.

Adding an antimilitarist plank to the highly developed campaigns around weapons—as debated periodically by the nuclear freeze movement—is not an adequate response. The former is far more important than the latter, and the two are not linked in the ways that some theorists of the "deadly connection" contend.[12] That is, stopping new U.S. nuclear weapons systems is unlikely to demilitarize conventional U.S. foreign policy by curtailing interventionism or support for aggressive client states. U.S. leaders may well purchase both strategic and tactical nuclear weapons in part because they *hope* that these will increase their capacity to project power. But in practice, nuclear force balances have little military import, and, as we have said, political leaders do not consider them in making real politico-military decisions.

Interventions, whether in Grenada, Afghanistan, Lebanon, or Poland, are almost certainly undertaken, rather, on the basis of perceived interests and opportunities specific to each situation, within the broad context of each superpower's global ambitions. Preventing the deployment of MX, for example, would have little if any direct effect on the United States' hazardous Middle East policies. These can be altered only through a specific effort aimed at those policies themselves.

A frontal effort must be launched, then, against conventional state violence, which not incidentally causes massive human suffering among the victims and should be opposed on that basis alone. This, and the politics which breeds it, should constitute the overwhelming focus of efforts to prevent nuclear war.

Some would say that this is self-evident and has long been accepted. But while everyone sees political dimensions to the nuclear problem, the overwhelming attention given to the weapons themselves by all sides to the debate cannot be denied. Despite the *Bulletin*'s significant coverage of conventional militarism, for example, in recent years a large number of articles, including almost half its cover stories, have focused on nuclear hardware, primarily new weapons systems and arms control. In addition, five of the eight changes in the hands of the *Bulletin*'s "doomsday clock" since the Cuban missile crisis were in large measure responses to developments in weapons technology or arms treaty negotiations. The hands moved to their most hopeful setting ever (12 minutes to midnight) because of the SALT I treaty in 1972; they advanced to their most frightening position since the invention of the hydrogen bomb (three minutes to midnight) two years ago, largely in response to the "accelerating nuclear arms race" and the suspension of arms control negotiations.[13] The editorial of the recent fortieth-anniversary issue approvingly notes that "the need to end the arms race has become widely recognized as the overriding issue of our time."

Other critics counter that while militarism and the conflicts underlying it may in fact be far more important than the arms race, these are so deeply engrained that their elimination is a very long-term if not completely hopeless task, and certainly a poor way to deal with the pressing problem of nuclear war. A comparable argument would be that eliminating nuclear weapons is almost certainly impossible over anything but the longest run, and therefore that it should be abandoned as an anti-nuclear-war strategy. In fact, definite short-term steps are possible both to limit conventional state violence and to limit nuclear stockpiles, although neither can be fully accomplished over a short period and without major socio-political change. Since, as we have argued, incremental changes in hardware stockpiles are almost meaningless, it is only logical to seek whatever brakes on militarism are practical at the present time.

While underlying causes of international violence—such as the nation-state system, the imperialisms of East and West, ethnic hatred, and mass poverty—can be addressed only gradually, decisive action can be taken now to limit many volitional acts of state aggression and repression. Some of the required changes in foreign policy can be advanced through bilateral negotiations with the Soviets about political arrangements and the use of conventional force in the rest of the world. For example, an agreement to ban direct superpower military intervention in the Middle East, along with commitments by both to restrain their clients from offensive use of the massive conventional military hardware they have supplied, would substantially reduce the likelihood of another superpower crisis in that region.

The 1982 Israeli invasion and subsequent occupation of Lebanon clearly illustrate the dangers of current policy, with U.S.-backed Israeli troops and Soviet-backed Syrian troops actively engaged. U.S. intervention in the war through extensive naval shelling and bombardment raised even graver possibilities. Going deeper into the political origins of Middle East conflict, the superpowers could agree to condition further aid upon sincere efforts by all parties to reach a fair agreement concerning the underlying political conflicts, such as the rights of Israelis, Palestinians, and other Arabs to secure coexistence on the basis of national sovereignty.

Even more important, for Americans, is action to change the role of this country in:

• sponsoring or supporting regimes that murder, repress, and starve their people, and that must ultimately use great violence to remain in power, or those that aggress against other peoples;

• sustaining regional conflicts and blocking peace efforts in order to advance U.S. corporate or state "interests";

• armed interventions to prop up friendly governments or overthrow unfriendly ones; and

• other actions which enflame conflict, produce large-scale political violence, and draw the superpowers into unnecessary conflict. Most of these have nothing to do with any concrete Soviet threat. They must be addressed through political action here at home, and not just concerning South Africa and Central America, where current peace efforts are most developed.

One small step in the required educational effort might be the invention of "nuclear war impact statements," to expose for the public the depth of the now invisible connections between U.S. foreign policy and the nuclear threat. Policy for each region could be evaluated for its likely effect on local tensions and conflicts, the likelihood that these could erupt into a head-on confrontation between the superpowers or other nuclear powers, and less hazardous alternatives for regional policy. Other practical steps will be possible as well once we acknowledge that controls on nuclear weapons must be decisively subordinated to the limitation of state violence generally, and the resolution of the grievances that often produce it.

The disarmament movement cannot accomplish such things. This is a job for a full-fledged peace movement.

1. Speech at Boston College Graduate Student Association symposium on the arms race and nuclear war, Oct. 12, 1983. See William Schwartz, "U.S. Nuclear Policies Increase Threat of War," Boston College Heights, Oct. 17, 1983.

2. Dean Rusk, et al., "The Lessons of the Cuban Missile Crisis," Time (Sept. 27, 1982), p. 85.

3. Marc Trachtenberg, "The Influence of Nuclear Weapons in the Cuban Missile Crisis," International Security, vol. 10, no. 1 (Summer 1985), pp. 137–63. Supporting documents are in the same journal, pp. 164–203.

4. Richard Nixon, RN: The Memoirs of Richard Nixon (New York: Grosset and Dunlap, 1978).

5. McGeorge Bundy, "The Unimpressive Record of Atomic Diplomacy," in Gwyn Prins, ed., The Nuclear Crisis Reader (New York: Vintage, 1984), p. 51.

6. Bundy, "To Cap the Volcano," Foreign Affairs, vol. 48, no. 1 (Oct. 1969), p. 11.

7. Dusko Doder, "A Comeback by Ex-Soviet Military Chief," Boston Globe, July 18, 1985, p. 13.

8. David Jones, "Is Arms Control Obsolete?," Harper's, vol. 271, no. 1622 (July 1985), p. 44.

9. Steven Kull, "Nuclear Nonsense," Foreign Policy, no. 58 (Spring 1985), pp. 28–52.

10. George Rathjens, "First Thoughts," unpublished manuscript, pp. 8–9.

11. Noam Chomsky, "Interventionism and Nuclear War," in Michael Albert and David Dellinger, eds., Beyond Survival: New Directions for the Disarmament Movement (Boston: South End Press, 1983), p. 259.

12. See The Deadly Connection: Nuclear War and U.S. Intervention (Philadelphia: New Society Publishers, 1986).

13. The Freeze Focus, vol. 4, no. 3 (April 1980), p. 19.

# Communications

The relations of people around the world are being transformed by a revolution in global communications. The development of the high-speed computer and satellite communication systems is having unforeseen consequences, redefining many aspects of the international political, economic, and social systems. This revolution has caught most observers by surprise. It is the classic case of new technology setting the agenda, forcing basic institutions to respond rather than to lead. Instantaneous communications, high-speed data processing, satellite resource surveys, and improved weather forecasting are just a few aspects of the communications revolution. Information has replaced more traditional sources of power (e.g., military capabilities and natural resources) as a key factor in determining a country's strength.

Advocates of this revolution point to the many positive benefits that the new technology provides, not only to the modern countries who produce these goods and services but also to Third World countries. A country such as Indonesia, which is composed of thousands of islands, could never afford to develop hard-wire telephone communications; it would simply be too expensive. However, satellite technology makes it possible to bypass the old technology, resulting in improved communications between Indonesia's widely dispersed people. The same is true for China. That country could not afford to install telephones for its population which numbers more than one billion; yet, in the near future, advanced technology will allow people to carry wireless telephones on their wrists. Television is another example. As satellite receiving dishes become smaller and less expensive, it will be possible to transmit programs to even the most remote village, which, in the long run, will facilitate nation-building. Implementing programs on reading, math, and public health will no longer require training teachers and building educational facilities. One dish and one television would be sufficient to serve a community, thereby conserving resources for other purposes.

The communications revolution, however, is not without its critics. The question remains whether the cost and benefits of the new technology will be equally shared. A satellite that uses scanners to map the natural resources of Africa, for example, can provide information to Western mining companies that is far superior to that which the governments of the area possess. Thus, the mining companies might have the upper hand when negotiating contracts for mineral rights. Since more and more international transactions take the form of "soft trade," such as banking and insurance services, those people who control the computers and satellites of the world have a tremendous advantage over those firms without access to these facilities.

There is also a cultural dimension to the communications revolution. The real costs in the television industry are not the distribution and receiving costs. Television sets and broadcast transmission systems are not that expensive. The real cost is in the production of the programs. The United States is the principal supplier of the world's television programming. The American values portrayed in its television programs have affected the values of the nations where those programs are shown. Critics describe this as "cultural imperialism." They question how governments in the Third World can ever meet the demands for consumer goods that have occurred because of exposure to American television programming.

The final criticism of the communications revolution is that its benefits are creating a new social class system. On top is a technological elite, who benefits from the services of the new communication systems. The vast majority of people, on the other hand, are not only left out of this system but, in fact, experience direct costs as more and more wealth is shifted into the hands of the technological elite. This has raised numerous questions: Do the workers in overseas plants that assemble integrated circuits benefit from the new industry? Do blacks in South Africa benefit from improved police surveillance? Who consumes the resources that are discovered by using satellites? Critics adamantly believe that the communications revolution is unfair in its distribution of costs and benefits; in fact, they claim, it is a new form of imperialism.

### Looking Ahead: Challenge Questions

How have technological developments changed (or how will they change) basic social structures within and between countries?

How has the revolution in communications affected the nonindustrial countries of the world?

What are the primary criticisms leveled at the so-called communications revolution, and what are the counter arguments?

How is life likely to be different 30 years from now if current communications trends continue?

How does control of the media affect political power and social change in the Philippines, the Soviet Union, and so forth?

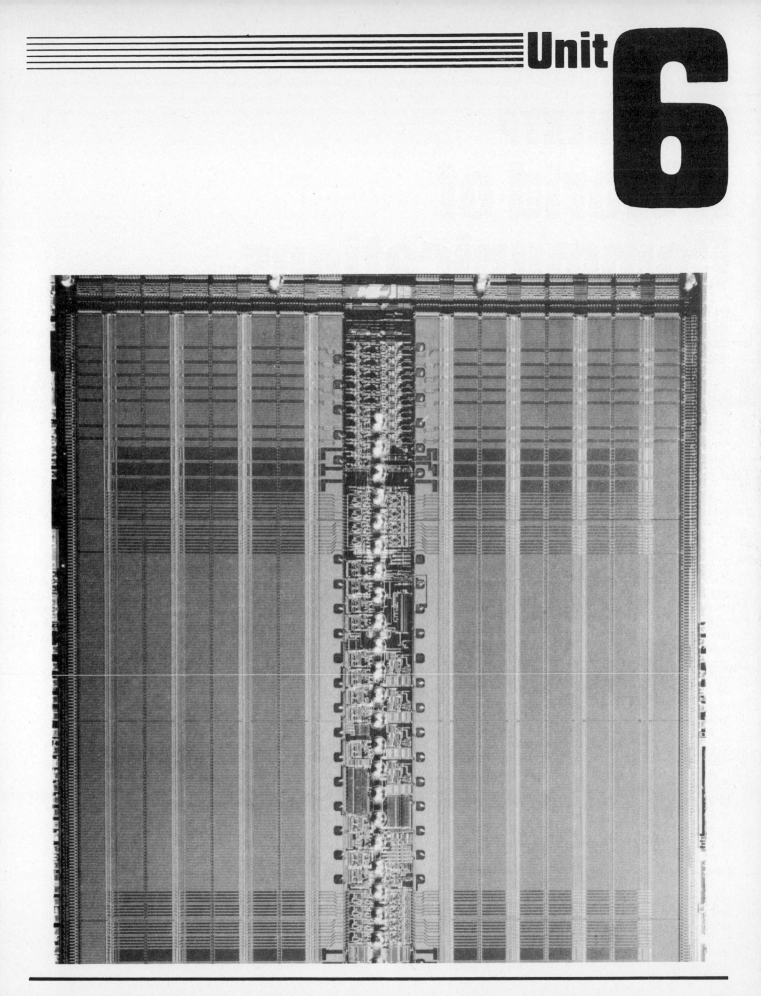

# WHAT NEXT?
# A World of Communications Wonders

**A phone in every pocket, a computer in every home: That and more await consumers as astonishing Information Age techniques start to pay off.**

A global telecommunications revolution is poised to bring astonishing changes to virtually every American—especially anyone who picks up a telephone, switches on a television set or logs on to a computer.

Growing out of the marriage of communications links with modern computers, the new technologies are spreading lightning fast. Experts say that the upheaval won't end until anyone anywhere can reach out and touch anyone else—instantly and effortlessly—through electronics.

Among the extraordinary possibilities in store for consumers by the end of this century:

● The standard telephone console will become the only computer terminal most people will need. Text and pictures will be viewed on a video screen attached to the phone, and additional data will be delivered as electronically synthesized speech. Phone users also will be able to see who is calling before answering.

● Automobiles will have not only telephones as standard equipment but also satellite navigation devices to pinpoint a vehicle's location and guide the driver to any destination.

● Combining laser optics and computers, three-dimensional holographic images will bring TV features from football games to political debates into living rooms with almost lifelike clarity.

● Automatic-translation devices will allow people to insert a text in English and have it delivered in minutes to a distant point in Japanese, Arabic or one of many other languages.

Such feats, some of which still are in the drawing-board stage, now are considered feasible by scientists who have seen the pace of communications technology move ahead dramatically in recent years.

"We are seeing a technological watershed—a sweeping away of long-established traditions and the opening of enormous business opportunity," says Charles Lecht, chairman of Lecht Sciences, Inc., a communications consulting firm in New York City. "State-of-the-art technology that once would have lasted 30 years is becoming obsolete almost as soon as it is installed."

Already, the conduits of yesterday—copper wires, radio signals, ground antennas and even electricity itself—are giving way to glass fibers, microwaves, satellites, laser beams and the pulsating digital language of computers.

The economic potential of such unprecedented changes in communications technology is practically limitless: Sales of hardware alone reached 60 billion dollars in 1983, according to estimates by Arthur D. Little, Inc., and will grow to 90 billion annually by 1988.

Added to that will be fees for communications services and software development that will add at least 50 billion dollars a year by the end of the decade.

The international stakes are enormous: Such American giants as AT&T, GTE, MCI Communications and Rolm—plus hundreds of smaller firms and entrepreneurs—are in all-out competition with experienced manufacturers in Japan and Europe.

Like a summer vine that shoots out in every direction without discernible pattern, the telecommunications grid also is spreading uncontrollably. Never before have so many individuals and organizations been able to interact on such a vast scale. By the end of the century, electronic information technology will have transformed American business, manufacturing, school, family, political and home life.

"No one anticipated how fast the demand for communications technology has accelerated in the last three or four years," says William McGowan, chairman of MCI Communications Corporation. "Telecommunications is one business today in which you don't need losers to have winners. There is enough for everybody."

The instruments in this sweeping electronic upheaval—computers, electronic links and video technologies—are the interlocking parts of a communications network undreamed of only a decade ago.

"Even five years ago, I would not have predicted in my wildest imagination how far we would be today," says Howard Anderson, president of the Yankee Group in Boston and a well-known authority in telecommunications research.

## TELEPHONES AND COMPUTERS
## Made for Each Other

Within a few years, telephones will be everywhere—in cars, airplane seats, boats, even coat pockets. Also likely: Individuals can have one phone number throughout life that will permit them to be called anytime, no matter where they are. High-tech networks will enable a telephone subscriber in a car in London to communicate by voice, data or facsimile to any other fixed or mobile phone in the world.

Such a network also will allow a variety of interacting banking and retail services, open up access to a wide range of specialized information, provide home-security alarm services and even deliver newspapers and magazines to subscribers through a computer terminal and printer.

Commenting on the trend, one technology analyst notes: "Computers and phones are going to be fused together so tightly that they will be almost indistinguishable."

These possibilities result from the advent of a global linkup known as ISDN, or integrated-services digital network. Already in operation, the network uses high-capacity optical cables and sophisticated computers to transmit a wide variety of information, including voice, data or graphics, in the same way.

This "supernetwork" converts traditional electrical waves into a stream of on-off pulses, the digital code understood by computers. Once equipment is updated to handle everything in digital form, huge quantities of data can be squeezed onto copper or glass cables or carried by satellites and microwave radio. The result is not only an increase in signal quality but also a dramatic lowering in the cost of sending everything from a simple telephone call to computerized airline reservations and TV pictures across vast distances.

Advocates concede that setting worldwide standards for ISDN will be difficult, comparable to converting the world to the metric system. However, most agree that the economic benefits of a compatible global system will force all nations to get on board quickly.

"We think ISDN will be the biggest hurdle in the communications race," says Warren Falconer, director of the Transmission Network Planning Center at AT&T Bell Laboratories. "But already, business and home users can choose from 150 specialized digital services to customize their communications needs, and more are on the way."

Some companies also see profits in coupling communications lines with powerful computers that could automatically translate spoken or written text into another language. A few systems can make technical translations now, but their creators say it will be many years before a commercial version is widely available.

Another technology on the verge of taking off is cellular radio, a new kind of mobile-phone network that will put full-service telephones in any vehicle on the road.

Car phones have been available for years, but the old transmission severely limited the number of subscribers. Cellular radio uses computers to make better use of radio frequencies, thus opening up thousands of new mobile links.

In Chicago, for example, where the first system is being installed, the existing system allowed fewer than 1,000 mobile users at one time. Using cellular radio, some 20,000 simultaneous conversations could take place.

In designing a system, a local phone company divides a city into cells. Computers track each call and pass it from one low-power transmitter to another as a car travels from one zone to the next, making sure that there is no interruption in the connection. Cellular phones offer more privacy than typical radio links, and calls can be made without the waiting needed when a human operator is involved.

"We think there will be between 1 and 3 million subscribers in the U.S. by the early to mid-1990s," says James Caile, marketing manager for Motorola's cellular operations, a major provider of mobile-radio equipment. Cities expected to be licensed in the next two years include Miami, New York, Los Angeles, Dallas, Washington, Philadelphia, Seattle, Atlanta and Detroit.

The price of a cellular phone now runs about $3,000 for installation, plus a monthly fee of around $100. Initial buyers are expected to be sales personnel and executives, but manufacturers foresee lower prices as demand increases.

"Once people realize how nice it will be to have phones in their cars, the auto manufacturers will begin to offer them as options," says a spokesman for GTE Mobilnet, Inc. "At that point, the prices should come down fast."

Already, Buick is offering cellular phones in some 1984 models, and Ford plans to introduce the devices in 1985.

## FIBER OPTICS
## Light Lines to the World

Gossamer strands of ultrapure glass, as thin as human hair, are fast becoming the nerve pathways of the burgeoning telecommunications grid.

Already, a half-inch cable containing 30,000 miles of tiny optical fibers runs between New York and Washington. The link will carry 240,000 simultaneous conversations—twice as many as can be carried by a copper cable as thick as a wrist.

"We are at the start of the light-wave era in long-distance communications," says Robert Kleinert, president of AT&T Communications, which is building an optical-fiber network across the nation. "Light pulses, rather than electrical signals, will be the workhorses of the Information Age."

Optical fibers have greater transmission capacity because they carry tiny staccato pulses of light generated by lasers that can turn on and off 90 million times a second. At such a pace, the entire contents of the 2,700-page Webster's Third New International Dictionary could be transmitted over a single fiber in 6 seconds.

Besides major cost benefits, fiber optics offer other advantages, too. They are immune to electrical interference, difficult to wiretap and cheap to produce. A mile-long thread of optical fiber, for instance, can be created from a single tablespoon of raw material.

Experts say the market for fiber optics could reach 3 billion dollars worldwide by 1990. Already, plans are under way to lay 3,500 miles of undersea cable between the U.S. and Europe by 1988, with a cross-Pacific cable later to Japan. Banks and other businesses are building "local-area networks"—intracity optical links to carry all phone and computer data between branch operations. Television and phone links for the 1984 Summer Olympics will be transmitted through a just completed fiber-optics system in Los Angeles.

Meanwhile, technology is bringing even more optical advances. One major step is a lengthening of the distance between the electronic relays that boost light signals before they dim in intensity. Bell Laboratories recently sent 1 billion bits of data—the equivalent of 100 novels—over 75 miles of cable without any electronic boosting.

Although most optical fibers use silicon dioxide, or sand, as their raw material, researchers at Corning Glass Works and elsewhere are experimenting with clearer types of glass. So flawless are some of the new glass compounds that a pane 1 mile thick could be made perfectly transparent.

In time, say researchers, light-wave communications will reach into individual homes and offices, delivering TV and radio entertainment, computer programs, videogames, teletext messages and two-way conduits all through a single optical cable. Such a system also would allow for televised phone conversations with higher quality than the Bell Picturephone displayed at the 1964 World's Fair but never put into commercial production because of high cost.

# SATELLITES
## High-Flying Birds of High Tech

In a sense, it's not an unusual scene: The boss calls a prospective employe into an office, interviews the person at length and finally announces, "You're hired." The difference is that the boss is 1,000 miles away, and the interview is being carried live and in color between offices by a satellite link.

Communications experts say such electronic conferences soon will be commonplace via satellite. Already, businesses and homeowners are learning to appreciate the services that

PHOTOS BY GARY L. KIEFFER—USN&WR

**Long-distance video conference is carried by Satellite Business Systems antenna.**

unmanned orbiters can provide. Mushroom-shaped dish antennas have sprouted atop skyscrapers and in suburban back yards, and new communications satellites are expected to go into orbit at a rate of 200 over the next 10 years in the U.S. alone.

"The fact is, businesses have been bypassing the traditional and more expensive transmission facilities in the U.S. for years," says Robert Hall, president of Satellite Business Systems (SBS), a joint venture of IBM, Comsat and Aetna Insurance. "Satellites have accelerated that trend because they are superb information handlers."

The carrying capacity of the newest satellites has increased more than a hundredfold since the first carriers went into space in the early 1960s. The latest generation of Intelsat VI satellites will carry more than 33,000 simultaneous phone conversations plus two TV channels between the U.S. and Europe.

"Satellites also will eliminate the need for phone lines in most developing nations," notes John Evans, head of Comsat Laboratories. "The smallest, most remote villages will be able to have a satellite phone link."

Businesses have been quick to use this resource, sending vast amounts of computer data from one point on the continent to another in a quarter of a second.

An American Express Company computer center in Phoenix, for example, uses a combination of satellites and phone links to approve 250,000 credit transactions a day from around the world, in an average of 5 seconds or less.

A large insurance company routinely sends computerized material by satellite in 12 minutes that would take 31 hours to transmit by land lines.

A service called Eyesat records new techniques in eye surgery at the St. Louis University School of Medicine, then transmits the video by satellite to physicians elsewhere.

In many cities, businesses are building special satellite-dish fields called teleports to transmit information into space without interference from competing satellite users. One such teleport is being built on Staten Island to alleviate congested airwaves over Manhattan.

Another prospect already being tested in an experimental car produced by Ford: An antenna trained on navigation satellites that display a car's location—within 30 feet—on a video screen mounted in the dashboard.

The newest major use of satellites is teleconferences, in which employees of corporations, educational institutions and government agencies gather around video monitors to hold meetings via satellite linkup around the world. Instead of traveling to meetings, executives can speak to and watch one another without leaving their office buildings.

"Video conferencing is the next best thing to being there," says an official of SBS. "It allows people to see each other on closed-circuit hookups and at fairly reasonable cost."

Conducted on large-screen projectors, video meetings cover questions and discussions by all participants, can be international as well as national and need run only long enough to handle the agenda. Some firms are considering setting up stockholder meetings via satellite links.

Last year, wine critics in France and the U.S. met through satellite to taste and compare notes on recent vintages. The link allowed wine merchants to get expert opinion, but only the wines had to be flown across the ocean.

Atlantic-Richfield Company has installed a 17-million-dollar video-teleconference system to connect its Los Angeles headquarters with offices in Philadelphia, Denver,

# Coming—Ways to Stay in Touch Nearly Anywhere

Imagine that you are an executive in a country where terrorist acts occur frequently. Your company suspects that you could be a target of kidnappers.

Now, communications technology may offer you some degree of protection. The solution: Implant a transmitter in your body that can be triggered to alert a satellite to your exact whereabouts.

Such a bizarre procedure is exactly what Carmine Pellosie, a New York electronics expert, intends to do. It is one of several novel spinoffs made possible by communications technology used in tandem with satellites and computers.

Many of the devices being studied will protect or keep track of individuals and therefore have application in law enforcement and personal safety.

Pellosie's transmitter, placed surgically beneath the rib cage, could be activated by the kidnap victim to beam a signal skyward. A satellite then would locate the hostage, possibly even within hours.

**Waiting list.** Pellosie says that he has some customers, including diplomats and celebrities, lined up and waiting to be wired. "It would be as reliable as a heart pacemaker and a lot less complicated," he says.

Another similar system—this one tied to telephone technology—is being used to keep criminals off the streets. In New Mexico, some drunk drivers are being confined to their homes through the use of an electronic bracelet that is a high-tech version of a scarlet letter. If the wearer ventures more than 200 yards from home—or removes the device—a signal is sent immediately through the person's phone line to the police.

"We wanted to punish convicted drunk drivers without sending them to jail, which probably wouldn't help them much," explains Jack Love, district judge in Albuquerque, N.M.

"Using this system, drunk drivers cannot drive or even ride in a car," Love pointed out, "yet they can stay with their families instead of being incarcerated."

Another law-enforcement communication prospect: On a busy highway, a trooper sits in a patrol car and trains an optical-scanning device on passing license plates.

**Fast tracker.** The scanner "reads" the plates and transmits the numbers to a central computer, which checks the numbers against lists of stolen cars. Within 15 seconds, the computer can verify that a stolen car has passed and alert the police officer to give chase.

One of the most visionary examples of personal communication is being offered by Geostar, a private satellite company. The device will allow individuals to stay in touch with others anywhere.

For example, backpackers or skiers in the wilderness can carry a small receiver-transmitter that allows family or friends to send them a brief message printed on a video screen. The recipient then can punch out a return message. Because of the satellite link, the system also can pinpoint the vacationer in case the person is lost.

"We think many people will want this service because so many individuals simply don't feel comfortable being completely cut off from their home base," says Gerard O'Neill, head of the Princeton, N.J.-based company.

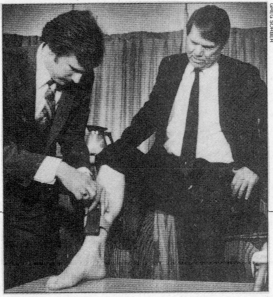

**Electronic anklet, being demonstrated, keeps drunk drivers out of jail and off the road.**

GREG SCHBER

Houston, Dallas and Washington. And the J.C. Penney Company recently set up a laser system linking two New York City skyscrapers to conduct video meetings, and plans to expand the system nationwide.

Despite such efforts, some analysts have doubts about the growth of video conferences. They point out that such companies as SBS have yet to make a profit and note that many people do not like to "perform" on a video monitor.

One breakthrough that would clearly aid all video services would be a higher-resolution television screen that would sharpen the often hazy, dull visual qualities of today's TV screen. "TV's are being used for many more things now—for the computer, VCR, teletext services and video conferences," says a Sony Corporation official. "The U.S. broadcast standard just doesn't allow for the higher resolution that is possible with today's electronics."

Now, scientists at Bell Labs and elsewhere are using digital technology to create a much higher-definition picture. "We can get images that are so crystal clear it's almost like 3-D," says one executive.

CBS and Philips Corporation are developing a high-definition satellite-TV system that would deliver cinema-quality signals to the home screen. Now, the television industry has formed the Advanced Television System Committee to

persuade the Federal Communications Commission to write regulations allowing such techniques.

But even advocates of new technology concede that getting consumers to discard old TV sets for new equipment will be a lengthy process, as will convincing government regulators to change existing broadcast standards. "It's not a matter of technology," says a scientist at RCA Corporation, "but of politics and economics."

Telecommunications-industry officials are clearly excited about the potential that new technologies hold out for consumers and business. How fast fiber optics, satellites and computer-enhanced techniques will surpass conventional methods is uncertain, but experts are optimistic that the world will shrink even further by communications advances.

Sums up Anderson of Boston's Yankee Group: "The next five years will surprise us, too. There will be price wars, a vast array of competing technologies and complex choices to be made. Consumers will benefit from the revolution with better service, cheaper prices and more control. Consumers will be the engineers of their own custom-designed communications centers."

*By STANLEY WELLBORN*

# DETECTIVES IN SPACE

*Sensors mounted on satellites send a stream of invaluable scientific information back to earth; now the US is in danger of losing its commercial lead just as important new applications are emerging.*

## Donald L. Rheem

*Staff writer of the Christian Science Monitor*

### Washington

Bolivian drug authorities obtain maps of illegal cocaine-processing plants. US news networks release photos of secret Soviet military installations. UN aid officials are able to predict crop failures in Africa and divert food aid to stricken areas. Multinational mining companies find potential ore deposits under dense jungle and pay little for the exploration rights because the host government has no idea of the land's value.

All of this is happening by using satellites hundreds of miles in space that produce detailed images of Earth. The issue of satellite remote sensing is gaining attention for these reasons:

• Remote-sensing technology will play a major role in predicting natural disasters, avoiding famine, mon-

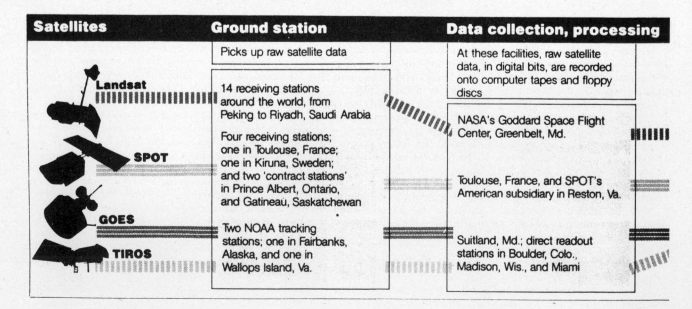

| Satellites | Ground station | Data collection, processing |
|---|---|---|
| | Picks up raw satellite data | At these facilities, raw satellite data, in digital bits, are recorded onto computer tapes and floppy discs |
| Landsat | 14 receiving stations around the world, from Peking to Riyadh, Saudi Arabia | NASA's Goddard Space Flight Center, Greenbelt, Md. |
| SPOT | Four receiving stations; one in Toulouse, France; one in Kiruna, Sweden; and two 'contract stations' in Prince Albert, Ontario, and Gatineau, Saskatchewan | Toulouse, France, and SPOT's American subsidiary in Reston, Va. |
| GOES TIROS | Two NOAA tracking stations; one in Fairbanks, Alaska, and one in Wallops Island, Va. | Suitland, Md.; direct readout stations in Boulder, Colo., Madison, Wis., and Miami |

itoring global pollution, and surveying inaccessible areas, such as the Chernobyl nuclear plant site, tropical rain forests, and foreign military installations.

- The United States, industry experts say, is not transferring its primary remote-sensing system to the private sector fast enough, and is at serious risk of losing its technological and therefore its market lead.
- The French launched a commercial satellite that surpasses US technology, and competitors in other countries—namely Canada, Japan, West Germany, and India—are setting launch dates for their own advanced remote-sensing satellites.
- The unofficial policy of "open skies"—agreed upon by the US and other Western powers—compels commercial satellite owners to sell images to anyone who can afford them.
- Some third-world countries object that satellite data, used by governments and multinational corporations in developed nations, leave them open to exploitation.
- The Pentagon is concerned with the national-security implications of the next generation of remote-sensing technology.

There are two basic types of remote-sensing satellites: government (intelligence gathering) and civilian or commercial (weather, communication), although some foreign government systems are also commercial.

Commercial remote sensing began when the US government turned over its Landsat satellite system to the Earth Observation Satellite Company (EOSAT), a joint venture of Hughes Aircraft Company and the RCA Corporation. The French are competing with their own satellite, launched in February 1986, called SPOT. Both Landsat and SPOT are able to produce images of virtually any location on Earth and are directed by the "open skies" policy to sell those images to whoever can pay the bill. But some analysts contend that images of certain Western military sites will be "unavailable," because of cloud cover or other "technical" reasons.

## MILITARY vs. CIVILIAN USES

The biggest difference between military and commercial remote-sensing satellites is the degree of detail—or resolution—of the images. For example, if you bought a picture of a city block from Landsat, you would be able to pick out any building or object bigger than 30 meters (about 100 feet). SPOT could pick out much smaller buildings, anything over 10 meters (about 30 feet). Military satellites, by contrast, could detail objects in the 3- to 4-inch range, such as a lost tennis ball stuck on a rooftop.

The military doesn't sell its satellite images. But for $100, EOSAT will sell you a black-and-white photo covering an area 110 miles edge to edge. SPOT will sell you a black and white print for $470; its better resolution covers a more detailed 37 miles edge to edge. You can get color prints from EOSAT for $300 and from SPOT for $515.

With each new satellite built, the sensors improve. "I think that over the next decade you will see resolutions improve," says Peter Zimmerman, a physicist at the Carnegie Endowment for International peace. "To go to 5 or 2.5 meters requires no scientific breakthroughs. It could be done in the commercial sphere as soon as anybody found a market for it."

But according to Charles P. Williams, president of EOSAT, there is no current market for the finer resolution. "To go to a very fine resolution similar to what some government may have . . . simply doesn't have commercial utility. You would be investing $500 or $600 million in an instrument that could not possibly be recovered." A finer-resolution satellite would generate considerably more data, significantly increasing processing and other costs.

---

**Data analysis** — **A sampling of satellite data applications**

Information from **Landsat** or **SPOT** is then turned over directly to the customer, or analyzed by the satellite company to meet the customer's specific needs. For **GOES** and **TIROS** data, NOAA freely provides weather information to all interested parties, including the news media, regional weather stations, and the military.

**Water resource management** (Identifying flood plains)
**Forestry and rangeland assessment** (Fire damage and recovery planning)
**Fish and wildlife analysis** (Snowcap mapping)
**Land resource management** (Lakeshore management)
**Environmental monitoring** (Detecting oil spills)
**Agricultural yield analysis** (Crop predictions)
**Geological mapping** (Oil exploration)
**Media applications** (Foreign military and secret site photography)

**Urban planning**
**Population density studies**

**Weather forecasting**
**Desertification tracking**
**Crop predictions**
**Atmospheric analysis**

# 6. COMMUNICATIONS

## PRESIDENT CARTER'S SECRET DIRECTIVE

More than economic viability is limiting the resolution of commercial satellites. According to government sources, President Jimmy Carter signed a secret presidential directive in 1978 that set 10 meters as the limit for nonmilitary remote sensing. Pierre Bescond, president of SPOT's American subsidiary, says that the next two SPOT satellites now in development will remain at 10-meter resolution, but he maintains it has nothing to do with the secret directive. The next Landsat satellite, if Congress upholds its commitment to help fund it, advances to only 15-meter resolution.

Industry analysts, however, believe that markets for less than 10-meter resolution will develop, and if US companies are held to 10 meters, America will simply lose its lead in this technology.

The Pentagon is worried about the geopolitical effects of widely available high-resolution images. It is currently opposing, on national-security grounds, a consortium of media interests which wants to launch its own 5-meter-resolution satellite (Mediasat).

"There were terrible fears of geopolitical problems [with] the first TIROS weather satellite," says Mr. Zimmerman. He points out that each improvement in resolution has raised fears, but eventually the fears subside. "This is a technology which is unregulatable and unrestrictable," he says.

But the US could lose its technological edge before the next series of satellites is even off the launch pad. The Reagan administration and Congress have made enormous cuts in the funding promised when EOSAT signed the contract to take over the Landsat program.

## THIRD WORLD OBJECTIONS

Since the market for remote sensing is in its infancy, EOSAT asked for transition funding to maintain the government's satellite system until revenues rise to cover expenses. This the US government originally agreed to provide until 1989.

"The threat itself is extremely serious," says EOSAT president Williams, "If the government portion of the investment is not provided . . . it would mean the end of new satellite construction for Landsat and a termination of the . . . US technological thrust sometime in the early 1990s. It will allow the French and Japanese to take the lead in the '90s and beyond, and become the governing factors in the sales of satellite data."

Many countries have raised objections in the United Nations to being "sensed" and then having the satellite data available on the open market.

There have been reports in the European press, for example, that satellite date were being used by mining companies headquartered in London to determine potential mineral deposits under inaccessible jungle areas. Several countries complained that the mining companies were able to buy the mineral rights from them at a very low price because these governments had no idea of the land's value.

"Now, that is always a possibility," says Mr. Williams, "before they allow anyone to come in and mine or exploit any part of their natural resources they must do an adequate investigation . . . into what they may or may not be giving away."

At a 1982 UN conference on space, developing countries took the position that the "dissemination of [remote-sensing] data to a third party should not be done without the prior consent of the sensed country." But their wording did not survive the UN's final draft, which offers only a set of general principles on the use of remote sensing.

"The UN simply will have little role to play except advisory," says Zimmerman, "perhaps consensus building, perhaps smoothing of ruffled feathers."

To help prevent exploitation, however, and to assist domestic planning and management activities, the UN and the US Agency for International Development now purchase and supply data to third-world countries for their own use.

All large-scale environmental changes, caused naturally or by human activity, leave what photo interpreters call a "signature."

Current satellite technology can detect signatures like soil erosion as the result of poor agricultural practices, toxic waste sites, locations of ocean dumping, clear-cutting in forests, massive development projects that destroy tropical rain forests, and the effects of acid rain. "It won't make polluting more difficult," says Carnegie's Zimmerman, "but it will make getting away with it more difficult."

In the future, commercial remote sensors will not only be able to detect pollutants leaving a factory, but determine what the factory is producing. Opportunities for industrial espionage, one company spying on another, are also possible (cases involving aerial reconnaissance have already hit the courts).

Environmental programs at the UN, NASA, and NOAA, and dozens of individual programs at universities and research institutions around the world, are now using remote sensing for environmental purposes.

It's more than a convenience. Hundreds of thousands of lives have been saved as a result of the disaster-prediction capacity of remote sensors. For example, in May 1985, US weather forecasters predicted a hurricane in the Bay of Bengal, off the coast of Bangladesh.

Computer programs combined the data from meteorological stations in Bangladesh with "real time" (as it actually happened) information from the GOES and TIROS weather satellites, general hurricane behavior data, tidal predictions, and storm-surge records for the bay to predict when and where the storm would strike.

This allowed for the evacuation of much of the coastal area. While more than 5,000 people lost their lives, a hurricane in 1970, before the early-warning system, killed 300,000.

## 'I SEE OPEN SKIES'

Perhaps even more important than predicting weather disasters is the ability to assess food production around the world. Using the TIROS and Landsat satellite, yield predictions can be made a month before harvest, enough time to adjust pricing and marketing policies, import and export plans, and economic programs for farmers. Longer-term drought and disaster preparedness plans can also be developed to select drought-resistant crops and optimum planting times.

Mining and oil exploration companies have joined agricultural interests as the biggest commercial users of remote sensing. Images can be specially processed, for example, to highlight areas with high concentrations of iron oxide and clay, which would indicate the presence of an ore deposit. Similar spatial processing can highlight areas with potential oil deposits.

"Commercial competition is what will govern remote sensing in the future," says the Carnegie Endowment's Zimmerman. Even without the US, remote sensing may become one of the most useful technologies ever developed.

Asked what he sees in the future as a result of remote sensing, Zimmerman pauses and then smiles: "I see very little way for any nation to hide any threatening activities from anybody. . . . I see open skies."

# The regional solution to a global problem

Since the BBC first began broadcasting more than 50 years ago radio and television have become the most powerful communications tools in the world. In one instance, one-sixth of the world's population – a billion people – can gather in their homes before their television sets to hear the same person talking or to watch the same event. Billions more, many of them illiterate, receive virtually all their information from the transistor radio.

By contrast to the print media, the overpowering superiority of both is that their audiences do not have to be literate to understand the messages they receive. Such a force is a propagandist's dream weapon. By using contrived images and simply stated ideas he can wield more power of persuasion over his subject, perhaps a peasant farmer in the Philippines or a refugee in the Sudan, than a thousand printed manifestos could ever hope to exert.

It raises many questions. Chief among these must be the manner in which these media manipulate public thinking and influence events: even, as some argue, to maintain the existing economic and political status quo between North and South.

For more than two decades, this question has been at the forefront of the South group's determination to change the international information order; although admittedly this has been consistently aimed at international text news agencies – like Reuters, United Press International and Associated Press – rather than the broadcasting agencies. Perhaps this is because broadcast agencies by comparison with these organisations represent a much newer phenomenon: syndicated sight and sound.

The largest of these agencies is Visnews. Based in London with bureaux in all the world's major cities linked together when necessary – and increasingly – by satellite, Visnews provides a 24-hour television news service to virtually all the world's broadcasters. Its majority shareholder is Reuters which bought out most of the BBC's shareholding last year.

In terms of people reached, World Television News – WTN – ranks near the top. Major national networks in Europe and America, for instance, also offer their news and feature programming to stations around the world. Simply by virtue of the investment which has been spent on it, the quality of this news output is much higher than anything a small broadcasting organisation can normally hope to achieve.

But is it relevant? This question is repeatedly asked in Third World countries where the broadcast media are normally used as the major propaganda arm of governments, particularly in explaining policy – and often for indoctrinating ideology – among the illiterate masses. In such countries, the use of the electronic media for entertainment is very much a secondary function – whereas in the industrialised world it is at least as important.

After 25 years in broadcasting – all of it dealing with hard news which I regard as the prime material of any broadcasting unit – I have conflicting views about whether Third World countries should place so much store on the use of electronic media for propaganda and indoctrination, often euphemistically called education. Certainly the first function of broadcasting in a society where 80 per cent or more of the population is illiterate must be to educate and inform – the more entertainingly, the better.

The big international television news agencies like Visnews provide frequent, regular and economical access to the world's major news stories, but too often, like the traditional text news agencies, the news is selected, reported, written and presented from the narrow perspectives of western interests.

Not too long ago, for instance, Visnews abandoned one service which I thought essential to Third World countries in Africa. This was their Africa service through which viewers in, say, Kenya or Zambia, could follow events in other African countries; events perhaps which did not merit international coverage, but certainly warranted regional attention.

Whose judgement – and what values – decide the newsworthiness of an item for a Third World audience? More often than not it is a news editor sitting in suburban London or New York more concerned by the rate of inflation and the size of his overdraft.

Last November, in my acceptance speech at the University of Southern California's journalism alumni awards ceremony, I said that the reports which had earned the award were "of half a million deaths which need never have happened". That raised two questions: How long would political differences be allowed to obstruct the supply of food and medicine to the needy? Does television (broadcasting) react responsibly to Third World problems – or simply exploit them for their emotional impact?

Too often news crews arrive in a country with preconceived ideas and set political attitudes so that their reporting is narrow and subjective. All this makes many Third World governments reluctant to allow access to foreign broadcast crews – which in the end only increases the measure of estrangement between South and North. Some people complained that my reports from Ethiopia were superficial and implied that drought alone caused the famine. They said that the causes should have been stated as well as the consequences. Some critics suggested that the pictures of dying children and adults were in bad taste.

Nonetheless, the tragedy established beyond doubt that the electronic media consistently underestimate the amount of public interest which exists in the West about the Third World. When my first film report about the Ethiopian famine was offered by Visnews to Europe's major broadcasters it was turned down! The way that syndication works in Eurovision is that broadcast-

Reprinted by permission from *South: The Third World Magazine* (London), August 1986, pp. 100-101.

ers and agencies in the network offer their contributions during the Eurovision telephone news conferences held three times a day. Initially, all the stations rejected the offer but the BBC, the exception, showed my pictures for more than seven minutes and such was the public response in Britain that by next morning all the European broadcasters were demanding the same story to show on their networks.

The situation in the US was identical. News executives said that there were too many presidential election campaign items to include it. Fortunately, better judgement prevailed. NBC viewers lost a few minutes of the 1984 campaign trail but they also saw the massive tragedy which was unfolding on the other side of the world in Ethiopia.

The reaction of Western viewers proved that their attitude was not as small-minded as some of the people who run the Western media. It is the immense influence the networks of the US and Europe have over the Western world which makes it imperative for them to change their attitude to Third World coverage. They have a moral obligation to inform one-third of the world, the North, about what is happening in, and to, the other two-thirds, the South. And not just the disasters. There must also be room for coverage of the successes. Third World governments have come to believe, rightly, that the West fails to report their nations seriously. If the electronic media had a positive attitude to reporting the Third World, it is virtually certain that disasters like the Ethiopian famine would not have such serious and tragic consequences.

However one potential benefit has arisen out of the narrow perspectives which exist as Third World broadcasters have formed their own regional communications groupings along the lines of Eurovision, such as the television news exchange group Asiavision in Asia and ArabVision in the Middle East. Those still to be set up in the rest of the South should help to make electronic media reporting of the Third World more relevant, objective and comprehensive.

This will depend on whether they are allowed to perform as professional news gathering outfits. URTNA, the African network, functions but is ineffective. It has offices in some member countries and a staff of 12 operating out of Nairobi with about 90 minutes a week of URTNA exchange programmes on the Voice of Kenya. However, many countries do not make any contribution and so far the exchange exists between only five or six countries. If Pan-african exchanges are seemingly distant, there can be no arguing against the case for a regional exchange of news, which would be handier to organise. The real obstacle to URTNA's development arises from conflicting political beliefs and lack of real communication resources in the member countries. If this obstacle could be removed the way would be open for URTNA to become the major television and radio news agency of the African continent.

**Mohamed Amin**

*Mohamed Amin has been head of the Africa bureau of Visnews since 1966. His work in Ethiopia has won him several awards and among his publications are **Portraits of Africa** (1983) and **Insight Guide, Kenya** (1985).*

# Uprising in the Philippines

## Could There Have Been a Revolution Without Television?

A firsthand account of the medium's influence on the

dramatic showdown between the Marcos and Aquino forces

Jonathan Kolatch

**N**ot in an ordinary lifetime does a country on the brink of losing its last hope for a future halt a seemingly irreversible tide by the sheer will of its people. Not in an ordinary lifetime does flesh stand up scornfully to metal and best it; does autocracy turn overnight to democracy without bloodshed, without shortage, without looting, without inflation, without a power-blinded, lingering strongman.

The days of cloud-walking have passed now and the 55 million people of this vast nation of 7100 islands are just beginning to ask how something so magical could have happened. Sometimes, in scrutinizing momentous events from a short-term perspective, factors tend to be distorted to suit the purposes of the observer. In the case of the Philippine revolution we have only recently witnessed on our television screens—here even better than in Manila—there is no need to exaggerate. From the Marcos interview with David Brinkley on ABC's *This Week* on Nov. 3, 1985, that forced the Feb. 7 election, to the Aquino-Marcos "debate" on ABC's *Nightline* on Feb. 5, to the capture of government station Ch. 4 that cut Marcos's lifeline, television played a pivotal and participatory role. Without it, history would have been written differently.

*Anong nangyari sa mga* TV announcers *noong gabi ng halalan?* asked a columnist in one of Manila's mass dailies, mixing English and Tagalog, as is the local custom. *Nakakahiya sila!*

"What happened to our TV announcers on election night? They were a disgrace!"

Most of them knew it; the best of them did something about it.

In a country where TV news anchors do not yet enjoy the celebrity status they have here, Tina Monzon-Palma stands alone throughout the Philippines as a professional and a symbol. A tall woman, in her mid-30s, with a strong, no-nonsense voice that sometimes lapses into an Irish lilt acquired from a childhood teacher, Tina Palma was until recently the news director and principal anchor at Ch. 7, the only one of five Manila flagship stations that could claim nominal independence from the Marcos government.

The day preceding the presidential election between opposition candidate Corazon C. Aquino and Ferdinand E. Marcos, her superior handed her a 30-page memorandum prepared by the government Office of Medja Affairs entitled "Talking Points for Feb. 7 Radio-TV Coverage." Its purpose: to tell radio and television announcers what to say as the vote was being tallied in order to convince the public that there was nothing questionable about the balloting or the tabulation. To read that memo, with its subtle audacity, is to begin to understand the brilliance with which Ferdinand Marcos hoodwinked this nation for 20 years: Cory Aquino had made a secret deal with the Communists; President Cory would cede the southern part of the country to the Muslims; vote buying is the *normal* Philippine way of conducting elections; *all* the polls favor F.M. and those that don't are haphazard and unscientific; The New York Times admires Marcos's boldness. Each point at best "selectively" true and, with no voice to answer it, cumulatively suffocating.

For most of those who received the memo, no coercion was necessary. Compliance was a term of employment. Tina Palma took it home, flipped a few pages, and put it aside. The next morning, she simply didn't show up for work. A few hours later, Ch. 7, without its news star, without its credibility, abandoned planned nonstop election coverage and reverted to regular programming.

To appreciate the absolute control Ferdinand Marcos exhibited over Philippine television, it is necessary to step back to Sept. 21, 1972. When he declared martial law on that date, there were seven stations operating out of Manila—reaching, as now, irregularly into the provinces through relay and replay arrangements. Immediately, Marcos closed all but Ch. 9, in which he had purchased a controlling interest through a friend, Roberto Benedicto, in 1969. The two top-rated stations, ABS and CBN, belonging to Eugenio Lopez, were seized without compensation and integrated into the state-run Maharlika Broadcasting System airing on Ch. 4. Channel 7, owned partly by an American, Bob Stewart, through his Filipino wife, was permitted to resume broadcasting with a 60-per-cent share reapportioned to a close Marcos associate, Gualberto Duavit. Duavit in turn assigned half of his interest to two executives at Ch. 7, Menardo Jimenez and Henry Gozun. In 1984, with Ch. 7 the only solidly profitable station in the country, First Lady Imelda Marcos spearheaded an attempt to reacquire all the shares originally given to Duavit, but was foiled by Jimenez and Gozun. Marcos thus retained leverage in Ch. 7 through Duavit, but no equity.

The Marcos family by that time had expanded its television empire to three stations (Chs. 2, 9 and 13) with a minority share held by Roberto Benedicto and a controlling share by Far East Management Incorporated, whose acronym, FEMI, is known to have more properly derived from *Fe*rdinand *E*dralin *Mi*rcos. The three stations would have been profitable but for misappropriations by Benedicto, who would borrow money for the stations, use it for non-station purposes and then declare a loss for the stations. In 1984, in the face of increasing losses, Marcos's eldest daughter, Imee Marcos-Manotoc, took an active role in the stations and brought in Ramon Monzon, a friend of her husband, to put the books in order and keep a stern eye on the news department. He proved more adept at the latter.

Thus, with government ownership of Ch. 4, with family ownership of Chs. 2, 9 and 13, and with Duavit holding an ever-present rod over Ch. 7's news-coverage policy—by threatening to cut off the foreign-exchange allowance needed to import equipment and programming; by threatening to make it difficult to free film from customs; and by threatening to pressure Marcos crony advertisers to place their buys elsewhere—Marcos domination of the television airwaves was complete.

From the opening of the campaign on Dec. 11, 1985, to the official campaign closing date of Feb. 5, the election bid of Aquino received at best 20 per cent of the television coverage given Marcos. If on American TV screens it was all "Cory! Cory! Cory!" on Philippine television it was "Cory *who*?"

On and off the government station, television discrimination against the Aquino campaign was blatant: minutes for Marcos, seconds for Aquino; face shots of Marcos, profiles of Aquino; live sound for Marcos, paraphrases for Aquino; lead stories about Marcos, tail-enders about Aquino. You appreciate the bias better, though, by comparing the candidates in the field with the view on the screen.

I followed the Aquino campaign for two full days, one in Manila and a second in Batangas Province, two hours to the south, and looked in vain for television mention. You don't have to be a media expert to know that crowds of 20,000 or 30,000 or 40,000 stopping traffic dead in the middle of a busy city highway—with stenciled T-shirts of every description, with pigeons streaming yellow ribbons (the Aquino campaign color) on their tail feathers, with kids banging drums and waving flags—make for first-rate television. Or that Cory Aquino taking Communion in a jam-packed small-town church early on a Sunday is worth 15 or 20 seconds. CBS was there and NBC was there and Japanese television was there; Philippine television was not.

I saw Ferdinand Marcos speak before an indifferent audience of business executives at the Intercontinental Hotel in Manila with every word reported live on television. A day prior, I saw Corazon Aquino outline her political program before the same forum, only to find the speech reported far down on the evening-news lineup with almost no live sound and no hint of her thunderous reception.

I saw extensive television reports of a Marcos campaign visit to Zamboanga City, 540 miles south of Manila, at the western tip of Mindanao, where major agreements and administrative changes important to the local population were presented to crowds said to reach 150,000. But, when I traveled there a few days later I found that the crowds had been "b(r)ought in" at 25 to 30 pesos (about $1.25) a head. "We're no fools," Mario Santos, who works at one of the hotels in the area, told me. "We take the money and vote for Cory. It's *our* money."

In orchestrating television coverage of the Marcos campaign, the government Office of Media Affairs maintained maximum control over its footage, often limiting camera access at speeches, at presidential news conferences and on the stump to government crews and then editing the tape and distributing it to other stations for airing. With no other source of presidential material available, stations had no choice but to present the president as the president wished to be seen.

Attempts were made by individuals to insert balance, and isolated discussion programs such as "Viewpoint" and "Tell the People" approached objectivity, but in the end the system proved too tight. In the early stages of the campaign, Tina Palma at Ch. 7 aired the opposition's Christmas and New Year messages and showed their rallies, which far outdrew those of Marcos. When the Presidential Palace called her on the carpet, she replied that if Marcos wanted more exciting coverage on Ch. 7, he should organize a more exciting campaign. Within days, she was stripped of her news directorship and reduced to news reader, without any editorial input.

Lawyers for the Aquino campaign petitioned the Commission on Elections—Comelec—to enforce the "Omnibus Election Code" requirement that television stations provide equal time and prominence to all candidates. They documented that Marcos speeches and rallies were receiving full TV attention, while the opposition was receiving almost nothing. The presidentially appointed commission convened hearings and took testimony, but never rendered a decision, and coverage of Marcos campaign activities continued on government Ch. 4 unrestricted through the duration of the campaign.

A larger result, however, was that noncoverage of the Aquino campaign became a news story in itself, reported widely in the international press. This forced minimal concessions, and in the final two weeks of the campaign, Ch. 4 assigned a reporter and crew to the Aquino trail for the first time. But this never translated into anything approaching equal coverage. For the voter in the provinces, the debate over equal access had little impact. All he saw on his screen was Marcos, Marcos, Marcos.

Local television denied her, Cory Aquino played heavily to the American television audience, hoping that the coverage would rebound through the local press and radio and through word-of-mouth. Even more important, she hoped that it would help her in obtaining U.S. Government support in the anticipated political struggle following the campaign.

Marcos, too, nuzzled up to American television. For him, however, it was as much a personal as a political need. Though he railed against American meddling in Philippine affairs at every opportunity, he relished his American connection. His World War II medals were the linchpin of his legitimacy, American aid a vital source of his wealth, the American bases his *personal* contribution to world stability. Like large numbers of Filipinos, he seemed to struggle with a deep-seated feeling of inferiority. All other interests aside, he had a genuine need to be liked in the United States, and the American networks, with their instant, living-room-to-living-room capability, provided the perfect platform. What he never seemed to grasp even to the end was that the American television public was not buying his story.

As was the case with news coverage, a similar morass—over law and substance—developed regarding paid political advertising. In a different country at a different time it would have erupted into a major scandal. In the Philippines, it was just one of many.

The overriding theme of Marcos's TV ad campaign was fear: of the Communist New People's Army, of the Muslim Moro National Liberation Front. If the country didn't want to end up like Vietnam, like Iran, like Iraq, it had better give the job to a counter-insurgency expert. Eerie scenes of battle and mutilation, accompanied by martial and patriotic music, a hail of spots featuring students saying that they just couldn't take a chance with Corazon Aquino, rehabilitated rebel officers telling how Marcos had put them back on the track . . . and a flustered and frustrated "Housewife Cory," *in simulation*, admitting:

"I'm a woman and naturally I have a woman's disposition. . . . To entrust the lives of millions of Filipinos to a woman like me. *Ako'y magtatapat sa inyo*—Let me confess to you. I would never give this responsibility over to a woman. It's a man's job." (*A man's voice*): "President Marcos is the only one."

Aquino ads, produced on a shoestring, were flat in contrast: two 30-second spots in her monotone voice on the themes of hunger and repression, concluding with her campaign plea: *Sobra na! Tama na! Palitan na!* "Stop it! It's too much! Let's change!"

Philippine election law requiring that paid air time be made available to all candidates equally, the Marcos government decided it could not simply deny the Aquino campaign commercial time. Instead it instructed all stations to insist that before any Aquino time-buy be executed, it carry the approval of the Movie and Television Review and Classification Board (MTRCB). It then instructed the Board, housed within the government Ch. 4 complex, to sit on each request.

Lawyers for Aquino petitioned the Commission on Elections, arguing that, under the election law, MTRCB approval of campaign ads was unnecessary. The Board responded by quickly approving two 30-second commercials that began airing Jan. 21—eight days after they were first scheduled to appear and five weeks after the Marcos TV ad campaign began. The relief was only temporary. Two additional Aquino commercials submitted Jan. 24 were never approved and never aired. The Board claimed it had no quorum.

The Aquino media campaign in any case was hamstrung by budget limitations, a problem the Marcos camp did not face. The independent Philippine Monitoring Services reports that between Dec. 14 and Feb. 5 the Marcos campaign had roughly 10 times the television advertising time of Aquino, and estimates, using standard rate cards, that this should have resulted in billing in excess of 21-million pesos (about $1.1 million). The Aquino campaign, in contrast, spent 2,170,310 pesos (about $110,000). (On the final night of the campaign alone, Marcos had more ad exposure on television than Aquino managed during the *entire* campaign.) While the Aquino campaign paid for its spots in cash, however, all available evidence indicates that at best the Marcos campaign paid for only a fraction of its time, contrary to the election-code provision that commercial time be billed to parties at equal rates.

Resolution 1731 of the Election Code specifies that before any campaign spot be aired, the contract for that spot *must* be registered with the Commission on Elections. However, my investigation of existing files at the commission revealed, and commission officers confirmed, that the only contracts on file are for time purchased by the Aquino campaign. Each of television stations 2, 7, 9 and 13 (government station 4 did not run commercials for either side) filed required documents for Aquino political advertising. They filed *nothing* for Marcos.

Industry insiders confirm that at Chs. 2, 9 and 13—each controlled financially by the Marcos family—commercials were simply presented to the station and run, without paper work or payment. At Ch. 7, financially independent of the Marcoses, the situation is more complex. Senior officials at Ch. 7 initially told me, two days before the close of the campaign, that Marcos spots, many of which ran up to two minutes, were being billed (illegally) at the same amount as 30-second Aquino spots. I made further requests, after the change of government, to Graciano P. Gozun, the senior vice-president in charge of finance at Ch. 7 (whose authorization appears on Aquino campaign contracts) to see the documentation regarding Marcos campaign buys. They were denied. "There are other stations," he told me. In fact, there were not.

In addition to standard campaign commercials, the Marcos campaign had the benefit of a full battery of "political ads in another dress"—19 different "public-service" plugs on the accomplishments of the Marcos regime, paid for by government businesses or agencies:

● "Twelve years ago, volcanoes meant nothing but trouble for Filipinos. Now, they work for you, making the Philippines the second largest producer of geothermal energy in the world."—*The Philippine National Oil Company.*

● "After five years in Saudi Arabia I was able to save enough money for my children's education."—*The Philippine Overseas Employment Association*, "joining in the president's program for national recovery."

Corazon Aquino, for her part, never expected anything from the local media. Speaking at a dinner stop at the provincial town of Balayan after a long day of

campaigning, she told me that she felt that "in a way this overkill of Marcos on local television is working to my advantage. Since very little of my activities have been reported, when people hear that I

will appear somewhere, they make an extra effort to come out and see me."

How, then, did she reach the people? To counteract minimal visual exposure, through videocassettes. Her "Beta Laban" (*Beta* for "Betamax," *Laban* for "fight," the name of her party)—a 45-minute inspirational message that told the story of her slain husband Benigno—was circulated throughout the country. Anyone who donated two blank tapes would receive a recorded tape in exchange. Through pro-opposition newspapers, which went unmuzzled by the government (but, at 10 cents per copy, were too expensive for most Filipinos). Through radio, which enjoys a strong tradition in the Philippines, and in sufficient cases carried news of her appearances. And, most of all, through word-of-mouth.

With Ch. 7 abandoning election coverage even before the polls closed on Friday, Feb. 7, Panawagan '86 (Campaign '86) fell completely to government Ch. 4. At various times, Chs. 2, 9 and 13 used the same feed as Ch. 4 and Ch. 4's signal was hooked up to national radio. The entire coverage carried an incestuous tone and, in the days that followed, the three-pronged government team of Deputy Minister of Media Affairs Ronnie Puno, Ambassador J.V. Cruz and Ronnie Nathanielsz, director of public affairs for the Office of Media Affairs, was seen time and again, alone or in a group, on any of the channels. Their scorn for the foreign press carried no veil and no sophistication. Ronnie Puno: "Tom Brokaw and Peter Jennings aren't going to come here to report quiet." J.V. Cruz on Ted Koppel: "His name should be pronounced *kupal*'—an uncomplimentary word in Tagalog, meaning "a person without shame."

But even with government monopoly of the airwaves, outside factors forced concession. For one thing, ballots were being processed at an excruciatingly slow pace and, by 9 the morning after the voting, Ch. 4 had to admit that it could not establish a trend. For another, the tally of the National Citizens' Movement for Free Elections (NAMFREL) was being reported by Radio Veritas (the voice of the Catholic Church) and its nonstop updates establishing an early trend for Cory Aquino had the nation's ear.

Initially, television reports ignored the NAMFREL count—which Ferdinand Marcos called "spurious"—insinuating that NAMFREL was funded by the CIA. Instead, they relied on broadcast and press surveys of uncertain origin that were showing a slight lead for Marcos. But as NAMFREL's lead for Cory Aquino held through Saturday, viewers started to question why it was not being reported, compelling Chs. 2 and 9 to show a 950,000-NAMFREL vote lead for Aquino at sign-off on Saturday night.

By Sunday, U.S. Sen. Richard Lugar's allegation of massive voting fraud occasioned Election Commissioner Jaime Opinion to convene a live press conference for foreign and local journalists of a tenor rarely seen on Philippine television. He admitted that Comelec had a credi-

bility problem and blamed it on the Western media. Soon after, he abruptly closed the news conference, citing a lack of order. That day American television watchers saw interviews with 30 Comelec computer operators who had walked off the job because the figures they were asked to tabulate were being manipulated.

The more important story, though, was out on the streets, where tens and hundreds of thousands of volunteers stood vigil over their ballots day and night in what later came to be known as "people power." Chains of human beings—drawn in common purpose—locked arm in arm to protect something sacred; rich and poor, holy and profane, forgetting their stations for the first time in their lives. Their heroism was collective. Philippine television made no mention of it.

National will was one thing; the Marcos machine yet another. The canvassing stretched out and five days after the election—with Aquino still ahead in the NAMFREL count and her supporters still smarting over President Reagan's remark that *either* side could have cheated—faces at Aquino campaign headquarters took on a drawn look. The votes were coming in too slowly, and they knew that late votes would not be Cory votes. The campaign continued almost as if there had been no election: rallies and marches in Manila,

in Angeles City, in Tarlac. A 20-year-old Aquino supporter was shot dead during a protest procession and Radio Veritas appealed for donations to ship his body home 540 miles south. A Harvard-trained Aquino campaign chief was assassinated by six masked men.

Philippine television ignored the huge crowds and the violence as government Ch. 4 gave gavel-to-gavel coverage of the final canvassing in the Batasang Pambansa, the National Assembly, where a 2-to-1 Marcos advantage turned back every opposition protest. Some talked of prolonged protest; others of civil war. I packed my bags and penciled in my tentative concluding paragraph: "The elections are over now and many in the Philippines feel that they have lost their last chance. Philippine television has reverted to its former diet of soap operas and celebrity gossip and American serials. . . . They deserve much, much more." Ten days later, within hours of a last-leg flight home, I rerouted, arriving in Manila just before the airport closed down. Two hours later, I was on the streets in the midst of a revolution.

# For the First Time the People Could See What Was Happening

## As the Aquino forces took control of Filipino TV stations, the public got an uncensored look at what was really going on.

If by Saturday evening, Feb. 22—two weeks after the election—the seeds of revolution were firmly set, you would never have known it from Philippine television. There was President Ferdinand Marcos, the ultimate in calm, telling the people he was "in control of the situation," and calling on the renegades to "stop this stupidity." In the streets of Manila, however, a different tale was unfolding.

To be sure, what we saw in the U.S. of those critical days of Feb. 22-25 was truthful, as far as it went. Torrents of people dressed in yellow, manning barricades, sleeping in the streets, standing up to tanks. What television could not show was the continuum, the sense of suspended time and place. A carnival, with multiple venues. There were hawkers selling peanuts and soft drinks and cigarettes. There were public prayers and street Masses. There were mini-rallies and impromptu processions, graced by nuns in habits and statuettes of the Virgin Mary. No doubt there was some fear, but it rarely showed and never dominated. Mostly, the people had answered "the call" and were awaiting further instructions.

There developed a battle of radio versus television. At the same time that Marcos was telling turncoats Defense Minister Juan Ponce Enrile and Lt. Gen. Fidel Ramos on television to fall in line or face attack, Enrile was telling Marcos over Radio Veritas that his time was up. Radio Veritas—the voice of the Catholic Church and the voice of the opposition—had become the lifeline of the revolution, carrying messages to the nation from opposition leader Corazon Aquino, who considered herself duly elected and was in hiding; transmitting the latest information on troop movements and defections; and, most important, rallying the people to take to the streets.

By 5:30 Sunday morning the challenge had become unacceptable to the Marcos camp and a band of armed men knocked out Radio Veritas's main transmitter. An antiquated backup transmitter was pressed into service, but by nightfall it had burned out. For six long hours on Sunday evening, events stood still as people scoured their radio bands in vain.

But this, Filipinos like to think, was a revolution orchestrated from Above, and its "Angel of the Airwaves" was a woman by the name of June Keithley, a children's-show host who resigned her Ch. 4 position a week before the election and anchored election returns on Radio Veritas. With the assistance of two young boys, a few volunteer professionals and a priest, she took over an abandoned radio station. By midnight, it was back on the air. By morning, it was a radio network. By midday it was part of a television network.

If Philippine television missed the election, it reported, orchestrated, cheer-led the revolution.

On Monday morning, Feb. 24, at about 9 o'clock, Ferdinand Marcos went on state-run Ch. 4, with his wife, children and grandchildren in the background, the latest in a series of calming appearances. But this time there was a greater urgency. Earlier that morning, Radio Veritas had broadcast a "confirmed" report that the president had left the country. At the barricades, on the streets, throughout the country, the celebration was primed to begin. His television appearance was geared to head it off.

It was an extraordinary show. Solemn adult faces, little children scampering about. Marcos telling his chief-of-staff, Gen. Fabian Ver, that only small arms should be used to disperse the crowds. Ver countering: "I cannot go on all the time withdrawing."

Forty-five minutes into the press conference, the transmission STOPPED . . .

Those of us crowding around television sets at Camp Crame, in the northeast sector of Manila, mere yards from the nerve seat of the revolution, weren't sure what we were witnessing. Across the hall, though, where Fidel Ramos and Juan Ponce Enrile were receiving minute-by-minute reports of the battle for Ch. 4, the picture was clear: Marcos had lost his lifeline. Now, it was only a matter of time.

Fact and fancy have a way of melding in the Philippines and, not infrequently, once they have fused, it becomes very difficult to separate them. For his decisive role in the capture of Ch. 4, Col. Mariano Santiago became an instant hero in the Philippines; it took me almost a week to find out that he had been falsely crowned.

Anxious to tell his story, but too much the professional soldier to come out and complain that he and his comrades had been dealt out of their glory, Lt. Col. Teodorico Viduya, sitting in his spare narcotics-division office at the edge of Camp Crame, outlined the details in clipped military fashion:

*At 8:30 Monday morning, a 130-man force commanded by Viduya and two fellow officers (Col. Eduardo Matillano and Lt. Col. Francisco Zubia) received orders from the office of General Ramos at Camp Crame to capture Ch. 4. The combat-ready strike force had assembled the day before to guard Radio Veritas.*

One of the least explained aspects of the revolution is that for all the tight reins he kept on the administrative, propaganda and financial bureaucracies, Marcos proved totally unready to defend his reign militarily. The force about to attack Ch. 4, armed with M16s and rifle grenades, was primed for stiff resistance. The station proved to be lightly protected: just five duty soldiers and 12 scout rangers.

*The attackers arrived in 17 vehicles. At 9:30, the defenders began sporadic fire. At 9:50, Ch. 4 went off the air. By 10, heavily outmanned, the defenders were talked into surrendering. For the next hour, the soldiers searched floor to floor, finding 40 frightened employees huddled individually throughout the building. By 11, the premises were cleared. At 1:25 P.M., the station went back on the air. On several occasions on Monday and Tuesday, small bands of loyalist troops made moves toward Ch. 4, but each time were repulsed by the masses of people who had surrounded the roads to the station.*

While the loss of Ch. 4 severely crippled his propaganda effort, it did not completely cut Ferdinand Marcos off from the nation. When Ch. 4 was lost, a group of loyalist troops immediately seized nearby Ch. 7, which remained on the air until mid-afternoon. And Ch. 9 continued on the air through the following morning, Marcos using it that evening to announce a 6 P.M.-to-6 A.M. curfew. What the loss of Ch. 4 meant to Marcos more than anything was a loss of legitimacy and a loss of control. For the first time, the reformists had a direct, orthodox, uncensored avenue to the people. And for the first time the people could *see* what was happening around them.

After its capture on Monday morning, the area surrounding Ch. 4 became a focal point of the revolution—a place where people gathered to safeguard their gains, but also a place where people gathered just to gather. When I arrived late Monday afternoon, I found them praying. When I left them toward midnight, they were sleeping, many of them, curled up on newspapers in the middle of the street. The next afternoon they were singing "Tie a Yellow Ribbon 'Round the Old Oak Tree"—Cory Aquino's theme song—led by the country's top entertainers (who pitched them cakes and soft drinks from the station's roof between refrains). And late that night they were dancing in the streets, celebrating the ultimate victory.

Within the Ch. 4 complex, meanwhile, the frantic business of putting a station on the air was unfolding, manned strictly by volunteers. With the political situation still unclear, a nonstop entertainment, talk-show, information format was adopted that would continue for the next few days: politicians, entertainers, commentators—with no line between them—urging people to continue to take to the streets and appealing to reluctant loyalists to come over to "our side."

The phone lines were kept open and anyone with useful information received air time. There were patches to General Ramos and press conferences with Juan Ponce Enrile coupled with thanks for donations of 150 boxes of Kentucky Fried

Chicken and 600 bags of Prince potato chips. In the backdrop, a sign: *Mabuhay Ang Kalayaan*—"Long Live Freedom." And up in the newsroom, where—"Believe it or not," said the announcer—not one still photograph of Corazon Aquino could be found, the final touches were being put on the 7 o'clock news, the first uncensored newscast in 14 years.

The final blow for Marcos—the aftershock—came on Tuesday morning, Feb. 25. Though his situation was rapidly deteriorating, he insisted on going through with his inauguration and insisted that it be broadcast on television. The evening before, four snipers still loyal to the president had climbed the tower of Ch. 9 and, backed by 60 soldiers below, had used pulleys to hoist ammunition and supplies to a midpoint platform. By morning, they were still there.

The inaugural began. That is all that can be said. At the very moment that the master of ceremonies announced, "And now, the moment you have been waiting

---

## What the loss of Ch. 4 meant to Marcos...was a loss of legitimacy and a loss of control.

---

for...," the transmission ceased. Several hours later, a reformist helicopter blew the last of the loyalists out of the Ch. 9 tower, and the troops below surrendered.

That same day, just a mile from Camp Crame, Corazon Aquino held her own inauguration. For her there was no live television either, several hours elapsing before the tape could be played to the nation on Ch. 4. That same evening, Ferdinand Marcos left his palace for the last time, en route to Hawaii.

Did American television play more than an observer role in the Philippine elections and transfer of power? Certainly both the Marcos and Aquino camps were equipped to serve American television: Marcos, with a television studio inside Malacañang Palace; Aquino, with a media staff headed by her sister-in-law, Lupita Kashiwahara (the sister of Aquino's slain husband, Benigno), a producer at KGO-TV in San Francisco. And just as certainly, because so many Filipinos speak English and because Marcos left the foreign press to do its work unencumbered, the American public got a view of foreign politics it has never had before. Almost to the end, though, Marcos succeeded in what he set out to do: he let the outside world into his living room and kept his countrymen hanging by the gate.

He drew the line at what was dubbed "The Great Philippine Election Debate of '86."

Neither Aquino nor Marcos was anxious for a face-to-face debate on local television. She feared that he would manipulate the interrogators and that he would distort the camera angles. He feared the unknown: an innocent-looking lady in a yellow dress who could call him a liar to his face without blushing. So, each side laid conditions the other could not meet.

The pressure for a debate originated from Ted Koppel of ABC's *Nightline*. The weekend before the Feb. 7 election each candidate agreed to a live 60-minute interview, following the *Nightline* format, to be aired Wednesday night (Feb. 5) U.S. time, Thursday morning Manila time.

But Marcos never intended to go through with a debate with his opponent, not if there were any chance that it would be shown on Philippine television.

On Monday, Feb. 3, in a major speech in Manila, Aquino announced that at last she and Marcos would be appearing together on *Nightline*. The *Nightline* debate carried the lead on Philippine television news that evening, exerting tremendous pressure on Marcos to allow it to be aired in the Philippines. This he did not want. So, the next day, Tuesday, Marcos announced that the Commission on Elections had ruled that a live debate aired on Wednesday night in the U.S. (Thursday, Feb. 6, in the Philippines) would violate the election law prohibiting campaign activities after Feb. 5.

*Nightline* offered to move the broadcast up one day, but Marcos set an additional condition: the Koppel broadcast would have to be preceded by a local debate, with local interrogators. Aquino refused. So on Wednesday, Marcos ran a one-candidate "debate" with four local television interviewers—announcing, "This lightens my conscience, because now I have been interviewed by the local press"—and then taped an individual interview with *Nightline*. That evening ABC sped two hours north, to Tarlac, Aquino's home province, completing its interview with her at 11:55 P.M.—five minutes before the midnight cutoff. The Feb. 5 edition of *Nightline* juxtaposed the two interviews. There was no debate.

Later, during the period of revolution, American television had a more direct hand. In the critical days of Feb. 23-24, each network managed interviews with Enrile and Ramos, and NBC with Marcos. The audience might have been the American public, but the target was the American Congress and President; to hasten American support for the new government or to encourage the United States to continue to "wait and see."

And, for Ferdinand Marcos, by now under siege in his own palace, there was an additional element. For, to be sure, in his final hours in power, those around Marcos, if not the president himself, were monitoring American television reports, which they could pick up from nearby Clark Air Force Base, and the universal predictions of their leader's imminent downfall could only have added to their growing sense of isolation.

People ask if the election in the Philippines was really as tainted as American television reported, the response of the people as moving.

I spent election day, Feb. 7, in the Fort Bonifacio section of Manila, at Precinct 3, in a place called Cembo. At nearby Guadalupe, there was gunfire, but from all appearances, Cembo was a peaceful polling place, perhaps because—the election law be damned—it lay within the gates of an armed military camp. But it was not an honest polling place. Of the 404 names and addresses of "registered" voters posted outside the one-room schoolhouse at Precinct 3, 104 were listed at house numbers that didn't exist. It was easy to verify.

I followed the 161 ballots cast at Precinct 3 to the canvass point at city hall. It coursed a very crooked route. First, to the school principal's office nearby, where the ballot box was opened and closed. Then, to the courtyard outside city hall where, in fading light, tally sheets were separated from ballot boxes and placed in drawers. Then, to the offices of the Board of Canvassers, whose chairman sat in his air-conditioned office, while in the adjoining room dozens of unsupervised hands sorted 853 precinct envelopes, first into three piles and then into 10.

At 11 P.M., with tally sheets still dribbling in from the courtyard eight hours after the close of the polls, Chairman Marcelo emerged briskly from his office and announced that it was time to move to the chambers of the city council to begin the canvass.

Almost on cue, hundreds of people chanting C-o-o-ry! . . . C-o-o-ry! . . . C-o-o-ry! locked arms to form a cordon—two human chains 3 feet apart. I found myself in the middle. Several hundred feet they snaked, the ballot box weaving between them . . . through the darkness and up two flights of stairs to the mouth of the chamber. From time to time I would steal a glance at their solemn faces. About what went on in shadowed places, about what went on in closed forums, perhaps they could do nothing, but here at least—within their view—there would be no switching, there would be no snatching.

For a week they watched and I watched as the tallying went on. I met a young woman, soon to be a lawyer, an opposition supporter from a political family. Just weeks before, her brother had been shot to death right in front of her house. Just days before, two bullets had found their way into her living room. *A campaign message.* "We will not tire," she told me.

"People Power?" Perhaps it required just the right storybook mixture of ingredients: a relentless yet engaging dictator bluffed by an American TV interviewer into calling an election early one Sunday morning; a nouveau riche First Lady with 3000 pairs of shoes; a martyred exile who would not die in vain; his fiercely determined widow with 12 yellow dresses; a suffocated yet proud people who had finally had enough. . .

And a smile from Above.

# GAMBLING ON GLASNOST: A CHRONICLE OF CURRENT EVENTS

## an interview

**Editors' Note:** Recent developments in the U.S.S.R. led us to assemble a panel of Soviet watchers to help explain them. These experts ply their trade in the Munich offices of Radio Free Europe and Radio Liberty. Keith Bush is director of Radio Liberty Research, Vladimir Kusin is acting director of Radio Free Europe Research, Elizabeth Teague is a specialist in Soviet politics at Radio Liberty, and Vera Tolz is a specialist in Soviet media at Radio Liberty. RFE/RL president Gene Pell, a distinguished journalist and foreign correspondent who has worked in the U.S.S.R., conducted the interview.

**Gene Pell:** *One of the most striking aspects of Mikhail Gorbachev's rule has been the transformation of the Soviet media. Party officials and government institutions that were once immune to criticism are, to varying degrees, now being criticized in Soviet newspapers and on television. Even the KGB has received its share of negative reporting on the front pages of* Pravda—*something that would have been unthinkable a few months ago. Subjects that were once taboo, from drug addiction to prostitution, from dismal grain harvests to official corruption, are being discussed. Natural and man-made disasters have been reported with a speed and in*

*a detail never undertaken before. Soviet television screens now show everything from battle scenes in Afghanistan to favorable reports on McDonald's hamburgers in America, from Soviet emigrants criticizing the country they left behind to performances of heavy metal rock groups.*

*This new mood of public tolerance is by no means confined to the media. In the human rights area, Andrei Sakharov has been freed from internal exile and more 200 political prisoners have been released.*

*What is going on, and why, and what are the potential consequences of this phenomenon known as "glasnost"—or openness—to the USSR, its people, and to the West?*

**Vera Tolz:** Mikhail Gorbachev did not invent glasnost. Lenin talked about it as a tool for controlling management and directors of enterprises. Gorbachev started this campaign to control the same people.

Soviet intellectuals support openness as a tool not for controlling bureaucrats, but for reinvigorating Soviet society. Without openness, without truth, they believe Soviet society will continue to be demoralized, and productivity affected.

Glasnost reappeared in the Soviet Union in a new context in the mid-sixties. It was one of the main demands of

the newly born human rights movement. A group of Moscow and Leningrad intellectuals started to emphasize the need to tell the truth about the history of Russia, the history of the Soviet Union, and to publish more books by Russians, including forbidden classics. During the Brezhnev era these voices were not heard at all. The result of the Brezhnev period was stagnation in all spheres of Soviet life. The leadership began to understand that without some kind of fresh air, the Soviet Union would become a second-rate country. That view was shared by many dissidents and was emphasized in Sakharov's writings.

These concerns were taken into account, and they have now become official policy. The first signs appeared under Andropov, but the formal campaign, glasnost, began with Gorbachev. Its main purposes have been well specified in his speeches.

In one speech, he connected glasnost to the country's economic performance. He said that without telling the truth, you can't boost morale and, therefore, productivity.

**Pell:** *Is economic reform the motivating factor?*

**Keith Bush:** Yes. On several occasions

## 6. COMMUNICATIONS

Gorbachev has said explicitly that glasnost is a precondition for bringing the Soviet Union up to the technological level of the West. He has tied economic progress to access to information.

**Elizabeth Teague:** We now know the enormous extent to which statistics were falsified by managers in the Brezhnev era. Moscow itself couldn't believe the statistics. The system was becoming a victim of its own monopoly on information.

In your introduction, Gene, you mentioned the transformation of the media. It is important to understand the role the press plays in the Soviet Union. It is openly propagandistic, and its purpose is to shape public opinion, not to respond to it.

At the end of the Brezhnev years, as the Soviet population was becoming better educated, the gap grew between reality and what appeared in the press. As more people got television sets, the fact that Soviet television was late with the news gave Western radio broadcasts an edge over the Soviet version of events. The population grew more cynical. People simply did not believe what they read and they turned to Western broadcasts and Western ideas. That was thought to be a very dangerous trend. Among Soviets, there is a tremendous thirst for knowledge of the outside world, particularly the West. A credibility gap existed.

**Pell:** *It's one thing to talk about the release of accurate economic data as a spur to development, or to talk about unmasking corruption that impedes development. But to go beyond that to the public tolerance that now seems to be evident is quite a leap, is it not?*

**Teague:** There's been a big change in the Soviet population over the years, and the Soviet media have not kept up with it. People now have some sense of their rights, and of what they want out of life. They're not living at a subsistence level anymore. The gradual introduction of modern technology into the workforce has meant that you cannot terrify people into working as Stalin did.

To work on a modern production line, you need intelligent, well-educated workers with initiative. Chernobyl is cited often as an example of people acting irresponsibly in a devil-may-care way. Because people had nothing to believe in, they didn't give a damn about the consequences of the slackness, the idleness, and the carelessness that run throughout Soviet society.

**Bush:** This has had a profound impact on Gorbachev's thinking. His chief economic adviser is A.G. Aganbegyan, the noted reformer. He headed the Siberian section of the Academy of Sciences and has run the most informative Soviet economic journal for years. He is aware of these problems. One of his closest associates, Tatiana Zaslavskaya, has put forth the thesis that Liz enunciated. The workforce has changed qualitatively; it's not enough any more to give people orders and minimum subsistence. They're better educated, more sophisticated, and much more demanding.

**Vladimir Kusin:** Glasnost is yet another Communist attempt at self-repair. Gorbachev himself is reputed to have said the Soviet ship of state was not sinking,

ation of censorship or augmentation of the amount of information is possible, without necessarily exposing the system to undue risk. Communism is a very wasteful system, and waste can be cut without harming the basis of the system.

**Pell:** *What are the effects of the criticism and/or the new flow of information?*

**Teague:** Gorbachev seems to have succeeded in gaining support from certain significant members of the intelligentsia. But the masses still feel some antipathy. For decades any criticism of the system—or even of the people above you—was regarded as dread dissent and was harshly punished. It's very difficult for ordinary people to adjust to glasnost. They're confused by it.

---

> Several of Gorbachev's recent moves have been acts of desperation. The Sakharov move was one. Although the reforms he's trying to introduce are not new and do not go far enough . . . they are running into monumental resistance . . . . At every single level, there are people putting up as much resistance as they can.
>
> **Elizabeth Teague**

---

but it certainly was taking on water. Glasnost is only one of several instruments that Gorbachev is using to set it upright, and on course.

In saying that, one is also defining the limits of glasnost as an instrument. It is seen neither as a human right, nor as something intrinsic to Soviet society. It's a tool that's being used to attain certain goals. There are other such instruments.

There are two major components of glasnost: criticism and information. Both are connected to individuals and also to the institutional performance of the state, the economy, and the party.

Criticism is not new. What's new is who's using it and for what purpose. Glasnost is mainly an instrument in the hands of a group of new Soviet leaders to get rid of a group of old Soviet leaders.

In a system where even the innocuous and the silly have long been considered taboo, and where the obvious has been kept away from the public, where black has been consistently painted pink, and where the efforts to seal the society off from foreign-based information have largely failed, a certain relax-

**Pell:** *There's one group that is supporting the policy and one that is displaying antipathy, but is there any open resistance?*

**Kusin:** Yes. The recent riots in Kazakhstan point to two problems Gorbachev faces. One is the implementation of glasnost and the other is the friction, often outright hostility, of Soviet ethnic groups toward the Russian leadership.

**Teague:** The resurgence of nationalism presents a threat to the regime in the republics, in the western borderlands, and particularly in the Baltic states. There are already signs that people are using glasnost to press for the use of their native languages and not the Russian language. That's not what Gorbachev had in mind. The regime may feel obliged to limit glasnost because of nationalism.

### Is the Party Over?

**Pell:** *There have been a few suggestions that the glasnost campaign has gone too far. Gorbachev reprimanded* Pravda *a few months ago for criticizing the special privileges that the nomenklatura (the party elite) enjoy.*

**Tolz:** When openness threatens the in-

> When openness threatens the interests and privileges of the most powerful people in the country, or when it undermines the basic elements of Soviet ideology, it is not tolerated.
>
> **Vera Tolz**

terests and privileges of the most powerful people in the country or when it undermines the basic elements of Soviet ideology, it is not tolerated. In a country where atheism is part of the ideology, some of the intellectuals tried to praise religion in the Soviet press. They were strongly reprimanded. Even the poet, Yevgeny Yevtushenko, who has more personal freedom to talk about what he wants than other Soviet citizens, was strongly criticized for advocating freedom of religion in Soviet society.

**Pell:** *What are some of the other taboo areas? Military subjects, of course, are not discussed.*

**Bush:** Almost half of Soviet history is still taboo.

**Teague:** The party is still sacrosanct and immune from criticism. But there is pressure to rid the party of the inert bureaucratic layer that everybody admits is at its center. Gorbachev is pushing to get these people out, but without destroying the party in the process. He can't wash too much dirty linen in public without having to admit that the one party system itself has become a brake on development. That's very difficult.

**Bush:** Once you let the genie out of the bottle, it's very difficult to put it back.

**Kusin:** Having seen glasnost wax and wane in front of my very eyes, I wouldn't agree that it is irreversible. It is not.

**Teague:** Glasnost is, in a way, the leadership deciding what the population needs to know. The idea that people have a *right* to know is simply not accepted in the Soviet Union.

In the Soviet Union, any right or privilege can be taken away. The leadership may decide that you no longer need to know this year what you needed to know last year.

**Pell:** *In other words, whether you're permitted to say more or say less, you still need permission.*

**Tolz:** One of the main reasons this campaign started was their lack of control over information coming from the West. Glasnost was one way to limit it. The Soviet leadership realized that it's better to supply people with information in the shape the government prefers and to distract them from Western broadcasts, where information is provided in a way the government does not like.

**Bush:** They cannot stop the flow of VCR cassettes. There are about 300,000 VCRs now in the country. If they can't beat them, they join them. So they are now making their own.

### The Cultural Arena

**Pell:** *The new mood of public tolerance is not limited to the information sphere. What about the cultural arena—the rehabilitation of authors, a new permissiveness in the theater and the cinema? Are these part of the same picture?*

**Tolz:** Because the Soviet people are deprived of traveling, and even of normal social and political activity, these cultural initiatives are very important. Culture is always a top priority for the Soviet people.

Many Soviet intellectuals who had never cooperated with the regime started to praise official Soviet policy, because Gorbachev allowed liberalization in cultural affairs.

**Kusin:** Cultural expression is a fundamental human need. Some of the films that were apparently shelved for a number of years are now coming to the cinemas. It will take several years to see whether this move is genuine or a short-term measure to obtain the support of an important group, the intellectuals.

**Tolz:** Russian culture stimulates people's pride in their homeland. There is less and less reason for many Soviet people to be proud of their country. Liberalizing the culture was designed to stimulate pride.

### Eastern Europe Reacts

**Pell:** *Has glasnost created a ripple effect in Eastern Europe?*

**Kusin:** Certainly. There were times when, if they had colds in Moscow, all the East European countries sneezed obligingly and, if possible, in unison. That was that.

Slavish imitation is not the rule now, for Eastern Europe is no longer the monolithic projection of Soviet power that it was thirty years ago. In Hungary and Poland, glasnost existed long before Gorbachev.

In Hungary, glasnost is a spinoff from economic reform, only gradually becoming something more political. Glasnost was not decreed there, but it arose from the nooks and crannies of the reform process.

In Poland, of course, they had a tremendous upsurge of openness and freedom of expression during the Solidarity period. Not all of that could be taken from the people when Solidarity was crushed.

Paradoxical as it may sound, the Polish press is perhaps the freest press in Eastern Europe. In Poland there's a mixture of the officially tolerated glasnost and tolerance of independent sources of information—Solidarity and the Catholic church.

East Germany rejects glasnost. They consider Gorbachevian reforms as inapplicable simply because there is no need for them. They have not opened their press at all.

Rumania is paying lip service to glasnost. There is obviously more in the press now than there was before, but at a very low level.

Bulgaria and Czechoslovakia attempt to imitate the Soviet Union, but one has the feeling that glasnost and reform are two different things there. Glasnost is just another duty that, because it comes from Moscow, has to be followed.

Unlike the Soviet Union, the leaders of yesterday are still leaders of today in Eastern Europe. Gorbachev is using glasnost to get rid of people in the establishment. That tendency must be blunted in Eastern Europe lest it cut into live flesh.

### Sakharov's Release

**Pell:** *Why do you think Sakharov was released, and how does that fit into the pattern we've been discussing?*

**Bush:** Again, Gorbachev wants the intelligentsia on his side, because he faces a tremendous and protracted battle to break through bureaucratic obstacles—the Party and state apparatchiks. He needs the intelligentsia. One clever move is to release Sakharov and the other political prisoners. I wouldn't be surprised to see further amnesty for other prisoners of conscience.

**Pell:** *And the effect in the West is positive?*

**Bush:** When you stop doing something you shouldn't have done in the first place, you get tremendous kudos in the West.

**Pell:** *But is the purpose to influence opinion in the West or is that only a useful byproduct?*

**Bush:** It's a by-product. Glasnost itself is primarily internal. The Soviets have conducted extremely effective public relations policies in the West, not only in projecting their image, but also in interviews and press conferences. They are being friendly and accessible. Sometimes they've outperformed the West at their own game.

**Kusin:** They are now selling glasnost to the West as a great attainment.

**Teague:** Some role is being given to public opinion in very circumscribed areas. Where it's fashionable at the moment is in ecology. Most of the left wing parties in the West are strongly biased ecologically, so Soviet efforts in this area do give them a boost with certain elements of Western public opinion.

**Pell:** *In Reykjavik, Gorbachev said that the American people were not well informed about the Soviet Union because they have no access to Soviet media. That is sort of turning the world on its head, but nonetheless, it's an argument he's making.*

### Monumental Resistance

**Teague:** Several of Gorbachev's recent moves and actions have been acts of desperation. The Sakharov move was one. Although the reforms he's trying to introduce are not new and do not go far enough to right the wrongs of the system, nonetheless they are running into monumental resistance. No one in Soviet society really favors the reforms. At every single level, there are people putting up as much resistance as they can.

The working class is not helped by glasnost. Workers are not interested in books and movies. What does it matter to a worker in a town with one 300-seat cinema if films about Stalin are shown in Moscow? They're interested in better housing and food. Under the new reforms, their wage differentials are going to be widened, their pay packets are going to be cut. If Gorbachev does what he wants, Soviet workers will experience job insecurity. They're going to

have to put up with unemployment, shift work, and transfers. They will be moved from places where they're happy to cold places away from their roots.

Party members are going to have to work a lot harder, too. They're going to have to do without their privileges. There's this new mood of Puritanism. And it's very uncomfortable for them.

Plant managers are going to have to pay for their mistakes through their pay packet, something they've never had to do before.

Ministries' powers are being cut back, too. A lot of Moscow bureaucrats are going to lose their jobs if the reforms go through.

In seventy years of Soviet power, almost everybody—one way or another—has managed to find a niche in the system. They don't have our freedoms, our choices, or our standard of living, but they cling to what they've got. They've found a way to survive with the system, mostly by going around it, not by working within it.

**Pell:** *If it takes three to five years to determine the consequences of glasnost, and if the short term is fraught with danger, one might not be too surprised if at some point a new general secretary were selected.*

**Tolz:** Gorbachev understands that in the short run it will be difficult. But he hopes that in the long run glasnost will bring good results.

Still, some of the intelligentsia are against liberalization. For example, the Soviet writer Georgi Markov said that the system doesn't need any changes. Obviously, he is a very bad writer. When Pasternak's *Dr. Zhivago* is published, it will become more obvious that Markov is a bad writer. If good books aren't published, then bad writers like Markov can survive.

**Kusin:** Gorbachev has set out on the right road—perhaps the only one that he can take short of a revolution or a war.

**Pell:** *Is too much being made of glasnost in the West?*

**Kusin:** The proposed changes are profound. But the road to Heaven is paved

with good intentions, and Soviet leaders have paid the price for this before. If Gorbachev could push through half of them—it would be magnificent.

**Pell:** *No one around the table believes that glasnost is simply another ploy for Western consumption?*

**All:** No.

**Teague:** They can't really afford that.

First, the more the Soviet Union looks like Western societies, by covering up or blurring the most glaring discrepancies, the more the outside world may give credence, or at least a favorable hearing, to their propaganda efforts.

Second, it may have a positive effect on their own people. Cynicism at home about leadership may decrease if the new men in the Kremlin continue on this course, and if they alleviate or eliminate the sore points—human rights and Afghanistan, for example.

Third, they could make human rights and emigration issues less prominent in the Western media. The world's attention span is limited even in the best of circumstances.

**Pell:** *Do you let Sakharov out because you want to make a good impression on the West, or do you let him out because you think he may support your reform policy at home?*

**Teague:** You certainly don't let him out from the goodness of your heart, but externally, it's a good thing.

**Tolz:** Sakharov formulated the position well when he was asked how the West should react. He said that the West should put pressure on and criticize the Soviet Union. On the other hand, it should encourage the reforms, and give some support to Gorbachev.

In a situation with this much built-in resistance, Gorbachev needs anyone, especially famous people, to support him. He expected Sakharov to support and to participate in this campaign.

**Kusin:** The last thing that he expects or needs is Radio Free Europe/Radio Liberty praising him.

**Pell:** *Well, you just did.* [Laughter]

**Teague:** There is a quotation from Nikolai Chernyshevsky in the 1860s about a glasnost campaign that was going on

---

> When you stop doing something you shouldn't have done in the first place (imprisoning Sakharov and others), you get tremendous kudos in the West.
>
> ### Keith Bush

---

The destiny of glasnost depends on the fate of Gorbachev, and I give him a 50/50 chance to succeed.

Vladimir Kusin

then. He said that glasnost was a bureaucratic substitute for free speech. While I would like to be optimistic, we've seen the genie put back in the bottle before.

**Bush:** By traumatic means, like Stalin's terror of the 1930s or the war.

**Pell:** *How far do you think they will allow glasnost to go? There have been suggestions that Western newspapers will be sold in Moscow kiosks, and that there will be further exchanges of radio and television programs.*

**Bush:** I wouldn't be surprised if they stopped jamming certain Western broadcasts, but they will continue to jam others. I would be surprised if they sold the *New York Times* or *Washington Post* in kiosks. But, they have published longer articles from Western newspapers in Soviet journals, something not done a year ago. So this is a step forward.

**Teague:** I'm pessimistic. I would like to see the initiative and creativity of the people given room to grow. But I think the atmosphere of fear and deprivation in which most people grew up is still the biggest opposition to the modernizing changes that Gorbachev wants to make, not only the radical changes that let people's initiative and creativity blossom.

**Tolz:** It is very difficult to predict, because with this country, you can't know what will happen tomorrow. I don't know if Gorbachev will survive and be able to continue this policy.

**Kusin:** Vera stole my line. I was going to say the destiny of glasnost depends on the fate of Gorbachev, and I give him a 50/50 chance to succeed. If he succeeds, then I feel it can go far, because he can take a lead in the positive and the negative sense, from the examples of Poland and Hungary. The limits of glasnost are now well defined. They must stop short of eroding the fundamentals of the Communist system. It's difficult to stop, because openness tends to have a life and logic of its own.

The fundamentals of the system are: The Communist party's leading role and absolute power over decision making; the preservation of the Soviet Union as a multinational state in its present borders, which includes the question of nationalism and the treatment of it; the preservation of the Soviet Union's status as a world superpower, and the prevalence at all times of collective or state property and a collectivist ideology.

Now when glasnost begins to encroach on these four areas, it will be resisted, and if they can't preserve the system, it will be stopped.

Can we expect the leopard to change its spots immediately? They have to start somewhere, so they start by dispensing information and imparting or encouraging criticism. It's a first step on a difficult, long road. Gorbachev may turn out to be another Brezhnev in three, four, or five years if the reforms do not work.

Glasnost is a different animal from the freedoms that are considered intrinsic and pertinent in the West. But I still thank God for what little the leadership has started doing. May God, in whom they don't believe, keep them on the same road.

# Human Values

The final unit of this book considers how humanity's view of itself is changing. Values, like all other elements discussed in this anthology, are dynamic. Therefore, as other factors change, so do values.

Novelist Herman Wouk, in his book *War and Remembrance*, notes that there have been many institutions so embedded in the social fabric that the people of the time assumed they were part of human nature. Slavery and human sacrifice are two examples. However, forward-thinking people have opposed these institutions. Many knew they would never see the abolition of these systems within their own lifetimes, but they pressed on in the hopes that someday these institutions would be eliminated. Wouk believes the same is true for warfare. He states, "Either we are finished with war or war will finish us." Behaviors such as warfare, slavery, racism, and the secondary status of women are creations of the human mind; history suggests that they can be changed by the human spirit.

The articles of this unit have been selected with the previous six units in mind. A good example of the inter-relationship of themes between articles is Prafulla Mohanti's description of village life in India in unit 4 and Professor Broomfield's analysis of Gandhi's role in traditional India in this unit. Gandhi's principal concern, Broomfield writes, was "the construction of an economic and political order in which the peasantry could have a full role." This struggle, to provide the disenfranchised with an opportunity to influence the events that shape their lives, continues today.

It was feminist Susan B. Anthony who once remarked that "social change is never made by the masses, only by educated minorities." The redefinition of human values (which, by necessity, will accompany the successful confrontation of other global issues) is a task that few people take on willingly. Nevertheless, in order to deal with the dangers of nuclear war, overpopulation, and environmental degradation, educated people must take the broad view of history. This is going to require considerable effort and much personal sacrifice.

When people first begin to consider the challenges of contemporary global problems, they often become disheartened and depressed: What can I do? What does it matter? Who cares? There are no easy answers to these questions, but people need only look around to see good news as well as bad. How individuals react to the world in which they live is not a function of that world but a reflection of themselves. Different people react differently to the same world. The study of global issues, therefore, is a study of people, and the study of people is a study of values. Hopefully, people's reactions to these issues (and many others) will help provide them with some insight into themselves as well as the world at large.

## Looking Ahead: Challenge Questions

What values helped to eradicate smallpox? Can the lessons from this success be applied to other global problems?

Are there any similarities between Gandhi's struggle for Indian independence and the efforts to overturn apartheid?

How do the values of the United States differ from those of other countries (e.g., Japan, China, etc.)?

Is it naive to speak of politics and economics in terms of ethics?

How will the world be different in the year 2038? What factors will contribute to these changes? What does your analysis reveal about your own value system?

# Smallpox: Never Again
## (The Lessons Learnt)

## Dr Donald A. Henderson

Dr Donald A. HENDERSON is the Dean of the School of Hygiene and Public Health at the Johns Hopkins University, Baltimore, USA.

Smallpox is the first disease to have been eradicated through a concerted global effort. Although this is a stupendous achievement in itself, it also has broader implications for health policy in demonstrating the impact which a community-based programme can have in the field of prevention, the considerable resources that can be mobilised for such an effort, the value of setting measurable goals and monitoring the incidence of disease, and the remarkable cost-benefit advantages of prevention programmes. It is in part because of smallpox eradication that increased emphasis is now being given to disease prevention and health promotion programmes throughout the world. Specific, measurable goals in national and local health programmes are being more widely identified and used in management, and health authorities are increasingly adopting surveillance and sample survey techniques that were elaborated during smallpox eradication.

It was in 1958, that a Soviet delegate to the World Health Assembly proposed that global smallpox eradication be undertaken by WHO, and this was unanimously approved at the following year's Assembly. At that time, 60 per cent of the world's population still lived in areas where smallpox was endemic. During the succeeding seven years, some progress was made in improving vaccine quality and a number of countries became free of smallpox, but the disease, often in epidemic form, continued to be widespread.

Delegates at the Nineteenth World Health Assembly (1966) allocated special funds for an intensified programme starting in January 1967. They proposed a ten-year goal for the achievement of eradication. At that time, an estimated 10 to 15 million cases of smallpox were occurring annually in 31 endemic countries with a population of more than 1,000 million persons. Given that programmes would have to be conducted in most of the least developed countries, that disruptions due to civil strife, famines and floods were inevitable, and that more than a century and a half had already elapsed since Edward Jenner's discovery of a vaccine, the goal was an optimistic one. Nevertheless, the last known endemic case occurred just 10 years, 9 months and 26 days after the programme began.

The strategy of the programme was two-fold: to vaccinate at least 80 per cent of the population, and to establish systems for surveillance (case detection) and containment of outbreaks. Between 1967 and 1971, WHO-supported national programmes began in all endemic countries and in others that were at special risk of importations. All programmes functioned within the public health structure and each differed from the others in order to cope best with different epidemiological patterns of smallpox, national administrative practices and socio-cultural conditions.

After the occurrence of the last known smallpox cases, health officials in all countries had to be sufficiently confident of eradication that they could stop vaccination. So surveillance programmes and special search activities were conducted for at least two years in every country after the last known case had occurred. At that time WHO-appointed International Commissions visited and verified the absence of smallpox. Finally, a WHO Global Commission, through a variety of studies, satisfied itself that eradication had been achieved, and its conclusions were endorsed by the Thirty-third World Health Assembly in May 1980.

It is sometimes suggested that the programme should serve as a template for other disease control or eradication compaigns. This is not

Reprinted from *World Health*, August/September 1987, pp. 8–11. World Health is the official illustrated magazine of the World Health Organization.

Photos WHO

within the existing public health structure rather than as an entirely separate entity as was the case with the earlier (and unsuccessful) malaria eradication campaign. It was thus obliged to work with and through the existing administrative health structure and to coordinate its activities with other programmes.

In addition, a specially dedicated and trained professional smallpox eradication programme staff was necessary at all levels to design and coordinate the programme; to develop reporting and surveillance systems; to undertake case-detection and containment measures, and to train local health staff. There was a need to seek the support of village leaders and, through them, the acceptance and participation of the population.

The observations have important implications to the strategy for providing what is called primary health care. Such care is usually regarded as a closely related set of services, all delivered in a similar manner, but experience suggests that it would be better conceptualised as consisting of two different but complementary components. One of these involves the traditional, primarily curative activities; the second involves those services intended to reach individuals throughout a community, including both preventive interventions (such as immunization or family planning) and curative ones (such as oral rehydration therapy). The traditional health care system may serve as the base for both functions but different types of programme, different personnel skills and different methods of assessment are required for each activity. Traditional, curative services can be provided in established health units by clinically-trained physicians and nurses, and are usually appraised in terms of the training of the practitioners, the quality and sophistication of facilities and the numbers treated. Community-wide programmes require active outreach by persons skilled in management and public education in order to ensure ac-

feasible, because each disease has its own epidemiological characteristics and methods for control which require strategies and tactics unique to that disease. But the rapid progress in eradicating smallpox after so many decades of persistent transmission provides principles and lessons which have implications for other health initiatives.

For a global programme to be undertaken, universal political commitment is necessary and, for this purpose, the World Health Organization and the World Health Assembly were essential. The Assembly uniquely provides the necessary forum for countries to agree on global health policies. WHO, alone among the international organizations, has the requisite scientific expertise and channels of

communication with national authorities for the monitoring and coordination of health programmes.

Smallpox eradication could not have been achieved were it not a targeted, time-limited special programme with funds specifically allocated for it, both in the WHO budget and in most national budgets, and with full-time technical staff responsible for its supervision. Yet some argue, even today, that special programmes are inherently poor policy, serving only to divert resources and attention from the development of primary health care systems. That such programmes can make important contributions to the development of national health services was demonstrated by the smallpox eradication programme. In part, this is because it functioned

More rapid progress might have been possible if, from the beginning there had been special staff to handle... public information. Wide publicity was needed to encourage national programmes and to recruit support from donors but WHO's public information office was inadequately staffed to... stimulate coverage by the mass media, thereby informing a broader public audience. Not until 1977 was a full-time public information officer added to the smallpox eradication unit. His value was immediately apparent. As a result of his efforts, it was eventually possible to foster public confidence that eradication had been achieved so that vaccination could be stopped.

*Dr D.A. Henderson, then chief of WHO's smallpox eradication unit, examining vaccination scars during casefinding operations in Ethiopia.*

ceptance; the provision of services at a site and time convenient to their clients; and methods such as surveillance to measure success in diminishing morbidity, mortality or fertility.

Special purpose programmes identifying the achievement of certain objectives, usually within a finite period of time, are generally better supported and financed than are programmes with less explicit goals. Experience shows that a programme to eradicate smallpox or to prevent poliomyelitis, for example, has more popular appeal than one to develop the basic health services. Such special-purpose programmes are particularly important to public health because it is almost always more difficult to obtain support for public health programmes than for curative services. This reflects a reality that political leaders are usually more readily persuaded to provide funds for the more tangible curative services (hospitals and health centres) than for community-based programmes.

*Surveillance teams tirelessly tracked down every case, no matter how remote the community.*

A finite end-point–the nil incidence of smallpox–undoubtedly was important in motivating staff and sustaining interest. Though few health programmes have such an end-point, comparable levels of achievement, interest and morale should be possible where specific goals are identified, where progress is monitored and where programme staff are fully supported in their efforts.

Extraordinary achievements are possible when countries throughout the world pursue common goals within the structure provided by an international organization. WHO played this role in the eradication of smallpox. It now offers a unique–although only partially realised–potential in promoting other efforts in disease prevention and health promotion. It is an organization which can demonstrably catalyse achievements far out of proportion to the resources it commands. The extent to which it is successful will depend upon the confidence it merits from its Member States, on the effectiveness of its leadership in enunciating clear and measurable objectives and in mobilising support to attain them, on the number and competence of its professional staff, and on its ability to set aside extraneous political agendas. WHO's ability to respond appropriately will determine the degree to which it succeeds in the future in providing improved health and a better quality of life for all the world's people.

# Children in South Africa's Jails

*Tales of detention and abuse suggest the crisis is far from over*

## Gay McDougall and James Silk

*Gay McDougall is the director of the Southern Africa Project of the Lawyers' Committee for Civil Rights Under Law in Washington, D.C. James Silk is a student at the Yale Law School and a summer intern in the Southern Africa Project.*

Imagine what it is like to be a parent in South Africa's black townships.

You cannot send your children to the grocery store without worrying that police will stop them, beat them, and arrest them for no reason.

If your children play in your own yard, they may be shot by police or military patrols roaming the neighborhood.

Police may come to your home in the middle of the night and take your sons and daughters away. Or troops may surround your children's school and arrest the entire student body.

Children in custody, who may never even be charged with a crime, can be beaten and tortured; you would be unable to learn if and where they are being held.

"Every mother is crying about what is happening in our country," said Sylvia Dlomo Jele, a South African mother whose 16-year-old son was held without charges for six months in 1986. Fighting to control her emotions, she spoke last month at a symposium on the detention and abuse of children in South Africa.

Mrs. Jele was one of the 15 witnesses who came from South Africa to testify at a recent summer symposium sponsored by the Southern Africa Project of the Lawyers' Committee for Civil Rights Under Law. Members of Congress and other United States panelists, as well as an audience of several hundred, heard testimony from South African doctors, lawyers, ministers, a psychiatrist, a social worker, a teacher, parents, and children.

They presented a restrained, yet moving and detailed, account of the many children rounded up, abused, held without charge or notification of relatives and often held in solitary confinement and tortured by the South African security forces.

The government of South Africa would have the world believe otherwise. But its pronouncements cannot overcome the grim evidence of the continuing detention of young people.

On June 2, the government announced that it had released 269 children under the age of 16 who were being held without charge under the state of emergency regulations declared June 12, 1986.

For the 269 children, release from the cruel and mostly hidden cells of the South African security system was, of course, welcome.

Unfortunately, like so much in the "reform" proclaimed by the government of South Africa, these releases are far too little, too late.

- It is so for the children released. For them, unjust detention has already taken a heavy physical and emotional toll.
- The same holds true for an estimated 10,000 others, those children under the age of 18 detained under the emergency decree of a year ago. Their scars have been well documented by South African, international, and U.S. human rights groups.
- And it is clearly too little, too late for the 200 children who, according to the New York-based Lawyers Committee for Human Rights, were killed by police in "unrest" incidents in 1985 alone.

Countless South African children continue to be brutalized by the repressive instruments of apartheid.

A representative of the Detainees'

Parents Support Committee, the most reliable detention monitoring group in South Africa, estimates, based on the government's own figures, that approximately 1,000 young people under the age of 18 are still in detention under the year-old emergency regulation.

That figure does not include children who have been jailed without charges or trials under other repressive laws, such as the Internal Security Act. The figure does not include young people who have been charged with political offenses such as distributing banned literature or attending an "illegal" gathering.

And more children are being taken into custody every day.

The stories of detention, torture, and killing have a horrible redundancy. In time, no one story stands out from the others.

Patrick Makhoba testified at the symposium about his detention. He was 16 when security forces surrounded the school where he and six of his friends were talking.

Patrick was kept in solitary confinement for 39 days. He was interrogated nearly every day, mostly to get the names of students involved in anti-apartheid activities like school boycotts. Sometimes, he said, he was handcuffed and pinned against a wall with a table pushed against his waist; police sometimes jumped up on the table and beat him as they asked questions.

At one point, Patrick said, police officers told him that his parents were in detention and that his little brother had been shot. It was not true, but Patrick had no way of knowing that.

After 42 days in detention, Patrick was told to go. He was never charged with any crime, nor given an explanation as to why he had been detained.

Documents tell the story of an 11-year-old who was awakened by policemen at 2 A.M. one day last October. They took him and his 14-year-old sister to a van already holding eight other children. They were driven to the police station, put in cells, and deprived of food for 16 hours.

The next day, the 11-year-old was interrogated. Even when he said he was not involved in the burning of cars and schools in the township, a policeman beat him. He lost four teeth. After almost four weeks, he was transferred to a prison. His face was swollen and he was unable to eat, but he was never allowed to see a doctor.

There were 28 other detainees in the same cell, 20 of them adults. One day the police took him back to the police station, put him in a dark room, attached wires to his hands and feet, and turned on the current. Two months later, he was released. He was never charged with a crime. He never appeared in court.

The stories appear endless. One child is beaten with fists and rifle butts. Another simply disappears. One is tortured with electric shocks to the spine. Another is threatened with being burned alive. One is hit by police buckshot while playing in the street. Another is shot in the back while under arrest.

No, despite the impression the South African government seeks to create, the crisis of children in South Africa's jails is far from over.

Under South Africa's draconian Internal Security Act and the State of Emergency regulations, renewed and tightened on June 11, people—minors included—can be detained because they are a "threat to state security" or for purposes of interrogation.

They can be held indefinitely, incommunicado, and with virtually no recourse to the courts. Legal protections that most people take for granted such as "due process," even for criminals, are denied to innocent children in South Africa.

As a result, parents go from police station to jail to hospital looking for their young sons and daughters. The children are often held in inhuman conditions for long periods of time and are tortured and denied access to their families, lawyers, and medical care; when they are released, eventually, they are charged with no crime but have been deeply wounded, physically and emotionally.

It is difficult to talk of justification for these horrible acts. In the words of a report issued by the Detainees' Parents Support Committee, the aim is "to strike fear and terror into the hearts and minds of the children detained and those who escape the detention dragnet. Part of this is the deliberate humiliation and denigration of the children who are detained."

The National Medical and Dental Association, an independent South African organization, whose doctors have examined hundreds of ex-detainees, found that children who have been detained tend to live in a distorted world, unable to play or socialize in normal ways. "Especially devastating," the group concluded, "is that they are hurled into an adults' world that is violent, abusive, and destructive and in which they are at the receiving end in a helpless and powerless state."

South Africa presents itself as a Western-style democracy trying to solve its problems. But a country that aims to rob its children of their hope, their dignity, their promise, can make no claim for the respect or patience of other nations.

Sen. Barbara Mikulski (D) of Maryland, Rep. William Gray III (D) of Pennsylvania, and Rep. Cardiss Collins (D) of Illinois have introduced resolutions calling on the government of South Africa to release immediately all children detained under the state of emergency regulations. Congress should pass these resolutions without delay.

Beyond that the U.S. must stop giving comfort and support to South Africa. The U.S. must see South Africa's victimization of its children for what it is—one piece of the desperate effort to maintain apartheid. The U.S. should reject all ties with the South African regime.

Congress, by passing the new comprehensive sanctions legislation that has been introduced this year, would send a strong message to South Africa: Let the children go.

# How the Japanese Beat Us in School

## Fiercely competitive academics come first

GREG SHERIDAN

THE AUSTRALIAN

The U.S. and Australia, dissimiliar in so many ways, are similar in two deceptively linked spheres. Both are facing an economic crisis that grows out of international competitiveness, and both have remarkably similar school systems.

Both countries are experiencing enormous trade deficits, especially with Japan, Taiwan, Hong Kong, and South Korea. And both the U.S. and Australia have experienced similar education reforms in the past 10 to 15 years, reforms that make their education systems almost the opposite of the Japanese system. The question is: Do education and economic performance interact?

Increasingly, cultural explanations are being advanced for the economic miracle of Japan and the other east Asian societies, as indeed they must be for the success of the West Germans. It is not just the effective use of governmental macroeconomic tools that produces economic and social success, but also the ability of the people to respond to opportunities.

More and more U.S. business leaders believe their education system is contributing directly to their economic woes and that it is threatening to bury the U.S. in a trough of intellectual and cultural mediocrity from which it may never emerge. In 1983, a special presidential commission produced a bomb-

Excerpted from the conservative "Australian" of Sydney.

shell report entitled, "A Nation at Risk," which sparked a move for education reforms. Its broad conclusions were endorsed by similar studies conducted by the Association of American Principals and, most recently, in a comparative study of the U.S. and Japanese education systems.

The reports have all found the same things: U.S. education has abandoned academic excellence as its primary goal. It has substituted therapeutic and social goals for intellectual ones; it tries to make children feel good about themselves, effectively encouraging them to take courses that are not too demanding and, therefore, do not carry the threat of failure, thus blurring the distinction between success and failure.

The irony is that the U.S. system is not working as a tool of therapy either. Japan's fiercely competitive and rigorously academic school system is often blamed for putting so much pressure on students to succeed that many teenagers commit suicide. In fact, Japan's rate of teenage suicide is lower than America's. While strong discipline and pressure to succeed may cause anxiety and stress, so can a lack of discipline and the associated problems of playground violence and drug abuse.

One stark fact is that Japan's schoolchildren and teachers work much, much harder than those in the U.S. or Australia. While Japan's school year is about 240 days long, in the U.S. it is about 180 days long. In their short summer break, Japanese schoolchildren must complete many homework

assignments; U.S. and Australian schoolchildren do no schoolwork over their long summer break.

The Japanese education system is structured around a series of competitive examinations. No matter how well or poorly a child has been doing in school, it is the child's performance in these external exams that determines his or her future. If a child does well in the exam at the end of primary school, he or she will go to an academic high school or a prestigious private school. If the student does poorly, he or she might go to a vocational or technical school.

This system is anathema to modern U.S. and Australian educators. They believe that a child's options should not be limited when the child is young. Therefore, in the U.S. and Australian systems, the student gets chance after chance to re-enter the academic stream and to achieve high results. Virtually anyone who matriculates in Australia or the U.S. can go to college; this is not the case in Japan.

Yet the paradox is that the Japanese system, partly because of its rigidity, does much better in providing high-quality education to everybody. The exams, which have their down side in shunting off students to non-academic schools for doing poorly on one exam, nonetheless provide the incentive for sustained effort that is utterly lacking in the Australian and U.S. systems. In trying to craft a painless school system, American and Australian educators have come up with a vacuous system.

By Greg Sheridan, The Australian, Sydney. Reprinted from World Press Review, May 1987, pp. 32–33. World Press Review, 230 Park Avenue, New York, N.Y. 10169.

Japanese students study demanding subjects such as languages, mathematics, and physics in proportionately much greater numbers than do U.S. students. Only 6 percent of U.S. high school students study calculus.

"A Nation at Risk" concluded that the radical decline in the numbers of U.S. students studying intellectually demanding subjects was caused by the proliferation of choices in U.S. high schools. Students, being subject to the normal human impulse of laziness, tend to take soft subjects such as environmentalism or lifestyle courses or even, at the ridiculous extreme, disco dance appreciation, which was once an approved course in an Australian high school. For Japanese students these options do not exist.

Both U.S. and Australian pedagogical fashions dictate that subjects be immediately relevant to the students' environments so that students will find them interesting. This has been a catastrophic reform. It not only fails to broaden students' cultural horizons, but it clearly tends to favor the trivial over the substantial, the academically anemic over the key intellectual disciplines.

Similarly, the quality and training of Japanese teachers is better than that of U.S. or Australian teachers. In Confucian-influenced societies, education is valued very highly, and teachers and academics are greatly esteemed. High school teachers tend to have degrees in the subjects they teach, rather than in teaching methods. In the U.S. and Australia, the trend has been for more and more high school teachers to do their entire training in institutions dedicated to teaching teachers how to teach.

In Japanese society, the family — especially the mother — is intensely involved in the child's education. Married women with children participate much less in the Japanese work force than they do in the Australian or U.S. work forces. They are free to fulfill their traditional roles of educators and nurturers. Parents supervise homework and frequently forbid students much social life, for academic success is seen as the only road to financial and personal security. Even the best teachers in the U.S. and Australia are limited by lack of parental involvement and by homes that are not conducive to study.

In the past few years, the U.S. has seen a turning away from the education trends that have produced such disasters. There is more stress on a common curriculum. Some states have introduced longer school years, and others have introduced competence tests for teachers. Diversity is no longer the aim. A nationwide fight against slack discipline is underway.

Australian education generally apes U.S. education. We tend to do what the U.S. does, only a few years later. Whether Australia will follow the U.S. in this counter-reformation is unclear. Even in the U.S. the prospects of the new reform movement are not particularly good. It is easier to destroy a good education system than to recreate one.

In one key respect, the U.S. is much better off than Australia. U.S. students still do a series of objective tests, so that Americans at least have the data to plot their decline and on which to base a strategy to correct it.

Australia's education authorities, under the intimidation of militant teacher's unions, have refused to undertake this sort of systematic testing. It is the worst possible sort of intellectual cowardice, which prevents Australian education authorities from even determining the extent of the disaster.

As our trade problems and those of the U.S. continue to worsen, as the deficiencies of our work forces become more obvious, and as economic power flows from our societies and toward the industrious societies of Asia, we can reflect that a large part of the problem lies in the classroom.

# GANDHI
# A Twentieth-Century Anomaly?

John Broomfield

*John Broomfield is professor of history.*

Early one misty morning in January, 1941, a bearded figure, dressed as a Muslim, slipped away from a house on a Calcutta back street to begin what has become an epic journey in modern Indian history. Eluding the police and ultimately the British military on the frontier, he made his way across North India into Afghanistan, where he arranged with difficulty to be taken to Moscow and on to Berlin. There he persuaded the Nazis to provide him with the resources to raise an Indian regiment, which he hoped would spearhead the armed liberation of his homeland. When it appeared that the Japanese were likely to reach India before the Germans, he made another journey, by submarine, to Southeast Asia, there to raise an Indian National Army. His troops saw action against the British in Burma before their leader died in an air crash in 1945.

This heroic figure was Subhas Chandra Bose, and his life story is in many ways typical of the twentieth-century revolutionary nationalist. Western-educated, with a university degree, he went in his late teens to the imperial metropolis, London, to compete successfully for a place in the ruling Indian Civil Service. At the moment of triumph, however, he renounced the opportunity and returned to India to join the new mass movement of resistance to British rule. In his twenties he organized militant youth brigades, reaching the height of his popularity during the civil disobedience campaigns from 1930 to 1932. He advocated the violent overthrow of the British and led paramilitary formations in displays of opposition to their imperialism. He was arrested, imprisoned, and externed for long periods, but from his jail cell in exile he continued to exhort his countrymen to rise in revolt against their oppressors.

In Bose we can see the likeness of many other twentieth-century revolutionaries: Mao, Ho, and Sukarno in Asia; Kenyatta in Africa; Madero and Castro in Latin America;

Venizelos, Husseini, and Grivas in the Eastern Mediterranean; Trotsky, De Valera, Tito, and Hitler in Europe. All were practitioners of the politics of militant confrontation, and all earned their periods of imprisonment or exile. All shared an ambition to mobilize sectors of their societies to effect the overthrow of perceived imperialisms, internal or external. All were attracted by military styles of organization and discipline, and all had faith in the efficacy of violence.

How striking the contrast if we consider Mohandas Karamchand Gandhi. During that same civil disobedience campaign of 1930 in which Subhas Bose led his young stormtroopers against the police, we find Gandhi on his Dandi salt march: a walk of 200 miles through village India to the seacoast to make salt, as a symbolic gesture of resistance to British rule. What a quaint figure we see in the photographs: a skinny, knobbly-kneed little man, dressed in a loin cloth, granny glasses perched on his nose, barefoot, setting forth with only a walking stick to assist him on a trek that would daunt most men of sixty. Here was a man leading a great political movement with watch cries of truth, love, self-suffering, abstinence, and nonviolence. Surely anomalous watch cries for the twentieth century, with its dynamic emphasis upon revolutionary uprising and violence. Perhaps Gandhi is an anomalous figure in this century? "In an era that takes matters of religious faith lightly," Susanne Rudolph has written, "it is difficult to consider a man who is suspected of saintliness." Yet it is Gandhi, not Subhas Chandra Bose or the many other Indian proponents of violence, who is best known outside, as well as inside, India.

Let us recap the main features of Gandhi's life to draw out the characteristics of his ideals and achievement. He was born in Kathiawar, an isolated northwestern peninsula, where his father was a princely state official. The

From *LSA*, Winter 1984, pp. 16-21. From MOSTLY ABOUT BENGAL: essay in modern South Asian History (New Delhi, Manohar, 1982) by John Broomfield. Copyright © 1982 J.H. Broomfield. Reprinted by permission.

"My experience," Gandhi wrote, "has shown me that we win justice quickest by rendering justice to the other party."

environment in which he was raised was one of orthodox Hinduism, and he was strongly influenced by the quietous principles of Vaisnavism and Jainism. His was an educated but not, we may fairly say, an intellectual family. He was put into that most favored of professions for the nineteenth-century Indian elites, the law, and, as few Indians in that century could hope to do, he was enabled to go to Britain in 1887 for extended legal education.

Gandhi's first months in London were cold, lonely, and uncomfortable (as his photographs of the period suggest: flannel suit, starched shirt, Victorian high collar, and all). It was not until he abandoned his legal studies and began to associate with a vegetarian, pacifist group that he discovered some warmth and friendship in that alien city. It was in this company that he rubbed shoulders with such European minds as Tolstoy, and with the American Thoreau. The mixed metaphor of shoulders and minds is appropriate, for Gandhi does not appear to have gained any deep understanding of these thinkers. They influenced him, but mainly by reinforcing established beliefs. The basis of his philosophy is to be sought within his own Indian traditions.

In 1891, having belatedly resumed his legal studies and passed the bar examinations, Gandhi returned to Bombay, where he was an instant and spectacular failure as a barrister. Rising in court to plead his first case, he found himself at a loss for words, and he was quickly demoted to office paper work. In 1893 his firm received a lucrative but routine request for legal counsel from a member of the Indian community in the Transvaal. The partners looked around for their most dispensable clerk — and dispatched Mr. Gandhi.

The experience in South Africa, though in origin so humdrum, was to work a transformation in Gandhi's life — a transformation so spectacular that it may be compared with that of Saul on the road to Damascus. Gandhi arrived in South Africa to be met with racial discrimination of a kind he had never experienced in India and Britain. It shook his faith in the fundamental justice and goodwill of the British imperial system. For a time he was at a loss for a course of action, but finally in May, 1894, goaded by the imminent disenfranchisement of his compatriots in Natal, he formed the Natal Indian Congress. The inarticulate young lawyer was gone; in his place stood an outspoken and courageous crusader against racial injustice.

For the next twenty years, up to the outbreak of the First World War, Gandhi worked in South Africa. In this land far from India, step by step, he fashioned his new revolutionary technique, to which he gave the name *satyagraha:* "soul force," which he contrasted with "brute force." His basic principle was *ahimsa:* non-violence. Non-violence in thought as well as deed, for Gandhi drew on a philosophical tradition that does not recognize that hard distinction between thought and action with which we are familiar in the West. Angry thoughts injure the thinker as well as those against whom they are directed. So Gandhi

insisted that love, not hatred, must be the guiding principle of political, as well as personal, action. One must empathize with one's adversary, seeking the good in him and his cause, and trying to eradicate whatever is evil — in self or opponent. The aim in politics, Gandhi emphasized, is to help one's opponent escape his error, as much as to advance one's own cause. The objective must be to heal social wounds, to establish a new basis for reconciliation and positive political action in the future, not to antagonize and polarize. "My experience," he wrote, "has shown me that we win justice quickest by rendering justice to the other party."

This did not mean that injustice from others should go unresisted. Indeed, Gandhi emphasized that non-violent resistance to oppression was a duty. Urging his fellow Indians in South Africa to united action in defense of their communal rights, his call was: "Not to submit; to suffer." Again he drew upon the traditions of his native Gujarat in applying to politics a technique of moral suasion used there in familial and mercantile disputes. The method was for the aggrieved party to shame his adversary and win sympathetic support for his cause by display of self-abnegation, most commonly fasting. With this model in mind, Gandhi devised a succession of non-violent confrontations with the South African authorities. The issues were diverse, and time and place varied greatly, but there was a common aim: to provide those in power with opportunities to demonstrate the injustice of their regime by forcing them to retaliate against limited, non-violent and symbolic acts of protest.

Gandhi achieved a surprising number of victories, but the long-term gains for the South African Indian community were negligible. For this reason the real significance of this period of Gandhi's work must be sought in the experience it gave him: as an organizer, tactician, and publicist. His trips to India and Britain in search of finance and support provided enduring contacts for his later work with the Indian National Congress, and the attention his movement attracted in the press assured him of fame among politically-aware Indians. He left South Africa in 1914 after a striking success against the Union Government. His opponent of many years, the Minister of the Interior, Jan Smuts, breathed a sigh of relief. "The saint has left our shores," he wrote. "I sincerely hope forever." It proved to be so.

Gandhi in India had bigger fish to fry — if one may use so inappropriate a metaphor for a vegetarian! The Indian nationalist movement to which he returned, and in which he was clearly determined to play a role, had developed rapidly in the preceding decade. If, for comparison's sake, we use the familiar categories of American Black nationalism, the Indian movement had developed from its late nineteenth-century NAACP stage, of a liberal

For Gandhi it was a dictum of politics that an unjust regime is bound to enlarge the area of conflict by its over-reactions to protest.

union of right-thinking people, through a period of marches and sit-ins, to economic campaigns to "Buy Black," accompanied by cultural revivalism ("Black is Beautiful"), and finally to the revolutionary call to arms: "Burn, Baby, Burn." As one might expect, such radical developments had split the Indian National Congress. Growing disunity and the failure of the Congress leaders to win mass support had convinced many nationalists of the need for a structural reorganization of their movement.

Into this situation Gandhi came with striking advantages. He had an established public reputation, but, unlike other prominent figures, he was free of factional identification. Moreover, he was an experienced organizer, with his own patented technique of agitational politics. Circumspect as ever, he bided his time. He spent the war years extending his network of political contacts, but steadfastly resisted the temptation to be drawn into their factional squabbles. He chose his own distinctive point of entry into the Indian political arena, initiating a peasant *satyagraha* against the British indigo planters of northern Bihar in 1918. The indigo industry he attacked was uneconomic and had been maintained only by blatant exploitation of the peasant cultivators. His *satyagraha* was a rapid and complete success, and its publicity precipitated him into the front rank of nationalist leaders.

For Gandhi it was a dictum of politics that an unjust regime is bound to enlarge the area of conflict by its overreactions to protest. The months following his Bihar movement seemed to prove him right. Disturbed by industrial and peasant unrest, and with a weather-eye on Bolshevik successes in Russia, the government of India insisted upon arming itself with legislation to extend its war-time powers of summary action against suspected conspirators. Gandhi responded with a call to the Congress to organize nation-wide *hartals* (general strikes). April, 1919, brought mass protests in many cities of northern and western India, and, when violence erupted in the Panjab, a jittery British administration retaliated brutally. In the bitter aftermath, Gandhi was able to persuade the Congress to accept his blueprint for reorganization and his leadership of a mass campaign of non-cooperation.

It is instructive to observe the elements Gandhi emphasized in the program he advanced, for it will give some measure of the principles that were to guide his three decades of political work in India. In the first place he proposed that all participation in the activities and institutions of British Indian government should cease, and that Congressmen should devote themselves to the construction of national institutions: "a government of one's own within the dead shell of the foreign government." Resistance, non-violent and symbolic, might be offered to particular acts of British oppression, but the really important work was in national reconstruction. For the nation as for the individual, Gandhi taught, salvation could be gained only by internal reformation. Society had to be rid of its evils, especially those of dissension and human exploitation. As a first step he called for reconciliation between religious communities, and he took up the Khilafat issue as a means of cementing Hindu-Muslim unity. He also demanded that caste barriers be broken down and that the untouchables be accepted into the body of Hinduism. Congressmen of all castes should work with the Harijans (the "Children of God," as Gandhi called them) to help them rise from their degradation.

Similarly, there had to be an end to economic oppression. Gandhi was adamant that self-government for India would be a travesty if the mass of people were not freed from the exploitation of capitalists, landholders, and money-lenders. The nationalist movement had to be the people's movement, to benefit the mass of the people. He insisted that Congress demonstrate its concern for the welfare of the Indian poor by adopting a program of economic rehabilitation. Congressmen should leave their urban professions and go into the villages to start cottage industry. The local manufacture of cotton cloth should be revived. The spinning wheel should become the symbol of India's new life, and the wearing of *khadi* (homespun) a gesture of the nation's rejection of imperialism.

In its initial states in the early months of 1921, the first non-cooperation movement was a remarkable success. The unprecedented numbers participating in the agitation — Muslims as well as Hindus — raised serious alarm among British officials. To the perplexity of many of his colleagues in the Congress hierarchy, however, Gandhi seemed to value opportunities for confrontation with the government less than those for popular or political education and social reform. His insistence on continually shifting the focus of the movement, and his prohibition of what to others seemed logical areas of agitation, e.g., industrial disturbances, frustrated even some of his closest followers. In part these shifts reflected his mature judgment of the need to keep the British off-balance; in part they were the product of a determination to maintain his personal domination of the movement; but, most of all, they reflected his deep concern to preserve non-violence. It was the conviction that he had failed to do this that led to his sudden call in February, 1922, for an end to the agitation.

Gandhi initiated two other great campaigns and a host of minor actions in the years before independence. Always he put major emphasis on ethical considerations, insisting doggedly that he alone must be their arbiter. Always he was unpredictable in his tactical decisions and in his timing of the final withdrawal. As a consequence, there were some who became totally exasperated with his leadership — Subhas Chandra Bose being amongst the most outspoken. We need not follow Gandhi step by step through these years, but we must surely ask: how could he retain his following despite such apparently eccentric political behavior? The question is the more intriguing when we realize that on a number of occasions he withdrew from active politics for five or more years at a time and yet was still able to emerge at his chosen moment to resume the leadership of the national movement.

One answer is that Gandhi was a phenomenal scribbler, a fact readily verified by a count of the number of volumes of his *khadi*-bound collected works, now threatening to engulf all but the largest libraries. His polemical writings filled his own newspaper and the columns of many others, year in and year out. He produced books on politics, religion, social organization, and his own life. During his great campaigns, his scribbled battle orders poured from every halting place; and from his *ashram* during his years of retreat the flow of advice, praise, cajolery, and (forgive the heresy) moralizing never ebbed. Gandhi knew the value of a good communication system, and he spared neither himself nor his assistants in his efforts to keep in touch.

He also knew the value of good lieutenants. It is paradoxical that while Gandhi was not particularly responsive to criticism (being too assured of the quality of his own judgment), he was willing to tolerate strong differences of opinion amongst his associates. Indeed it should be put more positively: he worked hard (often through painfully devised compromises) to prevent disagreements over ideology or strategy from driving able men and women out of the Congress.

As these two points suggest, Gandhi was an organizer *par excellence*. We should not be misled by the sainthood conferred upon him by popular mythology into thinking of him as some impractical, dreamy visionary. This was the man who took the ramshackle Indian National Congress of the second decade of the century, and rebuilt it as an effective nationwide organization, extending from a full-time working central executive, link-by-link, to representative committees in virtually every district of British India. At the high points of participation during the civil disobedience campaigns, the formal organization reached even to the villages. Though periodically weakened by the removal to prison of its office-bearers, it survived to provide independent India with a nationwide institution parallel to, and reinforcing, the governmental structure.

Another of Gandhi's personal attributes — one which he undoubtedly shared with other great politicians — was extraordinary physical and mental stamina. The seemingly frail old man could outwalk, outsit, and outtalk others half his age. We have amusing accounts from the second Round Table Conference in London of British Cabinet Ministers wilting perceptibly as Mr. Gandhi, calmly and quietly, talked on into the small hours of the morning. His slow, tireless methods drove foes, and sometimes friends as well, to distraction.

Lastly, Gandhi had what we can only describe as an amazing mass appeal. He was known to, and revered by, millions in urban and rural India, like no other figure in historic times. Wherever he went, the news of his coming spread far beyond the reach of the mass media. How could this be? The easy thing to say is: because of his charisma. But that is no answer, merely a rephrasing of the statement about his mass appeal. Gandhi was a master of symbolism, and here we may have a key. To say he was "a master of symbolism" is to make him sound more manipulative than I would intend. Rather, he had a keen sense of the political, social, and ethical fitness of a variety of symbols and symbolic acts.

Let us take some examples: The Dandi salt march of 1930, already mentioned, was one of his most brilliant, yet simple, symbolic successes. All humans need salt, and in many places in India salt can be produced with the simplest equipment, or even scraped up from dried pools or marshes. The British Indian government, however, levied a tax on salt and prohibited its unlicensed production. Obviously an attack on this restriction would be universally popular and would serve as an indictment of a regime

that taxed the basic needs of its pitifully poor colonial population. Brilliant in conception, equally brilliant in execution: a long march through village India, gathering thousands of supporters, drawing the attention of the world press to the moment by the sea when the imperial policemen would be forced to arrest India's most revered leader, and unmanageable numbers of his adherents, simply for lighting a fire and heating a pan of salt water.

Gandhi's choice of the spinning wheel and *khadi* to represent the revitalized Congress was a similar attempt to find symbols that would have emotive appeal across the many levels of Indian society. To the urban professional classes it was a call for a return to a more pure and traditional way of life. Discarding imported cloth offered them a way to make a visible sacrifice for the cause, while striking a blow at British economic domination. It also offered them an opportunity (not welcomed by all) for a symbolic union with the masses by donning common garb. For the peasantry, the spinning wheel was among the most sophisticated of their familiar instruments of production, and one which had frequently provided a marketable product to supply an income above their minimum needs. For generations past the sale of homespun had brought them a few good times and good things, but all too often of late their spinning wheels had lain unused, unable to compete with factory-made goods. In Gandhi's symbols they saw the promise of a restoration of a more just order.

Gandhi himself was a living symbol. His lifestyle expressed a traditional philosophy. To many he appeared as a humble ascetic, the pure man of the soil, fearless of his environment, because his own physical survival meant little to him. Confident and courageous, yet devoid of all defensiveness, even the defensiveness of blustering arrogance. This idealized stereotype owed much to the Indian tradition of the ascetic leader, a tradition in which Gandhi himself believed implicitly. He was at pains to project the image of the *brahmachari* (celibate). Although his rejection of worldly comforts was sometimes ostentatious (a puckish disciple is credited with the comment: "You have no idea how much it costs to keep Mahatmaji in the style of poverty to which he has become accustomed"), there can be no question that he was thoroughly sincere in his conviction that strength came through a renunciation of sensual indulgence. He accepted traditional Indian theories of physiology and psychology, which hold that the bodily essences giving physical, mental, and moral strength are dissipated through such outpourings as sex and anger, but increased by pure foods, particularly vegetables and milk products, and through disciplined meditation. Gandhi shared this belief with the vast majority of his fellow Hindus. They saw that he was a disciplined *brahmachari*, and they had no difficulty in understanding the source of his superior stamina and moral virtue.

He earned for himself the title *Mahatma:* a great soul. It is a title he disclaimed, but significant nonetheless, for it suggests a link with an Indian tradition of religious leadership that has been disregarded in measuring Gandhi's impact on twentieth-century India. This is the tradition of the religious ascetic combining spiritual instruction for a peasant community with the leadership of that community in rebellion against its oppressors: against (in Eric Hobsbawm's words) the "special form of brigand," the government, and against the lesser, but regrettably more familiar brigands: tax collectors, policemen, landlords, and moneylenders. Many Hindu folk tales and many of the most popular epics concern such rebel *gurus*, leading the fight against injustice. In more recent times, under Muslim rule and in the nineteenth century, there are many recorded cases of religious teachers, *sufis* and *bhaktas* particularly, providing leadership for local revolt. Gandhi could easily be understood by the peasant community as a great leader, a *mahatma*, in this tradition of protest.

As Eric Wolf has observed in *Peasants:* "Simplified movements of protest among a peasantry frequently center upon the myth of a social order more just and egalitarian than the hierarchical present." By attacking the hierarchical present, by symbolizing a resistance to the economic oppressions worked by intrusive modern technology and its accompanying innovations in the organization of labor, by using the language and symbolism of the popular Hindu tradition, Gandhi mobilized rural mass India in a way that would never have been possible had independence from Britain been the sum total of the Indian nationalist movement. It was his genius to have seen the need, and to have provided the means, to link together the urges of India's peasant masses with the struggle to expel the foreigner.

Here we touch the tragic core of Gandhi's life. He used symbolism brilliantly. He was a master of emotive religious imagery and the historical myths associated with his religion. But in a multi-religious and multi-cultural society, such an emphasis on one tradition, even if it is an unconscious emphasis expressed through a lifestyle, must inevitably give offense to some groups. We cannot be surprised, given the structure of Indian thought in the twentieth century, that attempts at mass mobilization would involve the use of Hindu symbols, but equally we must expect the alienation of non-Hindu communities, most notably the Muslims, a quarter of all Indians before 1947. The Muslims felt increasingly threatened by Indian nationalism, and the Mahatma — for all his non-violence — was not a reassuring figure. Gandhi devoted his last ten years to a struggle to heal the wounds opened between Islam and Hinduism in the mass political movements of the century. It was tragic irony that he should be assassinated in 1948 by a Hindu nationalist who blamed him for the concessions to the Muslims that made possible Pakistan.

Let us return to the original question: was Gandhi a twentieth-century anomaly? Certainly he was out of step with much else in the twentieth century, but he was intentionally so. It was not that he was unaware of what was occurring around him. He emphasized "soul force" as a counter to what he saw as the omnipresent, twentieth-century brute force. He emphasized non-violence for a society he believed to be far too violent. He was not saying, as many have mistakenly suggested, that non-violence was *the* Indian tradition. Rather, he lamented that India had many violent traditions, and he warned his contemporaries not to let those traditions dominate. He charged them to take the most noble of their traditions — non-violence — and to work to ensure its dominance of their national life.

This invites the retort that he had little success: India, after Gandhi, remains a violent place. Similarly, many will question the general effectiveness of non-violence as an agitational strategy, and they can cite numerous instances of its failure. It would be foolish to suggest that non-violent movements are always victorious, but that claim could scarcely be made for violent struggles either. Perhaps, if we could draw up a score sheet, we would find that failure was no more frequent in non-violent agitations, and I suspect we would discover that in the former, means less often distorted ends.

What Gandhi contributed with *satyagraha* was an alternative model of revolutionary action. He extended the range of political options available to the twentieth-century activist. This was no mean achievement.

Perhaps Gandhi was an anomaly in another way: as a traditionalist leader in a modern world. Not so, I would argue. If we properly understand our twentieth-century world, we shall expect to find traditionalist leaders all about us. Such understanding, however, has been made difficult by the false dichotomy many social scientists (and journalists in their wake) have drawn between tradition and modernity. Modernization, we have been told, implies moving away from the traditional. On the contrary, I would argue that tradition is not something dispensed with as one becomes modern. Tradition is the cement that binds society together. If it is hard and inflexible, it may prevent change, or change may crack the cement and shatter the society. This has happened, but rarely. Usually the cement is flexible, for tradition is a malleable commodity. In the hands of traditionalist leaders it can be bent and reshaped in adapting the society to modern demands. Insight comes from understanding and interpreting the continuity of tradition: the strengths or weaknesses of diverse traditions for various social and political purposes. Because of our acceptance of the false dichotomy between tradition and modernity, we have equated modernization with change and neglected the equally valid equation between tradition and change. We have been taught to regard traditionalist leaders as reactionaries, when in fact many, like Gandhi, have been vigorous proponents of change. Frequently they have been most effective "modernizers," for they have understood the importance of presenting change in comprehensible, i.e., traditional, forms.

There is a final point to be made about Gandhi's relevance to the twentieth century. He recognized the critical need to deal with the problems of the peasantry — still a majority of the world's population, though so often treated as an anachronistic survival. I have already pointed to his attempts to evolve an economic program for the Indian nationalist movement that would relieve the economic hardships and social dislocations inflicted on peasant communities by industrialization. Through his criticism of urban elitism in the Congress, and, more im-

Far from being an anomaly in his twentieth-century world, Gandhi was wrestling (however unsuccessfully) with a crucial problem of that world: the construction of an economic and political order in which the peasantry could have a full role.

portantly, through his own labors in rural reconstruction, he attacked the dysfunctional and debilitating status inferiority imposed upon the cultivator by the cult of urban civilization. In his reverence for the tradition of the village *panchayet* (council of elders), and in his utopian hopes for the ultimate withering away of the central state structure, he faithfully reflected the peasantry's hostility to that "cold monster," the state, whose baffling complexity grew with every advance in communications technology. In his insistence that the Congress not become the inheritor of the institutions of British administration, he was trying to prevent in India what has happened almost everywhere else in the ex-colonial world: the transfer of the power to exploit the peasantry from an urban-centered imperialist regime to an urban-centered nationalist regime. Far from being an anomaly in his twentieth-century world, Gandhi was wrestling (however unsuccessfully) with a crucial problem of that world: the construction of an economic and political order in which the peasantry could have a full role.

# Agenda for the 21st Century

## Rushworth M. Kidder

*Staff writer of* The Christian Science Monitor

Boston

What's on humanity's agenda for the 21st century? In a series of *Monitor* interviews during the past four months, 16 leading thinkers have identified scores of items. Some of the items center on technological advances—the robots, electronics, and genetics that will reshape daily life in the next century.

Others focus on social, economic, and political trends—increased leisure, a heightening of international competitiveness, the burgeoning of the Asian nations, and a host of others. And some call for a higher vision of the heart, soul, and mind of humanity—better arts, finer journalism, sounder governance, greater compassion for the world's hungry and homeless.

But which are the first-intensity items—the "high leverage" issues (in former World Bank president Robert McNamara's phrase) to which humanity must devote its full attention and its unstinting resources?

Here, drawn from these interviews, are the six points on the agenda for the 21st century:

• The threat of nuclear annihilation.
• The danger of overpopulation.
• The degradation of the global environment.
• The gap between the developing and the industrial worlds.
• The need for fundamental restructuring of educational systems.
• The breakdown in public and private morality.

The list is not in order of priority—although the nuclear issue appears to rank first. Nor did every item arise in every discussion. And in some interviews several items appeared under single headings—with population, environment, and the North-South gap packaged into a bundle, for example, or morality and education lumped together.

Most surprising, perhaps, is the absence of two key items from this list: energy resources and international debt. Several of the people interviewed argued strongly for these points. To a number of others, however, they appeared problematic but not intractable.

Why these six? Here, in a nutshell, are some of the reasons.

## 1. NUCLEAR ANNIHILATION

There is widespread agreement that, as long-time labor leader Douglas Fraser says, "the consequences of not doing something" about this subject could be "horrible . . . beyond imagination." Others note that, if this item is not satisfactorily addressed, none of the others will matter. "Without peace in a nuclear age," as West Germany President Richard von Weizsäcker puts it, "it's not worth [talking] about preserving creation."

Few see a nuclear holocaust as arising from a calculated, all-out conflict between the superpowers. Rather, the greater danger appears to be from an accident, an irrational reaction on the part of a world leader, or a lashing out by a small nation driven to desperation.

For several thinkers, however, the possibility of a future physical disaster is of less concern than the immediacy of the mental impact. "Once you've said to people—and we have, to a whole generation—that you live in a world that can end at any moment," observes theater director Lloyd Richards, "it affects their sense of responsibility."

Or, as novelist Carlos Fuentes puts it, "the consciousness that nature can disappear along with us . . . really shakes your soul."

Not surprisingly, the discussion of nuclear peril was interwoven with calls for a rethinking of the basis of world peace—not as a standoff among frightened adversaries, but as what philosopher Mortimer Adler calls "a positive condition" in which "individuals and peoples can solve all their problems, all their conflicts, by law and by talk rather than by force."

## 2. POPULATION

The scope of this issue, unlike some of the others, can be assessed fairly accurately: All the people who will be approaching middle age in the early decades of the 21st century have already been born. Yet the real problem, except in some densely packed nations, is still in the future.

"You can live a civilized life with a much higher population density than we have [in the Untied States]," says physicist Freeman Dyson. He adds, however, that the world "can't go on growing at its present rate for very long." Yet size alone is not the problem. What causes the "human misery," as Mr. McNamara explains, is "the imbalance of population growth rates on the one hand and social and economic advance on the other."

How serious is the problem? Left unchecked, says former President Jimmy Carter, it will produce "increased dissension, increased animosity, uncontrollable numbers of refugees, [and an] increased tendency toward revolution or violence." In fact, several thinkers see the population problem as the cause of most of the world's ills: third-world hunger, disease, poverty, energy insufficiency, environmental damage, a reshaping of international trade and banking, immigration pressures.

## 3. ENVIRONMENT

"Every possible [agenda] item you're going to mention," said Mr. von Weizsäcker early in his interview, "has to do with my primary concern—namely, to preserve nature." For most of the people interviewed, the degradation of the environment comes second only to nuclear holocaust in its potential for destroying humanity and the natural world.

"This loss or deterioration of the natural world is probably the No. 1 problem," says historian Barbara Tuchman. "I think it's already more with us than is the nuclear."

While some thinkers raise issues associated with the industrial world—such as acid rain, air and water pollution, and the destruction of the ozone layer—the real concern centers on developing-world problems: the destruction of the rain forests, the erosion of topsoil through poor farming practices, the pollution of groundwater. Many thinkers draw clear connections between environmental and population problems. "The environment is going to determine, in the final analysis, what population can be supported," says business leader David Packard.

## 4. THE NORTH-SOUTH GAP

Here the problem is largely defined as a need to strike a difficult balance between opposing forces. For economist Marina Whitman the challenge is for developing nations to preserve national identity in a global marketplace. For University of Chicago president Hanna Gray, the problem is to "sustain both a world economy and the hopes for democratic and humanitarian governments . . . in the less-developed countries."

---

**"Every possible [agenda] item you're going to mention has to do with my primary concern—namely, to preserve nature."**

—*Richard von Weizsäcker*

---

There is broad agreement that the developed nations need to be doing more to help their less-developed neighbors—not simply for altruistic reasons, but because, Mr. Carter says, "We're all in the same boat." Unless such efforts are made, these thinkers generally feel that the problems of the South will spill over into the North. Unfortunately, the gap seems to be growing—"making the rich richer," as physicist Abdus Salam says, "and the poor hungry man's soul sink lower."

How can the gap be closed? The group is divided. For some, the UN provides a promising model. Others, sharply critical of such supranational mechanisms, see more promise in a freeing of world markets, a strengthening of the economies in the developed world, and an invigoration of international trade.

## 5. EDUCATION

Implicit in many of these discussions was the idea that, if the world is to deal with the first four agenda items, it will need to undertake a strenuous reappraisal of the last two: education and morality.

Because the developed nations provide the educational leadership, much of the discussion focused on education in the industrial world. How, then, do these thinkers assess Western-style education?

"Our educational system is absolutely inadequate—not relatively [but] absolutely inadequate—for the purposes of democracy," asserts Mr. Adler. He speaks more vehemently than the rest. But most of them touch on the subject, and most see significant changes coming: more developing-world students, older students, more life-long education, more on-the-job training, more leisure time to pursue knowledge, more difficulty finding the

bedrock of real wisdom under a blizzard of information. The consensus seems to be that the present system needs serious rethinking.

Dr. Gray says she finds it "astonishing" that so many undergraduates major in business—at the expense, she says, of learning about "basic science and the basic humanities and social sciences" in a liberal arts program. Michael Hooker, chancellor of the University of Maryland's Baltimore County campus, would no doubt agree. "I'd educate everybody in the humanities—literature, philosophy, poetry," he says, because "they tell the truth."

## 6. MORALITY

Asked to characterize the present, Mrs. Tuchman calls it "an Age of Disruption." And the greatest disruption, she says, is found in "the real deterioration of public morality."

---

**"Our educational system is absolutely inadequate—not relatively [but] absolutely inadequate—for the purposes of democracy."**

—*Mortimer Adler*

---

She touches on a theme that pervades these interviews. The failure of public truth-telling, the sale of political influence, the acceptance of illegality in stock-market dealings—such topics appear again and again in these interviews, sometimes prominently and sometimes subtly. For social philosopher Sissela Bok, morality is the central issue for the 21st century: Because she sees "trust" as the vital missing ingredient in so many negotiations, she foresees a time when public officials will

---

**"I am not against material progress. I am against the consciousness that [material] progress will solve our problems."**

—*Carlos Fuentes*

---

have to "take moral principles into account" in order to develop the trust necessary for negotiating towards solutions.

Closely related are questions of private morality. Dr. Whitman sees, in the 21st century, the values of strong family life. Mr. Hooker warns of a "growing intellectual and cultural and ethical anomie" in the teenage population.

To author and editor Norman Cousins the problem goes to the very core of survival: "We

move into the 21st century without the philosophy or the sociology or the politics that can keep the species going."

## CAN HUMANITY COPE?

These, then are the six items on the 21st century's agenda. Can humanity come to grips with them? Few think the road ahead will be easy. "Things are going to get worse," says Adler, "before they get better."

Why? Because, according to many of these thinkers, humanity's current institutions are designed to cope only with current problems. The need, voiced repeatedly, is to redesign institutions—of government, education, economics, business, and so forth—to bring them into line with the pace and complexity of 21st-century challenges.

The current structures, many say, are simply not working. "When [problems] are not in a crisis stage," says Mr. Packard, "no one pays any attention to them." Efforts to resolve long-term problems, says Carter, come about "almost entirely [as] a reaction to crisis."

Yet beneath the surface of most of these dis-

---

**"The real deterioration of public morality" is the greatest disruption in "an Age of Disruption."**

—*Barbara Tuchman*

---

cussions lay a quiet optimism. "I really don't know enough to be a pessimist," says Mr. Cousins, who says he is "optimistic about the intangibles that could be converted into assets."

Most of the people interviewed expressed a similar optimism. Richards called it "perspective." Whitman called it "balance." Gray saw it as "intellectual and personal integrity" in the face of "cheap and simple versions of life and history." Mrs. Bok thought of it as "a virtuous circle" spiraling up out of "defeatism and passivity."

All of them expressed a sense of urgency—that the problems were serious, and that there was no time to waste. But most of them shared the conviction that there were ways forward. Perhaps Mr. Fuentes spoke for the group when, in decrying the "great addiction to materialism," he touched on what he called "the moral rewards of progress."

"I am not against material progress," he said. "I am against the consciousness that [material] progress will solve our problems."

# Index

# Credits/ Acknowledgments

Cover design by Charles Vitelli

**1. Global Issues: A Clash of Views**
Facing overview—United Nations photo by Shelley Rother.

**2. Population**
Facing overview—United Nations photo by S. Jackson.

**3. Natural Resources**
Facing overview—United Nations photo by H. Null. 60—USDA. 61—Lookout Mountain Air Force Station. 98—Irene Pearlman. 114—Gamma-Liason.

**4. Development**
Facing overview—United Nations. 133–134—FAO.

**5. Conflict**
Facing overview—United Nations.

**6. Communications**
Facing overview—IBM Corporation.

**7. Human Values**
Facing overview—Save the Children by Joe Loya. 228—(top) WHO photo; (bottom) WHO photo by P. Almasy.

# ANNUAL EDITIONS: GLOBAL ISSUES 88/89
## Article Rating Form

Here is an opportunity for you to have direct input into the next revision of this volume. We would like you to rate each of the 51 articles listed below, using the following scale:

1. **Excellent: should definitely be retained**
2. **Above average: should probably be retained**
3. **Below average: should probably be deleted**
4. **Poor: should definitely be deleted**

Your ratings will play a vital part in the next revision. So please mail this prepaid form to us just as soon as you complete it.
Thanks for your help!

# We Want Your Advice

Annual Editions revisions depend on two major opinion sources: one is our Advisory Board, listed in the front of this volume, which works with us in scanning the thousands of articles published in the public press each year; the other is you—the person actually using the book. Please help us and the users of the next edition by completing the prepaid article rating form on this page and returning it to us. Thank you.

| Rating | Article | Rating | Article |
|---|---|---|---|
| | 1. Life on Earth Is Getting Better, Not Worse | | 28. Women on the Sidelines |
| | 2. The Cornucopian Fallacies | | 29. Children in Darkness |
| | 3. 5 Billion and Counting . . . | | 30. Rural Industry: China's New Engine for Development |
| | 4. The Politics of Population | | |
| | 5. Baby Makes Three—And No More | | 31. The Strategic Challenge of the Evolving Global Economy |
| | 6. Cities Without Limits | | |
| | 7. The Global Phenomena of Immigration | | 32. Japan 1987: A Question of Course |
| | 8. The Future of AIDS | | 33. Dismantling the 49th Parallel |
| | 9. The Heat Is On | | 34. Strains in the Welfare State |
| | 10. 46 Nations Agree on Pact to Protect Ozone Layer | | 35. The Great Siberia in the Sky |
| | | | 36. On the International Uses of Military Force in the Contemporary World |
| | 11. Transboundary Pollution and Environmental Health | | |
| | | | 37. Ambiguous War |
| | 12. The Lessons of Chernobyl | | 38. The Future Course of International Terrorism |
| | 13. State of the Earth: 1985 | | |
| | 14. Treasure Among the Trees | | 39. The Nuclear Arsenal in the Middle East |
| | 15. Converting Garbage to Gold: Recycling Our Materials | | 40. Foundation Stone, Stepping Stone |
| | | | 41. Arms Control: Misplaced Focus |
| | 16. A Crisis of Many Dimensions: Putting Food on the World's Table | | 42. What Next? A World of Communications Wonders |
| | | | |
| | 17. The Hidden Malice of Malnutrition | | 43. Detectives in Space |
| | 18. Grains of Hope | | 44. The Regional Solution to a Global Problem |
| | 19. Tomatomation | | |
| | 20. New Directions for Oil Policy | | 45. Uprising in the Philippines |
| | 21. The World's Shrinking Forests | | 46. Gambling on Glasnost |
| | 22. Power Without Nuclear | | 47. Smallpox: Never Again (The Lessons Learnt) |
| | 23. Shapes of a Renewable Society | | |
| | 24. A Village Called Nanpur | | 48. Children in South Africa's Jails |
| | 25. International Stratification and Third World Solidarity: A Dual Strategy for Change | | 49. How the Japanese Beat Us in Schools |
| | | | 50. Gandhi: A Twentieth-Century Anomaly? |
| | 26. Dance of Debt Isn't Over Yet | | 51. Agenda for the Twenty-First Century |
| | 27. The Next Earthquake | | |

*(Continued on next page)*

**ABOUT YOU**

Name_____ Date_____

Are you a teacher? ☐  Or student? ☐

Your School Name _____

Department _____

Address _____

City _____ State _____ Zip _____

School Telephone # _____

**YOUR COMMENTS ARE IMPORTANT TO US!**

Please fill in the following information:

For which course did you use this book? _____

Did you use a text with this Annual Edition?  ☐ yes  ☐ no

The title of the text? _____

What are your general reactions to the Annual Editions concept?


Have you read any particular articles recently that you think should be included in the next edition?


Are there any articles you feel should be replaced in the next edition? Why?


Are there other areas that you feel would utilize an Annual Edition?


May we contact you for editorial input?


May we quote you from above?

ANNUAL EDITIONS: GLOBAL ISSUES 88/89

**BUSINESS REPLY MAIL**

First Class          Permit No. 84          Guilford, CT

*Postage will be paid by addressee*

**The Dushkin Publishing Group, Inc.**
**Sluice Dock**
**Guilford, Connecticut 06437**